THE
INTERNET
IN CHINA

Routledge Studies in New Media and Cyberculture

Routledge Studies in New Media and Cyberculture is dedicated to furthering original research in new media and cyberculture studies. International in scope, the series places an emphasis on cutting edge scholarship and interdisciplinary methodology. Topics explored in the series will include comparative and cultural studies of video games, blogs, online communities, digital music, new media art, cyberactivism, open source, mobile communications technologies, new information technologies, and the myriad intersections of race, gender, ethnicity, nationality, class, and sexuality with cyberculture.

Series Titles

Cyberpop: Digital Lifestyles and Commodity Culture
Sidney Eve Matrix, University of Winnipeg

The Internet in China: Cyberspace and Civil Society
Zixue Tai, Southern Illinois University

Forthcoming Titles

Racing Cyberculture: Minoritarian Internet Art
Chris McGahan, Yeshiva University

Virtual English: Internet Use, Language, and Global Subjects
Jillana Enteen, Northwestern University

THE INTERNET IN CHINA

Cyberspace and Civil Society

ZIXUE TAI

Routledge
Taylor & Francis Group
New York   London

Routledge is an imprint of the
Taylor & Francis Group, an informa business

Routledge
Taylor & Francis Group
711 Third Avenue
New York, NY 10017

Routledge
Taylor & Francis Group
2 Park Square
Milton Park, Abingdon
Oxon OX14 4RN

© 2006 by Taylor & Francis Group, LLC
Routledge is an imprint of Taylor & Francis Group, an Informa business

International Standard Book Number-13: 978-0-415-97655-8 (hbk)
International Standard Book Number-13: 978-0-415-53588-5 (pbk)

Library of Congress Cataloging-in-Publication Data

Tai, Zixue.
    The Internet in China : cyberspace and civil society / Zixue Tai.
       p. cm. -- (Routledge studies in new media and cyberculture)
    Includes bibliographical references and index.
    ISBN 0-415-97655-3 (hardback : alk. paper) 1. Internet--Social aspects--China.
    2. Internet--Political aspects--China. 3. Civil society--China. 4. Information
    policy--China. I. Title.

HM851.T35 2006
303.48'330951--dc22   2006023496

Visit the Taylor & Francis Web site at
http://www.taylorandfrancis.com

and the Routledge Web site at
http://www.routledge-ny.com

Contents

List of Figures

List of Tables

Acknowledgments

Writing a book is an intellectual journey. I am grateful to a number of people for providing me with the much-needed road map. First and foremost, my profound thanks go to Professor Tsan-Kuo Chang, my adviser in the School of Journalism and Mass Communication at the University of Minnesota-Twin Cities where I completed my Ph.D. dissertation, upon which this book is based. Professor Chang's thoughtful input and encouragement at each step, through numerous stimulating conversations and communications, were indispensable to the successful completion of first my dissertation and then this book. Many thanks go to Professor Hazel Dicken-Garcia, also from the University of Minnesota, for being a constant source of inspiration. Hazel is an exemplary scholar, a wonderful teacher, and an excellent editor, and made insightful suggestions about an earlier draft of the book.

I also wish to thank two special friends, Tao Sun and Sheng-ping Tao, whose friendship and companionship made my experience at the University of Minnesota a much more pleasant one. The School of Journalism and Mass Communication at the University of Minnesota-Twin Cities, where I obtained the academic training necessary for the completion of this book, deserves a special mention here.

Most importantly, thank you (with a great sense of guilt) to my wife Lu, my daughter Ellinor, and my son Ethan, for their unconditional love and support that sustained me through the long process of writing this book. Their understanding and confidence helped me sit through numerous nights of reading, deliberating, writing, and revising. In particular, the evolution of this book coincided with the birth of Ethan, which meant that I had to spend a significant amount of time away from him during this time. For that, this book is dedicated to my whole family. Without them, this book would never have been what it is now.

Special thanks to my parents, my brother, and my sister — especially my father, who did not live to see the fruition of this book — for being a constant source of emotional support. To them I am forever indebted.

Finally, I would like to register my thanks to Matthew Byrnie, Rachael Panthier, and Devon Sherman at Routledge/Taylor & Francis for their vision and invaluable support throughout the process of the production of this book. Many thanks also to Rita Margolies for her admirable copyediting contributions. Any content of the book, needless to say, is my sole responsibility.

Introduction

The year 2003 has been widely acclaimed as the "Year of Network Opinion" in China,[1] because, for the first time since the introduction of the Internet into Chinese society in the 1990s, public opinion on the Internet from online bulletin boards, forums, chat rooms, postings, and Web blogs on numerous Chinese Web sites had prompted the Chinese government to take action on many occasions to address issues of concern to Chinese netizens. The following are some prominent and well-publicized cases in 2003 and 2004.

1. On March 17, 2003, Sun Zhigang, a 27-year-old college graduate from Wuhan and employed by a local graphic design company in Guangzhou, was stopped by the police on his way to an Internet café. When he was unable to produce a temporary resident ID permit, he was subsequently sent to the detention–repatriation center for vagrants. Three days later, Sun fell ill and was sent to a penitentiary hospital, where he was beaten to death by inmates and employees at the hospital. Sun's tragic death only caught public attention about one month later when his story was picked up by a local newspaper reporter in Guangzhou and then hit the Internet. Angry Chinese citizens expressed their outrage on the Internet, which exerted extensive pressure on the local and central authorities for swift action. The dozen culprits responsible for Sun's death were arrested and sentenced to prison terms or the death penalty in June 2003, and in the same month, China's State Council terminated its administrative measures that had been in place for two decades on the custody and repatriation of vagrants in Chinese cities (see Chapter 7 for an in-depth discussion of this case).

2. On the morning of October 16, 2003, farmer Dai Yiquan and his wife, Liu Zhongxia, were on their tractor to deliver green onions to residents in China's northeastern city of Harbin when the tractor swerved to the right to avoid an oncoming van and swiped the side mirror of a metallic-silver BMW X5, a symbol of status and wealth of the newly affluent class in China. The owner of the BMW, Ms. Su Xiuwen, flew into a rage and hurled insults at the farm couple and hit them with her handbag after they got off their tractor. The angry Su then got into her car, started the engine and drove through the crowded street lined with on-looking pedestrians, killing Liu Zhoungxia and injuring twelve others before the car crashed into a

nearby tree. Su was detained by the police, who later pronounced the whole incident to be a traffic accident.

On December 20, 2003, the Harbin District Court sentenced Su Xiuwen to a two-year jail term for traffic violations with a three-year reprieve. The victim's family was absent during the sentencing because they had settled outside of the court, getting a handsome amount of compensation from Su. There was an unquestionable imbalance in the equation in this case, which reflects the cruel reality of Chinese society today, with Su and her US$90,000 (Chinese market price) BMW at one end and the poor farm couple who had to make a living by selling green onions at the other. However, this whole event took an unexpected turn when the news of the incident, first reported by a local newspaper, reached millions of Chinese readers through the Internet. Angry Chinese Internet users flooded major portal sites with postings and messages, while rumors swirled in chat rooms and forums with allegations that the driver was a relative of a high-ranking provincial official (which later met with fierce denial from the official). This incident, along with the court rulings, quickly became the center of focus online nationwide, and a Google search in early January of 2004 turned up over 220,000 items about the story.[2] By January 6, 2004, more than 70,000 postings appeared on Sohu.com alone, a popular Chinese portal site, crying foul play and demanding a retrial and justice.[3] Mounting public interest and negative opinion on the Internet forced the provincial Party Committee to intervene by ordering a reinvestigation of the incident and the trial procedure through a third-party team. There was an official probe into the case, and the trial concluded in March 2004 that the driver did not commit manslaughter, and the original sentence was upheld. Public interest in the case resurfaced in July 2004 when a chief investigative officer and a district judge were arrested in connection with the case on the charge that both had attended a banquet hosted by the driver's relative.[4]

3. On December 22, 2003, for the first time since the Communist Party came to power in 1949, the Chinese Supreme People's Court heard a common criminal case and overturned the ruling from the second trial of a local court in the northeastern province of Liaoning. The case involved Liu Yong, an alleged mafia kingpin in the province who terrorized the region and whose personal assets were estimated to be worth RMB¥700 million (approximately US$87.5 million). Liu's rags-to-richness adventure started with a modest store in Shenyang, the capital city of Liaoning province, and quickly built a conglomerate that had interests in garments, restaurants, entertainment, retail, and real estate development. Liu's success story could be one

of the glorified examples extolled by the Chinese government in the past decades, with one significant exception — he built his personal wealth through bribing local government officials, forging close ties with law enforcement, injecting fear and terror into competitors, and recruiting gangsters into his personal army. His formidable network also landed him the enviable social status of delegate to the Shenyang People's Congress, the local legislature.

In July 1999, Liu ordered his henchman, Song Jianfei, to beat up a cigarette vendor who had been involved in a minor dispute with Liu. The vendor later died of internal bleeding as a result of the beating, and his death led to the arrest of Liu and Song in July 2000. On April 17, 2002, Tieling Intermediate People's Court gave Liu and Song the death penalty along with a fine of RMB¥15 million (approximately US$1.88 million) for willful killing; Liu immediately appealed to the provincial Higher People's Court. On August 15, 2003, the higher court overruled the lower court's decision and changed Liu's sentence to death with a two-year reprieve (but kept the fine) on the ground that Liu's confession had been extracted through torture. The retrial of Liu received plenty of attention from the national media, even though the local media mainly remained silent, apparently because of pressure from local authorities and concern that the coverage might offend local officials. Investigative stories from several reporters on the Internet about Liu's background and local official corruption fanned the flame of widespread anger among Internet users throughout China. The Internet quickly became the court of public opinion, which was an almost one-sided condemnation of what most believed was a mistrial. The denunciation of the higher court's decision on all major Chinese news and portal sites caught the attention of the Chinese central government, which ordered the Supreme Court to look at the case. Adding to the anger of Chinese netizens were stories by several reporters who revealed that they had received anonymous spoken or written threats ordering them to stop covering the Liu case or face death.

In response to public outcries on the Internet, the Supreme Court held an open trial of Liu Yong from December 18 to 22, and gave Liu the death sentence for crimes of willful bodily injury, organizing and leading a crime ring, property damage, illegal business operations, bribery, gun possession, and interference with law enforcement.[5] Liu was executed the same day under high police security. Liu's attorney, while facing the media, charged that Liu was executed by public opinion. Over a dozen public officials, among them the mayor of Shengyang and a few high-ranking police officers, were also sentenced to varying prison terms in connection with this case.[6]

4. Over 200 Japanese tourists arrived in the southern Chinese city of Zhuhai on the night of September 16, 2003, and left on the morning of September 18. It would have been just a routine sightseeing tour except for one thing — the Japanese visitors were all men, ranging from 16 to 37, and their sole attraction was Chinese prostitutes, and most important of all, their orgy was later exposed by the Chinese media and led to a national uproar.

The tourists were all employees of a Japanese construction firm, which paid all the expenses in connection with the tour in celebration of its fifteenth anniversary. Upon their arrival at a five-star hotel in Zhuhai, the group summoned hundreds of Chinese prostitutes to the hotel for sex services.[7] Drunken Japanese tourists were flirting with the prostitutes in the hotel lobby and the elevators, and left the doors of their hotel rooms open while engaging in sexual activity. Among the various Chinese witnesses at the hotel, Zhou Guangchun, an executive from a Hainan pharmaceuticals company, who stayed at the hotel at the same time, was so disgusted that he made dozens of calls to the police and the local government during the next few days, but to no avail. It is an open secret known to Chinese bureaucrats and civilians alike that red light districts have mushroomed throughout Chinese cities in the past two decades, and local government officials are quite tolerant toward, and thus sometimes silently promote, the sex industry (nicknamed the "yellow industry" in Chinese) to increase local revenue. Therefore, although Chinese laws forbid prostitution, local government and police forces generally take half-hearted measures in banning sex services. They only adopt some symbolic postures to suppress prostitution from time to time when it becomes too rampant or when there are specific instructions from superior authorities. However, no matter what they do, there is little incentive for the local officials to totally eliminate the sex industry in their jurisdiction.

So it was no surprise that Zhou's complaints only met with deaf ears from the Zhuhai government and law enforcement officials. Angered by their inaction and nonresponsiveness, Zhou decided to turn to the media for help. After being contacted by Zhou, three newspapers, all headquartered in Guangdong's capital city of Guangzhou, decided to run the story. The first paper to break this story was *New Daily Express News* (*Xin Kuai Bao*), followed by the *Southern Metropolitan Daily* (*Nanfang Dushi Bao*) and the *Nanfang Daily* (*Nanfang Ribao*) — two weeks after the whole incident was over. The story was immediately picked up by hundreds of portal and news Web sites throughout the nation, triggering a nationwide condemnation and uproar from Net citizens around the country.

The relationship between China and Japan, the two largest countries in East Asia, has always been a delicate one. Most Chinese people are still resentful about Japan's evasive attitude toward the Japanese invasion and occupation of China and the atrocities committed by Japanese soldiers in China during World War II; ups and downs in Sino-Japanese relations are often marked by nationalist sentiments resulting from scars of that particular historic period. Public response toward this three-day sex romp was no exception. That the orgy took place on the eve of September 18 was a good reason for the Chinese anger: on September 18, 1937, the Japanese attacked the Chinese industrial city of Shenyang and proceeded to take over the three northeastern provinces within the next three months. This became known as the "Mukden Incident" in the West and the "September 18 Incident" in Chinese history textbooks, and it has been called a "day of national humiliation" in modern Chinese history. After the sex orgy incident was publicly reported by the media, many Chinese citizens believed that the Japanese tourists had intentionally chosen the date in an effort to humiliate the Chinese people, and this belief in turn fueled the public outcry on and off the Internet.

Within the first few days after the news appeared on the Internet, an outpouring of invectives against the Japanese tourists and Japan flooded Chinese Web sites, and tens of thousands of protest messages were posted in chat rooms and on bulletin boards of each of the major Chinese portals and news sites. Some demanded an open trial of both the Chinese and Japanese individuals involved, some called for a boycott of Japanese goods, and others included the hotel's phone number and urged their fellow citizens to call the hotel in which this sex spree took place to protest (which many did). The immediacy and scale of public responses online made it hard, if not utterly impossible, for authorities to ignore the fermenting public sentiment. Soon after the story broke, the hotel involved was closed for "rectification," and Zhang Dejiang, the Party boss of Guangdong province, quickly ordered a top-level investigation into the allegations and promised the media that the case would be handled "in the strictest manner."[8] The incident also quickly evolved into a diplomatic juggling act, with the Chinese Foreign Ministry expressing "strong indignation" and calling on Japan to teach its citizens how to behave.[9] Chinese Foreign Ministry officials also summoned Japanese Embassy counterparts to protest.

In the following months, many Chinese citizens were arrested in connection with the incident, and fourteen were officially charged and put on a public trial by the Zhuhai Intermediate People's Court. On December 17, 2003, the court sentenced Ye Xiang, an assistant to the hotel manager, and Ming Zhu, another hotel employee, to life imprisonment; and prison terms for the other twelve individuals ranged from two to fifteen years. While the normal punishment for prostitution is a fine and a warning, these sentences are unprecedentedly harsh. Meanwhile, fifteen public security and tourist administration officials in Zhuhai were disciplined for negligence by the local government.[10]

5. On Wednesday, September 1, 2004, the opening day of the Russian school year, armed militants seized more than 1000 children and adult hostages in a Beslan middle school in the southern Russian republic of North Ossetia. The crisis came to a bloody end on September 3 as Russian security forces stormed the besieged school after failed negotiations, with nearly 400 deaths and hundreds more wounded. Throughout the crisis, the global media provided around-the-clock news of this tragedy to the shock of the global audience; leading the Chinese media coverage was the state-run China Central Television (CCTV).

During the primetime program "Today's Focus" (*Jinri Guanzhu*) on the night of September 6, 2004, while broadcasting a news update about the Beslan hostage crisis, CCTV 4 flashed text on the screen asking viewers to take part in a game quiz by text messaging their guess to the number of hostages that had been killed in the school siege. Audience members were given four choices ranging from 302 to 402. Participants who sent the right answers via short message services (SMS) to the listed numbers had the chance to win prizes.

At the start of 2004, China Central Television (CCTV), China United Telecommunications Corporation (China Unicom) and China Mobile teamed up in a joint business operation in text message games and quizzes. China Unicom and China Mobile are the two largest state monopolies specializing in wireless telecommunication services, while CCTV is the only state-run national television network in the country. The joint venture among the three is an effort to boost ratings for CCTV and to promote mobile services for the two telecom companies because users have to watch the program and subscribe to the wireless services either from China Unicom or China Mobile to participate.

The moment the hostage crisis quiz was aired, angry citizens throughout the country expressed their outrage at the heartless practice of profiteering from such a tragic event in popular chat rooms and on BBS and online forums.[11] As revealed in the postings, many people did not initially see the program and only got the information from other netizen's postings. However, most of them felt ashamed and shocked at such a scandal and called on their fellow citizens to act by protesting to CCTV or other Chinese authorities. On the official Web site of China's Xinhua News Agency, Xinhuanet.com, a commentary written by a journalist titled "Don't Seek Entertainment by Exploiting Others' Pain," which was read, reposted, and responded to both on Xinhuanet.com and other popular portal sites, openly challenged the hard-heartedness of cashing in on this brutal terrorist act.[12] Public outcries were also posted by Web bloggers and on popular news sites.[13] On www.163.com, a portal site owned by NetEase and ranked as one of the top three most popular news sites (the other two are Sina.com and Sohu.com), users posted over 700 messages in the next few days in response to this incident on its BBS, most of which condemned CCTV's practice.[14]

Spurred by the changing online and offline media environment, news about this incident spread quickly to Chinese audiences all over the country. Many citizens contacted CCTV and government authorities to express their disgust, and demanded punishment for those directly responsible. Spontaneous outpourings of public furor led to the dismissal of the two producers of the program and the firing of its editor in mid-September 2004,[15] and also resulted in the ban of SMS games and quizzes during news broadcasts by China's State Administration of Radio, Film and Television (SARFT),[16] the state regulator of Chinese broadcasters.

These cases are only five of over dozens of high-profile cases in 2003 and 2004 in which Chinese netizens flexed their muscles by exerting pressure on the government to change the course of events. In a country where authoritarianism is deep-rooted in the polity, a systematic and reliable mechanism for feeling the public pulse on key issues is lacking, and the Internet, which has fewer barricades to public participation, may be the closest viable alternative for gauging popular sentiments. In commenting on the role of the Internet in influencing government handling of these events, Yu Guoming, a noted public opinion scholar in China's Renmin (People's) University, said: "Two or three years ago, no one took these Internet postings or messages seriously, and regarded them as merely recreational. But now Internet polls, surveys and responses in [on] bulletin boards have a real influence."[17] Because there is no judicial independence in China and courts often collude with government officials, Chinese netizens may understandably redress what they perceive as unfair and unjustified by taking issues into the virtual court of appeal on the Internet and thus swaying the tide of public opinion.

Parallel with the rise of the Internet as a social force is the emergence of civil society in China after decades of economic development. Although the specific nature of the Chinese civil society that is developing is debatable, the indisputable fact is that economic openness and prosperity in China's reform era have led to the mushrooming of social organizations and social groups that serve a variety of purposes and functions. In the meantime, commercialization of the media industry has fostered a brand new audience–media relationship and has significantly expanded the public sphere that is so essential to the growth of civil society.

The explosive development of the Internet in China in recent years has meanwhile opened up a whole new milieu for the nurturing of civil society. The Internet is not only bringing about a new type of social space to Chinese netizens, it is also redefining existing social relations and propelling existing civil forces into new possibilities. Since the mid-1990s, the Chinese government has displayed an unusual level of enthusiasm for the Internet and has fully embraced the Internet age with two hands: on the one hand, it has implemented a set of policy initiatives that have prioritized the development of the Internet and related technologies in the nation's economic strategies; on the other hand, the Chinese authorities have reservations about the Internet and have sought to enforce a variety of legal and technical measures to put the Internet on short leash. But more often than not, things do not happen as designed or intended by the Chinese authorities. There is mounting evidence that the Internet is already fundamentally transforming the "Central Kingdom," and this important and challenging area calls for scholarly scrutiny.

It is the purpose of this book to examine the evolving interplay between the Internet and civil society in the Chinese context. An understanding of a concept can be better achieved by studying its origin and its evolutionary, historical trajectory — that is what I try to accomplish in the first two chapters. Chapter 1 first looks at the idea of civil society from Plato and Aristotle in its ancient and classical heritage to Hegel and Marx in early modern Europe, and then discusses the democratic potential of civil society and the historical conditions under which the idea of civil society resurfaced in contemporary debates. Civil society as a scholarly concept, of course, is heavily grounded in the Western social and philosophical tradition. How and to what extent it can be applied to the Chinese context, however, is another question that merits scholarly attention. Chapter 2 maps out the conceptual development of the idea of civil society as well as the evolution of Chinese civil society since the early modern era in Chinese history, and helps readers gain an understanding of how scholarly debates in relation to the Chinese context have adapted the concept of civil society to Chinese soil.

The next two chapters look at the Internet in China. Chapter 3 provides an examination of China's informatization effort in which new information technologies with the Internet at its forefront are vigorously promoted by the state for economic gain while control mechanisms are implemented at the state, institutional, and individual levels to ensure that only information desired by the authorities can be accessed by the Chinese audience. On the other hand, despite the government effort to control information flow in China's cyberspace, the Internet has increasingly become a liberating force for dissident and other social groups to challenge the government monopoly over information. An overview of the growth of the Internet in China from the early 1990s to the present is offered in Chapter 4. The purpose is to show that the popularization of the Internet among average Chinese citizens has become an irreversible trend, and that the penetration of the Internet in every aspect of Chinese society creates the precondition for the Internet to emerge as a revolutionizing force for Chinese civil society.

In Chapter 5, I first give a critical overview of the Internet as an empowering tool in opening a brand-new type of social space, and then discuss the implications of the Internet for civil society. The chapter concludes with an examination of how public opinion from different online groups in China has emerged as a formidable social force in government policy making and China's political juggling, and how the Internet has revolutionized public communication through nurturing a high level of online political efficacy and participation. The last two chapters (Chapters 6 and 7) illustrate, through in-depth analysis of some prominent cases, the use of the Internet by Chinese civil society in disseminating information, organizing online petitions and offline protests, extracting varying degrees of responsiveness and accountability from the authorities, and affecting government decision making concerning important social, political, and diplomatic issues.

Here, I would like to address the methodological approaches adopted in the book. Because the idea of civil society is so complex, versatile, and evolving, and because a multitude of historical, social, and cultural factors are intricately involved in the conception of civil society, this book tries to address the full dimensionality of the phenomenon of civil society by incorporating different methods and evidence from multiple fronts. The first two chapters (Chapters 1 and 2) are an explication of the idea of civil society, with Chapter 1 focusing on the Western context and Chapter 2 on the Chinese environment. In these two chapters, I conduct a historical review of the evolution of the concept of civil society and critically analyze the different theoretical strains in contemporary debates on civil society in the West as well as in China. In the next three chapters (Chapters 3, 4, and 5) — which examine government policy and information control, history and the transformative power of the Internet in China, as well as the use of the Internet by Chinese civil society — I have used a variety of sources, including extensive review of current research and debates, evidence from the popular press and other publications, secondary data (secondary analysis) in the form of surveys conducted by various institutions on different occasions, and industrial reports about China's Internet industry. Of course, the best way to research the Internet is to use evidence readily available on the Internet. Of the multiple Internet sources utilized throughout the chapters, some are physically hosted in China while others are dispersed in other parts of the world. Although physicality still matters in the Internet age, it only does so in a different sense. Innovation on the Internet is a never-ending process; as is shown in the chapters, information has a way of bypassing even the most sophisticated firewall system in the world. In Chapters 6 and 7, I have adopted a multiple-case approach to demonstrate the prevalence and relevance of the Internet to Chinese civil society, and the use of the Internet by Chinese civil society to effect change in the country. These cases, which took place under different settings and involved different players, offer corroborating evidence to the central arguments of this book.

Finally, just as the Internet and its technologies are on the fast track of change in the new millennium, so is cyberspace in a constant state of transmutation. Noticeably, cyberspace, a term coined and popularized by William Gibson, has achieved the status of a major intellectual currency as computerization and Internet connectivity become deeply ingrained in every aspect of human life. However, over the years, the uses and meanings of the term have diversified. Heavily grounded in human–machine interaction in the networked world, cyberspace can be and has been applied to the realms of human creation and imagination in relation to computer games, video games, text-based interactive systems, three-dimensional immersive systems, different types of virtual reality environments, computer hacking activities, digital artistic expressiveness — just to name a few. This book exclusively focuses on the domain of new information and communication technologies (ICTs), especially the Internet. While the Internet, which is center stage in the ongoing global digital revolution, is the focal point of examination in the book, emerging new communication technologies, such as cell phone text messaging services and other wireless personal communication devices, are also discussed in various sections. Indeed, the convergence of multiple platforms of communication media — computers, PDAs, cell phones, and other mobile devices, all with Internet access — is leading the next communication (and in all likelihood social) revolution. Consequently, academic inquiries into the social impact of the Internet cannot ignore this profound trend.

1

The Idea of Civil Society from Early Modern to Contemporary Social Thought in the West

Few concepts in the social sciences have appeared in theoretical deliberations, intellectual debates, and research programs as often as the idea of civil society in the past two decades. Yet even fewer concepts have been as undertheorized, controversial, and oftentimes confusing. An examination of the rich terrain of the genealogies of civil society can yield new horizons in our discussion of this concept within today's environment, and an explication of the long tradition in its conceptual development will help us critically evaluate the prevalent democratizing, liberating, and other claims in the anachronistic employment of the term "civil society" under various contexts. Thus it is appropriate that this book start with an overview of the historical, political, and philosophical evolution of the concept of civil society in occidental thought.

Although the genealogies of the idea of civil society can be traced to ancient Greece, immediate inspirations for contemporary debates come more directly from social theories in early modern Europe. Therefore, this chapter starts with a brief overview of the ancient and classical heritage of the idea of civil society, and then examines theoretical deliberations on civil society in early modern European social thought, followed by a review of the historical context in which the concept of civil society was revived in the twentieth century. Next, I analyze the different strands of theoretical foundations explicating the democratic potential of civil society. To rejuvenate the theoretical thrust and augment the practical utility of the concept, I end this chapter with some theoretical propositions on how to adapt the theory of civil society to the changing political and social conditions of the new millennium.

Ancient and Classical Social Thought, the Emergence of Modern Capitalism, and the Idea of Civil Society

It is generally believed that the notions of politics, democracy, and political theory were invented in the fifth and fourth centuries BC in ancient Greece, where the Athenians turned the practice of politics into an "art" (*techne*) (Finley, 1985; Wallach, 2001). John Ehrenberg (1999) summarizes succinctly the classic understanding of civil society in Greece as "a politically organized

1

commonwealth" (p. 3), which differentiated civilized Greeks from barbarians without any membership in political association. However, Plato and Aristotle, both masterminds of political discourse of their times, approached civil society differently.

The political commonwealth of Plato's Greece was organized into numerous relatively small separated regions of self-contained political units varying in sizes called *poleis*. The size of a *polis* (often translated as city-state; see e.g., Howland, 1993; Klosko, 1986) was typically small and its citizens were adult males, although the community as a whole included women, slaves, and foreign businessmen (who were confined to limited spheres outside the political world). The *polis* came into being for the following reasons:

> The origin of a city (polis) lies ... in the fact that we are not, any of us, self-sufficient; we have all sorts of needs ... Different individuals, then, form associations with one person to meet one need, and with another person to meet a different need. With this variety of wants they may collect a number of partners and allies into one place of habitation, and to this joint habitation we give the name "city" (polis).
>
> (*Republic* 369[b–c])[1]

These associations in Plato's *polis* were nothing less than civil society in the sense we use the term today. The *polis* was not only a geographic entity; it was a civic, social space where politics of the day was practiced (Ophir, 1991). The Athenian democratic politics was made possible by ennobling and energizing frank public discourse (e.g., *Republic* 557[b–d]). Plato's ideal city-state was organized into a system of classes comprising three types of men: "the lover of wisdom, the lover of victory and the lover of profit" (*Republic* 581[c]). The three classes of citizen would become Ruler(s), Guardians, and Ruled in the *polis*. Plato's political art strives for a unity of different interests of society into a God-orchestrated division of labor among the different classes, and civil society is made possible by the intellectual power of the Rulers in attending to the welfare of all citizens in a rigidly structured *polis* (Monoson, 2000; Nichols, 1987; Ophir, 1991). Different classes live within different specialized civic spaces, yet each contributes in its own way to the harmonized city-state.

Aristotle's intellectual undertaking was primarily developed in his *Politics*,[2] which, in combination with Plato's *Republic*, marks the start of political philosophy as a field of study. Aristotle shared with Plato the idea of the centrality of the polis in studying political communities. However, he attacked the aim of Plato's ideal polis as the highest degree of unity of individuals who compose the polis. For Aristotle, Plato's unity of individual human beings defeated the exact purpose of the polis: to unite people with distinctive differences. A community, of course, implies a sense of sharing. There are three possibilities of sharing in the polis, according to Aristotle: the citizens might share (1) in nothing, (2) in everything that can be shared, or (3) in some things but not others (*Politics*, Book II, 1261ᵃ). Aristotle quickly eliminates the first option because it is impossible for citizens to have nothing in common. Then the question comes to which is better, a state that has as many things as possible in common or a state that shares some things but not others? Plato's *Republic* obviously opts for the second one: an ideal state would allow its citizens to share as much as possible. Aristotle makes his position very clear from his arguments in Book II of *Politics*: an ideal polis allows its citizens to share some things in common but not others. For Aristotle, unity of the polis is not only undesirable but also practically impossible — by nature the polis is less of a unity than the household, which in turn is less of a unity than the individual. A polis with a high degree of unity ceases to be a polis (*Politics* Book II 1261). The survival of the polis depends to a great extent on the plurality of its citizens because only diversity makes it possible for individual citizens in the polis to exchange services and products, and only through this is the binding relationship among individuals created to let the polis maintain its self-sufficiency (Mayhew, 1997, Stalley, 1991).

The beginnings of Aristotle's polis can be found in the most primitive forms of association — "unions of those 'who cannot exist without one another,' man and woman, master and slave" (Bradley, 1991: 23). Plato would have been appalled at Aristotle's inclusion in the polis of the basic relationships of the family and villages as well as many other forms of association: schools and educational institutions, fraternal associations, religious communities, and more importantly, close personal friendships.

But families, villages, and other associations only become a polis when they are components of a whole with a common good as its end, a whole in which the individuals directly participate as virtuous citizens. Hence the polis exists by nature for the fulfillment of human perfection and assumes priority over individuals (Miller, F., 1995). Because humans are political animals and the polis as a political community is the natural affiliation for them to reach the common good, there is no distinction between the state and society or civil society. The polis combines them all — civil society *is* the state.

Both Plato and Aristotle were suspicious of the divisive acids of commercial activities and other private pursuits in the formations of civil society because they tend to place self-interest above the highest good. Religion for both Plato and Aristotle is tied intricately to the politics of the polis. The ideal state is a rule of virtue and therefore of God's will. Church as an exclusive religious sanctity is nonexistent because all religious activities are practiced in the public space of the polis toward the good life.

The downturn of Athens as the center of political discourse shifted the search for political thought and action to the Roman Empire in the Middle Ages. Christianity, which was instilled as the official religion of Rome, was fundamental to the development of political and philosophical ideas at the time. The Christian doctrine justifies the use of the political power of the state to save the fallen humanity under the guidance of the Church, and it finds full exposition in Aurelius Augustine (AD 354 to 430). The domination of Augustine's intellectual tradition continued until the time of St. Thomas Aquinas, whose legacy in moral and political philosophy still finds passionate followers today. For Augustine and Aquinas, civil society (city of man), which includes family and the state as well as other secular organizations, exists side by side with the city of God: the former fulfills the material, the immediate, and the temporal happiness while the latter is for the attainment of man's eternal and spiritual destiny of the Divine Order. Man's ultimate end, of course, takes precedence over his material well-being; but only the ecclesiastical power at the will of God can help man achieve his complete fulfillment (Benkert, 1942; Dyson, 2001, Elshtain, 1995; Finnis, 1998; Mueller, 1987; von Heyking, 2001).

During the second half of the eighteenth century, Scotland, the "great eighteenth-century incubator of intellectual innovation" (Muller, 1993: 16), was leading Europe to become a commercial society in which economic activities were at the center of human life. Adam Smith (1723 to 1790) was among the first to observe the hindrances created by classical Aristotelian philosophy, Christian rationalism, and medieval theology to emerging social conditions in an age of dynamism of economic growth and commercial activities, and he set out to develop a brand-new worldview with an intention to integrate economic motives and morals (Fitzgibbons, 1995). Spending most of his life in Scotland, Smith benefited enormously from many seminal ideas of the Scottish Enlightenment. Through his writings, Smith intended to demonstrate that acknowledgment and discovery of the "scientific" laws of Nature could solve both economic and moral problems (Fitzgibbons, 1995). Smith's writings not only provide a base line for economic and social theorists for generations to come, but they also establish his founding father status in the political economy of civil society (Madison, 1998).

First of all, Smith starts to conceive of his science of economics by frankly recognizing the motivating force of self-interest. This is best summarized in a passage widely cited by Smithian scholars:

> It is not from the benevolence of the butcher, the brewer, of the baker, that we expect our dinner, but from their regard to their own interest. We address ourselves, not to their humanity but to their self-love, and never talk to them of our own necessities but of their advantages (*The Wealth of Nations*, hereafter referred to as WN, Vol. 1, Book I, Chapter ii, p. 18).

> (Smith, 1976)

Man is by his very nature dependent on others. But Smith's social nature of man is bound by his commercial affairs: "In civilized society he stands at all times in need of the cooperation of assistance of great multitudes, while his whole life is scarce sufficient to gain the friendship of a few persons" (Cited in Muller, 1993: 71). This dependence is demonstrated by the capacity of human beings for exchange. It is the possibility of exchange that differentiates human beings from one another, because it "encourages every man to apply himself to a particular occupation, and to cultivate and bring to perfection whatever talent or genius he may possess for that particular species of business" (WN, Vol. I, Book I, Ch. Ii, p.19) (Smith, 1976).

Many have linked selfishness, egoism, or selfish passions to Smith's concept of self-interest. Contemporary scholars have challenged this reading of Smith (e.g., Fitzgibbons, 1995; Muller, 1993; Werhane, 1991). Smith believes, they point out, that the pursuit of self-interest is not without its restraint, and self-love can be virtuous. According to Smith in *The Theory of Moral Sentiments*, hereafter referred to as TMS, (1892), self-interest can be channeled, moderated, or redirected to produce socially desirable behavior, because "man's natural 'sociability' — his desire for the sympathy, attention, and approval of others — makes him capable of subordinating his egoistic desires to the demands of shared social rules" (Muller, 1993: 99).

One important concept in understanding Smith's idea of social interaction is "the impartial spectator." There is an element in human nature that leads us to pursue self-interest within limits and care for the welfare of others. The key to this realization lies in our imaginative ability to understand what others would feel if they were in our situation. The word Smith uses for this is "sympathy," a "fellow-feeling with any passion whatever" for other people (TMS, Part I. Ch. I., p.5) (Smith, 1892). In a similar vein, other people display concerns for our feelings. Thus the desire for a shared sympathy serves as a social motive for people to accommodate to one another's sentiments. Because sympathy allows people to disengage themselves from their own feelings and to evaluate the actions and motives of selves and others without any bias, a standard of what Smith calls "the impartial spectator" is reached. It is through acting as "the impartial spectator" that individuals measure their behavior by the imaginative standards of others to gain the approval of others in their social behaviors. So human passions can be disciplined by the market, which is comprised of buyers and sellers freely engaged in day-to-day commercial activities, and civil society, rather than government, creates what Smith calls the "natural order" in society.

Another important notion of Smith's civil society is his metaphor of the Invisible Hand, which refers to the positive unintended consequences in civil affairs resulting from cooperation in economic activities necessitated by a free market economy. It appears only once in the *Wealth of Nations*:

> As every individual ... endeavours ... both to employ his capital in the support of domestic industry, and so to direct that industry that its

produce may be of the greatest value ... He generally, indeed, neither intends to promote the publick interest, nor knows how much he is promoting it ... and he is in this ... led by an *invisible hand* to promote an end which was no part of his intention ... By pursuing his own interest he frequently promotes that of the society more effectually than when he really intends to promote it. (WN, Vol. I, Book IV, Ch. II, 477–478).

(Smith, 1976. Emphasis added)

So through self-seeking operations, each individual also makes a contribution to the common good of society. Thus the moral promise of commercial society lies in its capability in civil society to channel individual self-interested passions into positive directions that benefit the society as a whole.

Smith again uses the term "Invisible Hand" only once in his *Theory of Moral Sentiments*, echoing his theme in the *Wealth of Nations*. Although the rich are driven by their "natural selfishness and rapacity" to accumulate and purchase, they unwittingly distribute a large residue of their goods to the poor.

They are led by an *invisible hand* to make nearly the same distribution of the necessities of life that would have been made had the earth been divided into equal portions among all its inhabitants; and thus, without intending it, without knowing it, advance the interest of society, and afford means to the multiplication of the species. (TMS, Part IV, Ch. I, p. 264–265. Emphasis added).

(Smith, 1892)

Thus, the Invisible Hand helps us achieve the natural harmonious order in civil society.

Although Smith argues against direct government interference with the economy, he also thinks that the state is the most important institution on which commercial society depends. The state is essential, according to Smith, because it provides the authority and security for the survival and functioning of commerce. On the one hand, there is the potentially destructive force of group self-interest in civil society that the state has to reckon with. In every state, Smith writes, there are numerous orders and societies of civil affairs concerned more with their particular interests and privileges (TMS, Part VI, Sect. II, Ch. II.) (Smith, 1892). Because all these civil institutions invariably go to the state for prosperity and protection, it is the responsibility of the state to balance among these orders and societies to maintain the stability and permanency of the whole society. On the other hand, civil society also provides the necessary balance and check on state power. Where there is a paucity of civil associations, an arbitrary and despotic government results (Muller, 1993).

So Adam Smith believed in the beneficial effects of the economy of competition, the profit motive, and the free market on the moral developments and public virtue in society, as well as their contributions to freedom and civilization (Reisman, 1976). This is Smith's idea of, to use his own words, "commercial humanism." But this is only made possible by a panoply of nongovernmental institutions that channel individual passions toward socially desirable outcomes. The role of civil society, therefore, is its capability of transforming the base human desire of self-interest into promoting not only the materialistic but also the spiritual and moral wealth of the nations.

Georg Wilhelm Friedrich Hegel (1770 to 1831) explicitly made the conceptual separation of civil society and the state as we understand it today for the first time (e.g., Cohen and Arato, 1992; Seligman, 1992). Indeed, this separation is one of the most important features of Hegel's political philosophy. Prior to Hegel's time, in ancient Greek and medieval thought, there was no distinction between the political and the civil — "civil society" was used interchangeably with "political society" (Riedel, 1984). Hegel's conceptual scheme of the distinct sphere of civil society was to answer the call of the changing socioeconomic conditions of his time.

Hegel defines civil society in the following well-known passage:

> Civil society is the [stage of] difference which intervenes between the family and the state, even if its full development occurs later than that of the state; for as difference, it presupposes the state, which it must have before it as a self-sufficient entity in order to subsist itself ... In civil society, each individual is his own end, and all else means nothing to him. But he cannot accomplish the full extent of his ends without reference to others; these others are therefore means to the end of the particular [person]. But through its reference to others, the particular end takes on the form of universality, and gains satisfaction by simultaneously satisfying the welfare of others. Since particularity is tied to the condition of universality, the whole [of civil society] is the sphere of mediation in which all individual characteristics, all aptitudes, and all accidents of birth and fortune are liberated, and where the waves of all passions surge forth, governed only by the reason which shines through them.
>
> (Hegel 1991, Elements of the Philosophy of Right [hence referred to as PR] §182: 220-21)

The emergence of a social sphere of private interactions distinct from family and state where individuals pursue their particular interests in Hegel's characterization corresponds to "the development of capitalism, the beginning of industrialism, and the rise of the bourgeoisie" (Hardimon, 1994: 189). Then why is there the modern need for a separate sphere of human ethical life intervening between the family and the state? The starting point to understanding the Hegelian civil society is Hegel's conception of the natural unity of family.

For Hegel, the family represents a unit of ethical or spiritual unity because it is a substantial whole or universal in which the individual finds his or her self-consciousness. In Hegel's words,

> The family, as the *immediate substantiality* of spirit, has as its determination the spirit's *feeling* of its own unity, which is *love*. Thus, the disposition [appropriate to the family] is to have self-consciousness of one's individuality *within this unity* as essentiality which has being in and for itself, so that one is present in it not as an independent person but as a *member*.

(PR, §158: 199. Emphasis original)

Hegel departs significantly from the classical and medieval conception in that he does not regard the family as entering into the political arena of the state. Instead, "[t]he family as an institution provides [a] stable, continuing source of capital on which the economic system of civil society can be built and a nascent civic-mindedness on the basis of which the political state can be secured" (Brod, 1992: 65). This is Hegel's idea of the "ethical quality" (PR, §170–172), which produces propertied individuals to lay the ethical foundations of the state. So the family is the "primary basis of the state" (PR, §255) and the "ethical root of the state" (PR, §265).

Civil society is the sphere that is beyond the patriarchal connections of the family and below the universality of the state. It is the social configuration where the individuality and self-interest submerged in the family and the state become liberated, and where men, as individuals, pursue their separate and particular (mainly economic) interests. The emergence of an autonomous sphere of self-interested, individual activity independent of the family and the state was a development in Western Europe in the eighteenth century, especially after the French Revolution of 1789 (Pelczynski, 1984). Or, in Hegel's own words, "the creation of civil society belongs to the modern world, which for the first time allows all the determinations of the Idea to attain their rights" (PR, §182: 220).

Hegel, as an important forerunner in the conception of civil society, used the term in a noticeably narrower sense than most contemporary scholars (Franco, 1999; Hardimon, 1994). This point will become obvious in the discussion that follows. Instead of being an all-inclusive term for the vast array of associations mediating the family and the state, as used by many researchers today, Hegel's notion of civil society primarily falls into three sections: the system of needs, the administration of justice, and the police and corporation.

The first aspect of Hegel's civil society, the system of needs, is the economy proper where human needs are satisfied by individuals exchanging goods and services. Unlike animals, whose needs are purely natural and biological, the needs of human beings multiply and refine as the system develops (PR, §191 and §192), and human needs are subjective and social in nature (PR, §192). So needs are generated and satisfied through the spirit of recognition and cooperation. The particularity and universality of human needs are embodied in human work, and in this particular aspect, Hegel focuses on the division of labor that instills a sense of interdependence and social acceptance. The division of labor not only divides individuals into groups of particular skills and talents; it also voluntarily links them into something larger and more universal than their individual self-interest: social groups or "estates" based on their affiliations with specific trades (PR, §201).

The second major component of Hegel's civil society is the administration of justice, wherein, as Inwood (1992: 54) summarizes, "abstract right is codified in laws that are definite, promulgated and known, and are designed to protect individuals against injury." The administration of justice, Hegel insists, provides the legal structure necessary for the regulation of the system of needs by offering protection of property and contracts that are essential for the functioning of the market economy. The administration of justice educates individuals of civil society to the importance of respecting each other's rights and honoring contract; it also regulates the pursuit of individual needs by codifying, promulgating, and enforcing the law of individual rights; finally, it confers the status of property on the products individuals produce, exchange, and consume (PR, §208 and §218; see also Hardimon, 1994, and Verma, 1974 for a summary).

Because the administration of justice only concerns abstract rights, it fails to take into account the subjective particularity and welfare of the individual. Hegel's solution to this problem is his third component of civil society: "But since I [as an individual] am completely involved in particularity, I have a right to demand that, within this context, my particular welfare should also be promoted. Account should be taken to my welfare, of my particularity, and this is the task of the police and the corporation" (PR, §229: 259).

Hegel's use of the term "police" is much broader than merely the maintenance of public order or the enforcement of law as now understood. It involves a host of activities initiated by the government to intervene in the market and to regulate and control civil society. Hegel's *Polizei*, therefore, is often translated into "public authority" to differentiate its meaning from today's counterpart (e.g., Hardimon, 1994: 195; Westphal, 1992: 43). In addition to crime prevention and control, Hegel's police are also responsible for a wide range of public services that are performed by public institutions today: "the provision and operation of public utilities and works ... the regulation of the market ... consumer protection, public health, public education, welfare, and prevention of unemployment" (Hardimon, 1992: 195). For Hegel, policing in a modern civil society, as clear from the above inclusions, involves the creation of a healthy environment for the proper workings of the economy.

Similarly, Hegel's use of corporation (*Korporationen*) has little to do with what is understood as corporations of industrial or financial conglomerates today. Instead, "Hegel sees the *Korporation* as representing the interests of a particular industry in general" (Cullen, 1979: 92). Therefore, Hegel's corporation, which is formed in the service of particular interests, is tantamount to the network of associations that are considered so crucial for today's democracy in contemporary political theories. Corporations include not only economic organizations, or "trade guilds" as Hegel called them, but also such noneconomic associations such as religious bodies, learned societies, and sometimes town councils (PR, §270 and §288).

The dual nature of modern Man is important in understanding Hegel's theory of civil society and the state (Cullen, 1979). On one hand, there is the particular aspect, which motivates individuals to pursue their own selfish ends and to look after their own interests; on the other hand, there is the universal aspect, which makes people interdependent upon each other in a community. Man's particularity is actualized in civil society, where individuals compete with each other to further their own interests:

> Particularity in itself is boundless extravagance, and the forms of this extravagance are themselves boundless. Through their representations and reflections, human beings expand their desires ... But on the other hand, deprivation and want are likewise boundless, and this confused situation can be restored to harmony only through the forcible intervention of the state.

> (PR, §185: 223)

Separate individuals in civil society are integrated into their universality in the structure of the rational state. Thus, the state is the political arena in which particularity and universality are harmonized into a unity. Hegel's state is strictly political in nature and is designed to deal with nothing but purely political affairs as well as to promote the common good of the community, which should be distinguished from the particular interests of individual members.

When Hegel died in 1821, he had attained the status of an intellectual giant who brought worldwide acclaim to the German intellectual and had bequeathed an elaborate philosophy to his disciples — a philosophy that was unsurpassed in its breadth and depth but yet difficult and ambiguous sometimes. Karl Marx (1818 to 1883), whose ideas are among the most influential in social theories in the twentieth century, joined in his youth a group of radical enthusiasts calling themselves the Young Hegelians (Breckman, 1999). Marx shared the Young Hegelians' ambition to rethink Hegel and go beyond him without completely turning their backs to him.

Marx's idea of civil society began with his criticism of what he perceived as flaws and inconsistencies in Hegel's concept of civil society. As Jean Cohen points out, "Hegel excelled in grasping the 'positive side' of the emergence of civil society; Marx's main contribution consisted in accounting for its 'negative side' — the new forms of domination and stratification proliferating on its terrain" (Cohen, 1982: 25). While Hegel's doctrine provided the general parameters for Marx's intellectual inspirations, Marx arrived at his own social theory primarily after a negative criticism of Hegel (O'Malley, 1970). Many scholars have called attention to the original German term that Hegel and Marx used, *bürgliche Gesellshaft*, which means both "civil society" and "bourgeois society" (e.g., Rauch, 1981). While Hegel's use of the word includes both the civil and the bourgeois aspects, Marx used the concept to focus on the bourgeois side by reducing civil society to the capitalist mode of production.

Marx's critical examination of Hegel's political philosophy led him to believe that the political state represents not universal but particular interests. Private and special interests do not only find expression in civil society; they actively seek representation through "organs of the state" in the political state (Teeple, 1984: 46). The hold of power by material interest in the political state, Marx concludes, makes the political state not unify but stand against civil society. Marx's criticism of Hegel is found mainly in his commentary on the *Philosophy of Rights*, Hegel's major work in political philosophy, and his manuscript is usually referred to as the *Critique of Hegel's "Philosophy of Right."*

First of all, Marx takes issue with the self-contradictory nature of the state in Hegel's own statements. At one place, Hegel claims that "the state is contrasted with the spheres of family and civil society as an external necessity," and elsewhere, Hegel understands this "dependence" to be "of internal dependence." "At the same time, however, he subsumes this dependence under the relationship and opposes it, as another aspect, to that relationship wherein family and civil society relate to the state as to their immanent end" (Marx, 1970a: 5). External necessity, by and large, must dominate that which is subordinate or secondary. "Precisely because subordination and dependence are external relations, limiting and contrary to an autonomous being, the relationship of family and civil society to the state is that of external necessity, a necessity which relates by opposition to the inner being of the thing" (Marx, 1970a: 6). But the family and civil society are "presupposed by the state as particular spheres" of an autonomous unity. So "external necessity" is contrary to the essential relationship of the whole and the parts, which characterizes the relationship between the state at one end, and the family and civil society at the other end. As a result, wrote Marx, "Hegel sets up an unresolved antinomy: on the one hand external necessity, on the other hand immanent end" (Marx, 1970a: 6).

Marx's criticism of the "external necessity" extends over several sections of the *Critique*. Marx's focus is on the contrarieties of Hegel's argument concerning the relation of the state to the family and civil society. As presuppositions of the state, Marx contends,

> Family and civil society are actual components of the state ... they are the modes of existence of the state; ... According to Hegel they are, on the contrary, made by the actual Idea ... they owe their existence to a mind other than their own ... This is to say that the political state cannot exist without the natural basis of the family and the artificial basis of civil society ... but the conditions are established as the conditioned, the determining as the determined, the producing as the product of its product.
>
> (Marx, 1970a: 8–9)

So here Marx pinpointed Hegel's unsolvable inconsistency: he inverted the subject and predicate, and thus the nature of the transition of the family and civil society into the political state.

Marx in a large part accepted Hegel's presentation of the state as an organism, one in which the whole and its parts are unified. However, Marx argued, Hegel's idealism creates some logical inconsistencies in his actual presentation of this discovery. The problem for Hegel is, Marx demonstrated in the *Critique*, that he cannot bridge a transition "from the universal idea of the organism to the particular idea of the organism of the state or the constitution of the state," and therefore Hegel can do "nothing but resolve the constitution of the state into the universal, abstract idea of the organism" (Marx, 1970a: 14).

The general interest of the state, Marx argued, has no content other than the particular interests of civil society. To put it another way, the actual content of the political state is none other than the material interest. However, Hegel's characterization of the bureaucracy remains an abstraction and there is no content in his "formalism of the state." The bureaucracy, Marx points out repeatedly, presupposes the separation of the state and civil society; consequently, the reuniting of the two in the bureaucracy can only spell the end of the bureaucracy. Here is Marx's own solution to Hegel's contradiction: "The abolition of the bureaucracy can consist only in the universal interest becoming really ... a particular interest; and this is possible only through the particular interest really becoming universal" (p. 48). This subsumption of the particular and general into one, as Marx would show us later, is only possible in the communist state.

One concept at the center of Marx's political philosophy is that of man as a species being, which means that man is aware of being not only his individual self but his species-character as well. This doctrine permeates all his political writings from his early political journalistic essays to the *Germany Ideology* to the *Capital* (e.g., Kain, 1993; McCarthy, 1990). It also serves as the conceptual basis for Marx's critique of Hegel's civil society. As a species being, man is a social as well as political being; he consciously performs his social and political functions. It is because of his species character, writes Avineri (1975: 33), that "[m]odern civil society, based on individualism, violates, according to Marx, man as a social being." As species beings, the full development of individual elements is only possible with the development of the whole species. The very nature of the capitalist mode of production represents these relationships in the exchange of products and services; and the separation of the state from the family and civil society inevitably leads to the alienation of man, Marx observed.

Human beings as a species are characterized by their productive powers and practices. "The whole character of a species resides in the nature of its life activity, and free conscious activity constitutes the species character of man" (Marx, 1975: 328). In capitalist society, productive activities by the working class have a dualistic role, and this is Marx's concept of labor. On one hand, labor is "conceived as a process of *objectification* through which individuals create their needs, abilities, and world" (Cohen, 1982: 69. Emphasis original). In this sense, labor is a liberating force through which the individual worker develops. On the other hand, "[i]t prevents him from recognizing himself in his product, it separates and atomizes him from his fellows, it turns his free life activity into a forced and deforming means of survival, and it subjugates him to the domination of another — the capitalist" (Cohen, 1982: 69). This estrangement or alienation, the condition under which the proletarian becomes the victim of its creative powers, gives it the emancipatory potential as a universal class for the realization of species capabilities in the future.

Marx borrowed from Hegel's notion of a universal class, "a class within society whose interests are identical with the interests of society as a whole, and therefore of man himself as a naturally social, species-being" (O'Malley, 1970: lii). However, Marx did this with a significant twist: he substitutes Hegel's bureaucracy with the proletariat as a universal class. The universal character of the proletariat as a class derives from the fact that it is

> a class in civil society that is not of civil society, a class that is the dissolution of all classes, a sphere of society having a universal character because of its universal suffering and claiming no particular right because no particular wrong but unqualified wrong is perpetrated on it ... a sphere, finally, that cannot emancipate itself without emancipating itself from all the other spheres of society.

> (Marx, 1970b: 141)

So Marx sees in the proletariat the solution to the problems of civil society. After examining the nature of the state and civil society in capitalism by analyzing private property, production relations, bourgeoisie and proletariat class relations, and alienated labor, Marx intended to show that the antinomy of the state and civil society is an inevitable consequence of the capitalist mode of production. After his dismissal of Hegel's model of civil society, Marx constructed his own vision of the sociopolitical ideal of the state–civil society.

Civil society, the source of the contradictions in the modern state, creates a universal class, the proletariat as its own "grave digger," Marx declared. Nothing less than a fundamental transformation of civil society can eliminate the contradictions — a transformation that can only be accomplished by the proletariat, the only class that can unify the particular and the general. The proletariat embraces the emancipation of humanity as its historic mission, an emancipation in which, for the first time in history, there is a union of the man as individual and citizen. In Marx's vision, conquest of the political power by the proletariat will lead us to the communist state — a state in which civil society, along with private property and class, is abolished. As a result, all mediating instances between state and society are dissolved into the state, and individual and community are reconciled into unity (Marx & Engels, 1976; 1992).

It is hard to overestimate the influence of Marx's thought on modern social and political theory. His analysis of the capitalist socioeconomic relations continues to have relevance today. However, as many have noted (e.g., Cohen, 1982), Marx has left much unsaid in his theorization. It is partly for this reason that Marx's ideas have been subject to misconceptions and misinterpretations since their inception. Partly thanks to Marx's sweeping and deconstructive criticism of Hegel's theory, the idea of civil society to a great extent fell into intellectual limbo (e.g., Madison, 1998) until its contemporary revival in Eastern Europe. Oddly enough, this revival was paralleled with a decline, if not total demise, of Marxism as a state ideology worldwide.

Democratic Implications of Civil Society

The democratic terrain of civil society has not been a part of the conceptual framework in the political philosophies mapped out by the thinkers examined above. Popular political participation in a democratic polity is not an attribute of Hegel's conception of civil society because the atomized nature of civil society will, if left unchecked, split the state into competing, and often mutually hostile, factions. Bureaucracy (i.e., estate-constituted legislature) is the mediating class to reconcile community, individual, and social interests. Political democracy, instead, is replaced by participation in nonpolitical institutions of civil society, such as corporations or professional associations, and no distinction is made between the rights of men from the rights of the citizens (Benhabib, 1984).

It is because of the separation of the man in civil society from the citizen in the state that Marx criticizes the capitalist civil society as antidemocratic. Accepting Hegel's corporate organization of civil society, Marx sees modern civil society, which seeks representation in the state via the estate system, as running against the principles of its own making uncovered by Hegel — the principles of free association and independence. This led Marx to believe that the opposition between civil society and the state is irreconcilable (Cohen, 1982). As a result, Marx dispels the potentiality of democratic effects of any institutions of civil society. According to Marx, true democracy is marked by the direct participation of free, self-determining, and autonomous individuals in the political affairs of the state. Because civil society is seen by Marx to be created by the modern capitalist mode of production and to be the cause of political alienation, and because civil society is by its very nature separated from the state, Marx only envisions the reunification of state and civil society, of man and citizen, in a classless society of communism that opens politics to mass participation and deliberation (e.g., Gilbert, 1991). So Marx's solution to the antidemocratic tendencies of civil society is its total abolition.

The consensus in contemporary theories of civil society that the viability of democracy is contingent on the robustness of voluntary associations finds its first inspiration in the writings of Alex de Tocqueville, who was the first one to articulate the compatibility of civil society and democracy — in *Democracy in America* published in 1835. Thus Tocqueville was the forerunner of what Ehrenberg (1999: 201) calls the "pluralist foundations" of the theories of civil society. Arguably, the *Federalist Papers* and *Democracy in America* are called the only two classics of American political theory (Wolin, 2001: 3).

Right at the beginning of *Democracy in America*, Tocqueville wrote, "nothing struck me more forcibly than the general equality of condition among the people ... I soon perceived that the influence of this fact extends far beyond the political character and the laws of the country, and that it has no less effect on civil society than on the government ... " (Tocqueville, 1985a: 3). Against the backdrop of equality is Americans' obsession with individualism, which "is a mature and calm feeling, which disposes each member of the community to sever himself from the mass of his fellows and to draw apart with his family and his friends, so that after he has thus formed a little circle of his own, he willingly leaves society at large to himself" (Tocqueville, 1985b: 98). Then, how do Americans overcome the danger that equality and individualism will split society apart? By free institutions, Tocqueville observed. "The Americans have combated by free institutions the tendency of equality to keep men asunder, and they have subdued it" (Tocqueville, 1985b: 103). Here we see the essence of Tocqueville's conception of civil society.

Associational relations are voluntary and contractual, Tocqueville notes. "An association consists simply in the public assent which a number of individuals give to certain doctrines and in the engagement which they contract to promote in a certain manner the spread of those doctrines" (Tocqueville, 1985b: 192). Rousseau said that freedom is obedience to laws we prescribe ourselves (Plamenatz, 1992: 163). This declaration wins Tocqueville's total support:

> The most natural privilege of man, next to the right of acting for himself, is that of combining his exertions with those of his fellow creatures and of acting in common with them. The right of association therefore appears to me almost as inalienable in its nature as the right of personal liberty.

> (Tocqueville, 1985b: 196)

Amazed by the prevalence and multiplicity of associations ingenuously formed by Americans, Tocqueville came to this illuminating conclusion: "In democratic countries the science of association is the mother of science; the progress of all the rest depends upon the progress it has made" (1985b: 110).

It is through associations that Americans learn the spirit of cooperation, because association brings men out of their own confines and teaches them the need to "surrender their own will to that of all the rest and to make their own exertions subordinate to the common impulse" (1985b: 116). One premise that is of great relevance today is Tocqueville's argument for a reciprocal connection between political and civil associations: the vitality and vigor of one kind depends on the other and vice versa. Referring to political associations, Tocqueville wrote that "instead of directing the minds of the community of public affairs these institutions serve to divert them from such reflections, and that, by engaging them more and more in the pursuit of objects which cannot be attained with public tranquility, they deter them from revolutions" (1985b: 118). He ridiculed those governments that abhor political associations, because "these governments do not attend to the fact that political associations tend amazingly to multiply and facilitate those of a civil character, and that in avoiding a dangerous evil they deprive themselves of an efficacious remedy" (1985b: 118).

Associations not only combat individualism, they also provide a buttress against the central power of the government elected by the general will of the people. "At the present time the liberty of association has become a necessary guarantee against the tyranny of the majority" (1985b: 194); it is the existence of a vibrant civil society that brings about the decentralized administration and a weak state in the United States (i.e., strong society, weak state, which is the idealized model for many scholars today), Tocqueville (1985a: 59–97) points out. Thus freedom of association is the defining feature of a stable, well-ordered democracy because the civil society of voluntary associations provides balances and checks against the political power of the state. We see a continuation of this Tocquevillean theme in present-day discussions.

Of particular interest to journalism scholars is the intimate connection Tocqueville builds between freedom of the press and associations. In addition to circulating ideas to scattered individuals for "intercommunication and combination" (Tocqueville, 1985b: 113), newspapers bring association into being. "A newspaper can survive only on the condition of publishing sentiments or principles common to a large number of men. A newspaper, therefore, always represents an association that is composed of its habitual readers" (Tocqueville, 1985b: 113). In a word, "newspapers make associations, and associations make newspapers," Tocqueville (1985b: 112) nicely summarizes. Almost two centuries later, Tocqueville's theme is echoed by Benedict Anderson (1991), who asserts that "all communities ... are imagined" (p. 6) and claims that early American newspapers "created an imagined community among a specific assemblage of fellow-readers" (Anderson, 1991: 62).

Tocqueville's premises in *Democracy in America* have had enduring significance and have found perennial appeal in Western political thought. The publication of the first volume of *Democracy in America* in 1835 and volume two in 1840 brought Tocqueville instantaneous fame. Interest in Tocqueville in Europe and America declined from the late nineteenth century until the 1930s, when the age of totalitarianism and the subsequent cold war revitalized interest in *Democracy in America* (Eisenstadt, 1988: 4–12). The full Tocqueville revival in the United States came in the 1940s and 1950s, when American scholars, with the vantage point of hindsight, realized the prophetic power of Tocqueville in the wake of a series of historic events in the century following the publication of *Democracy in America* (Rodgers, 1988).

That the American democratic polity is deeply entrenched in associational life also finds voluminous support in John Dewey. Dewey challenges the individualistic philosophy in the Lockean tradition and warns that to conceive of the individual as isolated and possessed of inherent rights "by nature" apart from association would be a great mistake, because "[m]en have always been associated together in living, and association in conjoint behavior has affected their relations to one another as individuals" (Dewey, 1946: 97). According to Dewey, democracy "is not an alternative to other principles of associational life. It is the idea of community life itself" (Dewey, 1946: 148). The democratic government chosen by the majority vote is justified only in its function as a state machinery force to first help the inchoate and unorganized public to define and express its common goods and interests, and then make them the supreme guide and criterion of all governmental activities. The only path to the realization of those objectives is to create the conditions in which associative groups can interact flexibly and fully in connection with each other. Democratic ideas, such as fraternity, liberty, and equality, are hopeless abstractions when taken out of associational life (Dewey, 1954).

Robert N. Bellah and his associates keep alive Dewey's caution about the destructive effects of "Lockean individualism" on creating the "good society" of republican ideals and civic virtue. To shift the focus of public debate from a concern for maximizing individual interests to the "central problems of a sustainable future in our society" (Bellah et al., 1991: 143) — that is, a search for a common good that benefits everyone in the long run — we must generate a constellation of institutions, both public and private, which strive to strengthen "bonds of a nonpecuniary kind" (Bellah et al., 1991: 169) that will be of little interest to the market or interest groups. It is herein that civil society can create organizational and physical spaces where constructive argument can take place. As Bellah et al. note,

> [T]he organizations of the "third sector" — such as schools and universities, religious organizations, theaters, museums, and orchestras, voluntary associations of all kinds — have given the collective purposes of justice, mutual aid, enlightenment, worship, fellowship, and celebration some substance in metropolitan life. They have civilized commerce and enhanced metropolitan life and have saved the market from its own worst consequences. But they have done more. They are points of "focal structure," places where people can meet to focus their attention and gain a sense of the whole of life through the cultivation of memory and orientation.
>
> (Bellah et al., 1991: 169)

The democratic effects of the associational fabric of civil society stressed in the Tocquevillian paradigm were fully revived in what has now become a modern classic in democratic theory in Almond and Verba's *The Civic Culture* (1989). First published in 1963, this book seeks to explain differences in democratic governance in five nations through an examination of a particular set of political values, attitudes, and skills believed necessary in democratization and democratic stabilization. According to Almond and Verba, the development of a democratic form of participatory polity requires a political culture consistent with it — the "civic culture" of which Britain stands as a model for the world. The civic culture is first and foremost "a participant political culture in which the political culture and political structure are congruent" (Almond and Verba, 1989: 30). But more importantly, in the process of political participation, individuals retain their subjective and parochial political orientations in civic culture. As a result, "... attitudes favorable to participation within the political system play a major role in the civic culture, but so do such nonpolitical attitudes as trust in other people and social participation in general" (p. 30).

Almond and Verba also attest to the proposition that the existence of voluntary associations increases the democratic potential of a society: organization membership leads to more civil cooperation and higher political competence. Moreover, patterns of participation in voluntary associations display a cumulative effect: the number of organizations with which an individual is affiliated affects his or her political competence positively — this is what Almond and Verba call the "cumulative effect of participatory experiences" (p. 297).

Noticeably, Almond and Verba demonstrated that citizen participation in a democratic polity is not limited to political institutions alone; rather, it materializes in a complex process that involves many social organizations, such as family, peer group, school, and workplace, as well as the political system itself. Indeed, as many have cautioned in different historical periods, excessive political activity by citizens could endanger the existence of a democratic society. The more successful democracies, Almond and Verba conclude, are marked by a nice equilibrium in the civic culture: "It is a mixture in the first place of parochial, subject, and citizen orientations ... The result is a set of political orientations that are managed or balanced. There is political activity, but not so much as to destroy governmental authority; there is political cleavage, but it is held in check" (p. 360). Only this kind of subtle mixture in the civic culture, Almond and Verba argue, can sustain a stable and effective democratic political system.

The emphasis on democratic participation in the pluralist tradition elaborated in *The Civic Culture* recaptured scholarly attention, in part, through an impressive survey by Verba, Scholzman, and Brady (1995) in *Voice and Equality, Civic Voluntarism in American Politics*. They examined the nature of participation of civil society in American politics in times of accelerating unequal distribution of economic, social, and political resources among citizen groups. Their "civic voluntarism model" first demonstrates that "both the motivation and the capacity to take part in politics have their roots in the fundamental non-political institutions with which individuals are associated during the course of their lives" (Verba et al., 1995: 3). Thus factors that foster political engagement are stockpiled over the course of a person's lifetime in civil society. However, Verba et al. skillfully show that the disposition to participate bears the unmistakable marks of cleavages of race, ethnicity, education, class, time, money, and other available resources. Robert Putnam also draws on the Tocquevillean tradition in his *Making Democracy Work* (1993) by analyzing the nature and effects of voluntary associations in amassing social capital in northern and southern Italy. The publication of Putnam's research has spurred a wave of theoretical debates and empirical studies of the key role played in maintaining effective political governance by a vibrant civil society of secondary organizations with social capital at its center.

Couto (1999) traces the origin of the use of the term "social capital" to James O'Connor's (1973) *The Fiscal Crisis of the State*. However, the theoretical framework within which O'Connor employs the term is drastically different from the current understanding of social capital in political theories. O'Connor's intellectual heritage is tied to Marxist economics, which maps out the twofold character of the capitalist state's basic functions into social capital and social expenses. Social capital, O'Connor explains, "is expenditures required for profitable private accumulation; it is indirectly productive" (as against social expenses, which are not indirectly productive) (1973: 6). Putnam's use of the term is directly borrowed from Coleman (1990), who turns it into a central explanatory factor for the control of individual and collective behavior among a system of interdependent social relations: "Like other forms of capital, social capital is productive, making possible the achievement of certain ends that would not be attainable in its absence ... Unlike other forms of capital, social capital inheres in the structure of relations between persons and among persons" (p. 302). The usefulness of the concept is that it identifies the value of certain aspects of social structure to individual actors "as resources that can be used by the actors to realize their interests," and it allows "showing how such resources can be combined with other resources to produce different system-level behavior or, in other cases, different outcomes for individuals" (Coleman, 1990: 305).

Putnam's definition of social capital — which "refers to features of social organization, such as trust, norms, and networks, that can improve the efficiency of society by facilitating coordinated actions" (Putnam, 1993: 167) — clearly is deep-rooted in Coleman's theoretical construct. There is, however, one significant differentiation in Putnam's treatment of the concept. Coleman essentially limits his theoretical exploration of the production and maintenance of social capital to a series of economic functions and market relations, and he tries to model the decision-making process involving social capital in a set of mathematical equations. This give-and-take approach to social capital as private, divisible goods leads Coleman to argue that social capital is subject to the "free rider" dilemma commonly noticed in game theory. Putnam, on the other hand, calls special attention to the public nature of social capital. "One special feature of social capital, like trust, norms, and networks, is that it is ordinarily a public good, unlike conventional capital, which is ordinarily a private good" (Putnam, 1993: 170). Therefore, there is a moral dimension to social capital. Putnam incorporates Hirschman's (1984) work on "moral resources" into his conceptualization of social capital and argues that "[o]ther forms of social capital, too, such as social norms and networks, increase with use and diminish with disuse. For all these reasons, we should expect the creation and destruction of social capital to be marked by virtuous and vicious circles" (Putnam, 1993: 170).

Another significant effort by Putnam is the role he assigns to the civic culture as espoused by Almond and Verba in the production and sustenance of social capital. Drawing on Tocqueville's classic interpretation of American democracy, and Almond and Verba's description of civic virtue, Putnam concludes that "the civic community is marked by an active, public-spirited citizenry, by egalitarian political relations, by a social fabric of trust and cooperation" (Putnam, 1993: 15). Trust is an essential component of social capital, and it is necessary in sustaining civic cooperation among voluntary associations. "Social trust in complex settings can arise from two related sources — norms of reciprocity and networks of civic engagement," Putnam (1993: 171) summarizes. Reciprocity, the most important of all norms, is of two sorts: the "balanced," which involves a simultaneous exchange of items of equivalent value, and "generalized," which involves a continuing relationship of exchange that is at any given time unrequited or imbalanced but a benefit granted now that is expected to be repaid in the future. The latter, the norm of generalized reciprocity, is a more productive component of social capital, Putnam contends.

Networks of communication and exchange fall into two categories. "Some of these networks are primarily 'horizontal,' bringing together agents of equivalent status and power. Others are primarily 'vertical,' linking unequal agents in asymmetric relations of hierarchy and dependence" (Putnam, 1993: 173). Only networks that represent intense horizontal interaction, such as "the neighborhood associations, choral societies, cooperatives, sports clubs, mass-based parties" (Putnam, 1993: 174) (in other words, civil society of voluntary organizations), contribute to civic engagement; vertical networks, such as patron–client relations, cannot build social trust and civic collaboration.

Putnam further makes the distinction between two types of social capital: bridging social capital and bonding social capital. The former connects people of different groups while the latter links people within the same group who share similar backgrounds and beliefs. These two types of social capital play different roles in social networks:

> Bonding capital is good for undergirding specific reciprocity and mobilizing solidarity ... Bridging networks, by contrast, are better for linkage to external assets and for information diffusion ... . Moreover, bridging social capital can generate broader identities and reciprocity, whereas bonding social capital bolsters our narrower selves ... . Bonding social capital constitutes a kind of sociological superglue, whereas bridging social capital provides a sociological WD-40.

> (Putnam, 2000: 22–23)

Most social groups serve both bridging and bonding functions, although civic networks typically fall closer to either the internality or externality end of the spectrum.

As early as the 1950s, Robert Nisbet made pioneering observations on the role of associative structures as balances and checks against the excessive power of the capitalist market and government. Nisbet agrees with John Dewey that individual freedom is a social, not biologically derived, process. Family, church, and local community — what Nisbet calls "intermediate associations" — play a central role in forming individual allegiance, loyalty, and moral values, the kind of social capital in Putnam's term. The collapse of intermediate associations in a society will lead to totalitarianism, a state of spiritual and cultural vacuum, when individuals have lost "their accustomed roots of membership and belief," Nisbet writes (1969: 204). As demonstrated by Hitler's Nazi Germany and Stalin's Soviet Union, the totalitarian state is an absolute, total, and political community made possible "by the removal of all forms of membership and identification which might, by their existence, compete with the new order. It is, further, made absolute by the insistence that all thought, belief, worship, and membership be within the structure of the State" (Nisbet,

1969: 204–205). The elimination of intermediate associations in totalitarian states "can lead only to social and cultural death" (Nisbet, 1969: 211).

Totalitarianism is not the only enemy of intermediate organizations; the enlarged and centralized economy in the capitalist age has also posed a threat to associative relations. Nisbet attributes the alienation he has observed among individuals to changes in both the economy and the state. "The recent history of capitalism, especially in its vast corporate forms, has tended to weaken steadily the symbolic and the normative aspect of economic life," Nisbet (1969: 239) points out. We face two alternatives, Nisbet says: "Capitalism is either a system of social and moral allegiances, resting securely in institutions and voluntary associations, or it is a sand heap of disconnected particles of humanity. If it is, or is allowed to become, the latter, there is nothing that can prevent the rise of centralized, omnicompetent political power" (Nisbet, 1969: 241). Nisbet's points are echoed by Paul Hirst, albeit more radically, in his proposed democratic framework of "associative democracy." Hirst conceives voluntary self-governing associations as the primary means of democratic governance of economic and social affairs, reversing the tradition of liberal democratic theories, which view voluntary bodies as "secondary associations" whose role as the social foundation of pluralistic politics is to ensure the democratic nature of the "primary association," the state as the central political community (see also Cohen and Rogers, 1992).

To be sure, not all associations are conducive to the democratic experience. In his effort to develop a "democratic ecology of associations," Mark Warren (2001) analyzes the pluralism of potential effects that different types of associations exert on a robust democracy. The full range of democratic effects and the norms necessary for a democratic ecology of associations, according to Warren, are individual autonomy, political autonomy, and institutional democracy; however, no single kind of association can provide all of these effects and norms. Ideally, in a democratic ecology, no single democratic effect should marginalize other effects and hence there will be a state of associational balances. In actuality, imbalances may result if some associations are empowered to "deprive individuals of autonomy, or to bypass accountability to the publics affected by their actions, or to dominate representative institutions" (Warren, 2001: 208). Other examples of antidemocratic associations are vested associations lacking internal or external checks and balances, groups with incentives to represent commonalities while suppressing differences, and associational ties that mirror cleavages of education, income, and race and/or ethnicity (Warren, 2001: 210–213). Similarly, Nancy Rosenblum (1998) notes cases of "incivility" and antidemocracy (i.e., compelled religious and racial groups, greedy business corporations) among various associations in cultivating a pluralism of moral dispositions in the "democracy of everyday life." Nonetheless, the general democratic tendency of associational life is not to be doubted. As Warren (2001) remarks, there is nothing inherently antidemocratic in most associative organizations, and the antidemocratic potential of the other associations can be identified and minimized while their democratic possibilities are maximized through state involvement, cultural developments, and economic initiatives. The reciprocal role of civil society and the state watching over each other is best summarized by John Keane (1988b: 15) who claims that "civil society and the state ... must become the condition of each other's democratization."

To conclude my discussion in this section, if the democratic potential of the associational life of civil society has been largely marginalized in classic and early modern social theories, it has entered the center stage of contemporary theoretical debates on voluntary associations and civil society. This is particularly so after the recent reinvigoration of the term "civil society" in the political lexicon of Eastern Europe as an oppositional idea and a liberating force in toppling dictatorial rules. However, in most of the theoretical traditions examined in this section, scholars (with the noticeable exception of Tocqueville) tend to mention the mass media only in passing, and sometimes negatively (as Putnam does). The role of mass media in civil society is addressed later in this chapter.

Revival of the Concept of Civil Society in Eastern Europe

The current understanding of the concept of civil society in a variety of uses and definitions has roots in the attribution of the demise of communism and dictatorships in Eastern Europe in the late 1980s to the revolt of civil society against the state by a significant number of intellectuals both in and outside of the region. Many have concluded that the history of the democratic transformation in East Central Europe, led by countries such as Poland, Hungary, and the former Czechoslovakia, may be written as a struggle by various social forces within these countries for the rebirth of civil society crushed by decades of communist rule (e.g., Ash, 1989; Bernhard, 1993; Curry and Fajfer, 1996; U.S. Helsinki Watch Committee, 1986).

Civil society emerged as an important concept in political discourse in or about East Central Europe in the 1970s, when political activists opposing the communist system shifted their strategy "from dissidence to opposition" (Bernhard, 1993: 7). The oppositional resistance strategy involved a critical change of focus: "It ceased to be preoccupied with telling the party state authorities how to act, and instead, concentrated its efforts on society" (Bernhard, 1993: 9).

Prior to the 1970s, dissidents in the East Central European communist block did not break away from the fundamental Marxist–Leninist Soviet model of communism; they had aimed to reform from within, but not to totally abolish, the one-party communist state as specified in the Marxist political vision (see Ekiert, 1996 for an overview). For instance, dissenting intellectuals in Hungary in the 1960s, as Tamas Aczel summarizes, "had still retained their faith in the viability of certain Marxist ideals: the conviction that society's moral force would eventually triumph over the party's physical power and that only a truly socialist-humanist transformation of society could answer the questions left unanswered by totalitarian regimes" (1978: 31). By addressing grievances to the communist party-state, dissidents strived for changes in its political behavior without challenging the political framework of the Marxist–Leninist state.

The inability of dissenting forces to develop a consistent alternative political discourse and redistribution of political and social power had led to the failure of first the Hungarian Revolution of 1956 and then the Prague Spring Movement of 1968. The immediate aftermath was that revisionist Marxists were marginalized or kicked out by the ruling party, thus ending any hope of reform efforts to build any sort of "Socialism with a Human Face" (Ekiert, 1996: 162–97). Because of the failed attempts to reform the communist party from within, dissident groups in East Europe resorted to a new oppositional strategy: to appeal to the forces of society from outside the framework of the party state.

The shift of focus was the most prominent in Poland in the 1970s, with the Workers' Defense Committee (KOR for the Polish equivalent) being the first group to effectively translate strategies into practical politics. The KOR's line of action is nicely summarized by Jacek Kuron in his well-known essay "Reflections on a Programme of Action," in which Kuron concludes that the best way to initiate change in Polish society is to let social movements exert pressure from below (Kuron, 1977). The KOR set up the model for oppositional activities throughout Poland and later East Central Europe that is best expressed in Kuron's famous dictum "Don't burn down committees, found your own" (Ekiert, 1996: 232). As a result, a multitude of independent social organizations emerged in various cities in Poland in the mid-1970s (e.g., Bernhard, 1993; Curry and Fajfer, 1996; Ekiert, 1996; Raina, 1981). The culmination of Polish social movements during this period was the birth of Solidarity (a Polish trade union federation primarily engaged in the anticommunist movement in the 1980s) in September 1980.

The unusual makeup of the social movements was an alliance of intelligentsia with workers and professional groups in standing against the state. Indeed, the KOR was first started by a group of thirteen intellectuals with the goal of providing legal and material support for prosecuted workers. The intellectual origins and development of these activists, articulated in their writings at various stages, had a direct impact on the course of the KOR action. Besides Kuron, another prominent member was Adam Michnik, whose political writings had influence well beyond the KOR milieu.

After analyzing the failure of two resistance strategies in the aftermath of de-Stalinization, the "revisionist" and "neopositivist" as Michnik called them, Michnik argues that the failure was attributable to their shared conviction that change would come from above, by means of the party or state apparatus.

"Both the revisionist and neopositivists counted on positive evolution in the party, to be caused by the rational policies of wise leaders, not by incessant public pressure. They both counted on the rational thinking of the communist prince, not on independent institutions that would gain control of the power apparatus" (Michnik, 1985: 136). Michnik came to a conclusion similar to that of Kuron — that only pressure from below could limit state power and make it more responsive to society. This was "a new evolutionism" that would require a new set of tactics emphasizing oppositional power from nonstate, independent organizations.

> "New evolutionism" is based on faith in the power of the working class, which, with a steady and unyielding stand, has on several occasions forced the government to make spectacular concessions. It is difficult to foresee developments in the working class, but there is no question that the power elite fears this social group most. Pressure from the working classes is a necessary condition for the evolution of public life toward democracy.
>
> (Michnik, 1985: 144)

Thus, the reform-from-below strategy involves the creation of "self-managing" social movements in producing pressure to force great concessions from the state (Kuron, 1977). First, Kuron argues that a totalitarian system (like the Polish political system at the time) separates the power and the people, and the power "to initiate, to think, to decide" exclusively belongs to the government and the people are reduced to the status of "an amorphous mass, with no personal rights of any kind" (p. 54). The government, however, would not start reforms on its own initiative; it could only be forced into genuine negotiations for change when enough social pressure was built: "If the Government is not willing to take the necessary steps, the only way to save the country from the worst is for the people to join in a movement strong enough to force the Government into genuine negations" (p. 66). It stands to reason, therefore, that the only feasible course of action for any oppositional effort should "immediately start organizing a number of linked groups representing the widest possible spectrum of views" (p. 67).

Then, Kuron argues, it is the responsibility of the intellectuals to help the initiatives of other social groups and classes in realizing the kind of self-managing form of democracy envisioned by him. This kind of direct democracy is only possible with a solidaristic, pluralistic civil society organized on the level of "corporations, cooperatives, consumer associations, economic self-managements; different cultural associations, sponsorships, etc.; an organized farmers' movement, a movement of citizen's initiatives, of discussion clubs designed to work out certain concepts, centers whose tasks it would be to integrate individual programs. And, of course, also unions" (interview with Kuron, cited in Bernhard, 1993: 94). The communist regime in Poland, of course, would not easily relinquish power without a fight. The election of a noncommunist government in 1989 only came about after the communist elite realized the futility of governing the country without social endorsement in the face of increasing power as a result of the flourishing of consolidated organizations outside of the control of the party state.

A pronounced antagonism that is characteristic of the Polish oppositional movement is its "self-limiting" nature — or "self-limiting revolution," as it has been called (e.g., Schell, 1985; Staniszkis, 1984). It is self-limiting because, despite the overwhelming support it enjoyed from the general public, it refrained from attempting to overthrow the government or to control state power. Instead, it set out to bring about changes to the state structure through the reconstruction of an autonomous and vibrant civil society. This self-limitation is summarized by Schell thus:

> Though schooled in opposition to totalitarian rule, the Polish movement has not grown to resemble its opponent; its answer to totalitarian violence and deception has not been violence and deception with some new twist, some new political coloration. Instead, in a radical break, it has ceded those ageless instruments completely to its governmental foe, and sought its strength in altogether different sources, including, above all, the multitudinous peaceful activities of a normal civic life.

> (Schell, 1985: xviii)

Indeed, the self-limitation of civil society has given rise to a new thread of contemplation of its self-organizing, self-defensive, and self-reflexive natures in contemporary discourse of civil society in a variety of political–cultural contexts (Cohen and Arato, 1992; Ehrenberg, 1999).

The oppositional politics pioneered by KOR made it the first autonomous nonreligious organization to achieve notable social impact on the buildup of grass-roots associations as a viable form of social defense against totalitarianism (Lipski, 1985). Its strategic shift of emphasis from the state to society outside of the state power or state institutions as a target of democratization was continued in Solidarity's mode of politics. After the dissolution of KOR in 1980, many of its leaders, activists, and participants went on to assume important positions in the creation of Solidarity and other oppositional groups (Bernhard, 1993: 191–208; see also Ekiert, 1996). Membership and participation in KOR, Solidarity, and other workers' organizations played a pivotal role in the cultivation and revitalization of civic identity and citizenship values among Polish workers (Cirtautas, 1997; Goodwyn, 1991), and it is no coincidence that Poland became the first post-communist nation in Eastern Europe to engage in democratic reform of its local government in 1990. KOR's successful strategies set the stage for a theoretical breakthrough in oppositional political deliberations in Poland as well as other nations among the former Soviet block. By the 1980s, the self-liberation and reconstitution of civil society had become an explicitly stated objective of oppositional movements in Poland and Eastern Europe (e.g., Tismaneanu, 1990; U.S. Helsinki Watch Committee, 1986).

The transformation of Eastern Europe was the principal terrain that popularized the term "civil society" in the 1980s. Oddly enough, when Eastern European nations embarked on the road to democracy after the collapse of communism, interest in civil society started to fade in the 1990s, Hann (1996) contends. I find this hardly to be the case, though. Instead of fading, the concept has significantly expanded from the 1980s to the present in application to a vast array of different social and cultural conditions and political life across the globe, as can be attested by the rich literature cited throughout this section. For example, the concept of civil society has been explicitly associated with the expansion of democracy in Latin America (e.g., Alvarez, Dagnino and Escobar, 1998; Cardoso, 2001; Oxhorn, 1995; Stepan, 1988), Asia (e.g., Schak and Hudson, 2003a), and sub-Saharan Africa (e.g., Cohen and Goulbourne, 1991; Ndegwa, 1996; Wiseman, 1996; Zoubir, 1999) in transformations from authoritarianism to democratization in recent years. There have also been numerous attempts to examine the potentiality of civil society as a positive social force and as a spark to enhance or revitalize democratic practices in the new millennium in Western democracies, especially in the United States (e.g., Deakin, 2001; Edwards, 2004; Fullinwider, 1999; O'Connell, 1999).

Thus far, the most fertile ground for the development of the theory of civil society has been cast in Western democracies, which already enjoy a high level of industrialization and capitalism. Scholars have noted the problematics associated with the applicability of the idea of civil society to other parts of the world under vastly different historical, social, and political conditions. Because national development and modernization have become the priority above everything else, third-world nations champion a "compliance ideology" among their citizens through the co-option of state policy-making and state-led economic growth initiatives. A compliance ideology, according to Wilson (1992: 20), "is infused with conceptions of justice that involve broad definitions of the appropriate interests of individuals and of the community. In this sense, a compliance ideology is an ethos that always subordinates some interests that might otherwise be acted upon." As a result, specific and autonomous individual and group interests are subsumed in a communion of national interests defined by the state. So as Reis (1998) and Post (1991) point out, in Latin America and Africa, the incentives for joining civic associations are almost nonexistent and individuals resort to immediate kinship–tribal groups for the protection of their private interests. This distrust in the community and the retreat to the private realm for the short-run material gain is called "amoral familism" by Banfield (1958); lack of solidarity at the community and national level thus excludes collaboration outside the restricted family circle.

These problems among many developing nations should not lead to the conclusion that civil society does not exist or cannot fulfill its function as a democratic force in those nations. Rather, civil society should be conceptualized with somewhat different boundaries, taking into account the terms and conditions under which it exists. The degree of the applicability of the idea of civil society to the Chinese context, or whether the idea can be applied to China at all, has been a topic of heated debate, and is addressed in the ensuing chapter.

Civil Society, Mass Media, and the Public Sphere

In the days when the ancient masters were deliberating about the important issues of the day in relation to civil society, face-to-face (nonmediated) communication was the dominating mode of debate and discourse. It should then come as no surprise that those early thinkers did not mention the role of mass media either in communicative functions or as part of civil society. Alexis de Tocqueville was the first major political philosopher to have conceptualized the importance of mass media (i.e., newspapers in his days) in Americans' love affair with associations during his travels to the United States in the 1830s. Tocqueville, however, only afforded newspapers a limited role in civil society in that he mainly saw newspapers as facilitator to, and playing a supplementary role in, associational life. Most contemporary scholars (with the understandable exception of some in the communication disciplines) in the civic culture tradition tend to give the media a marginalized role in the civil society of voluntary associations. Robert Putnam (1995; 2000) even goes as far as to blame television as part of the cause for the decline of social capital, which is so vital to the vibrancy of civil society.

The scholars who have placed the media of communication at the center of their discussion are those that view civil society as a public sphere that contributes to rational debates and public deliberation in pursuit of common interest among citizens and individuals (a good example is McNair, 2000). As life in modern society has become increasingly mediated, these scholars argue, the functioning of mass media is indispensable in establishing and sustaining democracies. A key issue for many scholars in this tradition, then, is the mounting threat from increasing commercialization and concentration of the media industry to the foundations upon which the public sphere is created (e.g., Boggs, 2000; Hoynes, 1994; McChesney, 2004).

In a recent overview of the rich and diverse origins of contemporary (practical and theoretical) understandings of the concept of civil society, Michael Edwards summarizes the different theoretical and policy underpinnings into three distinctive yet interrelated schools of thought — "each useful and legitimate but incomplete" (2004: vii). Scholars in the first school, which he calls "the analytical models of civil society," see civil society as associational life which, as a distinct sector from the state and the market, is conducive to "civic engagement" or the "civic culture." The second set of theories, "the normative models of civil society," view civil society as the good society that "represents the institutionalization of 'civility' as a different way of being and living in the world, or a different kind of society in which all institutions operate in ways that reinforce these positive social norms [such as tolerance, non-discrimination, trust, cooperation, and non-violence]" (p. 39). Although the second set is closely related to the first set, key differences exist, Edwards notes: the second school sees civil society as sharing a core set of normative values and agendas that do not exist in the first school; furthermore, the normative models place much emphasis on the civil (civic-minded) aspect of civil society, while the first school tends to classify all social groups that mediate between the state and the market as belonging to the terrain of civil society.

Edwards's third school of theories sees civil society as the public sphere that provides the forum and arenas in modern society for legitimate, normative consensus to be reached through rational debates and open discussion. Scholars in this tradition recognize the high degree of mediation in present-day society and invariably assign communication (and more often, mediated communication) a central role in the functioning of the public sphere. Understandably, communication scholars have taken a great interest in, and have made significant contributions to, debates in this school.

Each of the three schools, standing alone, is incomplete, Edwards argues. What is needed, he contends, is an integrated approach that combines elements from all three models so that there is a chance "that their strengths and weaknesses can be harmonized, and that all three can benefit from a positive and conscious interaction" (p. 91). In Edwards's integrated approach:

> An inclusive and well-articulated associational ecosystem can be the driving force of the good society, but the achievements of the good society are what make possible the independence and level playing field that underpin a democratic associational life. Without a functioning public sphere neither would be possible, since there would [be] no space for associations to operate in defining the good society's ends and means.
>
> (Edwards, 2004: 91)

An integrated approach, Edwards contends, increases the utility of the idea of civil society both as a tool for theoretical explanation and as a vehicle for practical action. For social activists who have resorted to the idea of civil society as a rallying cry for programmatic action, there has also been a noticeable difference in their strategies, as Edwards notes:

> Devotees of associational life will focus on filling in the gaps and disconnections in the civil society ecosystem, promoting volunteering and voluntary action, securing an "enabling environment" that privileges Non Governmental Organizations (NGOs) and other civic organizations through tax breaks, and protecting them from undue interference

through laws and regulations that guarantee freedom of association. Believers in the good society will focus on building positive interactions between institutions in government, the market and the voluntary sector around common goals such as poverty reduction, human rights and deep democracy, and collective strategies to reach them. Supporters of civil society as the public sphere will focus on promoting access to, and independence for, the structures of communication, extending the paths and meeting grounds that facilitate public deliberation and building the capacities that citizens require to engage with each other across their private boundaries.

(Edwards, 2004: 94)

Again, all those are for worthy causes but each of them is insufficient for policy purposes. Edwards's integrated approach calls for positive interactions between the three models to generate "*an inclusive associational ecosystem matched by a strong and democratic state, in which a multiplicity of independent public spheres enable equal participation in setting rules of the game*" (p. 94. Emphasis original). However, the specific paths to realizing this ideal remain debatable.

The different schools of theoretical positions on civil society as observed by Edwards all contribute to theoretical discussions about the democratic experience, but in different ways. The first two schools place an emphasis on associative democracy in the Tocquevillean tradition, which is defined by Paul Hirst to be "a normative theory of society the central claim of which is that human welfare and liberty are both best served when as many of the affairs of society as possible are managed by voluntary and democratically self-governing associations" (1993: 112; see also Hirst, 1994; Warren, 2001). The theory of public sphere, on the other hand, stresses deliberative democracy in the Aristotlean tradition that emphasizes the importance of a free public sphere which, free from the apparatus of the state and economy, values public discourse, open debates, rationality, and grass-roots participation (e.g., James, 2004; Miller, 1993). Both associative democracy and deliberative democracy stress active citizen participation (although deliberative democracy is also said by many to be direct, or participatory democracy) — the former is more concerned with unrestricted participation in social life while the latter is more concerned with unfettered access to, and the quality of, public participation in the deliberative process of decision-making.

The American political philosopher John Dewey was among the first to develop the concept of public sphere as an essential component of democracy. In the introduction to a special issue of *Argumentation and Advocacy* devoted to John Dewey and the public sphere, Asen and Brouwer thus characterize the relevance of Dewey's ideas on present-day understanding of the public sphere:

Communication scholars interested in public sphere studies will find much to consider in Dewey: his assumption of the primacy of communication for identity formation, his concern for the constitution and character of publics, his commitment to engaged public discourse as a dynamic force in democratic polities, and his attention to relations among political, educational, and economic issues. Moreover, Dewey's reflections on the public prefigured issues arising in contemporary scholarship.

(Asen and Brouwer, 2003: 158)

Dewey, however, was interested in both the associational and the deliberative aspects of the democratic life. Dewey proposed two points to measure the worth of a form of social life: "the extent in which the interests of a group are shared by all its members, and the fullness and freedom with which it interacts with other groups" (1966: 99). For Dewey, a sphere of free public communication is based on the human capacities of deliberation:

Democracy is a way of personal life controlled not merely by faith in human nature in general but by faith in the capacity of human beings for intelligent judgment and action if proper conditions are furnished ... For what is the faith of democracy in the role of consultation, of conference, of persuasion, of discussion, in formation of public opinion, which in the long run is self-corrective, except faith in the capacity of the intelligence of the common man to respond with commonsense to the free play of inquiry, assembly and free communication?"

(Dewey, 1981a: 227)

The free and communicative spirit of the public sphere was reemphasized by Dewey later:

In short, a primary, perhaps *the* primary, loyalty of democracy at the present time is to communication ... The freedom which is the essence of democracy is above all the freedom to develop intelligence: intelligence consisting of judgment as to what facts are relevant to action and how they are relevant to things to be done, and a corresponding alertness in the quest for such facts.

(Dewey, 1981b: 275-276. Emphasis original)

Yet, there is an overreliance on face-to-face communication in Dewey's conceptions, as Asen observes: "Dewey articulated a creative and consequential notion of communication, which he regarded as most fully realized in face-to-face communication" (2003: 187). How public engagement can be achieved through alternative modes and the mass media remains a challenge to contemporary scholars who try to adapt Dewey's ideas to the present-day environment. The role of the media in the public sphere, however, finds full expression in the German thinker Jürgen Habermas, who elevates the theory of the public sphere to a much higher level.

Much recent discussion about the communicative power and the rational–critical discourse civil society helps generate is inspired by Habermas and his historical study *The Structural Transformation of the Public Sphere* (first English version was published in 1989) (Habermas, 1989). In the book, Habermas asks a question crucial for democracy theory that is summarized by Calhoun as: "What are the social conditions … for a radical–critical debate about public issues conducted by private persons willing to let arguments and not statuses determine decisions?" (Calhoun, 1992: 1).

Habermas traces the historical emergence of a bourgeois public sphere of the seventeenth and eighteenth centuries in Europe — a sphere in which private people came together and for the first time engaged in critical rational debate about the general issues governing commodity exchange and social labor. The significance of those debates is that what was valued was the merits of one's ideas, not one's identity or status. As a practice of rational–critical discourse, citizens entered the public sphere to influence the affairs of the state as well as society in general. This is how Habermas defines the public sphere:

> The bourgeois public sphere may be conceived above all as the sphere of private people come together as a public; they soon claimed the public sphere regulated from above against the public authorities themselves, to engage them in a debate over the general rules governing relations in the basically privatized but publicly relevant sphere of commodity exchange and social labor. The medium of this political confrontation was peculiar and without historical precedent: people's public use of their reason.

> (Habermas, 1992: 27)

Habermas's concept of the public sphere delineates a social space of institutions and practice that mediates between the private interests of the individuals and families on one hand, and the state on the other, which often exerts arbitrary forms of power and domination on the former. The public sphere provides the social arenas for individuals and groups to discuss public affairs of common concern and to organize against the coercive and oppressive forms of social and state power. While in the bourgeois public sphere, Habermas's ideal type, consensus and public opinion were formed in open, rational debates from private individuals regardless of their race and class, a fundamental transformation of the public sphere has taken place. In what Habermas calls the "welfare state capitalism and mass society," debates are dominated, and public opinion is administered, by political, social, and media elites as part of "systems management and social control." Thus the structural transformation of the public sphere came about when the distinction between public and private realms was eroded with the interpenetration of state and society through organized interest groups and corporate actors, and rational–critical public discourse gave way to the mass consumption of culture (Habermas, 1989; 1992).

Habermas's work has triggered important debates about the progressive potential of emancipatory possibilities of modern society. Search for public space has been an ongoing focal area of contention in today's conceptions of civil society. Civil society, it is hoped, may very well be the source for a regenerated or rehabilitated public sphere (e.g., Calhoun, 1992; Cohen and Arato, 1992 Fraser, 1992; Howell and Pearce, 2001). Warren (2001: 77) calls this the "public sphere effects" of associational life, which provide "the means for forming opinions and developing agendas outside the state, as well as outside the structures of economic markets."

Scholars following the Habermasian tradition do not necessarily limit civil society to the public sphere, but they tend to agree that the public sphere is the most crucial element of civil society today because of the high degree of mediated communication. Habermas himself is highly critical of the role of mass media in the debased, media-saturated public sphere of modern state capitalism, where the function of the media has degenerated from facilitating rational public debates in the bourgeois public sphere to shaping and limiting public discourse to those themes and agendas approved by the media corporations. Thus what used to be an open space of public debates and individual participation has been mutated into a realm of political information and spectacle, and accordingly, what used to be citizens who actively participated in public debates are now passive mass consumers and spectators of highly controlled media information. "Inasmuch as the mass media today strip away the literary husks from the kind of bourgeois self-interpretation and utilize them as marketable forms for the public services provided in a culture of consumers, the original meaning is reversed," Habermas observes (1989: 171).

The "refeudalization," or corruption, of the public sphere in present-day society then poses a serious threat to civil society, and a revitalization of civil society calls for a revitalization of the public sphere. That can be accomplished, according to Habermas, by setting "in motion a critical process of public communication through the very organizations that mediatize it [the public sphere]" (1989: 232). Other contemporary scholars have called for revitalizing civil society through media literacy by raising public awareness about critical issues and by providing the public with important skills of public communication (e.g., Cohen, 1998; Hobbs, 1998; Milner, 2002). These efforts are well summarized by Salvador:

> Effective communication in a participatory democracy demands that citizens are able to have a voice in the discussion, that they are able to consider the voices of others, and that they can recognize the many

subtle forces that impact how those voices are communicated in our mediated and technological world.

The processes and products of communicating about matters of common interest, of deliberating about public issues, make up what we call the *public voice* ... To talk about the public voice is to address the awareness, values, knowledge, and skills that citizens must have to constructively contribute to the process and outcome of civic deliberation.

(Salvador, 1989: 4. Emphasis original)

All of these, it goes without saying, have to be accomplished by working through the media.

A more radical formula by some scholars and journalism practitioners under the civil society–public sphere umbrella is the public journalism (or civic journalism) movement (for a discussion of the theoretical and practical connections of public journalism to the theories of communicative action by Dewey and Habermas, see Compton, 2000). Public journalism is called by Michael Schudson "the best organized social movement inside journalism in the history of the American press" (1999). In response to the public lethargy to public life and the acknowledged failure of conventional journalism to constitute a public sphere where people can gain an intelligent understanding of and have a voice in public affairs:

Public journalism is a new kind of journalism that puts main emphasis on the people's participation in journalism and government. For the public journalists, "the people" are at the center of their program. They are interested in opening the press to the people, motivating the people for the community service, stimulating a civic conversation for the people, further democratizing the people, encouraging them to set their news agenda, facilitating message outlets for the people, and creating a public sphere in which the people can talk and act.

(Merrill, Gade and Blevens, 2001: 126)

The philosophy of public journalism is summarized by Sirianni and Friedland (2001: 186) thus: "Journalists must assume responsibility for helping to constitute vital publics with the usable knowledge that enables them to deliberate about complex issues and to engage in common problems solving." Thus the objective of public journalism is not simply to be neutral observers of events, but rather to engage citizens in public life. Public journalists see their role as inextricably interwoven with the vitality of the public sphere: they must not only provide essential information upon which public deliberation can happen, but they should also frame issues and provide perspectives that are conducive to public engagement and bring people together for active and productive public deliberation (Lichtenberg, 1999; Merrill, Gade, and Blevens, 2001; Merritt, 1998).

As was pointed out earlier, contemporary scholarship about the public sphere has invariably assigned a critical role to the media, and has examined the various aspects of the media, in the formation and functioning of the public sphere today. It is no wonder, then, that the Internet, as the newest tool of mass communication, should trigger new debates about its role in the transmutation of the public sphere. As the history of its theoretical evolution has taught us, the idea of civil society has always risen to the tides of the day; and as "the 'big idea' for the twenty-first century" (Edwards, 2004), civil society will again become an important theoretical construct for us to understand emerging issues faced by society in the new millennium. Now as the Internet continues to penetrate every aspect of society, social scientists need to address new important questions, such as the ones raised by Alan Wolfe (2003: 12): "Can these newly emerging forms of civil society [in cyberspace] act as a buffer between the market and the state, protecting Americans from the consequences of selfishness on the one hand and coercive altruism on the other? Will they encourage people to practice political participation, learning through the local and the immediate what it means to be a citizen of the nation and even the world? Are they sufficient to encourage in people a sense of responsibility for both themselves and those with whom they share their society?" Likewise, Putnam sees new potentialities in the socializing effect of the Internet: "Like plazas and parks, local newspapers, and neighborhood libraries, Internet technology could create social spaces within which we see how our numerous networks of interest and interaction overlap and intersect" (Putnam and Feldstein, 2003: 293–294). These issues are the focus of Chapter 5.

Civil Society Defined (Revisited)

Assigning a proper meaning to the concept of civil society is no easy matter. While everyone agrees on the importance of civil society in contemporary social life, there is also a growing frustration among scholars about its lack of clarity and rigor, both as an intellectual currency and as a social and political practice. While theories of civil society have benefited from scholarly works in a plethora of disciplines across national and cultural boundaries, the idea of civil society has also inherited an accumulated stockpile of ambiguities, confusions, and sometimes contradictions from these sources. Some use the concept of civil society as an *ideal type* against which different social settings and systems can be measured; others treat it as existing social realities that can help us reach a better understanding of pragmatic social and political complexities; and still others employ the language of civil society to recommend pragmatic courses of social and/or political action. Moreover, political camps from both Right (Conservatives) and Left (Liberals) have used civil society as a slogan to gain political points against each other (e.g., Cahoone, 2002). As a result, civil society has quickly become one of the most overused or abused terms in the social sciences.

It has been widely acknowledged that the development of the idea of civil society has been an essential part of the history of Western political philosophy. As Adam Seligman (1992: 16) points out, "the very idea of civil society touches on and embraces the major themes of the Western political thought." As demonstrated early in the chapter, the concept of civil society has always been invoked by great thinkers to answer calls of the day and to meet challenges posed by disrupting social or political structures at times of unusual convulsions and social transformations. The popularity of the term in the seventeenth and the eighteenth centuries among Western intellectuals was tied closely to the tumultuous death of the feudal and aristocratic order and the birth of democracy and capitalism in Europe. Within this context, the notion of civil society was readily adopted to "help society respond to this new social reality: either by embracing it and finding new and more appropriate forms of civil virtue, or by finding ways to preserve the best elements of the older forms of social order" (Beem, 1999: 4; see also Seligman, 1992). Likewise, the contemporary burst of interest in civil society is necessitated by attempts to restore and maintain social order in existing Western democracies in the midst of mounting political and economic upheavals as well as global trends of traditional authoritarian and totalitarian regimes to democratize in a growing number of third-world nations. The biggest challenge for the various interpretations and articulations of civil society is how to adapt the concept with such a rich intellectual tradition to different socioeconomic and cultural settings to address an emerging set of different problems and concerns.

The biggest tension among the numerous strains and mutations of the theories of civil society centers on the role played by the economic sector in the formations of civil society. These disputes are summarized nicely by Khilnani (2001: 13–14) into three camps:

> One response, which for convenience might be called a "liberal" position, sees the effective powers of civil society as basically residing in the economy, in property rights and markets where such rights may be freely exchanged. Another view, a "radical" position, locates civil society in a "society" independent of the economic domain and the state, where ideas are publicly exchanged, associations freely formed, and interests discovered. Finally, a "conservative" position prefers to see it as residing in a set of cultural acquisitions, in historically inherited manners of civility which moderate relations between groups and individuals: unlike the previous two positions, adherents of this view do not see these acquisitions as being necessarily universally available.

Jeffrey Alexander (1998) suggests that the terrain of civil society has undergone three ideal-typical forms in historical time in Western intellectual discourse. When the modern conception of civil society first developed in the late seventeenth century, Alexander argues, it "was an inclusive, umbrella-like concept referring to a plethora of institutions outside the state" (Alexander, 1998: 3). The first important phase of modern understanding of the concept is called by Alexander "civil society I (or CSI)" and "was endowed with a distinctively moral and ethical force" (Alexander, 1998: 3). The free-wheeling capitalist market was assigned a special place in civil society because the processes and organizations of the capitalist mode of economic production and trade were believed to induce desirable self-discipline, senses of responsibility, bonds of trust, public virtue, and propriety of market life. The emerging capitalist market was perceived to be a force that liberated society from feudal and aristocratic vices.

The positive tone attributed to the capitalist market took a dramatic turn near the middle of the nineteenth century and was replaced by the pejorative association of capitalism with exploitation, domination, and instrumentality (Hirschman, 1977). The concept of civil society in social theory fell victim to this drastic transformation and was associated with the fateful aspects of market capitalism alone, devoid of any democratic, cooperative, and virtuous ties. This is the second version of civil society (CSII) by Alexander. The mastermind of this categorization of civil society is, of course, Karl Marx and his adamant followers, who associated civil society with ravages of industrialism and regarded it as a field of rampant private interests and class domination. As a result, the profanation of the idea of civil society in social theory led to the disappearance of this term in social scientific discourse in the later half of the nineteenth century.

In the 1970s and the 1980s, revolutionary social and cultural forces worldwide created a new environment for the renewal of intellectual engagement with civil society: collapse of command economies in the Soviet blocs, search for democracy from forces within society among Eastern European nations and countries in other regions that had experienced decades of dictatorial or authoritarian regimes, failure of big state theories within Western democracies. The decline of the prestige of the state as a solution to the variety of global problems means scholars have to look into informal ties, voluntary social organizations, and cooperative relationships for answers. Thus understanding of civil society has been cast in a refreshing perspective. In the place of the all-inclusive CSI and the reductionist CSII, this is the "civil society III, or CSIII," as called by Alexander, which is dominating current research agendas. In this emerging line of theoretical discourse, civil society is increasingly recognized "as a sphere that is analytically independent of — and, to varying degrees, empirically differentiated from — not only the state and the market but other social spheres as well" (Alexander, 1998: 6).

Alexander argues that there is no reason to single out the market in our deliberation of civil society because each of the noncivil spheres — economy, the state, religion, science, the family — maintains its own criteria of justice and its own system of rewards and must be differentiated from the distinctive sphere of civil society.

> Civil society should be conceived as a solitary sphere in which a certain kind of universalizing community comes gradually to be defined and to some degree enforced. To the degree that this solidary community exists, it is exhibited by "public opinion," possesses its own cultural codes and narratives in a democratic idiom, is patterned by a set of peculiar institutions, most notable legal and journalistic ones, and is visible in historically distinctive set of interactional practices like civility, equality, criticism, and respect.

> (Alexander, 1998: 7; see also Alexander, 1997)

In the prevalent understanding of the role of civil society in its potential as a democratic force within former communist nations, importance is attached to the freedom civil society enjoys from the state and to the freedom for individuals to pursue their own destinies in voluntary associations with others. In much of Western literature, the "Hegelian" way of viewing civil society as the intermediate public realm between the state (i.e., political life) and the sphere of purely private life (i.e., the family and/or the individual) still prevails. True to the Hegelian legacies of bourgeois society, the emphasis is often placed on those social relations that are mediated by the market. The following definition of civil society by Larry Diamond (1994: 5) is typical of this view: *civil society* is

> an intermediary entity, standing between the private sphere and the state. Thus it excludes individual and family life, inward-looking group activity (e.g., for recreation, entertainment, or spirituality), the profit-making enterprise of individual business firms, and political efforts to take control of the state.

Another important scholar who has contributed to contemporary discussions of civil society is John Keane who posits a civil society-versus-state dichotomy.

> [C]ivil society can be conceived as an aggregate of institutions whose members are engaged primarily in a complex of non-state activities — economic and cultural production, household life and voluntary associations — and who in this way preserve and transform their identity by exercising all sorts of pressures or controls upon state institutions.

> (Keane, 1988a: 14)

As an ideal-typical category, civil society "both describes and envisages a complex and dynamic ensemble of legally protected non-governmental institutions that tend to be non-violent, self-organizing, self-reflexive, and permanently in tension with each other and with the state institutions that 'frame,' constrict and enable their activities" (Keane, 1998a: 6). Noticeably, Keane and Diamond differ on whether to include the domain of the family in the terrains of civil society.

Keane's idea of civil society as a counterbalancing power against the state echoes Ernest Gellner's conceptual development of civil society as "that set of diverse non-governmental institutions which is strong enough to counterbalance the state and, while not preventing the state from fulfilling its role of keeper of the peace and arbitrator between major interests, can nevertheless prevent it from dominating and atomizing the rest of society" (Gellner, 1994: 5). In other words, the state checks extremes of individual interest in civil society whereas civil society, predominantly embedded in economic activities, in turn checks the state from enforcing an ideological monopoly on its citizens.

Gellner's emphasis on the separation of the polity from economic and social life in his model of civil society even leads him to claim that civil society is "the social residue left when the state is subtracted" (Gellner, 1994: 212). A similar view is found in Tester, who says that "[c]ivil society is about what happens to us when we leave our family and go about our own lives. It is about the relationships I have with my colleagues and the person who crashed into my car" (Tester, 1992: 8). I will agree with many that this overinclusive approach does not offer much help in clarifying an already muddy situation in current debates about civil society.

Jean L. Cohen and Andrew Arato are the leading contemporary scholars in advocating a three-part framework that distinguishes civil society from both state and the economy. In their influential work *Civil Society and Political Theory*, they define civil society as

> a sphere of social interaction between economy and state, composed above all of the intimate sphere (especially the family), the sphere of association (especially voluntary associations), social movements, and forms of public communication. Modern civil society is created through forms of self-constitution and self-mobilization. It is institutionalized and generalized through laws, and especially subjective rights, that stabilize social differentiation.

> (Cohen and Arato, 1992: ix)

In their reconstruction of the theory of civil society, Cohen and Arato have heavily relied on Jürgen Habermas's structural components of the lifeworld and have borrowed from Talcott Parsons's and Antonio Gramsci's triple model of society–economy–state relations. "Parsons and Gramsci were the first to see that contemporary society is reproduced not only through economic and political processes, or even their new or renewed fusion, but through the interaction of legal structures, social associations, institutions of communication, and cultural forms, all of which have a significant degree of autonomy," Cohen and Arato (1992: 425) write.

There are two distinctive advantages with their three-part model, Cohen and Arato argue. First of all, the dichotomous model of state and society mapped out by Hegel and Marx "represents a quintessentially nineteenth-century figure of thought" (p. 421) and is inevitably out of tune with today's society. By equating society with a self-regulating market mechanism, Cohen and Arato assert, this model tries to reduce all social relations to economic ones. Secondly, their framework has an advantage over the dualistic model because "it allows a clarification of the structural interrelations among civil society, economy, and state by severing the ideological, one-to-one correlation of civil society with the private sphere and of the state with the public sphere," Cohen and Arato (1992: 430) claim. Cohen and Arato's triple model has been subsequently embraced by some while challenged by others. For example, scholars that have embraced the three-party model have defined civil society as a "third sector" that mediates between our individuality as producers and consumers of the market and our abstract identity as members of a sovereign state (e.g., Barber, 1998). Palmer, on the other hand, contends that efforts to define civil society as "between state and market" has at least two serious defects:

> [F]irst, they represent a break from the long tradition of understanding civil society, generating confusion rather than illumination; second, to the extent that they identify the state with coercive power and the market with self-interest, they divide up the various possible forms of interaction in terms of nonexclusive categories. Coercion is a way of treating others, while self-interest is a motivation.
>
> (Palmer, 2002: 57)

Instead, Palmer contends,

> [C]ivil society is that kind of human interaction made possible by equality of rights that are protected by institutions/organizations that exercise delegated, enumerated, and thus limited powers, such that those members of civil society not tied to one another by kinship, friendship, love, faith, or even geographical proximity can nonetheless interact in a "civil" manner.
>
> (Palmer, p. 57; see also Alexander, 1998)

This brief examination of some of the current multiple, and often conflicting, definitions of civil society testifies to the ongoing tension in contemporary scholarship on the idea of civil society. The "paradoxes of civil society," Trentmann (1999) argues, are attributable to its double life unparalleled by any other concept in the social sciences: as a prescriptive norm on one hand and as descriptive of social realities on the other. "The modern history of civil society has been a story of dynamic tension between these two lives, for ideal and praxis never found a perfect fit," Trentmann (1999: 3) points out.

What further complicates the situation is that the idea of civil society developed in the West, and, either as an ideal type or as an expanded reality, it has been "predicated on a fundamental ethnocentricity" (Hann, 1996: 1). It is then only natural that there have been various challenges in the recent application of this concept to an emerging array of developing nations in various non-Western settings, as evidenced in current debates about the concept of civil society in the Chinese context to be reviewed in Chapter 2.

However, these competing views and perspectives may not necessarily be a limitation in the scholarship on the idea of civil society. The current proliferation of intellectual activities on civil society as a social concept from scholars with diversified academic backgrounds and disciplinary foci across national and cultural boundaries is testimony to its importance, vitality, and adaptability. Contributions from different scholarly traditions are essential for the concept of civil society to obtain its full-fledged status as a theoretical framework.

Here, I have no intention of developing a brand-new definition of civil society, as hard and challenging as that may be. Instead, I elaborate on several important concepts that I think are essential in understanding civil society as a subject of social inquiry.

Talcott Parsons contributed much to contemporary discussions of associational life. He argues that while primordial societies were organized on bases of religion, ethnicity, and territoriality, modern social systems have fostered three dominant types of societal relations, namely, the markets, bureaucratic organizations, and associational structures (Parsons, 1971). Parson's influence is apparent in Cohen and Arato's three-part model of civil society. What is of most interest to us is Parson's conception of associational structures or associational organizations, in which memberships are primarily based on consensual and voluntary relations. Parsons identifies three major characteristics or trends of modern associational structures: first, they display a trend toward a certain egalitarianism; second, they show a tendency toward voluntariness; third, there is the increasing importance of procedural institutions (Parsons, 1971: 22–26). These three trends are invariably tied to one another. Egalitarianism involves expanding equalities among members who participate and disassociates membership from ethnicity, social status, and other individual symbols of identity. Voluntariness means that members are not permanently bound by any sworn allegiance to any social relations by compulsion or coercion, and are free to accept, retain, or exit an association. Parsons specifies two levels of proceduralism — discussions and decision-making — with each governed by a code of rules. Proceduralism is fundamental to the formation and maintenance of associative relations in which members can exit in the face of conflict because only by working out procedures to discuss and resolve differences can associations renew their normative consensus.

There are elements of associationalism in some government and market institutions, as Parson acknowledges, but it is not the dominant organizational principle within these organizations. There is the need to highlight the point that *it is only within civil society groups that associational relations become the axial principle; it is the defining feature of civil society.* In this regard, a relevant definition is offered by Warren, who says that civil society is "the domain of social organization within which voluntary associative relations are dominant" (Warren, 2001: 57).

It is also useful to borrow one term from Ernest Gellner to understand the flexible and tolerant nature of civil society in fostering individual attitudes and values in the formation of social relations. Because people have the ability to join and leave multiple associations without binding themselves to a totalizing mode of life, this creates what Gellner calls the "modular man": one who is

> capable of combining into effective associations and institutions, *without* these being total, many-stranded, underwritten by ritual and made stable through being linked to a whole inside set of relationships, all of these being tied in with each other and so immobilized. He can combine into specific-purpose, *ad hoc*, limited association, without binding himself by some blood ritual. He can leave an association when he comes to disagree with its policy, without being open to an accusation of treason.
>
> (Gellner, 1994: 99–100. Emphasis original)

It is this modularity of man that brings about civil society; it transforms atomized and helpless individuals into adjustable social relations that are responsive to mutually agreeable criteria.

In his *An Essay on the History of Civil Society* (remarkably, the first book that bears the title of civil society, initially published in 1767), Adam Ferguson, one of the intellectual leaders of the Scottish Enlightenment, has provided significant theoretical underpinnings for modern civil society discourse by basing his conception of civil society as a natural condition for moral development and the progress of society. Because of the innate human sociable nature, or the "amicable propensity in the human mind," men "act in society from affections of kindness and friendship" (Ferguson, 1995: 38–39). Civil society is the mode of existence in which our moral development and material life are realized through intimate relationships with others: "in … various appearances of an amicable disposition, the foundations of a moral apprehension are sufficiently laid, and the sense of a right which we maintain for ourselves, is by a movement of humanity and candour extended to our fellow creatures" (Ferguson, 1995: 38).

It is within civil society that "[n]ot only the individual advances from infancy to manhood, but the species itself from rudeness to civilization"

(Ferguson, 1995: 7). Civil society, as a "polished" or "refined" form of society, is a natural stage in the long process of human evolution from an early stage of "savage" primitive tribes and transient military leadership to the "barbarian" phase in which property was established, Ferguson claims.

"It is in conducting the affairs of civil society, that mankind find the exercise of their best talents, as well as the object of their best affections" (Ferguson, 1995: 149). In the battle between material progress and moral advance, in polished, commercial society, Ferguson opts for an institution of civic virtue in the modern state. It is in a vigorous public life that citizens can resist the temptation of a selfish private life marked by accumulation of wealth.

It is worth noting that while Hegel's conception of civil society makes the distinction between "civil society" and "state," Ferguson saw an integration of the economic man and the political man in the single polity of civil society. Ferguson's emphasis on the social and benevolent side of nature has been revived in contemporary debates about civil society in the stress that a number of scholars have placed on the rudiments of civic virtue in civil society (e.g., Bryant, 1995; Seligman, 1995). *As an important stage in human elevation to civilization, civil society, therefore, excludes the domain of such social organizations as fanatical groups, hate groups, criminal mafias, or collectivities, among others, that advocate violence or antisocial behavior because of their uncivil nature.* In his discussion on civil society and fanaticism, Colas thus characterizes the key differences between civil society and fanatical groups:

> The moment that the government of a civil society is recognized as having the right to exercise political domination, the moment that civil society becomes the legitimate arena in which each person seeks the personally useful, fanaticism moves into absolute opposition to such society, mobilizing those faithful to a prince not of this world or who, oppressed, proclaim the prophecy of a just realm. For to promote civil society as a positive value is to promote both tolerance and "bourgeois" values, the free market as well as freedom of thought ... . Fanatics, who by definition reject mediation and representation and wish to establish a new world without delay and without institutions, may be disciplined militants marching lock-step at the command of a supreme sovereign or anarchists, iconoclasts revolted by the complacency of the guardians of the temple, who they see as idol worshipers. They may be servants to an inflexible law or relentless utopians, activist assassins or asocial outcasts moved by impatient hopes.

> (Colas, 1997: 6)

So the defining feature of fanaticism is its rejection of representation and mediation (i.e., "stand-in" role fulfilled by social or political institutions or forces) and its hatred of civil society such as in totalitarianism. It is precisely because of this that communism is destructive to civil society — it tends to replace all the associations and activities of civil society with the omnipresent and all-powerful party-state.

Likewise, John A. Hall makes a strong case for the argument that "civil society should be seen not merely as the presence of strong and autonomous social groups able to balance the state but also *as a high degree of civility in social relations*" (Hall, 1999: 48. Emphasis added; see also Hall, 1995). Civil society is an umbrella term that refers to distinctive types of self-organizations taking shape in early modern Europe that placed a particular emphasis on openness, equality, and tolerance and thus broke away from earlier closed societies based on rank, religion, guild, or clan (Hall, 1998). Likewise, Shils (1991:16) writes, "[t]he virtue of civil society is the readiness to moderate particular, individual or parochial interests and to give precedence to the common good."

One unfortunate fact in the recent discourse about civil society has been the emphasis on its antistatism, Hall argues, because "antistatism will not do as a general characterization of civil society, either in the abstract and as a description of the ways in which the term has been used in the past" (Hall, 1999: 50–51). The flaw with the claim that antistatism is the defining feature of civil society is evident now in the recent development of the former communist block in Eastern Europe and the former Soviet Union. The removal or absence of a predatory state does not ensure decency in civil society. *A responsive and cooperative state is necessary for the emergence of a healthy civil society*, as more and more have realized. Thus one urgency in current discourse about civil society is the restoration of civic virtue.

Chapter Summary

From the trajectory of the evolution of the idea of civil society from Plato to Hegel to Marx to contemporary social thought, we can see that the conceptualization of civil society has borne the hallmarks of the particular social and political life of different eras.

The concept of civil society was revived in the 1970s and 1980s in the East European context in which democratic transformation was made possible by the revolt of civil society against the totalitarian state. The demise of communism in Eastern Europe and the former Soviet blocks in the 1980s triggered widespread interest among scholars from a variety of backgrounds and disciplines; subsequently, there have been significant expansions in the theoretical terrain and the application of the idea of civil society to different social and cultural contexts across the globe.

The democratic potential of civil society, which was absent in the thought of classical and early modern political philosophers, has been at the center of contemporary debates on civil society. It is generally believed that a robust civil society is an indispensable part of democratic life today. In general, the idea of civil society has been related to two different but interrelated types of democracy: associative democracy and deliberative democracy. The former focuses on the freedom of individuals to form voluntary, associative relations with others while the latter is primarily concerned with the freedom of citizens to engage in open, public, critical debates on issues of common concern. In terms of associative democracy, voluntary associations of free-willing individuals not only contribute to the plurality of society; they also cultivate civic virtue and accumulate social capital. In terms of deliberative democracy, a central theme in the discussion of civil society has been the communicative power and the rational–critical debates civil society helps to generate in present-day society. This line of research has benefited mainly from the various conceptions of the public sphere — a social space where private citizens freely engage in public discourse on important issues of the day. The role of mass media and mass communication has occupied a central place in debates in the birth, degeneration, and rehabilitation of the public sphere. The rise of the Internet as a mass communication tool in the last decade has opened up both new challenges and new opportunities in the theoretical debates about the public sphere in the new millennium.

Gellner (1994) rightly notes that civil society has become a powerful slogan for people on many fronts. Yet for scholars across different disciplines and areas of interest to have a meaningful dialogue with one another, it is necessary to explore the different theoretical positions and thereby build some common ground while recognizing the differences. As Michael Edwards notes, "[w]hat is important about the civil society debate is not that one school of thought is proved correct and others exposed as false, but the extent to which different frameworks can generate insights that lead to more effective action" (2004: vi–vii). It is my contention that civil society, from its numerous versions of historical evolution, should be regarded as a fluid arrangement in which it tries to adapt to different cultural, political, and economic conditions. Alan Wolfe's comments are right on the mark here:

> It is certainly useful to inquire into the origins of the term civil society and to be reminded of its context in 18th-century Scotland or 19th-century Germany, but just about all the terms we use today meant something different when they were introduced ... The question is not whether academics and politicians are using the term civil society correctly; it is whether the reality they are trying to capture when they use the term is accurate.
>
> (Wolfe, 2003: 10)

As this Western-bred concept becomes more widespread and adopted worldwide, we must pay special attention to the voluntary (or associational), civil, and democratic implications of civil society as well as its potential as a public space of deliberative action in our theoretical approaches.

2
The Idea of Civil Society in the Chinese Context

Grounded deeply in Western social theoretical tradition and capitalist development, civil society has become established as a key concept in the trio-relationship among the individual, the state, and the society. In addition, as Howell and Pearce (2001) demonstrate, civil society has also been recognized as a paradigmatic concept in the field of development practice and policy-making in the contemporary reinvention of the idea worldwide. "Since the late 1980s multilateral development agencies, international financial institutions and nongovernmental organizations, environmentalists, feminists, neo-liberals, social democrats, and radical grassroots activists have all, in their own and diverse ways, appropriated the language of civil society," Howell and Pearce (2001: 1) note.

Within this broad context, starting from the late 1980s, there has been a renewed interest in the role of civil society in national development not only in Western democracies but also in the vast majority of third-world nations entrenched in different historical, political, and cultural traditions. This took place at a particular moment when development theory, which had guided state thinking and policymaking in many nations struggling to induce social change on the road to industrialization and modernization until the late 1970s, had reached what some called an "impasse" (Schuurman, 1993; see also Leys, 1996).

Development theory was the answer to the call after World War II for third-world countries to embark on the transitions to development and democracy following the route of the few Western industrial powers. Proponents of the theory afforded the territorial and political unit of the nation-state a central role in the process of national development in initiating and advancing the agenda of development, and they assumed that a strong state was essential in promoting change and facilitating the process of industrialization and urbanization (which was thought to be the only path to social and national development) (e.g., Lerner, 1958; So, 1990). Often cited examples as successful cases were Germany, Japan, and the four little dragons: South Korea, Taiwan, Singapore, and Hong Kong.

However, failures of these development models to materialize in developing nations and births of strong, authoritarian state bureaucracies in countries that tried to follow these models, followed by global recession and financial crisis, led to challenges to the basic assumptions of development theory from all sides in the 1980s. As a result, a major paradigm shift occurred in thinking about development.

> The state, as it had taken shape in many parts of the South, came to be seen as part of the problem, not part of the solution, to the process of development. It was criticized on many grounds, ranging from lack of accountability and representativeness, militarism and authoritarianism, corruption and venality, wasteful investment and expenditure, distorting market forces, protection of uncompetitive national industries, and the creation of large-scale state monopolies.
>
> Howell and Pearce (2001: 14)

The discourse on development in the West in the 1990s started to focus on redefining the relationships among state, market, and society, and looking for alternatives beyond the state (i.e., Soviet-style socialism) and market (i.e., free market or laissez-faire capitalism). The elaboration is best explicated in the framework developed by Anthony Giddens (1994; 2000) in his ideas of the "Third Way," or socially responsible capitalism, which articulates a path incorporating civil society, citizen participation, and responsible businesses into partnerships with the state in achieving equilibrium in the capitalist market. Meanwhile, encouraged by positive effects initiated by social forces outside of the state and market in Eastern Europe, Latin America, and sub-Saharan Africa, developing nations see the prospect of civil society as a transforming force in inducing social change, as elaborated in Chapter 1. It is only natural, therefore, that the role of Chinese civil society in the transformation of Chinese politics and Chinese society in the new century should attract considerable attention among scholars, politicians, and social activists.

Current Debates on Civil Society in China

Within this global resurgence of the idea of civil society, it is no wonder that China scholars both in the West and in China have tested the usefulness of the civil society paradigm, despite its basic European orientation, as applicable to China and an expanding public sphere associated with it in a variety of ways since the late 1980s. In particular, civil society has been an emerging concept in the formulation of research questions about China in the wake of the massive student prodemocracy demonstrations in the spring of 1989 in major Chinese cities (e.g., Calhoun, 1994; Ding, 2001). For example, Thomas Gold notes, "[t]he ruthless campaign of suppression that began on June 4 revealed in turn the degree to which the [Chinese Communist Party] remains unwilling and unable to accept the reality of nascent civil society in China" (Gold, 1990: 31).

Nonetheless, there is no consensus as to the implications of the failed massive student movement for the study of civil society in contemporary China. Cheek, for example, attributes the failure of the movement to the absence of civil society in China — no independent labor unions, no democratic parties, no dissident intellectual circles, no autonomous church (Cheek, 1992). By the same token, while civil society provided the institutional base for social movements against the monopoly of the state in East European nations in the late 1980s, China was depicted "as devoid of the institutional stage upon which the revolutions of 1989 were played out elsewhere in the communist world" (Perry and Fuller, 1991: 663). Because autonomous organizations composed of city dwellers and workers were not able "to build a significant membership or to coordinate work actions in support of the student protests" in 1989, Walder (1989; 35–40) contends, "[i]t is tempting, but misleading, to characterize Beijing's popular rebellion as a movement by 'society' against the 'state.' " Walder, of course, bases his conclusion on the comparison between the Beijing rebellion with the Polish Solidarity Movement. But we must not ignore the fact that the Tiananmen Movement was largely a spontaneous event triggered by mourning for Hu Yaobang, the former Party General Secretary who suddenly died of a heart attack in Beijing, and quickly evolved into a series of protests against official corruption and public calls for political reform within three months. The Solidarity Movement in Poland, on the other hand, was an organized and well-coordinated program of action involving concerted, planned actions by social forces from many fronts for many years. Wank (1995) also questions the usefulness of applying the East European view of civil society to the Chinese context. I review and comment on more literature relevant to this debate in the later part of this chapter.

Some bluntly question the relevance of civil society as it has been theorized in the Western context to the Chinese experience. Indeed, Habermas, whose work has been a major inspiration of scholarship on Chinese civil society, contends that the public sphere, as a direct result of an active civil society, is a historical phenomenon that is not only temporally but also culturally specific: it emerged at a specific moment in the seventeenth and eighteenth centuries in Europe. As he puts it in the preface of *The Structural Transformation of the Public Sphere*,

> We conceive bourgeois public sphere as a category that is typical of an epoch. It cannot be abstracted from the unique developmental history of that "civil society" originating in the European High Middle Ages; nor can it be transferred idealtypically generalized, to any number of historical situations that represent formally similar constellations.

> (Habermas, 1989: xvii)

Philip Huang (1993), for example, argues that the concepts of "public sphere" and "civil society" as developed in the West are inapplicable to China because they presuppose a dichotomous opposition between state and society. Instead, Huang proposes the term "third realm," which is "a third space conceptually distinct from state and society," to describe the particularities in Chinese sociopolitical life (Huang 1993: 225). The need for a different term, Huang reasons, is that, "[c]ontrary to the vision of the public sphere/civil society models, actual sociopolitical change in China has never come from any lasting assertion of societal autonomy against the state, but rather from the workings out of state-society relations in the third realm" (Huang, 1993: 238). However, before we can make the third realm a helpful approach in evaluating the Chinese situation, important questions remain to be answered as to how, in essence, Huang's trinary conception with a third intermediate space between state and society in China differs conceptually and functionally from the idea of civil society as proposed by a host of other scholars and how the third realm maintains its autonomy from the state and society.

Along a similar vein, Wakeman (1993) concurs with Huang in flatly rejecting the practice of applying the concepts of public sphere–civil society to China as "poignant," because, according to Wakeman, although the public realm has experienced significant expansion, it has not produced the desired effects of a surging civic power over the state. "Instead, state coercive power has continually grown, and most Chinese citizens appear to conceive of social existence mainly in terms of obligations and interdependence rather than rights and responsibilities" (Wakeman, 1993: 133–134; see also Wakeman, 1991). This pessimistic characterization by Wakeman, however, is totally out of line with what many other scholars have observed happening in the state–society reconfiguration in modern and contemporary China, where economic transformations, especially since the reform era initiated in the late 1970s, are believed to be continuously contributing to the rejuvenation of society and weakening the power of state control (see, for example, the edited volumes by Brook and Frolic, 1997; Rosenbaum, 1992 for an overview). I come back to this point later.

In response to the contention by Huang and Wakeman, among others, that the Habermasian model of the public sphere–civil society cannot be usefully applied to the Chinese scenario, it bears stressing that Habermas never intended to imply that the bourgeois public sphere is the only model out there. Instead, there have always been multiple, competing and sometimes overlapping public spheres in the arenas of public communication (see Baker, 1992; Eley, 1992; Fraser, 1992 for elaborations). As a normative, ideal type, Habermas (1989) himself acknowledges that the full utopian potential of the bourgeois public sphere was never realized in practice. But in actuality, variations of the public sphere have always existed because of accommodations to different historical, cultural, and societal conditions. In clarifying his model of the bourgeois public sphere, Habermas (1992) points out that "it is wrong to speak of one single public" (p. 424) (and one single public sphere for that matter); rather, there is a "coexistence of competing public spheres," because "the same structures of communication simultaneously give rise to the formation of several arenas where, beside the hegemonic bourgeois public sphere, additional subcultural or class-specific public spheres are constituted on the basis of their own and initially not easily reconcilable premises" (Habermas, 1992: 425). Thus, Habermas pictures an evolving public sphere based on a changing set of premises. So the conception of public sphere should not be treated as immutable; rather, it must be conceptualized as fluid, adapting to new formations of political, social, and institutional forces. If one agrees with Habermas that there is a typology of public spheres, then why cannot the Chinese scenario be contextualized and historicized as but one variant type? As Timothy Brook points out, civil society as constructed in the West is a model, not a reality. On the other hand, "[c]ivil society in China is not a reality but a concept" for the reason that "many of the elements associated with this European-derived concept can be traced in the Chinese past and present" (Brook, 1997: 21). Therefore, civil society is a model against which meaningful comparisons involving different cases can be made and useful analytical perspectives can be obtained.

Civil society as a concept is functional rather than normative, and it must be understood in dynamic terms by taking into consideration the different socioeconomic, political, and historical conditions under which it is used. In the previous chapter, I have pointed out that the idea of civil society has evolved to adapt to different historical eras; it is a fluid, rather than static, concept that has always risen to the challenge of the day. This is one way in which a concept achieves a status of vitality and maintains its theoretical and practical usefulness. A similar view is expressed by Schak and Hudson, who make the following comment while discussing the applicability of the concept of civil society to Asian societies:

> Civil society is not all or nothing, either existing or not existing. It may appear and make some advances, then stall or go backwards, and this pattern varies with the different levels of authoritarianism as opposed to democratization in the societies concerned. Moreover, it is not unilinear, but path dependent. Thus, while there is some convergence between societies with or in the process of developing civil societies, each will have its idiosyncrasies … This opportunity to observe civil society at various stages of becoming and in a variety of polities provides a crucial corrective to Western perspectives and may eventually lead to a differently modulated theorization of civil society altogether.

(Schak and Hudson, 2003b: 1–2)

Thus, instead of imposing a unified model of civil society on different societies, our focus should be on how to adapt the concept to the different contexts under which it is analyzed, and its convergences and divergences across various historical and analytical conditions.

Baogang He shares Huang's assessment that there is a lack of autonomy with Chinese autonomous organizations as an intermediate space between state and society. Because these organizations are neither completely autonomous from the state nor completely dependent on the state, He develops the notion of a "semi-civil society in China" (He, 1994; 1996; 1997). "It is the feature of partial autonomy and overlapping with the state that makes Chinese social associations a semi- or quasi-civil society" (1997: 8), He writes. Furthermore, this semi-civil nature is driven by the need to adapt to the Chinese political landscape:

> Significantly, the notion of semi-civil society does not imply a low level of development of associational life, but reveals a strategy employed by members of associations. They deliberately "blur" the demarcation between the state and associations, or "sacrifice" their autonomy in order to survive and develop, or to change the structure or policy of the state from within. In political-sociological terms, the very uncertainty of the distinction between the state and civil society is a protection for civil society in the face of oppression; that is, semi-civil institutions can be defended as part of the state's institutions.
>
> (He, 1997: 8)

He is certainly not alone in pinpointing this feature of lack of total autonomy in the Chinese civil society (re)configuration. This state–society interpenetration in the hybrid pattern of Chinese civil society, many tend to agree, generally runs against the idea of an independent, self-organizing civil society as conceptualized in the West. Solinger, for example, notes that China's economic reform since the late 1970s has not

> hewed out any sharp and novel borderline between the "state" and a distinctive sphere of "society" among its subjects ... [There has been no] genuine formation of a "private" realm truly separate from the still enveloping "public" one for those who make their lives in the marketplace. Instead, the essential economic monolith of the old party-state now shapes official and merchant alike; both have become dependent, mutually interpenetrated semi-classes, even as both share a new kind of dependence on the state.
>
> (Solinger, 1992: 121)

In characterizing the interactions between the state and business associations, White, Howell, and Shang (1996: 207) conclude that these relations are "complex and contradictory, containing elements of co-operation and conflict, control and contestation, incorporation and resistance, conservatism and innovation." However, they also see a new trend of more and more business associations seeking greater autonomy from the restrictive control of the state. Elsewhere in an investigative case study of contemporary Chinese civil society, White (1994: 208) also detects "complementaries as well as conflicts in the emergence of a dualistic mechanism of institutional integration" in the state and social sectors. What is particular about this integration is that it is "both vertical and horizontal: vertical in that the state and an increasingly disparate economic structure are brought together through the intermediation of a social organization, and horizontal in that a social organization can act to bring together both the scattered elements within a complex economic field and the unco-ordinated state agencies which may be involved in that field" (White, 1994: 208).

Here I would like to borrow Kevin O'Brien's twin concepts of "entwinement" and "embeddedness" to illuminate the particular situation in China's organizational culture. Because of the omnipresence of the state power of influence, social organizations may voluntarily give up part of their autonomy in exchange for advantages in influencing state policymaking or maintaining legitimacy. O'Brien sees entwinement as the effort by social forces to harmonize their relations with the state by subordinating themselves to the established centers of state power. Through the strategy of entwinement, social organizations can enmesh themselves in the political system and avoid potential confrontations with the state, and thereby acquire viability and legitimacy. According to O'Brien (1994: 99), embeddedness "occurs as leaders, staff, and allies of an [organization] redraw the formal and informal rules of a political system to win a valued place for their organization." "In an organization seeking to become embedded, the agents of change seek proximity to existing centers of power [i.e., entwinement] rather than distance. They are quite willing to sacrifice control of membership and opportunities to embarrass regime leaders to gain ... organizational capacity" (p. 101). By maintaining only limited autonomy, embeddedness brings about organizational development as a result of attention and support from the state power, thus O'Brien observes "that meaningful organizational development is possible and may be occurring within current constraints and that growth can continue for some time without significantly increasing conflict with established authorities and without winning autonomy" (p. 86). Although O'Brien limits his discussion to the early stages of Chinese legislative development, he tries to show that the process of embeddedness is important for the understanding of organizational development of all institutions in China. What this tells us is that newly emerging social forces strategically tie their fortunes to the state by adopting a strategy of voluntary co-option. O'Brien's process of "entwinement" and "embeddedness" can be instructive in helping us to understand the institutional mechanism that drives some secondary associations to actively seek the co-optive power of the state to protect and expand their own interests. Consequentially, one sees to varying degrees the loss of total autonomy with these types of organizational structures at the gain of much-needed state support in organizational expansion.

X.L. Ding introduces the concept of "institutional amphibiousness" to describe the nature of associations existing in China and similar countries. Institutional amphibiousness, according to Ding, is defined by the following characteristics:

> First, the boundaries between institutional structures are ambiguous. Institutional structures are so interwoven with each other in their operation that the formal demarcation of the scope of each other's activities or powers becomes insignificant. Secondly, the nature of individual institutions is indeterminate. An institution can be used for purposes contrary to those it is supposed to fulfill, and the same institution can simultaneously serve conflicting purposes.

> (Ding, 1994: 298)

In the case of transition from communism, Ding contends, the notion of "institutional amphibiousness" especially refers to "institutional parasitism" (i.e., organizations formed a parasitic relationship with the party-state in that they depended on the official structures for legal protection and personnel and material support) and "institutional manipulation and conversion" (i.e., institutions were set up by the communist regime as part of the state system but were gradually co-opted by other forces for counter- or antistate purposes).

Because civil society represents a domain of civil affairs that is independent of, and on some occasions in opposition to, the state, autonomy is its most important feature, according to Ding, and the dichotomous conception of civil society versus the state has limited explanatory power in explaining the transition from postcommunism. "Where state-society relations are highly interpenetrated and interwoven, the concept of institutional amphibiousness becomes useful," Ding argues. "Amphibious institutional relations exist in many historical as well as cultural societies, but in late communism one finds their most colourful expression" (Ding, 1994: 318).

While the process of entwinement ensures that the state is incorporated into the institutional structure of social organizations and therefore becomes more responsive to society's demands and interests, it also makes sure that the state has a direct say in regulating social forces and secondary associations. It is in this sense that Shue (1994) describes this new evolving state–society relationship as "mutually empowering." The dual nature of Chinese associations both as a means to represent member interests and as a tool of state control (or intervention in some cases) has been well researched (see Ding, 2001: 52–62 for an overview). It is for this reason that many scholars have invoked the idea of corporatism to describe the evolutionary process of Chinese civil society (e.g., Baum and Shevchenko, 1999; Chan, 1994; Frolic, 1997; He, 1996).

Corporatism was initially associated with Fascist governments in the 1930s and revived later by Philippe C. Schmitter in identifying the way in which the state came to control and regulate interest groups in the 1930s and 1940s in Brazil. The essential elements of corporatism have been identified by Schmitter as follows:

> Corporatism can be defined as a system of interest representation in which the constituent units are organized into a limited number of singular, compulsory, non-competitive, hierarchically ordered and functionally differentiated categories, recognized or licensed (if not created) by the state and granted a deliberate monopoly within their respective categories in exchange for observing certain controls on their selection of leaders and articulation of demands and supports.
>
> (Schmitter, 1974: 93–94)

Corporatism, therefore, is an institutional arrangement in which corporations are created and sanctioned by the state and are kept as auxiliary and dependent organs of the state, and through which the state maintains control over and intervention in the management of these corporations (Schmitter, 1974). Corporatism is not certainly a unique feature in Chinese civil society only (see, for example, Bianchi, 1989; Howell and Pearce, 2001; Stepan, 1978 for discussions about other regions), but the corporatist paradigm to some extent captures the emerging elements in the pluralizing Chinese socioeconomic structure induced by decades of economic reform. The state is no longer exercising absolute dominance over society, so corporatism "posits the existence of clear limits imposed by the state upon society, with the state setting both the terms of secondary group existence and the permissible limits of member activity" (Baum and Shevchenko, 1999: 348).

Anita Chan identified two types of corporatism: state corporatism and societal corporatism. State corporatism, one variant of which is the communist one-party system, creates vertical functional institutions and places them under tight control; horizontal coalescing of class interests is not permitted. "The logic of the argument [made by state corporatists] is that whenever central party-state control loosens up, the corporate institutions will dysfunctionally strive to expand their own interests" (Chan, 1994: 165). Societal corporatism, on the other hand, "is structured sectorally, but unlike state corporatism, it functions in a manner that represents grass roots interests ... Thus voluntary associations, semi-official organizations, or even government organizations could group and regroup horizontally while endeavouring through the corporatist structure to further their own interests and the interests of their assigned constituencies" (Chan, 1994: 171). In other words, state corporatism exercises power from above while societal corporatism exerts pressure from below.

Unger and Chan (1995) assert that China's state corporatism bears similarities to many of the attributes that had been common to Japan, Taiwan, and South Korea in their developmental stages, and identified an "East Asian model of state corporatism" (see also Zeigler, 1988). What China and its neighbors have in common, Unger and Chan argue, is a cultural bias favorable toward corporatist structures:

> In the Confucianist teachings that pervaded all of the East Asian cultures, giving primacy to private interests had been viewed as equivalent to selfishness. The greater good was ideally manifested in a consensus overseen by the moral authority of the leadership, reflected in a moralistic father-knows-best paternalism.

> The notion that individual and sectoral interests should be compromised for the greater good, as represented by a higher leadership, was conducive in the modern age to patriotic appeals, and East Asian governments have not been slow to wrap themselves in the garb of nationalism and 'national interest' in their promotion of corporatist solutions.

> (Unger and Chan, 1995: 33)

However, while Unger and Chan still see a domination of the role by the central or local state power in associational life in China, others have recently noticed a "transition from 'state-guided corporatism from above' toward 'corporatism from below based on unofficial relationships' " because of "increasing awareness of social group interests, and the resulting tension between an association's control and service functions" (Ding, 2001: 59). In other words, there is a clear shift from state corporatism to societal corporatism in recent developments as the influence of the state continues to be weakened by deepening marketization of the economic and other sectors in China.

From this discussions, it can be seen that except for those theoretical deliberations that treat civil society as a normative, prescriptive ideal type, civil society in a particular national setting should be contextualized and historicized. So, instead of approaching the subject of civil society as an either/or dichotomous category, I argue that it is best viewed as a continuum. At one end of the spectrum is the environment in which civil society is totally free of any state control and interference, and retains its complete autonomy; at the other extreme end is the situation in which civil society is incorporated into one unified national hierarchical associational structure under complete control of the state. In between those two extremes lie varying degrees of societal and state corporatist variations. In countries where civil society maintains its full autonomy and is free from any state control (in the face of a weak state), we see an unregulated competition among civil society groups for their own interests, and the most likely scenario is chaos in a factious society. By contrast, totalitarianism rules in countries where civil society is totally suppressed. A healthy, democratic society is one in which a vibrant civil society works hand in hand with a full-functioning state, with each acting as a balance to and check on the power of the other.

Indeed, when Habermas talks about the public sphere as a direct creation of a vigorous civil society, he is referring to it both as an ideal type and as a social reality grounded in peculiar historical terms (Baker, 1992; Calhoun, 1992; Eley, 1992; Fraser, 1992; Habermas, 1992; Hohendahl, 1992). The structural transformations in the twentieth century took place when the states and corporate actors started to instill their own motivations into civil society, and the public sphere began to lose its independence and became a bargaining place for different interest groups. Hence the degradation of the contemporary public sphere that Habermas has bemoaned.

Rather than applying the concept of civil society in the European sense and then testifying to the existence or nonexistence of a similar type of civil society in China, I believe a more fruitful path to follow is to examine what particular type of civil society existed or exists in China and what impact it has had or will have on the political arena. As was pointed out in the previous chapter, there has been no single, unified European concept of civil society, and a proper understanding of the idea of civil society must be historicized and contextualized.

As to research on civil society in China, there are three points that I would like to highlight here to clarify many of the ongoing controversies as reviewed in this section. First, the development of civil society in China has always been a fluid process adapting to evolving social, economic, political, and ideological conditions; its functions have also been varying to a great extent. As many have realized, throughout Chinese history, a strong state has been the dominating theme; however, it does not mean that the state has successfully strangled competing social forces in their various manifestations. As China has become more and more integrated with the world economy, it is increasingly clear that China cannot separate itself from many of the general trends in the globe. The social conditions that once contributed to the birth and prosperity of civil society in the West are also emerging in China after over two decades of economic reform and development (e.g., Zhang, 1997). Most of the changes in the social conditions that are thought to be favorable breeding grounds for a nascent civil society have to do with a dramatically improved economic environment in the reform era that helps elevate the quality of life for average citizens on one hand, and a drastically new information environment (both at the national and international levels) as a result of more access to a variety of information sources and increased contact with the outside world on the other. For example, as Feng Chen (2003) observes, the promotion of a capitalist-style market economy in China has intensified conflicts between labor and capital and management; workers' unions are gradually shifting their roles in solving work-related disputes and are more inclined to represent workers' interests. Lately, there have also been more and more cases of workers organizing themselves into unionlike arrangements to best represent their interests and to engage in protest against what are perceived to be unfair practices by the state. As the Chinese economic system becomes fully integrated into the world economy, a more diversified and plural Chinese society is becoming increasingly coterminous with global society. This creates the possibility for Chinese civil society to interact with global civil society in various ways, and the Internet undoubtedly weighs in as a significant, and oftentimes crucial, factor in this regard.

Next, most scholarly discussions, especially those on contemporary Chinese civil society, have focused heavily or exclusively on the interaction between business associations and the state. Most conclusions have been reached based on those limited observations. Independent intelligentsia, dissident groups, freelance associations, and overseas Chinese communities are most likely to be ignored in the configuration of Chinese civil society. Thus it must be admitted that Chinese civil society is much more wide-ranging and more colorful than has been acknowledged in most cases. Those two points should be obvious in my later discussions. In the later chapters, I demonstrate how the Internet has created an outlet for independent civil society groups to coordinate their activities and to communicate with the general public.

Finally, the state–civil society interaction is a two-way process, with each affecting the other in certain directions. While the Chinese Communist Party undoubtedly intends to incorporate social organizations into its domain of control, organized groups invariably want to tilt state decisions in their own favor and to seek state protection for their group interests. It is for this reason that Bruce Dickson (2003) argues that economic privatization has created an emerging class of "red capitalists" (i.e., private entrepreneurs that are recruited into the Communist Party) that exert pressure for political change from within the party. Dickson sees no prospect of these entrepreneurs acting as agents of democratization in the short run because the current economic and political systems work very much to their advantage. As long as their individual and group interests are not at stake, there are no incentives on the part of these red capitalists to challenge the party-state. However, as the existing Chinese political system grows more and more out of tune with the changing socioeconomic conditions in the country, the demand for change from these various social groups "embedded" within the party may grow. In that regard, change in the political system will be incremental rather than abrupt, and gradual diversification in representation of collective interests at the state level may be the preliminary steps toward democratization in the long run.

The Concept of Civil Society in the Chinese Language

The debates on Chinese civil society reviewed in the previous section are primarily based on research among China scholars in the West. Side by side with the surge of interest in the idea of civil society in the West has been an emergence of scholarship on Chinese civil society among Chinese researchers. In addition, the idea of civil society has also been embraced by Chinese politicians on various occasions in an effort to experiment with a viable Chinese model of democratic reform. Here I review the development of the concept of civil society on the Chinese soil. I start my discussion with an etymological evolution of the Chinese equivalent for the English term "society."

The Chinese word for society, *shehui*, is actually composed of two characters, *she* and *hui*. Of the two, *she* has a longer and more complex history. In a recent review of Chinese scholarship on the history of the term, Chen (1996: 1–5) summarizes its origin into five sources. The following discussion is based on Chen's summary.

First, the earliest use of *she* referred to the God of Earth and later to the sacrificial ceremonies for the God of Earth. Second, *she* was the basic administrative unit based on geographic location; it existed from ancient to early modern China, roughly from the Spring and Autumn and Warring States periods (770–221 BC) to the late Qing Dynasty (AD 1616–1911). Third, it was a festival gathering for sacrificial and god-worshipping ceremonies. Fourth, it referred to associations of like-minded people; its typical memberships were oriented toward poets or scholars, and its popularity reached its height in the Ming Dynasty (1368–1644). Fifth, it also referred to professional (mainly business) associations starting from the Tang Dynasty (618–907).

The origin of *hui*, on the other hand, has a much more limited meaning; it referred to a gathering of people with a common interest. Its earliest use was mainly limited to the associations of intellectuals whose purpose was the furthering of their artistic or literary pursuits. Historical annals indicate that the existence of *hui* was formally institutionalized at least in the North Wei Dynasty (386–534). The meanings of *she* and *hui* gradually overlapped and the two words were combined into one term, hence establishing its status as the Chinese equivalent of the English word "society" in the modern Chinese language as a nonstate sphere of activities.

Based on their functions (or orientations), Chen Baoliang then traced ancient Chinese associations in four categories: political, economic, military, and cultural. Political associations were established for the promotion of certain values and/or advocacy of social actions toward a claimed goal and later developed into political parties and oppositional groups. Economic associations included mutual-assistance groups, charity organizations, business associations, and chambers of commerce. Military associations were mainly locally organized groups for the purpose of protection against outside forces, and their existence and function were complementary to the state army. Finally, there were cultural associations that not only included gentries at various levels and scholars of all kinds, but also extended to gambling (e.g., cockfighting, cricket fighting) and entertainment groups, horticultural communities, and even organized groups renting out tear-shedding services for funeral ceremonies. Additionally, Chen also put religious (e.g., Buddhist, Taoist) groups in the last category. I regard those groups as a separate category and make them the fifth type in the categorization because of the distinctiveness of those religious associations, both in their formalities and in their historical functions.

From this brief summary, it can be seen that many (but definitely not all) of those associations were formed voluntarily and were in the domain of civil society as we understand it today. But the majority of these associations did not enjoy any royal recognition; there was no institutionalized protection of any kind and, indeed, they often were victims of persecution at the whimsies of the emperor.

While the Chinese language has a full-scale equivalent for the English word "society," that is not true for the English term "civil society." To understand the full ramifications of the intellectual debates on civil society in China, we need to start with an examination of the conceptualization of civil society as a linguistic construct in the Chinese context. Chinese philosophy since ancient times has attached a great importance to the controversies between *ming* (name) and *shi* (the actual world represented) because without a proper name there could be no substance. Intellectual development about civil society is no exception.

The exiled Chinese scholar Wang Shaoguang (1991) was among the first to call attention to the variations in the Chinese conceptions of civil society by way of its translations of the term into Chinese. Wang identified three intellectual strains in Chinese deliberations on civil society. First, civil society has been equated with and therefore translated as *wenming shehui* (which means civilized or enlightened society) and this conception acknowledges the essential role of the state in creating a new type of society that was a contrast with the crudeness or barbarianism in previous times. Second, the translation of civil society into *shimin shehui* (city or urban people's society) is tantamount to recognizing the role played by urbanization and commercialization (the Chinese word *shi* has a twofold meaning: market or city) in modern times in creating a social force of its own that is distinctive from the state. Third, the talk of *gongmin shehui* (public people's society or citizen's society) has also been associated with the idea of civil society; this form of thinking emphasizes the public good and good citizenship in the process of state-making. Wang himself opts for the second form because the first one is too broad and the third one is too utopian in nature. But the choice of *shimin* to represent the formations of civil society draws criticism on the ground that it excludes what might be an important component of the configuration: the peasants or rural people, which make up the majority of the Chinese population.

Wang's discussion has set the stage for a vigorous line of debates about the search for an appropriate linguistic concept in Chinese to define the nature of the society under discussion. Des Forges (1997) has borrowed Wang Shaoguang's three models of civil society in China and tried to place them in the larger context of Chinese history to glean various elements of intellectual traditions in civil society debates from ancient times to the present. He (1997: 60–62) gave a nice review of ongoing debates among Chinese scholars from the late 1980s to the mid-1990s and noted three popular Chinese renditions of civil society: *shimin shehui, gongmin shehui,* and *minjian shehui.* The first two versions have been discussed by Wang Shaoguang, and the third version, *minjian shehui* (nongovernmental or popular society), highlights the antithetical nature of civil society vis-à-vis the state. In commenting on the three uses, He (1997: 61) writes, "*Minjinan shehui* stresses the idea of the antithesis of state to society at the expense of the idea of civility. *Shimin shehui* highlights the role of entrepreneur and the market, but does not take autonomy into account. Even worse, duty to the state and even the public in the governmental sense is infused in the term of *gongmin shehui.*" I basically concur with He's critique. Liang (2001) has made similar comments about the use of the three terms.

Additionally, there are other popular terms in China's political language that also capture part of the civil society landscape. For example, *shehui tuanti* (societal associations) or *shehui zuzhi* (societal organizations), *qunzhong tuanti* (mass associations) or *qunzhong zuzhi* (mass organizations), can also be different components of civil society. But these are ambiguous terms at best: some of them are self-organized and voluntary in nature while others are government sponsored (or government sanctioned) and serve as an extended arm of the state. Clearly, not all of them belong to the domain of civil society and neither should they be categorized as such. Unfortunately, some current research (e.g., Gold, 1998; White, 1994) ignores this important distinction and puts all of these organizations under the broad umbrella of civil society; results from those findings tend to produce misleading (or conflated) conclusions or interpretations.

In short, civil society as an imported Western social construct lacks an exact, indigenous Chinese equivalent that can capture all of the various aspects associated with the theoretical dialogues about civil society. Each of the previous terms in Chinese conveys only part of the broad connotations embodied in conceptions of civil society in the Western tradition. Even today, there does not seem to be a consensus as to the choice of one term over another by scholars in China. This can be reflected by the decision of three leading Chinese social scientists in their discussions: Deng Zhenglai (1997) uses *shimin shehui* (because, he contends, it is an essential component of China's economic and political modernization process); Liang Zhiping (2001) chooses *minjian shihui* (because, he argues, what China needs most is a public sphere where private people can exchange opinions on matters of public importance free from the hand of the state); while Zhang Zuhua (2002) prefers *gongmin shehui* (because he believes that for a country with a long authoritarian political culture, civic awareness and a participatory culture are crucial for building a Chinese citizenship conducive to China's political future). Noticeably, all three stress the transitional role of civil society in China's ongoing transformation.

Search for Civil Society among Chinese Scholars

Triggered partly by the resurgence of the idea of civil society in the West and partly by the effort of Western China scholars to (re)conceptualize the interactions between the state and society in China within the framework of the notion of civil society, Chinese scholars have seized upon the idea in rethinking a host of issues closely related to China's economic reform and political future since the late 1980s. Generally speaking, while Western China scholars have been interested in the applicability of Western theories of civil society to the Chinese context, Chinese intellectuals have focused on the adaptability and domestication of a foreign concept to understand China's ongoing modernization drive and unprecedented social transformation in the reform era.

After reviewing major Chinese publications concerning the discourse on civil society from the late 1980s to the mid-1990s, Baogang He (1997: 38–64) and Shu-Yun Ma (1994) both suggest that Chinese scholars had actually conducted quite extensive theoretical deliberations on a number of important issues related to the concept of civil society during that period. The 1989 Tiananmen Massacre marked one major dividing line in the discourse.

Between 1986 and 1989, Chinese intellectuals enjoyed a relatively more liberal atmosphere during a time when the top leadership first under Hu Yaobang and then under Zhao Ziyang was willing to listen to different views on ideological matters. Several approaches to the discourse were identified: "the discovery of the value of civil society; the exposure of the negative consequences of 'mass society'; and the criticism of the ostensible incoherencies of the dominant official ideology" (He, 1987: 39). Some scholars had vehemently criticized the system failure of the totalitarian society in the Mao era and pointed out the impracticality of the type of socialist and communist framework openly advocated by the Chinese government, and a few even ventured to propose an alternative — calling for individual autonomy, individual rights, an independent and free public sphere, and voluntary associations. During this phase, "the focus of the Chinese domestic discussion of civil society was on the creation of a modern citizenry through inspiration of 'civic awareness' by the state among the people" (Ma, 1994: 185).

Unfortunately, this period of liberal thinking was curtailed by the heavy-handed suppression of the Beijing student-led prodemocracy movement in 1989. Many of the prominent advocates of ideological reforms were either persecuted or suppressed; there was a period of silence among Chinese scholars about civil society. However, the discourse on civil society in China was carried on and energized by Chinese intellectuals in exile.

Although the 1989 student movement failed to bring democracy to China, it dramatically shifted the tone of debates on civil society and its role in China's future. For one thing, it smashed any hope that many scholars might previously have had that the state would bring democracy to China; instead, these intellectuals started to look to the force of civil society for answers. Encouraged by the latest developments in Eastern Europe and the former Soviet republics, many of these theorists developed a model of civil society as a significant sphere independent from the influence of the state and as an effective check and balance against the power of the state. Meanwhile, inspired by the parallel developments in theories of civil society in the West, debates about Chinese civil society also became more sophisticated, more diversified, and more rational in perspectives and approaches (He, 1997; Ma, 1994).

Since the early 1990s, debates on civil society resurfaced among scholars in China, quickly gaining depth and intensity. One noticeable change is that scholarly attention to the idea of civil society is no longer constrained to the dissident circles only but has also spread to mainstream researchers in major Chinese universities. Many university departments in the social sciences have even started to offer courses and sponsor academic research in this area.[1]

Two phases can be detected in the development of theoretical debates about Chinese civil society within Chinese academia in the post-1989 era: phase one features the introduction of the different scholarly traditions and contemporary theories of civil society in the West (see Deng, 1997; Li, 1998; Lin, 1997; Zhang, 2002; 2003 for an overview of efforts to introduce the concept to the Chinese audience); phase two focuses on debates about whether it is possible and, if yes, how to implant a foreign concept to the Chinese cultural, economic, and political environment. An important step taken during the first phase was the translation into Chinese and publication of a handful of important works in the West on civil society in the early to late 1990s.

Fang Zhaohui's publication of a reflexive piece bemoaned the lack of critical perspectives on the discussion of civil society in China in the 1990s and called for scholarly attention to new models and the need to contextualize the concept of civil society in China's particular social, political, and economic conditions (Fang, 1999). This publication marked a turning point in shifting the emphasis from introduction of Western theories to localization and domestication of the idea of civil society on Chinese soil. Deng Zhenglai, of the Chinese Academy of Social Sciences (CASS), was among the first to recognize the necessity of inventing a theoretical framework to take into account the particularities of the Chinese sociopolitical reality. In a collection of essays on civil society in China, Deng (1997) first challenges the claim that the Western theoretical and institutional models are universally applicable and argues that the key to China's modernization is the building of a healthy civil society that can serve as a buffer against the power of the state. He further contends that a healthy civil society is essential to the building of a state–society structural relationship in which the state provides a legal system that can modulate civil society while civil society can provide an effective balance in checking the power of the state. Deng further mapped out two phases in constructing civil society in China: one is the installation of the state–civil society dual system, and the other is the active participation of civil society in state decision making.

Li Fan, being part of the civil society revolution in China himself by founding the independent, nongovernmental think-tank agency called the World and China Research Institute, notes four important transformations in China's march to a modern civil society: expanding autonomy and freedom of the individuals, increasing separation of the state and society, self-management of society, and mounting interaction between state and society (Li, 1998). Li says that this has set the stage for a "quiet revolution" in which the force of civil society will be irreversible. Zhang (2003) asserts that Chinese civil society is still at a nascent stage because, as key components of civil society, Chinese citizens have not enjoyed the full status of citizenship in the sense of rights and participation, and because civic awareness in China is still low. But Zhang contends that China is already embarking on a path to a mature civil society, and he further argues that the state can play a positive role in bringing Chinese civil society to its full capacity. Liu Xiaobo, the famed dissident known for his bravery in speaking out against the government during the 1989 student movement and who was later imprisoned for doing so, detects a clear trend in the weakening of the state and the strengthening of civil society during the past two decades. He pins his hopes on civil society in the eventual democratization of China (Liu, 2003).

Interestingly, in my review of current literature on the debates on civil society among Chinese scholars, I have seen none that has adopted the tripartite model of civil society as advocated by some neoliberals in the West in which the economy, the state, and civil society are conceptualized as distinctive spheres. The reason, I think, is that the long tradition of authoritarian rule in China has made the all-powerful state the primary factor in stifling the autonomy of social forces. The economy, which has gradually stepped out of the shadow of the state, instead of being a suppressing force, is likely to be the major friend of civil society in nurturing free-wheeling, autonomous groups independent of the traditional sphere of influence by the state — at least for the time being. This should be clear from the discussion in the remainder of this chapter.

Three points stand out in the ongoing debates about civil society in China among Chinese scholars. First, there is a general consensus among most scholars that civil society in China has experienced unprecedented development during the last two decades as a result of economic liberalization. Second, civil society will be a defining force in determining the future course of democratization in China, although there is still much controversy about the exact format of democracy to be seen there. Third, instead of the civil society-versus-state model as seen in Eastern Europe in the 1970s and 1980s, a much more complex model is needed for civil society in China — civil society assumes an adversary role to check the power of the state, yet at the same time it also needs to cooperate with the state (which is still a powerful force and will likely remain so for years to come) to put in place a framework in which civil society can enjoy institutional and legal protection.

Rebecca Moore (2001: 66), in commenting on the future of civil society as a force for democratization in China, writes:

> Civil society is unlikely to play the sort of role in China that it did in Poland in 1989. Rather, many China scholars and NGO advocates believe, China will democratize in an evolutionary rather than revolutionary way. Regardless of the pace of change, the evolution of liberal democracy in China will require that reform occur from the bottom up as well as from the top down — at the societal as well as the state level. A strengthened and increasingly autonomous civil society will serve not only to encourage reform at the top but also to ensure that reforms are firmly rooted in Chinese society — in its habits, institutions, and values.

Despite their differences on many important issues, this is a central point with which most China scholars in the West and within China seem to concur.

Confucianism, Neo-Confucianism, and the Idea of Civil Society

For a long time, it has been argued that the fundamental thesis in Confucianism was its denial of individual autonomy and the supremacy of the state. Max Weber, in his famous study of industrial capitalism, attributed the failure of modern capitalism to materialize in China to its lack of this worldly rationalization as represented by Protestant asceticism in Europe and the absence of individualism as a value that is so central to Weber's version of capitalism (Weber, 1976; see also Weber, 1951).

This interpretation of Confucianism as being hostile to individualism and as promoting unconditional surrender of personal interests to the state or group has influenced social research in relation not only to China but also to a number of nations in Southeast Asia that are considered to be traditional Confucian states. For example, Alexander Woodside makes such comments on Confucian values:

> Confucian thought essentially stressed the arrangement of relationships between people and people, but it paid far less attention to the combinations of different sets of people. It did not acknowledge the power and

influence of any abstract entity like "society" separate from individual existences, even though it did believe in a general moral climate which could degenerate.

(Woodside, 1976: 54)

There is no lack of similar views among contemporary China scholars. Schwartz (1985), for example, points out that although self-cultivation was highly valued, there was no place for liberty and individualism in the Confucian culture. Similarly, Donald Munro (1977) notes that there is no appreciation for the "private self" in Confucianism. What emerges instead is a selfless person who

submerges his own immediately experienced interests or wishes to those of a larger unit of which he is a part ... It is an old value in China, closely associated with mystical currents in Taoism, Confucianism, and Buddhism that proclaim the essential unity of individuals by virtue of their possession of some universal attribute ...

(Munro, 1977: 175)

Lucian Pye (1985) argues that in Confucian cultures government is viewed as an extension of the family and plays the role of a father whose authority and discipline is necessary as protector of the public good. Zeigler believes that as "one of many ideologies that speaks unambiguously about the desirability of negating the human error of individualism," Confucianism, combined with "the cultural collectivism of Asian societies," creates in those nations the "state corporatist political systems, Confucian variety." (Zeigler, 1988: 124–125). In such systems, the government plays an assertive role not only in infiltrating interest groups but also in creating its own "captive organizations"; nongovernmental organizations only gain legitimacy within the confines of state-sanctioned activities (Zeigler, 1988). Inevitably, civil society in those nations is constrained and encompassed by the omnipresent hand of the government. It is precisely this that leads Pye (1991: 443) to the conclusion that to understand the evolving state–society relationship in China, "it is necessary to recognize the massive weight of cultural inertia which favours the state and inhibits the growth of a vibrant civil society."

These assumptions have met with challenges from many fronts. Although China had "difficulty in developing a civil infrastructure by which to bridge the gap between local organization and a strong, centralized, authoritarian state," as de Bary (1998: 156) acknowledges, this should not give sufficient evidence to suggest that Confucianism is intrinsically alien to the idea of civil society. On the contrary, de Bary points out that (1988: 41–89) two specific cases in relation to Confucian thought, *shexue* (community schools) and *xiangxue* (community compacts), which were advocated by the neo-Confucian scholar

Zhu Xi (1130–1200) and his followers in an effort to promote popular education and moral uplift among the common people until the early twentieth century, are illustrative of a wide range of undertakings by Confucian scholars to "strengthen community life and build consensual fiduciary institutions" (p. 13). The community schools and community compacts envisioned by Zhu Xi were built upon "mutuality, reciprocity, and cooperation among community members" (p. 59), and they "sought to incorporate the principle of voluntarism into community structures that might mediate between state power and family interests" (p. 60). The fact that they eventually fell victim to the superior power of the state in adverse historical circumstances should not be evidence for their incompatibility with the idea of civil society; rather, "the noble failure of these Confucian experiments only underscores the very real difficulties of implementing ideal values" (de Bary, 1998: 13). This view wins support from the case of Korea, some argue, where disciples of neo-Confucians successfully used community compact associations as the organizational base for popular social movements in the nineteenth century (An, 1988; Setton, 1997).

The conscious improvement of self, or self-cultivation, was one of the top virtues in the teachings of Confucius, Mencius, and indeed, all Confucian masters. Thus, "the Neo-Confucians, advocates of universal education in furtherance of the people's welfare but unsuccessful in establishing schools for all, promoted popular education primarily through self-cultivation and disciplined self-governance in the context of family life and the local community …" (de Bary, 1991: 97).

The transformative power of self-cultivation extends not only to the individual and the family but also to the world at large in the Confucian state, as Wei-ming Tu (1988: 115) acknowledges:

> The logic of taking the cultivation of the self and the regulation of the family as "roots" and the ordering of the community, the governance of the state, and universal peace as "branches," may give the impression that complex political processes are reduced to simple relationships explainable in personal familial terms. Yet the dichotomy of root and branch conveys the sense of a dynamic transformation from self to family, to community, to state, and to the world as a whole. Self-cultivation is the root, and harmony attained in the family is the natural outgrowth, like the branch, of our cultivated selves. Family is the root, and harmony attained in the community, the state, and the world is a natural outgrowth of the well-regulated families. In this sense what we do in the privacy of our own homes profoundly shapes the quality of life in the state as a whole.

However, nowhere was the word "community" ever used by Confucius. So this insertion of community as an intermediacy between self or family and the state into what Tu considers to be a continuum is called by de Bary (1991: 96–98) "the fiduciary community" of the Confucian state.

Robert Weller also disputes the claim that Confucianism was basically antithetical to individualism. Instead, he concludes that "a firm sense of self was central to the philosophy" (Weller, 1999: 25). Confucian scholars were expected to reform themselves through self-cultivation and then to serve the state responsibly. So this self-cultivation encompassed a kind of "inner-worldly asceticism" not incompatible with Weber's Protestant asceticism — but with significant Confucian underpinnings (Chang, 1996).

Independent intellectuals who remain free from the coercive power of the state have made up an important part of current literature on civil society. Many have argued that similar values could also be found in the Confucian self-cultivation.

> The idea that men should cultivate the attitude of preferring "right" to material advantage continued to distinguish Confucianism from other schools of thought, and it subsequently had great political influence. It furnished the ideological underpinning of a famous governmental institution, the Censorate, whose officers in theory, were allowed to criticize all officials including the emperor, whenever they strayed from the right.
>
> (Munro, 1969: 93-94)

That Confucian scholars should cherish principles more than anything else, including their lives, has been an important part of Chinese intellectual culture. Weller (1999: 25) cites the example of Qü Yuan, who drowned himself in protest over an erroneous state over two thousand years ago and whose life has been celebrated with a traditional Chinese festival since, as evidence for this claim. Indeed, independent Chinese intellectuals have always been the pioneers in championing the discourse on civil society and spearheading revolutions in China from the start (e.g., Bonnin and Chevrier, 1991; Fogel and Zarrow, 1997; Gasster, 1969; Mok, 1998; Schwarcz, 1986).

Peter Nosco argues that the Confucian conception of civil society was not prescient teaching about what was to come, but rather was insight in response to changing historical conditions:

> Historically ... as societies in East Asia acquired the conditions of early modernity, a kind of "space" did indeed open between the state and the citizen ... As elsewhere around the world, though perhaps not to the same degree as in Europe or North America, this sphere has the character of a public space, distinguished from both official and private spaces, and attendant to the emergence of this space is a boundary of sorts between the government and other groups or individuals in society.

Confucianism cannot be credited with stimulating these changes, but it can be observed to respond to them in at least two ways. First, one notes an increasing priority within Confucianism given to those forms of praxis that privilege interiority and self-cultivation, at the expense of the study of either the external world or the traditional classics. "Look inside yourself" becomes the message of much early-modern Confucian thought, for there you will find all that you need to know in order to become a perfected person. And second, one finds the reemergence and increasing prominence of forms of Confucianism that assert historicist as opposed to naturalist ontologies, arguing that the Confucian Way is not an unchanging set of universal principles, but rather is comprised of social and political practices that are conditioned by time and place.

(Nosco, 2002: 339–340)

Another competing philosophy throughout Chinese history, Taoism, has also in many ways affected various aspects of Chinese culture, society, and governance. If Confucianism has been to a large part associated with advocating a paternalistic state in achieving harmony in society from above, then Taoism is just the reverse in offering a liberalized version of discovering the Great Way (i.e., the *Tao*) of life by giving full rein to the diverse power of the individual from below. While the key to the Confucian paradigm is conformity, the essence of the Taoist perspective is diversity (Roberts, 2001). Chinese individualism finds the fullest expression in the teachings of Taoism and its followers.

In Lao Tzu's conception, the best government is the one that governs the least. "Very great leaders in their domains are only known to exist. Those next best are beloved and praised. The lesser are feared and despised" (Tao Te Ching, 1999: 17–18). In other words, the best ruler is one who recognizes the full force of civil society and therefore undergoverns: "When the government is unobtrusive, the people are pure. When the government is invasive, the people are wanting" (Tao Te Ching, 1999: 36). So the dignity of the individual and the superiority of civil society are what help statecraft achieve perfection.

Enough attention has been paid to the concepts of *gong, guan,* and *si,* and their implications for institutional developments and civic discourse in Chinese history. *Gong* (public), which is a parameter of activity organized at the local level for the management of collective goods and social services distinct from the realms of *guan* (official) and *si* (private), has been associated with a local infrastructure that was claimed by some scholars to be closely comparable to the European concept of public sphere or civil society. Mary Rankin develops a tripartite model of *guan, gong,* and *si,* an apparent reconstruction of the Western state–civil society–individual conceptual framework in the Chinese tradition:

As I use the term here, "public" retains a considerable communal element but refers more specifically to the institutionalized, extrabureaucratic management of matters considered important by both the community and the state. Public management by elites thus contrasted with official administration (guan), and with private (si) activities of individuals, families, religions, businesses, and organizations that were not identified with the whole community.

(Rankin, 1986: 15)

William Rowe examines the historical developments of the concept of *gong* and suggests that "[t]he Chinese idiom of a 'publicness' outside the institutions of bureaucratic administration has been at least as well-developed historically, and perhaps more developed, than its analogues in the West" (Rowe, 1990a: 326). Strand, in his study of the expansion of the public sphere in Beijing in the 1920s, moves a step further in building the connection among the public sector, the media, and public opinion.

The high value tradition placed on the public realm (*gong*) of gentry leadership reinforced the modern notion of public opinion as a vastly expanded sphere of discussion and debate … [t]he trembling state in the 1920s, the weak legitimacy of private interests (*si*), and the positive moral and political evolution of *gong* as [a] zone of discussion and concern encouraged newspaper editors, new and old civic leaders and ordinary citizens to improvise tactics and strategies for expressing political views in public.

(Strand, 1989: 168; see also Schoppa, 1989 for similar comments)

However, some scholars have questioned whether it is stretching too far to make *gong* akin to a Chinese version of the public sphere. It is true that debates about *gong, guan,* and *si* have a long history in Chinese political discourse, but to what extent *gong* was functioning at any time as the public sphere remains controversial. The following comment by Weller is worth quoting here:

When *gong* was contrasted with officialdom, it still had implications that the elite were acting on behalf of the state, whose values and goals they shared even if they were not (yet) part of the world of officials. Given the lack of a strong distinction between state and society, gong could not have the same implications that "public" did in Europe. These were local elites acting in consort with the state/society, and generally not promoting their own interests to (or against) the state.

(Weller, 1999: 27)

I accept Weller's rendition as closer to the actuality in China's entwining state–society relationship up to the late imperial Qing dynasty. Furthermore, Weller (1999: 28) points out that "[g]*ong* indeed meant public, but more in the sense of 'public interest' than a Habermasian 'public sphere'." In addition, I would like to add that the Chinese *gong* promoted more the spirit of public service, or engagement in unselfish activities for the public good, rather than a rational discourse on issues of a public nature as assumed in the European public sphere.

Finally, it is important to bear in mind that culture is not immutable, neither is a philosophy. Confucian thought has always been interacting with social life of the day and has been a transformative force in Chinese society at various historical stages. Through this process, Confucianism itself has been reproduced and rejuvenated with new elements in the face of new social conditions and challenges.

The Development of Civil Society in China: A Historical Perspective

A historical trajectory of the development of associational life that is so important for civil society must be mapped out before we can glean a full view of the concept of civil society in Chinese life. The following offers a brief overview of the historical evolution of the different forms of civic associations in China.

As Chen Baoliang (1996) convincingly demonstrates through meticulous examination of historical records and documents, intermediate social organizations interacting between the family and state in their various manifestations — political associations, friendship connections, secret societies, community ties, economic cooperatives, credit unions, charity organizations, welfare organs, professional guilds, chambers of commerce, martial arts unions, military allies, poetry clubs, scholars' groups, game and entertainment leagues, religious and temple entities — have existed and developed throughout Chinese history. These associations played a variety of roles in Chinese society and not all of them were civil in nature. But there is enough evidence to suggest that Chinese associational life has been as rich and vigorous as in the West and to falsify the characterization of Chinese people as inclined to "trust only people related to them, and conversely to distrust people outside their family and kinship group" — and thus making it hard for "unrelated people" to form groups of any kind (Fukuyama, 1995: 75).

Borrowing the three concepts of civil society (i.e., civilized society, city people's society, and public people's society) in Chinese discourse as identified by Wang Shaoguang (1991), Des Forges (1997) suggests that there were antecedent embryonic forms of civil life associated with each of these three through different historical periods in Chinese history. The first type, civilized society, was most characteristic of social formations of Zhou (1100 to 256 BC), Tang (AD 618–907), and Qing (1616–1911) dynasties; the second type, city people's society, was more descriptive of voluntary groups in the Warring

States (770–256 BC) period, Southern Song (AD 1127–1279), and the Republic (1912–1949) eras; thirdly, public people's society was a more appropriate denominator for social interactions in the Han (206 to 220 BC) dynasty, the Ming (AD 1368–1644) dynasty, and the Mao (1949–1980) era.

A survey of auto-organizations in Shanghai from the sixteenth to the twentieth centuries led Brook (1997) to identify four principles beyond kinship by which Chinese social groups were formed: (1) locality; (2) occupation; (3) fellowship, and (4) common cause. Also roughly during the same period in imperial China, self-organizations led by local elites not only expanded in numbers but also in the areas of activities engaged in — some prominent examples are popular groups to promote Buddhist values, animal-life-saving associations, philanthropic activities to help the poor, the rise of the "gentry society" in the late Ming (Brook, 1993).

Closely tied to the flourishing of voluntarily organized activities was the newly commercialized economy during this phase of historical development in China (Smith, 1986). Understandably, influx of economic activities not only created the demand for some breathing space free from interference by the heavy-handed state, but also produced the necessary wealth for some emerging social groups to engage in various activities. This point is best illustrated by Kwan Man Bun's (2001: 9) fascinating study of "the salt merchants' carefully nurtured system of networks and cultural entrepreneurship" in the entanglements of the state, the public, and the private in Tianjin in the Ming and Qing dynasties, and by William T. Rowe's landmark exploration of the transformation of the Chinese inland commercial city of Hankow by long-distance trade from the late sixteenth century through the last decade of the nineteenth century and "the steady trend ... toward corporate-style institutionalization of philanthropic activities and the growing attachment of them to a depersonalized 'public sphere' " during this period (Rowe, 1989: 349; also Rowe, 1984).

Nosco notes that while China approached early modernity, developments that were comparable to those in Europe, which were favorable to the development of a public space intervening between the state and individuals, were also observable in China:

> ... increased urbanization, with individuals uprooted from traditional village communities, and endeavoring to create new forms of association to combat the anomie and alienation that accompany such changes; an expansion of surplus wealth and the market, with an ever-increasing volume of transactions, including the commodification of a broad range of cultural products; a developed communication and transportation infrastructure, which contributes to the spread of literacy throughout the society ... In a variety of ways, these developments reinforce a sense of the individual as competent on the one hand to negotiate the acquisi-

tion of an increasingly diverse range of material and cultural products, and on the other hand to enter into elective associations of an ever more variegated sort.

(Nosco, 2002: 339)

Three points in particular need to be recognized in understanding the historiography of civil society in imperial China. First, it has been pointed out earlier that corporatism is an important feature of social organizations. The two types of corporatism both stress vertical integration as an organizing principle: state corporatism calls attention to the practice of local interests or groups surrendering their integrity to the coercive power of the state (e.g., Chan, 1994) while local corporatism emphasizes that ordinary people give up their independence to the local elites and local authorities (e.g., Oi, 1992; R. Thompson, 1995). A key feature with self-organizations of this era was the role played by elites in initiating, organizing, coordinating, and directing actions; Brook (1993) identified this specific group as "scholar-gentry" and Phillip Kuhn (1980; see also Rankin, 1986) took account of the elite-led militarization as "elite activism."

Second, proliferations of self-organizing groups during this period also testify to the presence and sometimes strengthening of horizontal integration in the social hierarchy. While vertical integration aims for incorporation of social forces into the established state power structure, horizontal integration reflects the popular desire for voluntary cooperation on an egalitarian basis and the struggle to break away from the coercive power of the establishment. The former feature is more likely to be emphasized and horizontal ties tend to be ignored by scholars of social relations in China (Brook, 1997). Much of Chinese history has been marked by the state's effort to minimize horizontal ties and the people's urge to diminish vertical integration in shaping social relations. Indeed, Chinese history has been written by numerous occurrences of social upheavals, uprisings, rebellions, and chaos when tension between the state's attempt to verticalize social relations and the popular urge to break away from it reached a breaking point through different eras.

Third, as summarized by Weller (1999: 29), "[i]t is no accident that elite horizontal institutions like academies or charities thrived during periods like the Southern Song or late Ming, when politics was at its most chaotic." Although it is true that even the state at its most absolutist phase had not eradicated associational linkages completely, an unmistakable general trend is that the rise and fall of autonomous organizations has been tied closely to the fluctuations of the state power at various historical eras. Cracks occurred when there was a decline in the power of state mechanisms to control popular forces and demands, and this subsequently led to a more vibrant associational life. Scholarship on China's voluntary groups has lent support to this observation, and there is enough evidence to suggest that auto-organizations were more vigorous in the Southern Song, late Ming, late Qing, and the Republican eras when weakening of the state power had created enough breathing space for society. In particular, there have been more publications in relation to the civil society–public sphere polemics concerning the late Qing dynasty than any other era in Chinese history with the exception of the current reform era. This is perhaps not without good reason: the imperial bureaucracy was most limited in its effectiveness and state power was at the lowest, which created the natural conditions most conducive to the kind of institutionalized political and civic participation that makes up the hallmark of the kind of civil society we cherish today.

Much of this trend continued in the Republican era (1911 to 1949). "Late Qing urban elite movements for constitutionalism, self-government and reform, which contributed to much of the 1911 Revolution, fostered an emergent urban elite civic culture in the early republican environment," Rankin (1997: 263) notes. But there were also significant changes that made the Republican era a watershed in Chinese history, so this was both a time of continuation and innovation.

First, *dang*, or political associations of various kinds, had a long history in imperial China. Traditionally, *dang* was a formation of a group of like-minded people and was based on a commonality of either shared geographical or ideological ancestry (Chen, 1996). Starting in the early Qing dynasty, emperors issued edicts against political associations of any kind in the belief that factional parties led to the fall of the preceding Ming; commenting on affairs of the state was therefore forbidden to all but incumbent officials (Wakeman, 1985). Although concessions were made by the state in the last years of the Qing dynasty, the ban was not completely lifted until the collapse of the empire in 1911. As a result, "[p]olitics was no longer the exclusive preserve of elite mediation and government institution" (Strand, 1989: 197) and there was a noticeable intensification of political debate and participation by people from all fronts in the Republican era, and new forums for political discussions, such as in teahouses, bathtubs, parks, street corners, and restaurants, gave birth to an emerging public sphere unprecedented in Chinese history (Strand, 1989).

Second, the Republican era marked "the starting point of a forceful modernization drive" and was "a time of economic and cultural innovation and creativity" (Bergère, 1997: 309); it was a start of an unfinished revolution which was curtailed by decades of turmoil and instability in the ensuing years brought about first by the Japanese invasion in the 1930s and then by the internal warfare between the Communists and the Nationalists. Private entrepreneurs were nipped in the bud by Mao's collectivization campaign after the communist takeover in 1949. This unfinished revolution was again revived by Deng Xiaoping and reformers since 1978 more than half a century later. Since the early 1900s, flourishing factories in such major metropolitan cities as Beijing and Shanghai, and increasing foreign trade produced rapidly growing classes of merchants, capitalists, workers, and bankers, and this in turn created autonomous groups, such as trade unions, professional associations, chambers of commerce in defense of their respective interests and in negotiating with local and national authorities and organizing protests or strikes (e.g., Chesneaux, 1969; Fewsmith, 1985; Hershatter, 1986; Xu, 2001; Yu, 1993). Bergère (1989) calls this era "the golden age of the Chinese bourgeoisie."

Third, side by side with the emergence of new self-managing civic groups and remodeling of existing ones was a paradigm shift among leading intellectuals and elites in discourse on state–society relationships and the conception of citizenship in the Republican era (see Fogel and Zarrow, 1997, for a summary). Starting from late Qing and continuing throughout the Republican years, there had been an influx of all kinds of foreign ideas from Japan, Russia, and the West through translations, lectures, debates, and publications — mainly by a cohort of intellectuals and political activists, most of whom had studied abroad. Reviving the banners of science and democracy, they started the New Culture Movement, which reached its climax with the May Fourth Movement of 1919 (Doleželová-Velingerová and Král, 2001; Rowe, 1990b; Schwarcz, 1986). Part of the objective of the New Culture Movement was to rearticulate or redefine the role of citizenship in a brand-new constitutionalism in place of the old imperial system, and to carry forward much needed institutional reform that could strengthen the state and uplift the people at the same time. In particular, one of the leading theorists and reformers, Liang Qichao, among others, advocated a set of concepts analogous to the kind of civil society conceived today: "limiting state power; defining the freedoms, rights, and responsibilities of individuals citizens; maintaining rational and orderly public debate; and, in the most urgent way, encouraging voluntary associations which might legitimately seek to influence the state" (Zarrow, 1997: 232; see also Tsin, 1997).

Fourth, the Republican era was marked by political interruptions, instability, and fluctuations. The revolutionary provisional government (1912 to 1919), followed by military and warlord ruling (1920 to 1926), the Nanjing regime (1927 to 1937), the Japanese invasion (1937 to 1945), and then the civil war between Mao's Communists and Chiang Kai-shek's Kuomintang (Nationalists) (1945 to 1949), had brought about one political disaster after another to the nation; disappointment, fear, and uncertainty pervaded provincial and local bodies (e.g., Lary, 1985; Rankin, 1997; Sheridan, 1975). Under such circumstances, no strong central authority existed to unify social forces and local constituencies into a concerted program of action, and self-managing civil groups could not formulate any kind of established relationship — either supportive or oppositional — with the state. Alternatively, there was no institutionalized state protection for civic associations, and this in turn stifled the development of any fully fledged civil society. In that sense, Republican China was not only an unfinished revolution for constitutional reform but also an unfinished revolution for the development of civil society in the country.

Finally, the Republican era was also a time of crisis, as manifested in a sustained effort to search for a national identity on the one hand and the struggle to free the nation from decades of invasion, occupation, and humiliation by foreign powers on the other. Nationalism became the driving force and major organizing principle for many autonomous associations and voluntary civic participations (see the collected essays in Fogel and Zarrow, 1997 for an overview), and made limited cooperation between civil society and the state possible.

To sum up, the Republican era provided a fertile ground for all sorts of intellectual activities and social experimentation. Along with it was the creation of an environment conducive to civic participations, yet at the same time a weakened state was not able to provide a sociopolitical framework in which civil society could grow and prosper.

Unfortunately, any signs of a nascent civil society in the Republican era were circumscribed by the founding of the People's Republic by Mao's Communist Party in 1949. After decades of civil war, foreign aggression and humiliation, rampant official corruption and incompetence, people saw a glimmer of hope in a unified country led by Mao, who promised a prosperous and strong "new China" that would bring a bright future to everyone, and they without hesitation lent their full support to Mao's Communist Party. But Mao's Chinese Communist Party (CCP) set up a Leninist party-state, which equated the interests of the society with those of the state, and in turn were the sole responsibility of the party to manage (or mismanage) (e.g., Schram, 1985). Thus the Maoist absolutist state negated the right to any free associational life, and its destructive effect on autonomous independent organizations was disastrous: there was no tolerance of any effort to challenge the organizational monism of the party-state. The state control mechanism penetrated all sorts of social institutions at various levels, and the state, with Mao as the "Great Helmsman," turned all social organizations into a vertical hierarchical form to a degree unimagined by the dynastic empires (He, 1997).

China under Mao's rule adopted a centrally planned command economy in which labor, production, distribution, and consumption were all tightly controlled by the state. This family-based, community-confined self-sustaining agrarian economy was described as a "moral economy" by Daniel Little (1989), and it is an essential part of the social control structure. "The agrarian economy and its associated social institutions were characterized as a 'honeycomb' social organization that perpetuated the segmented and parochial structure of Chinese politics" (Wang, 1998: 107).

This lack of a powerful social force outside the administrative structure of the party-state in Mao's era was noted by many and has been considered to be a major contributing factor to hampering the emergence of a vibrant civil society in contemporary China (e.g., Ding, 2001; He, 1997; Rosenbaum 1992;

Wang, 1998). The state power as a destructive force to civil society reached its apex during the Great Cultural Revolution (1966 to 1976), when mass actions fervently responded to the supreme leader (i.e., Mao) in wreaking havoc in the nation and producing horrendous effects on civil society groups. Mass class struggle movements involving various sectors of society worked not in opposition to or separately from the state, but as part of the state mechanism (under the co-optation of the state power) to cause widespread individual abuses and catastrophic chaos in the social order, and took disastrous tolls on social groups that did not openly adhere to the party line — precisely the kinds of consequences civil society tries to act against.

Economic Liberalization and Media Reform: Implications for Chinese Civil Society

As revealed earlier in the chapter, the focal point in current debates on civil society in China is the transformation in China's social structure in the reform era started by the late Deng Xiaoping in 1978. The emergence of an affluent middle class and the relaxing economic environment has made it possible for individuals to make their voices heard by associating with others. James and Ann Tyson's (1995) *Chinese Awakenings* provides an excellent testimonial narrative of how independent conscious individuals may exert bottom-up pressures on the state to loosen its grip on people's lives and conform to popular demands.

Economic liberalization and the introduction of a Western-style market economy in China have allowed the Chinese people to enjoy a level of material prosperity that was hard to dream about in Mao's era. As the average citizens today enjoy an unprecedented degree of freedom to choose what to do and where to live, and as they become less and less dependent on the state bureaucracy in their everyday life, people are more likely to look to civil society groups or organizations for help with, and protection of, their individual interests and rights. As Liu Xiaobo writes,

> In the reform era, as personal interest has become the greatest source of motivation for the masses, the concepts of "public" and "national" have surrendered much of their status to the concepts of "popular" and "personal" ... The debased status of the public sector has been accompanied by a rise in prestige for people or organizations with populist tendencies. For example, international media and private news sources are treated with much greater regard and credibility than official media.

> (Liu, 2003: 16)

That partly accounts for the rising number of social movements and protests in the past decade in various regions of China involving diverse social groups and that explains why house churches are more trusted by some people than authority-sanctioned neighborhood committees. In this sense, the social conditions in present-day China are not unlike those in the early stages of Western capitalist societies when robust economic activities prompted individuals to seek protection for their material benefits through the power of voluntary organizations and associative relations. Economic reform has weakened the power of the state and created a dynamic milieu of autonomous social forces, thus leading to a "quiet revolution from within" Chinese society (Walder, 1995; see also Goodman and Hooper, 1996).

As was mentioned earlier, scholars in the West have put the market side by side with the government as potential threats to today's civil society forces in highly capitalized societies. In the particular case of China, because the state has enjoyed unchallenged monopoly of power for so long, the market at this stage acts as a friend, not a foe, to civil society because economic forces provide the best chance to crack open the state control of power and to create more and more living space for civil society groups. Indeed, many of the civil society groups are triggered by economic motives. The other reason that the market often works to the advantage of Chinese civil society is that free-wheeling economic activities have created a staple force of individuals and social groups that are relatively independent of state control. Current scholarship as reviewed in this chapter on Chinese civil society offers supporting evidence to this claim.

In a report recently released by the Chinese Academy of Social Sciences (CASS) based on a three-year national study of social mobility in twelve provinces, it was found that by the end of 2003, nearly one-fifth (19%) of mainland Chinese residents were qualified as "middle class" based on a combination of criteria involving occupation, income, lifestyle, and self-perception indexes, and that number will rise to 40% by the year 2020. The report also predicts a significant jump in the middle class in the next eight to ten years, reflecting the ongoing seismic shifts that are transforming the Chinese social structure (CASS, 2004). The emergence and expansion of an affluent middle class in China will serve as the bedrock of a vibrant civil society in the years to come.

Side by side with this development is the shifting role of the Chinese media as a result of both marketization efforts within the media industry and the changing relationship between audience and the media. As pointed out before, the media have figured prominently in contemporary discussions of civil society and the public sphere. In this regard, the Chinese media will likely play a significant part in the configuration of Chinese civil society. Some of the ongoing changes in China's "mediasphere" as called by Donald, Keane, and Yin (2002) — such as improved access, proliferation of information, decentralization of media control — will have profound implications for Chinese civil society. Market-oriented reforms in the Chinese media sector have not only democratized access to a variety of sources of information, but they have also cultivated a new way of life and a new ideological formation among Chinese audience. As Chang and Tai observe, "[w]hether the Chinese government likes it or not, the burgeoning public awareness and demand for a free press, the commercialization and internationalization of the Chinese media, and the increasing pressure from the world community may make the next step — what to say and what to publish without fear of state interference — irreversible" (2003: 43). Marketization of the media fosters a brand-new media–audience relationship and has led the media to be more responsive to audience needs and demands. This emerging trend is redefining the place of mass media in Chinese civil society. More discussion of this aspect appears in later chapters.

The quick rise of the Internet as the newest, and perhaps the most liberating, medium of mass communication in China in the past decade has brought new hope to the prospects of civil society in shaping political and social developments in the country. For example, the 2003 widespread outbreak of SARS in China, in which the Chinese local and central government officials initially attempted to cover it up but subsequently decided to adopt a more open strategy as a result of domestic and global pressure, was cited as the newest example in which the government had to conform to the pressure of society and public opinion in modulating its behavior.[2] In this particular case, the Internet played a pivotal role in opening up a brand-new channel for people in China as well as outside the country for gathering and exchanging information and countering official statements. The nature of this process is examined in greater detail in Chapter 6.

Chapter Summary

Alongside the revival of the concept of civil society first in Eastern Europe and then in the West have been vigorous debates among China scholars about the applicability of the European concept of civil society to the Chinese context. There is some general consensus that some form of (nascent, or embryonic, as some like to call it) civil society is taking shape in China outside the sphere of influence of the once all-powerful and all-inclusive state. The exact nature of this civil society, however, still remains debatable. It has been noted that Chinese civil society still lacks autonomy and is still interwoven with the parameters of the state arrangement (here one may wonder, of course, to what extent civil society in any national setting maintains its absolute autonomy). The entwining entanglement of civil society with the state in China allows it to be sometimes responsive to the state system of incorporation while at the same time being attentive to its own interests. That is, of course, a still-evolving process in which Chinese civil society is searching for its place and role in the overall social structure within a country of fast-paced changes in an era of unprecedented transformation. The most fruitful approach to studying Chinese civil society, it is argued here, is not from an either/or mentality wherein scholars debate about whether Chinese civil society exists. Rather, the most productive approach is to view the evolution of Chinese civil society as a dynamic, fluid process. The specific social, political, economic, and cultural conditions that have contributed, or are contributing to, this process need to be carefully examined to gain a better understanding of civil society in China.

While no exact equivalent of the concept of civil society exists in the Chinese language for its English counterpart, functionally comparable elements of civil society have existed as an integral constituent of society and evolved in the different eras of Chinese history, and their relationship with the individual and the state has gone through different configurations. The reform era in China since 1978 has created a fertile ground for the revitalization of civil society forces as a result of economic openness and prosperity. As the average citizens gain more economic freedom and benefit more from the economic booms, they are more likely to contribute to the formation of civil society forces and to seek help from civil society. Throughout the process, mass media, which are undergoing restructuring, play an important role in creating an information environment conducive for the functioning of civil society. The popularization of the Internet as a communication and socialization tool in China in the last decade, in particular, provides a new line of hope to empower Chinese civil society in an increasingly networked world.

3
Government Policy and State Control of the Internet in China

The worldwide spread of information and communication technologies (ICTs) led by the Internet in the last decade has intensified the global information revolution, and governments have struggled to come to grips with the economic, social, cultural, and political implications of this revolution. China has been quick to realize the great potentials and the underlying risks that are associated with the unprecedented scale of technological transformation; it has worked hard to map out an official strategy in embracing the latest waves of the information age. At the heart of China's official blueprint is a short-run and long-term plan of the envisioned role of ICTs in its national development. At the same time, the authoritarian regime has also put in place a sophisticated control mechanism with a combination of technical and policy initiatives to harness the destabilizing and disruptive potential of information technologies. Any discussion of China's Internet and new ICTs, therefore, is incomplete without a proper assessment of the bureaucratic regulatory apparatuses intended to solidify the party-state's political control of a fast-changing society. This chapter, then, starts with an examination of the multifaceted nature of China's official information infrastructure initiatives and is followed by a look at the rising trend of online campaigns against state control; it ends with a discussion of the theoretical perspective of fragmented authoritarianism, which, the author argues, helps us better understand today's information environment in the country.

Global National Information Infrastructures: An Overview

The acceleration of technological and industry convergence in telecommunications since the late 1980s and the early 1990s has not only created new opportunities for the fermenting and ever-evolving information revolution worldwide, but it has also posed unprecedented challenges to governments in every corner of the globe. Governments have exhibited different rationales, visions, policies, and strategies to advance developments of their National Information Infrastructures (NII). Examples are Singapore's "Intelligent Island" (Wong, 1997); Korea's "National Basic Information System" (NBIS) (Jeong and King, 1997); the United States's "Information Superhighway" (Kahin, 1997); and the models of European Union members: liberal (i.e., enforcing privatization, deregulation, competition, and information liberalization in the telecommunications industries), public service (i.e., giving priority to the rights of citizens to comprehensive information services and access to the communications network), and cultural–nationalist (i.e., stressing content policy over infrastructure policy and promoting cultural exclusiveness and expressiveness of communication content production and distribution) (Venturelli, 1997; see also the edited volume by Kahin and Wilson 1997 for more NII initiatives). Noticeably, the Internet has been dominating NII decision formulations in most nations for the past decade.

The complications for national policymaking in NII are manifold. First, they not only involve the national infrastructure by which telecommunications can survive and prosper but also necessarily touch upon the content and applications that exert a direct impact on everyone's life. In other words, telecommunications encompass a myriad of technical and economic issues as well as cultural and social ones. Second, engagement and conflict between public interest and the private sector feature prominently in the NII conception. Third, telecommunications are transnational in nature because the flow of information products often extends beyond national borders. Therefore, the information infrastructure not only has to address issues at the national level but must also take into account factors at the global level; intersections between the National Information Infrastructure (NII) and the Global Information Infrastructure (GII) make cooperation and competition the key themes in the development of national information frameworks (Baer, 1997; Spacek, 1997).

As Kahin and Wilson's (1997) edited volume titled *National Information Infrastructure Initiatives* illustrates, a nation's information policies reflect its economic, social, cultural, historical, and political circumstances, and are motivated by internal (domestic) as well as external (global) drivers in the areas of innovation, economic growth, and competitive edge. In evaluating the NII initiatives by a number of countries, the Organization for Economic Cooperation and Development (OECD) notes the following similarities and differences in their approaches:

> Without exception, governments have a positive attitude towards the developments in information and communication technology. The general conviction is that they will result in economic and social benefits: information infrastructures are expected to stimulate economic growth, increase productivity, create jobs, increase the quality of services, and improve the quality of life. The opportunities provided by the new technologies enable governments to react positively to economic and social challenges. Besides the similarities, however, there are also differences. First, programmes adopt different priorities for the development of information infrastructures. Some focus mainly on services

and applications while others primarily discuss networks and infra-structures. Second, the programmes take the country's specific economic, cultural and social situation as a starting point.

(OECD, 1997: 595)

A companion volume edited by Kahin and Nesson (1997) under the title *Borders in Cyberspace* demonstrates how the Internet has transformed the traditional concept of space by transcending and blurring geographic and political boundaries (interestingly, a defining feature of cyberspace is its space-lessness); it has thereby empowered individuals to bypass conventional regulatory mechanisms by creating a brand new realm of human communicative activity and connectivity (see also Nguyen and Alexander, 1996). Similarly, Haraway (1991) uses the word "cyborg" to depict the boundary (re)making potential of the cyberworld in brewing new relationships between "imagination and material reality": "The relation between organism and machine has been a border war. The stakes in the border war have been the territories of production, reproduction and imagination," Haraway writes (1991: 150). Thus for Haraway, cyberspace offers an opportunity to reconceptualize the ideas of emancipation and empowerment, and the transcendence of physical subjugation. It is herein that cyberspace has important implications for civil society at the national as well as the global levels.

Because the "permeability of national borders [by the GII] destabilizes territorial right," Reidenberg argues (1997: 86), "[n]ational borders and sectoral boundaries lose an important degree of relevance while network borders and network communities gain prominence." Therefore, what is needed is "a new network governance paradigm," which must "accord status to networks as semi-sovereign entities, and shift the role of the state toward the creation of an incentive structure for network self-regulation" (Reidenberg, 1997: 100; see also Frissen, 1997; Lenk, 1997). Likewise, Johnson and Post (1997) contend that cyberspace has distinctive boundaries of its own and should constitute a jurisdiction of its own. The new communication environment created by the Internet has remixed "universalism" (i.e., the global communication networks) and "particularism" (i.e., national and social realities, local cultural values, and so on), and has redefined "free speech" and "cultural sovereignty" in a global context (Volkmer, 1997). The global dimensions of network interactions erode the physical grasp of state authorities and have thus led to discordances in regulatory decision making and policy enforcement at the national level regarding a host of network issues, such as cyberjurisdiction (Baddeley, 1997; Froomkin, 1997; Loader, 1997; Perritt, 1997), free speech (Mayer-Schönberger and Foster, 1997; Shade, 1996), piracy (Burk, 1997), encryption (Barth and Smith, 1997; Denning, 1997), privacy (Gellman, 1997; Raab, 1997), and commercialization and consumer protection (Goldring, 1997; Weiss and Backlund, 1997). As a result, international perspectives and global cooperation are essential if nation-states intend to exploit the full potential of the network world (Allison, 2002; Kahin and Nesson, 1997).

Nation-states, however, are not totally irrelevant in the cyber age; they still matter in many ways and on multiple layers — often with new implications. Classical state theorists, such as Hobbes and Rousseau, have conceived of the state as a unitary object in relation to a particular setting of space and place. It is a physical entity that can be concretized in boundaries and borders and, to use Negroponte's words, is tied to "atoms" (mass media such as newspapers, magazines, and books that deliver information to people physically) rather than "bits" (digital media format that will be the future) (Negroponte, 1995). Negroponte argues that the "irrevocable and unstoppable" (p. 4) change from atoms to bits will redefine the role of nation-state which still measures trade and writes the balance sheet with atoms in mind, because "bits will be borderless, stored and manipulated with absolutely no respect to geopolitical boundaries" (Negroponte, 1995: 228). The triumph of the digital age is a foregone conclusion, Negroponte concludes, due to four powerful qualities of being digital: decentralization (i.e., the decentralizing of information, organization, and management), globalization (i.e., no limitations of geographic boundaries), harmonization (i.e., drawing people across different geographic borders and cultures into greater world harmony), and empowerment (i.e., the access, the mobility, and the ability to effect change).

However, Negroponte's ultra (and somewhat neo-Utopian) optimism in envisioning a new digital generation without "the baggage of history" and "released from the limitation of geographic proximity as the sole basis of friendship, collaboration, play, and neighborhood" and his attribution of technology to be "a natural force drawing people into greater world harmony" (Negroponte, 1995: 230) will surely raise eyebrows of politicians and dubious scholars worldwide. Jerry Everard, for one, counterargues that the state should be "conceived in a disaggregated form, existing as a function of its differences and dispersions, rather than as the rational, unified originary actor of modernist realist discourse" (Everard, 2000: 5). The multifaceted nature of the state means that sovereign identity is "comprised of bits rather than atoms" (Everard, 2000: 7). To follow Everard's argument, we note the Internet does not dismiss the relevance or significance of nation-states; rather, it rearticulates or re-creates nation-states in emerging sets of relations (e.g., rich countries that enjoy a high level of connectivity versus poor countries that lack online resources, people who are connected to the Internet versus those who are not, domination of the English language and Western ideas and their threats to other languages and cultures, the presence of global conglomerates and the implication for all nation-states) and functions (e.g., the role of the state is moving away from economics of goods and services toward "identity-economies," the preservation of local cultural values on the Net such as the effort put up by member countries from the Association of Southeast

Asian Nations, or ASEAN,). The Internet, therefore, may weaken some but strengthen other facets of state-making in the process of reconstructing relationships. In the minimal sense, the state is important in the enmeshed web of internetworked world communication structures because, as a geographic as well as political unit, it is here to stay and remains a principal player in the policing and national policy making concerning information and data flow on the Internet.

The Internet was basically invented by the U.S. military to break through conventional communication networks and regulatory frameworks to enable the free flow of information. In actuality, however, all governments have implemented policies aiming at censoring and controlling what is available on the Internet at national or transnational levels (e.g., Everard, 2000: 135–150; Kahin and Nesson, 1997). From the United States to the European Union to the Middle East to Africa and Asia, governments have articulated different rationalizations and implemented varying strategies for controlling the Internet. In his *Control Revolution*, Andrew Shapiro (1999) first reviews the parallel developments in the ongoing shift of power from institutions to individuals in the digital age with the disintermediation and decentralization of decision making in the online world on one hand and attempts by powerful entities (i.e., governments and large corporations) to set limits on individual digital autonomy through legislation and technological control on the other; he then proposes a balanced approach of governance to maintain an equilibrium both between individual well-being and public interest and between personal freedom and institutional power. He remarks:

> For our own sake, we need to see that living well in the digital age means more than just having complete dominion over life's decisions. Personal freedom requires knowing when to relinquish authority, either to chance or to the wisdom of others. Too much control will prevent us from seeing possibilities beyond our immediate desires. Too much order can stifle the restlessness of a truly open mind.
>
> For the sake of democracy, we need to forge a new social compact — not a starry-eyed declaration of cyber-independence, but a realistic compromise between personal liberty and communal obligation. Government has a role to play, but increasingly individuals will have to balance their new power with new responsibilities to society at large.

(Shapiro, 1999: 233)

Although Shapiro's discussion of the problems and his proposed solutions are U.S.-centric, his reasoning is internationally applicable. Indeed, the kind of balance advocated by Shapiro resonates with the proclaimed objectives of Internet control by most governments; however, nations differ a great deal in conceptualizing that balance and in the belief about how balance can be achieved within their territorial borders. Yet, notwithstanding the varying objectives and approaches of control attempts by governments across the globe, it is the potential of the Internet as an empowering technology that allows individuals or civil society groups to break away from government control and to negotiate newly found freedom online that brings new promise for civil society in the new age. This is especially the case for individuals and civil society living in authoritarian regimes like China.

Information Economy and China's Information Infrastructure

China's Internet initiative, like that of any other national government, reflects its strategic considerations on the short-term and long-term role of ICTs in its ambitious modernization drive. Since Deng Xiaoping decided to shift China's strategic focus from class struggle to economic development in 1978, there have been numerous debates among Chinese scholars and government officials about the parallel processes of industrialization and informatization, and the desirable path that should be followed in China's experimentation with market forces. An immensely influential book that has significantly shaped these debates has been Alvin Toffler's *The Third Wave* (1984), a popular reading among Chinese intelligentsia and bureaucrats in the 1980s, as many have acknowledged (e.g., Dai, 2003; Mueller and Tan, 1997; Zhao Hong, 1998).

In this primary work describing the information revolution, Toffler maintains that human beings started off as hunter-gatherers and have undergone three major revolutions: the first wave of change was led by the agricultural revolutions of 10,000 years ago when humans entered the peasant-based agrarian societies; the second wave of change was triggered by the industrial revolution of some 300 years ago and brought factory-centered civilization to human society. And the third wave — the information revolution — came out of the peak of the manufacturing era and replaces brute force with mental power in economic activities; information and knowledge become the powerful weapons of success (Toffler, 1983).

Another related area that has affected China's ICT decision-making is the discussion of the knowledge economy (see Dahlman and Aubert, 2001, for a detailed discussion). The earliest scholarly discussion of the production of knowledge as an economic activity was *The Production and Distribution of Knowledge in the United States* by Fritz Machlup (1962), who is the pioneer of the economics of information (or knowledge, which Machlup used interchangeably in most cases with information) and one of the founding fathers of the established area of study in what later came to be labeled information society and information economy. His works constitute a repository of inspiration and guidance in current scholarly activities in the field (see also Machlup 1980; 1982; 1983; 1984). A close follow-up was Daniel Bell's *The Coming of Post-Industrial Society* (1973), in which Bell presciently envisioned the arrival of a drastically different society marked by a growing information economy and explored the multitude of consequences of the shift from a manufacturing society to a knowledge society.

The monumental works of Machlup and Bell, among others, became popular readings for the Chinese intelligentsia in the 1990s and led to an important series of debates about the emergence of a knowledge-based economy in China and what role the government could play in the development of such an economy in the face of increasing global competition (see Dai, 2003 for more discussion). The former Chinese President Jiang Zemin told scientists from the Chinese Academy of Sciences (CAS) that the "knowledge economy and the sense of innovation are very important for China's development in the 21st century," and he instructed them to research and initiate projects in spearheading a Chinese national knowledge economy that could lead China's economic development.[1] In his speech to the Asia-Pacific Economic Cooperation (APEC) leaders in November 1998, Jiang noted that

> Promoting economic and technical cooperation (Ecotech) among its members is a major task of APEC and a primary way to common development. In the world of today, science and technology are progressing with each passing day and the knowledge economy is unfolding. To redouble the efforts to develop high and new technology and speed up the economic restructuring are the only way to promote a long-term and steady development of the economies of APEC members.[2]

Jiang reiterated the theme in his address to the APEC human resources forum in May 2001 and called attention to the fast-paced development of the knowledge economy and the challenges it poses to APEC nations.[3] Jiang's successor, Hu Jintao (who took over the Chinese presidency in March 2003), has continued the same official line. In one of his first important speeches after his inauguration, while addressing leading provincial and ministerial bureaucrats in September 2003, Hu stressed the importance of science and technology in general, the knowledge economy in particular, in building "comprehensive national strength" and in achieving "sustainable and balanced development."[4]

As a result of the direct encouragement from Jiang and other top Chinese leaders, many groundbreaking projects and intellectual works have appeared since the late 1990s. In 1998 alone, a dozen scholarly works were published in China on knowledge economy and its future in China's economic structure (e.g., Chen Yongxiang, 1998; Feng Zhijun, 1998; Wu Jisong, 1998; Zhao Hong, 1998). However, unlike Machlup who broadly classifies knowledge production into six major classes — education, research and development, artistic creation and communication, media of communication, information services, and information machines — and gives equal attention to each category, contemporary discussions on knowledge economy in China and in other developing as well as Western industrialized nations give substantial prominence to the emerging digital economy created by the computer networks with the Internet at its lead. Consequently, ICTs are believed to be the central nervous system of the so-called new economy in the twenty-first century, and Internet-related economic activities are thought to be vital for the development of national knowledge economies (e.g., Afele, 2003; DTI, 1998; Preston, 2001).

Having witnessed the impact of the Internet and Internet-related newly emerging industries on U.S. and European economies, the Chinese leadership believes that information technology offers a promise for China's economic, political, and social development in the new century that should be embraced at any price. In its "Outline of the 10th Five-Year National Economic and Social Development Plan of the People's Republic of China (Draft)," released by the Office of the Premier, State Council of the People's Republic of China, in March 2001, the Chinese government made clear to the world its determination to put the information industry at the top of its economic and social development strategies. An entire section, Chapter VI of the plan, titled "Accelerate the Development of the Information Industry, and Actively Promote the Widespread Application of Information Technology," was devoted to China's ICT ambitions. The beginning of the chapter stated:

> In keeping with the development approach of letting applications lead the way, being market oriented, with the joint development of networks, sharing of resources, technical innovation, and open competition, we must strive to achieve leapfrog development in the information industry in China, accelerating the promotion of information technology and increasing the proportion of the information industry in the national economy.[5]

The specific objectives to be achieved listed in the outline include widespread application of information technology, establishing an information structure, and developing the electronic and information products manufacturing industry. While the promotion of information technology by the state is primarily driven by economic considerations, for Chinese citizens and civil society groups this move means opportunities on a totally new platform of communication as a result of the popularization of new information technologies. As is shown in later chapters, this brand-new information environment has brought about new possibilities for individuals and social groups to access and distribute information, to form new relationships, and to organize or coordinate activities both online and offline.

Leapfrogging from Laggard to Forerunner

Although China embraced the Internet later than most Western nations, led by the United States, it has been under the strong belief that proper state intervention (and financial investment under some circumstances) can help the country catch up with, or in some areas even overtake, the Western powers in China's ICT development initiative. This belief has resulted in a national "leapfrog" strategy in its ICT industry, summarized by Wang Xudong, the newly installed Information Minister under the new government led by Premier Wen Jiabao, to be "characterized by the mutual reinforcement of informatization and industrialization."[6]

The idea of achieving possible leapfrog development in less developed nations was first proposed by Alexander Gerschenkron (1962), who developed the concept of "advantage of backwardness" in studying the process of European and Russian industrialization. Following Marx's grand generalization that the history of advanced or established industrial countries traces out the road of development for the more backward countries, Gerschenkron argues that this general pattern is observable (albeit not without specific changeabilities and peculiarities): "the tendencies in backward countries to concentrate much of their efforts on introduction of the most modern and expensive technology, their stress on large-scale plant, and their interest in developing investment-goods industries" (Gerschenkron, 1962: 26). So being backward gives some countries the advantage of being able to short-circuit the expensive historical contours undergone by developed peer nations and creates the possibility of high-speed economic development with the use of technologically superior equipment reinforced by an abundant labor supply.

Gerschenkron's concept has been further developed by recent endogenous economic growth models, which hypothesize that lagging countries may catch up with leading countries in the presence of knowledge and technology spillovers (Barro and Sala-i-Martin, 1995; Grossman and Helpman, 1991; Temple, 1999). The general thesis from these models is that it is possible for backward countries to take advantage of technology spillovers from the advanced countries to achieve economic growth, and direct foreign investment is one of the main channels of technology diffusion. Adaptation, rather than production, is the more desirable path to overcome technological backwardness. For example, the rise of Japan as a technological power in the world in microelectronics in the 1960s and 1970s has been largely attributed to its successful adaptation of a variety of technological breakthroughs mainly in the United States. The secret of Japan's success, in other words, is not in its innovativeness in research and development (R&D) of the technology, but rather in its sophisticated acquisition of technological spillovers from the United States (Alexander, 1990). If we look back at the two-plus decades of China's economic reform initiated by the late Deng since the late 1970s, no doubt the pattern of growth coincides with these arguments. By successfully upgrading its primitive industrial infrastructure and attracting global capital, China has been leading the world in its economic growth for this period. Absorption of foreign technology has been a key to China's glaring economic success. The fast-paced speed of economic development over the past two decades in China, in the mean time, has also led to major concerns over the possibility of an overheated economy, as can be testified to by the government's latest effort for a soft landing and the government's heavy-handed crackdown on unwanted investments in overheated sectors.[7]

Chinese leaders believe that the emergence of the Internet worldwide provides a unique opportunity for the country to fully utilize its "advantage of backwardness,"[8] or "competitive edge of late start,"[9] to use a quote from its Science and Technology Minister, to develop an information infrastructure that can play a pivotal role in its economic development strategies in the new century. By deploying cutting-edge technologies in its telecommunications industry, the Chinese government believes that the country will achieve a front-runner status in the latest ICT technological applications — without having to traverse the costly intermediary steps that the economically advanced countries passed through.

However, spillover from high-technology countries to low-technology countries cannot be taken for granted. For laggard countries to catch up, some important preconditions must be met. One central concept is "absorptive capacity," first proposed by Abramovitz (1986) and defined as a country's capability to access, learn, and absorb relevant overseas technology. Hence both access to advanced technology and a high level of absorptive capacity are essential determinants of the process of technological developments in technologically backward countries. Other development models have also examined the roles of human capital (the practical knowledge, acquired skills, and learned abilities of the labor force) (e.g., Barro and Sala-i-Martin, 1995), open trade (e.g., Coe and Helpman, 1995), and direct foreign investment (e.g., Xu, 2000) in the process of technological catch-up.

China's policy of economic reform and openness to the outside world for nearly three decades has certainly created a conducive environment for a major technological upgrade in its national economic infrastructure. In the past decades, China has surprised other countries in leading the world in its breathtaking growth in gross domestic products (GDP). After having overtaken the United States as the world's top destination for foreign direct investment (FDI), China now is experiencing a period of transition in which not only the quantity, but the quality, of investment is improving. While early investors were mainly attracted by the low cost in labor and raw materials, new foreign capital is coming to the country with long-term, sustainable funding commitments.[10] The integration of China into the global market may create a business culture that can step up China's official informatization effort. As I point out in Chapter 2, economic liberalization and expansion has been the primary contributing factor to the burgeoning of Chinese civil society in the past two decades. The globalization of the Chinese economy will in all likelihood accelerate that trend.

Inflow of Foreign Cash in China's Information Economy

The Chinese government's informatization initiative not only aims to implement advanced Western technologies but also to utilize much-needed foreign cash. In addition to creating a set of policies to attract direct foreign investment, the government has also initiated incentives for Chinese companies to get enlisted in foreign stock markets. China's domestic stock market, closed after Mao's collectivization effort following the communist takeover in 1949, was reopened in the late 1980s as part of Deng Xiaoping's bold effort to deepen China's reform. By the end of 2003, about 1200 Chinese companies had listed shares on its two stock exchanges, one in Shanghai and one in Shenzhen.[11] After its successful experimentation with the domestic stock market, the Chinese government started to eye the global market in the 1990s. For the Chinese government, pushing Chinese enterprises to the global stock market serves at least a threefold purpose: first, it shows the world China's determination to further open its market and to internationalize its enterprise financing mechanism; second, it boasts to the world business community the confidence of the Chinese government in allowing its companies to openly compete with its global rivals; and third, it gives Chinese businesses the goldmine opportunity of providing greater liquidity by using the larger pool of foreign capital. Another reason, although not openly admitted by the government, is that the failing official banking system in China has significantly lagged behind surging business demands.

To ensure that its first moves did not result in a fiasco, the Chinese government has adopted a stringent system to grant permission to selective companies to get listed overseas. Its first initial public offering was completed by a superstar enterprise, Tsingtao Beer, in Hong Kong in 1993. In the late 1990s, believing that the future lies in the Internet, the Chinese government started to shift its emphasis on emerging e-enterprises. China.com became the first Internet company to be listed overseas (on NASDAQ), followed by three other major portal sites a year later.

After the global dot-com bust in 2000, high-tech stocks were ready to stage a comeback in late 2003 as more and more Internet companies started to show profitability. The three Chinese portals, whose stocks were already listed on NASDAQ, sent their shares soaring in 2003 because of their ability to generate revenue from the huge base of Chinese web surfers. In October 2003, the shares of Sina.com, Sohu.com, and Netease.com skyrocketed 3,456 percent, 5,463 percent, and 11,571 percent, respectively, from their record lows on NASDAQ.[12] A closer look at this process ensues in the next chapter.

Regarding this astounding performance as solid proof of the profitability and scalability of China-focused Internet companies, Chinese Internet companies started a second round of efforts to seek overseas venture capital. In a forum appropriately titled "China: The Next Tide" in the Chinese city of

Hangzhou in November 2003, a group of prominent Chinese dot-com CEOs gathered to talk about preparing for initial public offerings on NASDAQ. Represented were dot-com upstarts Cstrip.com, Tom.com, Baidu.com, EachNet. com, and Shanda.com, all of which claimed they have found their own niche market in China for the new century.[13] In another significant development in 2003, Yahoo Inc. signed an acquisition deal to purchase 3721 Network Software Co. for US$120 million.[14] 3721 NSC developed the technology for the Chinese language search engine 3271.com, a popular search service site that allows users to type in keywords in Chinese. This highly publicized acquisition is just the start of more mergers and acquisitions among Chinese portals in the following year.[15] Indeed, Yahoo soon acted again in August 2005, this time offering to pay US$1 billion for a 40 percent of stake in Alibaba, the biggest online retailer in China with business operations spanning e-commerce, search, and communications services.[16]

In a recent report released by Shanghai-based Ploutos Investment Consulting Ltd, a company specializing in China's Internet industry, three "hot points" were highlighted: first, the fast-growing population of Internet subscribers; second, the exploding Internet game market; third, a new round of IPO's listed on the NASDAQ by many Chinese Internet companies.[17] The third "hot point," I think, will be the most significant factor in defining the future path of China's Internet development. Allowing Chinese Internet companies to go public — especially facing a broad pool of international investors — will fundamentally change the online information and service environment in China when those companies have to worry more about their stockholders than government demands. As Woesler (2002) points out, the Internet is transforming China into a Western-style information society — with its own modifications and adaptations, of course. These moves are going to reshape China's Internet for years to come because the Internet is a business, and with foreign cash comes the Western management models and practices. The inevitable integration of the Internet in China with the global network makes it possible for the emergence of an information environment that creates favorable conditions for the expansion of civil society forces in the country, despite the regime's sustained effort of information control.

Militarization of Information Technologies

Along with the Chinese government's interest in the technological and economic benefits of its national information initiatives comes its specification of the role of the Internet and information technologies in its military doctrine. Countries that have devoted significant resources to the study and development of information warfare strategies include the United States, Russia, and China (see Arquilla and Ronfeldt, 1997 for an overview). Chinese military strategists' conceptualization of information warfare has been to a great extent inspired and influenced by their U.S. counterparts (Mulvenon and

Yang, 1999), and it is largely an effort to adapt many of the American ideas to an indigenous culture and local conditions.

The Chinese military doctrine of information warfare follows closely the rationale of "leapfrog" development elaborated in its national information infrastructure initiative. Because China's military prowess lags significantly behind such major world powers as the United States and Russia, and it is unrealistic to expect the country to catch up in terms of conventional munitions and weaponry any time soon, military experts instead have focused on developing a pragmatic, feasible line of China's information warfare strategy that may give an unusual edge over the enemy (with the United States as the chief imagined opponent) in an asymmetric warfare. Major General Wang Pufeng, a chief architect and proponent of a Chinese information warfare theory, sees this as a driving force for modernizing China's military and achieving combat readiness in the new century. With due emphasis on information technology, Wang contends:

> [T]he thrust of China's military construction and development of weapons and equipment will no longer be toward strengthening the "firepower antipersonnel system" of the industrial age, but toward the strengthening of information technology, information weapons systems, and information networking. Our sights must not be fixed on the firepower warfare of the industrial age, rather they must be trained on the information warfare of the information age.[18]

The hallmark of information warfare is the involvement, training, and mobilization of a ubiquitous civil force in a time of emergency. If the first half of the 1990s was mainly a period of intellectual debates among military theorists, the Balkan conflict in 1999, during which the Chinese Embassy was "accidentally" bombed by the United States, sparked a dramatic shift in the pace of change in strategic thinking in the Chinese army. One of the immediate impacts was the formation of the idea among central military policymakers of what insiders call "Mao-style People's War in the new era." As a result, unprecedented resources would be devoted to preparations for what are called possible "hi-tech, information-based warfares" in the new century.[19] In the meantime, immediately after the Chinese Embassy bombing, coordinated Chinese hackers launched a series of powerful attacks against government computers and Web sites in the United States, wreaking havoc and disrupting services among pubic computing utilities. "Digital Armageddon," or "cyber warfare,"[20] in the network era led to widespread concerns about a possible "electronic Pearl Harbor" in the United States.[21] Since then, the Chinese military has staged several highly publicized information warfare exercises.[22] In its December 2004 Defense White Paper, the Chinese military introduced the concept "local wars under conditions of informationalization" and formally started to study the technological and tactical feasibilities of fighting and winning information- and knowledge-based wars.[23]

Informatization as Nationalism

Additionally, vigorous promotion of the Internet and related information technologies is considered by the government to be a necessary step in boosting China's national pride and bringing legitimacy to the rule of the Communist Party in the country. After decades of humiliation and subjugation by foreign powers up to the early part of the twentieth century, all Chinese leaders from Sun Yat-sen, Chiang Kaishek, and Mao Zedong to Deng Xiaoping and Jiang Zemin in the twentieth century have been determined to restore China's national grandeur and national pride, and they have been struggling for China's rightful place as a great power commanding due attention and respect from the world (Garver, 1993; S. Zhao, 2000). Meanwhile, they have been divided on how to realistically pursue the goal of national greatness (e.g., Chang, 2001). After the Communist takeover of China in 1949, Mao resorted to one massive social movement after another to mark a departure from the old society and to build a new society based on mass revolutions and class struggles. Deng, however, totally scrapped Mao's ideas of revolutions and decided to invest China's future in economic reform and openness. Deng's handpicked successors have continued his policy of economic development and are shifting the strategic focus to upgrading China's overall national power and thereby its competitiveness with world powers, not only economically but also geopolitically.

Under these circumstances, the Chinese government's stress on a "knowledge economy" and ICT, then, should come as no surprise. The Chinese leadership has felt a great sense of urgency after having witnessed the impact of information technologies on global economies in such industrialized nations as Japan and the United States, and in Europe. In addition, the Chinese leadership also feels the pressure from the neighboring economy in India — which, as a developing nation, has generally lagged behind in many of its traditional economies compared with China, but has emerged as a major global force in IT development. Successfully leapfrogging in its high-tech sector, the Chinese authorities hope, will not only increase Chinese economic prowess in the new century but will also legitimize the Communist Party's continued grip on power. One senior government official's sentiment summarizes the government's perspective well: "we in the government think we missed a lot of the industrial revolution. And we don't want to miss this (the IT) revolution" (quoted in Hachigian, 2001: 122). China's Internet initiative, then, is closely tied to the self-claimed mission of the Chinese Communist Party to revitalize the country's glorious past enshrined in a 5000-plus-year-old civilization. In both academic and popular cultures, there has been a rediscovery of Chinese nationalism since the 1990s (e.g., Swaine and Tellis, 2000; Wei and Liu, 2002; Zheng, 1999).

At the same time, Chinese Web sites have been flooded with nationalist sentiment, especially at times of major domestic or international incidents that involve China or overseas Chinese compatriots (e.g., Callahan, 2002; Hughes 2000). For an authoritarian regime that lacks an effective mechanism to gauge public opinion, the Chinese government from time to time uses cyberspace as a barometer of popular sentiment. However, the Chinese government is walking a delicate and occasionally dangerous line here, because, as Kalathil (2002: 350) points out, "(w)hen dissatisfaction and nationalism overlap, they can place significant pressures on the Chinese leadership, which has historically used nationalism to bolster its public support and divert attention from domestic problems."

China's strategy of developing ICT to promote regime legitimacy has won enthusiastic support of Chinese entrepreneurs. To the government and businessmen alike, software and information technologies are not only a matter of national pride; they represent a unique opportunity whereby Chinese inventors can break away from China's long-time dependency on Western technologies and take the lead in developing its own technological breakthroughs. In this respect, Chinese enterprises learned a good lesson from DVD technologies.

When DVD started to become popular and was poised to overtake conventional VHS as the next home entertainment technology in the late 1990s, Chinese entrepreneurs were quick to join the global bandwagon and China soon became one of the biggest global manufacturers of DVD players. A blow to the fledging Chinese DVD industry came in 2002, when the DVD Forum, an association of international DVD manufacturers mainly representing a few Japanese and U.S. companies owning core DVD patents, wanted to collect US$20 patent fees from Chinese DVD manufacturers for each DVD player produced in China.[24] After months of tough negations, Chinese DVD-player makers agreed to pay either US$6 or 4 percent of the selling price (whichever was higher) of every DVD player exported.[25] Since then, Chinese manufacturers have been vigorously promoting new-generation DVD technologies based on their own intellectual property rights. In July 2002, China successfully developed its own standards for a "Super DVD" product called Enhanced Video Discs (EVD), which promises five times the clarity of the conventional DVDs and enhanced sound quality.[26] China's State Trade and Economic Commission and its Ministry of Information Industry, two powerhouses in the country's efforts to promote rapid economic and technological growth, have played key roles in developing a state standard and in encouraging Chinese manufacturers in the launch of the EVD initiative. After much fanfare and some delay, the first 100,000 EVD players were released in major cities in China in January 2004.[27] A month later, multiple Hollywood companies announced that they have agreed to support the Chinese EVD standard in releasing future products.[28] As an indication that EVD is gaining ground in its uphill battle to win over consumers from the established DVD market, China's Ministry of Information Industry (MII) announced on July 8, 2004, that the homegrown EVD would be a national standard for the video disc player industry.[29] The standard became official in early 2005.[30] Thus China was able to use its huge market size and its latest technological prowess to spearhead IT standards to its own strategic advantage. The mass marketing of EVD players enters a new stage in 2005 as prices continued to go down and models diversified.[31] However, the situation has not been settled, as the thirty-two–member Shanghai Information Appliances Association (SIAA) formally unveiled the HVD (Holographic Versatile Disc) industry standard,[32] which is yet to be approved by the MII. With over 1 million players sold worldwide as of spring 2005, HVD poses as a serious competitor to the newly installed EVD technology.

For reasons of national security as well as national pride, China has joined a host of other countries, such as Germany and France, in adopting the free, open-source operating system Linux in hopes of decreasing its dependence on Microsoft products. With direct government support and involvement, Red Flag Linux, a domestically developed Chinese language operating system based on Linux, was officially released on August 10, 1999, in Beijing.[33] The system's universality, standardization, and multiplatform support make it a serious competitor to Microsoft's Windows product. Under the direct support of the government, China's Linux industry reached a turning point in 2004, with many players in the market reporting profitability for the first time in that year.[34]

In January 2000, a local newspaper in southern China reported that key Chinese ministries had decided to drop Microsoft's Windows 2000 operating system and to opt for Red Flag Linux for security reasons.[35] Although Chinese officials and Microsoft quickly dismissed any such moves on the part of the Chinese government, the circulation of this kind of rumor reflects China's ambivalence toward Microsoft products. Chinese newspapers ran a series of stories on the lack of privacy and the vulnerability to virus attacks of Microsoft operating systems, and they cited reports of the European Parliament that Microsoft and the American Secret Service have had an agreement that would allow the U.S. National Security Agency (NSA) to scan non-U.S. content worldwide using deliberate holes in Windows' security features.[36] Those stories, although not openly admitted by Chinese officials, partly testify to China's distrust of the software giant Microsoft. Starting in August 2000, Chinese PC makers opted to install Red Flag Linux instead of Microsoft Windows in its personal computers.[37] Recently, in a move that is likely to boost the home-grown Chinese operating system, IBM signed a deal to bundle a version of its database program with Red Flag Linux,[38] and Dell began to sell servers equipped with this operating system in the Chinese market.[39] For a market that will possess over a billion PCs in the next two or three decades, promotion of domestic products such as Red Flag Linux involves more than national pride; it promises a gold mine that the Chinese government does not want to sit on passively.

The full-arm embrace of the Internet and the knowledge economy by the Chinese authorities, however, does not mean that the Chinese leadership is willing to let the liberating and free-wheeling spirit of the Internet run its own course. Instead, the Chinese regime has taken a series of regulatory measures to ensure that the Internet is under the tight control of the state. By being able to reap the economic and political benefits of the Internet while suppressing its potential to challenge or threaten the communist government, the Chinese leadership believes that a well-developed and well-regulated Internet can work to its advantage in strengthening its grip on power and its capacity to win popular support. The flip side of the coin, however, is that the Internet, unlike any of the conventional media, was primarily invented as a technology to eliminate the possibility of a central control mechanism. Promotion of the Internet technology, of course, means promotion of accessibility to the Chinese public; once average Chinese citizens are exposed to a brand-new information environment spearheaded by the Internet, they very likely will not use the Internet in the way designed or desired by the regime. Here we see the potential of the Internet as an agent of change for Chinese civil society.

Government Policy Making, State Surveillance, and the Chinese Firewall

China's love of the Internet has been marked by its ambivalence toward the potentially liberating technology from day one. On the one hand, the government's enthusiasm about the Internet has been largely driven by the realization that the Internet represents a commercial gold mine for the country's economy in the new century; on the other hand, the government fully recognizes that an unregulated computer network will undermine the power and authority of the communist regime. Thus, as Hachigian (2001: 118) points out, the government has adopted a three-part Internet strategy: "providing economic growth and some personal freedoms, managing the Internet's risks, and harnessing its potential." The future of the Internet lies in the promotion of Internet technologies as a populist communication tool, and to encourage personal adoption of Internet use, the government knows well that individual users must be granted enough freedom in the cyberworld. Too much control will only kill individual desire to go online.

Over the years, China has cultivated a strategy of controlling cyberspace at multiple levels: state legislative actions in making laws targeting the various areas of telecommunications, technological implementation of the Great Fire Wall in controlling the flow of information on the Internet, coercive co-option of businesses, Internet Service Providers, and content producers to tow the state line, and monitoring of individual netizens (and occasionally punishing transgressors who cross the line) in their online behavior. In effect, this has created an "electronic panopticon," as described by David Lyon (1993), in which the invisible "Big Brother" is tracking one's digital footprints in every cybercorner. However, how successful or effective these measures have been is highly debatable (see, for example, the contrasting views from Deibert, 2002; Kalathil and Boas, 2001; Lacharite, 2002; Tan, 1999).

China has made clear to the world its intention to control the Internet from the very start. Its first official policy paper, titled "Regulations for the Protection of Computer Information Systems Safety in the People's Republic of China," was issued by the State Council on February 18, 1994, one year before the Internet was even commercially available in China. The 1994 regulations gave the Ministry of Public Security the overall responsibility to "supervise, inspect and guide the security protection" of computer information systems and "to investigate criminal activities" that undermine computer networks.[40] However, the focus of these regulations was on the physical entity and function of computer information systems in the country, and there was no specific mention of the type of content that was forbidden on the computer networks.

The most comprehensive and perhaps most important official ordinance is the "Temporary Decree on the Management of Computer Information Network International Connectivity in the People's Republic of China," first released publicly by the State Council on February 1, 1996 and revised on May 20, 1997.[41] A follow-up detailed "Implementation Measures for Enforcing the Temporary Decree on the Management of Computer Information Network International Connectivity in the People's Republic of China" was announced by the Informatization Leadership Group under the State Council on December 8, 1997.[42] The official decree forbids any units or individuals from using the Internet to create, replicate, retrieve, or transmit information that is "harmful," "subversive," "obscene," or "damaging to the state or state organs." Unauthorized connection to international networks is also not allowed. The significance of this set of regulations is that they make it clear that information considered to be deleterious on the Internet in China is punishable; yet no boundary has been specified as to what is injurious information and what is not. The government has the sole discretion to decide, in many cases after the fact, what it considers harmful and to punish individual violators accordingly.

Another important regulative directive is the "State Secrets Protection Regulations for Computer Information Systems on the Internet," issued by the National Security Bureau in January 2000. According to the circular, Internet users in China are prohibited from sending state secrets via e-mail or discussing state secrets in Internet chat rooms or on bulletin boards.[43] Moreover, it also said that China-based Internet service and content providers must undergo a "security certification" and are held liable for carrying materials that compromise state security. The problem is "state secret" in China is a notoriously ill-defined term.

In a major update to existing Internet laws, the State Council Information Office and the Ministry of Information Industry jointly issued the "Decree on the Management of Internet News/Information Services" on September 25, 2005.[44] It stipulates that news sites that publish stories from sources other than their own must obtain approval from the State Council Information Office, and that media attached to the central or provincial governments should not provide news to other online sites without approval. News sites that only publish their own stories must register with the provincial information offices. The regulatory measures apply to news, commentaries, and short message services (SMS) specializing in news content. Those who spread fabricated information, unhealthy content, pornography, and state secrets are subject to a fine, disciplinary and administrative action, and/or imprisonment.

As users at home and aboard have become more and more sophisticated in bypassing official blockages to spread "harmful information" on the Internet, the Chinese state has launched several campaigns to train special police task forces to deal with online rebellious behavior. On August 4, 2000, the first "Internet police" force in the nation was established in Anhui province with the responsibility to "administrate and maintain order on computer networks." Another 20 provinces, municipalities, and autonomous regions around China were ready to follow suit in establishing such police forces of their own.[45] The main regulatory arm of the state, the Public Information Network Supervision Bureau directly under the Ministry of Public Security, was reported to have been hiring an Internet police force of 300,000 personnel nationwide by the end of 2000.[46]

In addition to the regulations mentioned above are a dozen other official ordinances that target different groups.[47] Chinese laws have also shifted some of the responsibility of content control from the government to the Internet content and service providers. For example, Article Eight of the "Computer Information Network and Internet Security, Protection and Management Regulations" states that:

> Units and individuals engaged in Internet business must accept the security supervision, inspection, and guidance of the Public Security organization. This includes providing to the Public Security organization materials and digital document, and assisting the Public Security organization to investigate and properly handle incidents involving law violations and criminal activities related to computer information networks.[48]

On October 1, 2000, the Chinese government published regulations that require all Internet companies to apply for operating licenses from the Ministry of Information Industry within two months.[49] The regulations were finalized and officially published as the "Temporary Ordinance on the Management of Internet News Publishing" in November 2000,[50] and the deadline for Internet companies to register was subsequently extended to January 31, 2001. The ordinance applied to all Internet content providers (ICPs) who are in the business of carrying news content on their Web sites, and it required that all ICPs be licensed by national or provincial authorities. ICPs can only carry news stories from the officially sanctioned news media, and, other than the Web sites run by the news media, ICPs are not allowed to engage in the business of news collection; they can only publish news from officially approved news sources; Web sites cannot publish or link to news from overseas or foreign media sources without formal approval from the Information Office under the State Council.

Anonymity has been one of the hallmarks of online communication, especially on bulletin board services (BBS) and in chat rooms. But anonymity has also emboldened some types of online behaviors — in the case of China, criticisms of the government and grievances against officials. In the spring of 2005, government bureaucracies launched a series of campaigns to crack down on anonymous communications over the Internet on several fronts. It started with student-run discussion forums across college campuses in the nation. Bulletin boards on university-run computer networks are extremely popular among college students, the demographic group that is the most likely to be online. Discussions on these forums have been the liveliest in Chinese cyberspace, and topics range from the coolest course on campus to the most sensitive political issues of the day. Up to this point, many college forums had been not only open to students but also available to netizens from outside of campus. In January 2005, the Education Ministry ordered college campuses to deny access to these forums from outside and to require students to register with their real names while using the new, internal online bulletins. When Chinese universities started to enforce these rules in March 2005, students on several campuses angrily protested against these restrictions, prompting college officials to appeal to the Education Ministry for less tight controls.[51] Soon after, students managing popular BBS on some campuses continued their online services catering to internal and external users by hosting the BBS sites both on campus servers and public servers. The most popular BBS, Shuimu Tsinghua of Tsinghua University, reopened public services in May 2005 at several open addresses, including http://www.newsmth.net/, http://www.smth.org/, and http://bbs.tsinghua.edu.cn. The BBS averages 700,000 guest visits every day,[52] and continues to allow anonymous as well as real-name registration.

Meanwhile, as part of its efforts to step up Internet control, the Ministry of Information Industry announced measures in spring 2005 demanding that Web site owners and publishers register with Chinese authorities before or on July 10, 2005. Web sites that failed to register by that date or provided false information would be subject to closure. About 1000 Web sites were shut down for failure to comply with this demand in the following two months.[53]

The Internet laws in China stipulate that content and service providers are responsible for the content that their Web sites carry or that is available from the physical facilities in their jurisdiction. Those that are in violation may face fines or closure or both. As a result, individual service or content providers have set up their own monitors patrolling such relevant areas of cyberspace as bulletin boards and chat rooms, and deleting materials that may appear offensive to official censors. Almost all Chinese portals have appointed their own 24-hour cybermanagers to enforce the official rules to varying degrees. Internet café personnel routinely check which Web sites are accessed by individual users in their territories.

As an effort to protect themselves, a growing number of Chinese Web sites and Internet content providers have been trying to take precautionary measures so they walk a fine line between publishing materials that attract online traffic for commercial success and filtering out content that may be offensive to the authorities. As early as 1997, Prodigy Inc. had to sign an agreement to comply with China's policy of Internet censorship to sell Internet services to Chinese consumers.[54] The most important move came on March 16, 2002, when a group of Internet companies under the China Internet Association, a nonofficial self-governing body for the country's Internet sector, voluntarily signed the "Public Pledge on Self-discipline for China Internet Industry" designed to ban signatories from producing, releasing, or spreading material "harmful to national security and social stability" or "in violation of the law, " and to encourage Internet surfers to "use the web in a civilized way" and "avoid any content that breaches others' intellectual property rights."[55] More Internet companies have joined the "self-disciplinary pact" since then, including web giant Yahoo's Chinese language site. The effort to purge the web of content "harmful" to Chinese users has been condemned by many international media organizations.[56]

Those companies that do not want to please the Chinese government quickly learned a lesson. On August 31, 2002, Chinese web surfers suddenly found that their favorite search engine, Google, was no longer available to them. Instead, users were directed to alternative Chinese search engines. Google was blocked in China because it contained a lot of Web sites that are precluded by the Chinese authorities, and Google refused to bow to pressure from the Chinese government to filter content to its base of Chinese users. Amid a raging popular outcry of individual users, professional developers, and business organizations that immediately spread in almost all chat rooms and BBS services against this move, the Chinese government restored access to Google nearly two weeks later.[57] Publicly, Chinese officials even denied that they were behind this clampdown; a spokesman from the Foreign Ministry denied any knowledge of the Google ban,[58] and an official from the Ministry of Information Industry, the primary policy maker in regulating the Internet in the country, said the Ministry had no knowledge of the blocking and subsequent unblocking of Google in an interview with Agence

France-Presse (AFP).[59] The message from the government was that it has no qualms whatsoever about creating a Web that is fit for the Chinese citizens to see. Google, of course, changed its tactic later and decided to cooperate with the Chinese authorities in censoring sensitive content to users in China when it launched services (www.google.cn) specifically adapted to mainland China in early 2006.

Chinese Internet regulators also set up a set of rules for individual Internet surfers. All Internet users must register with a local police bureau within 30 days of signing up with an ISP, and all Internet traffic from and to China has to be directed through a few major national backbones such as ChinaNet, CERNet, GBNet, and CSTNet. Since the late 1990s, Chinese authorities have prosecuted a handful of individuals who have dared to challenge the official rules. The following are a few high-profile cases.

In March 1998, Lin Hai, a 30-year-old computer entrepreneur in Shanghai, was arrested for allegedly providing his database of 3000 e-mail addresses to VIP Reference, a U.S.-based news service organized by overseas activists e-mailing regular reports on politically sensitive topics and criticism of the Chinese government.[60] Although Lin himself was not a political activist, he was arrested and charged with subversion and was sentenced to two years in jail for inciting the overthrow of the state through the Internet.[61]

Huang Qi, a webmaster in the southwest Chinese city of Chengdu, was arrested on June 3, 2000, for posting dozens of articles on his Web site about the 1989 Tiananmen Massacre, mistreatment of Falun Gong members, and official corruption.[62] Huang started his Web site, www.6-tianwang.com, in 1999 to help people find missing friends and relatives. Huang was charged with subverting state power, and after his trial date was postponed several times, he was sentenced to five years in prison in a secret trial held on May 9, 2003.[63]

In another highly publicized case, Liu Di, a 22-year-old student from Beijing Normal University and known as "Steel-less Mouse" online, was arrested on November 7, 2003, for posting essays on the Internet criticizing the Communist Party's control over society and Chinese restrictions on the Internet. She also expressed her sympathy for Huang Qi in her essays.[64] Liu's arrest triggered widespread protest among Chinese and international netizens and a global call for her release. On November 28, 2003, Liu was freed a week ahead of Chinese Premier Wen Jiabao's visit to the United States.[65]

The simplest way to gain control over unwanted content is to completely block it. Indeed, this is the philosophy for the building of the Great Firewall in Chinese cyberspace (Yurcik and Tan, 1996). The Great Firewall is an attempt by the Chinese government to physically filter the kinds of content that can enter Chinese boundaries and is called by Yurcik and Tan the world's largest Intranet. By requiring all Internet traffic into and out of China to be funneled through the few major backbone Chinese networks, the government has been largely successful in territorializing China's computer networks into a controlled information environment (Deibert, 2002; Qiu, 1999/2000), although users have from time to time successfully bypassed the firewall by using proxy servers. Ironically, the development of China's firewall technologies has won technical support from major Western corporations, such as Sun Microsystems, Cisco Systems, Microsoft, Nortel Networks, and filtering software supplier Websense,[66] to name a few.

Over the years, China has adopted a regulative strategy of implementing content control at the macro (state), middle-range (Internet content and service providers), and micro (individual users) levels with the coercive power of the state. Unlike most countries, which allow Internet traffic to be distributed through a number of private and public national nodes, all online traffic into and out of China is directed through a limited number of national backbones that lie at the center of state control. So it is possible for the state to block most offensive Web sites at the macro level. In the middle, Internet companies have to "voluntarily" put in place self-regulatory measures to keep official censors at bay and to keep business going. At the micro level, individuals have to be registered with the Public Security Bureau and are constantly reminded that they are under surveillance with vigorous punishments of selective individual violators.

The Rise of Online Campaigns against Government Information Control and Crackdown in China

The incidents of Liu Di and Huang Qi show the government's determination to gain an upper hand in its tug-of-war with the emerging network environment by winning an all-out battle against the free flow of information on the Internet; yet the incidents also demonstrate the challenge that the Chinese regime faces in suppressing dissenting voices in the Internet age. While jailing a handful of well-known opposing voices is no major problem, it is virtually impossible or impractical to arrest thousands. It is a growing trend for Chinese Internet users to register their dissatisfaction with the authorities on the Internet. One recent example is a well-circulated posting by Jiao Guobiao, an associate professor in the Department of Communication at Beijing University, in which he chastised and denounced the bigotry, malpractice, abuse of power, and the blatant violation of citizens' free speech rights by the Propaganda Ministry of the Central Committee of the Chinese Communist Party.[67] Voluminous responses to Jiao's posting expressing support and dissension from an overwhelming number of users worldwide prompted Jiao to publish a follow-up online with clarifications and further vindications.[68] Jiao was suspended from his teaching responsibilities in September 2004 after his continued defiance against official admonitions, and was then reassigned the job of an archivist in Beijing University. In the spring of 2005, Jiao accepted a fellowship from the National Endowment for Democracy for a visit in the United States despite warnings from the Beijing University authority, and consequently lost his job at the university through "voluntary resignation."

Jiao is not alone in his fight for free speech in Chinese cyberspace. Other dissident writers that have established their fame among Chinese netizens include Wang Yi and Liu Xiaobo, who have found ways to publish numerous political diatribes on the Internet against official censorship and suppression of information. The biggest advantage of the Internet,[69] Wang Yi admits, is that it allows him to socialize and exchange ideas with like-minded intellectuals across the country, and that it provides an alternative platform for him to publish his writings. That more and more people like Jiao are willing to speak out on the Internet against the powers that be should be encouraging news for Chinese civil society in the new age. In this regard, the Internet has provided a brand-new platform for public campaigns among Chinese intellectuals and independent thinkers.

In their well-conducted analysis of the political use of the Internet by Chinese dissidents and the Chinese regime's counterstrategies to minimize the impact of the Internet through its information control effort, Michael S. Chase and James C. Mulvenon (2002) come to the conclusion that, although the Chinese authorities may be successful to a certain extent in the short term in controlling information flow on the Internet, the pendulum is swinging in the favor of the dissidents in the long run. Here is their summary:

> The arrival of the Internet has altered the dynamic between the Beijing regime and the dissident community. For the state, the political use of the Internet further degrades the Chinese Communist Party's (CCP's) ability to control the flow of information it deems politically sensitive or subversive into China and within China. The party, however, still uses Leninist methods to crush potential organized opposition, and as a result, no organization with the capacity to challenge the CCP's monopoly on political power presently exists in China.

> For dissidents, students, and members of groups such as Falun Gong, the Internet — especially through its two-way communication capabilities, e.g., e-mail and bulletin board sites (BBS) — permits the global dissemination of information for communication, coordination, and organization with greater ease and rapidity than ever before. Moreover, it allows these activities to take place in some instances without attracting the attention of the authorities, as exemplified by the unexpected appearance of an estimated 10,000 to 15,000 members of Falungong outside Zhongnanhai, the Chinese central leadership compound, in April 1999. The capability of even one-way Internet communication — particularly e-mail "spamming" — enables the dissident community to transmit uncensored information to an unprecedented number of people within China and to provide recipients with plausible deniability in that they can claim that they did not request the information. In part because of dissident countermeasures (such as the use of different originating

e-mail addresses for each message), the PRC is unable to stop these attempts to "break the information blockade." There is a trend toward more groups and individuals becoming involved in activities of this type, which some have dubbed a form of "Internet guerilla warfare."

Small groups of activists, and even individuals, can use the Internet as a force multiplier to exercise influence disproportionate to their limited manpower and financial resources. At the same time, however, enhanced communication does not always further the dissident cause. In some cases, it serves as a potent new forum for discord and rivalry among various dissident factions.

(Chase and Mulvenon 2002: xi–xii)

The last point, however, should not necessarily be interpreted as discouraging for civil society. A healthy civil society is one in which a plurality of viewpoints and practices can exist and be sustained. Vibrant and free-flowing debates on important issues, even among dissident groups, can help members resolve differences in a more productive manner, and hence promote their cause in the long run. It is herein that we see the liberating effect of the Internet for Chinese civil society.

In his analysis of the use of the Internet by the Falun Gong (or Falun Dafa), "the meditation exercise cum spiritual cultivation movement" (Tong, 2002: 6336) that has attracted millions of followers worldwide and has been outlawed and persecuted by the Chinese authority, Nan Lin argues that the ways in which practitioners around the globe organized, cooperated, and coordinated their activities in spite of the all-out efforts by the Chinese government to smear and eliminate the group in the country "provide a vivid and powerful demonstration, for the first time in history, of how cybernetworks were implicated in a major social movement and countermovement" (Li, 2001: 222). That the *Falun Gong* movement has not only survived but also continues to challenge the prevailing ideology and institutions in a highly controlled society shows the new possibilities of social movements in the Internet age. Nan Lin thus summarizes the impact of cyberspace on the *Falun Gong* movement in his conclusion:

Li [i.e., Li Hongzhi, the founder of the movement, who later fled to the United States] and his followers steadfastly denied that there was any organization (*zuzhi*), on the ground that they had no physical location, no visible leaders. But it was clear that Li had put together a most efficient organization, with sophisticated means of communication such as a cybernetwork [which is defined by Lin to be a social network in cyberspace, and specifically on the Internet], to recruit, train, retain, and mobilize followers and create collective social capital.

(Lin, 2002: 226)

Over the years, Falun Gong has established a sophisticated presence on the Internet, with its main page, www.falundafa.org, as the main port of entry and hub of global communication for its multitude of print media outlets, radio and television stations, and Web sites worldwide. In addition to publishing the latest news, member events and activities, commentary and deliberative pieces, testimonials, teachings of Master Li Hongzhi, the Internet has also allowed overseas Falun Gong members to establish a variety of communication channels with practitioners inside China and to publicize stories of government persecutions of individual believers in China to a global audience. Moreover, its well-orchestrated cybernetwork has also dogged the Chinese leadership with public protests and demonstrations wherever overseas visits by the top leaders are taking place.

Another prominent case that illustrates well the dramatic effect of the Internet on social movements in China is the Tiananmen Mother Group Campaigns. This is a group of parents who lost loved ones on the eve of June 4, 1989, during the brutal Tiananmen Square massacre. Collectively calling themselves Tiananmen Mothers, one hundred-plus members of the self-organized group have been collecting and disseminating information about victims of the massacre, issuing open letters to the government for formal dialogues with victims' families and an independent inquiry into the Tiananmen crackdown, and calling on authorities to redress the official verdict on the students-led movement (which has been branded as "counterrevolutionary" by the Chinese leadership). Leading the group is Ding Zilin, a former professor at China's Renmin (People's) University, whose 17-year-old son was killed on the night of the crackdown.[70] The group started in September 1989, when Ding Zilin met another mother, Zhang Xianling, whose 19-year-old son was also massacred on the same night. The two mothers immediately agreed to team up and started to recruit families of other victims into their movement.[71] As of early 2004, the number of members in the Tiananmen Mothers group had reached 124.[72] Since Ding and Zhang's meeting in 1989, Ding and her associates have been waging a sustained public campaign demanding accountability from the government despite continuous harassment, threats, surveillance, and detainment by the Chinese authorities. Their bereavement and love for their lost loved ones have made them strong and free from fear of the Chinese leadership.

The Internet has in particular become a powerful weapon for their campaigns in the following aspects. First, the Internet has become especially essential for the Tiananmen Mothers to communicate to the general public all over the world. They have published witness accounts, victim lists, and statements from victims' parents on the Internet that have been collected by the group over the years.[73] Meanwhile, the Internet has also provided the venue for the mothers to publish their open letters, public statements, declarations, and news releases on numerous occasions at different points of their campaign.[74]

All these activities, of course, would have been impossible without the Internet. As Wang Yi, a popular and influential essayist and freelancer who resides in China, has recounted, "were it not for the Internet, I would have been ignorant of all the audacious undertakings [of the Tiananmen Mothers]."[75]

Secondly, the Internet has also been an essential tool of communication for the public to express their support for the Tiananmen Mothers Campaign. On June 4, 2000, China Human Rights, an independent overseas organization for the promotion of human rights in China, established a Web site called Fill the Square: Support the Tianamen Mothers (at http://www.fillthesquare.org) to solicit e-petitions, invite friends to take part in the petitions, and recruit volunteers in support of the cause of the Tiananmen Mothers. Tens of thousands of people worldwide have joined the petition online. In addition to the numerous online petitions, signatures, and support letters from various groups and organizations, public support for the Tiananmen Mothers reached a peak when the group was nominated for the Nobel Peace Prize for 2002 by a concerted online effort involving a diversified group of scholars, dissidents, and people who were sympathetic to China's democracy movement.[76]

Because of the publicity and outpouring of support from all corners of the world, thanks to the Internet, the Tiananmen Mothers have won respect from a wide spectrum of global organizations. The leader and the most vocal member of the group, Ding Zilin, is the recipient of a number of prestigious awards, among them The Democratic Foundation Award (United States, 1994), Heinz R. Pagels Human Rights Award of the New York Academy of Sciences (United States, 1995), The Award of the Freedom Foundation (France, 1996), The Award of the Foundation of Freedom and Human Rights (Switzerland, 1998), The Award of the Alexandra Lange Foundation (Italy, 1999), The Award of Democratic Courage (Asia, 2000), and The Truman–Reagan Freedom Award (United States, 2000).[77]

Finally, the widespread interest in and support for the Tiananmen Mothers Campaign both on and off the Internet have exerted formidable pressure on Chinese authorities in their handling of the Tiananmen Mothers group. The Internet has played an indispensable role in that it provides people with the platform in cyberspace to exchange information and to voice their support for the vulnerable group. For example, in March 2004, three of the Tiananmen Mothers, Ding Zilin, Zhang Xialing, and Huang Jinping, were arrested by state security police for "harming national security," which was believed to be because of their video-taped testimonials regarding their efforts to seek justice for the victims of the 1989 crackdown. The testimonials were released in Hong Kong not long ago by a support group in Hong Kong and were to be presented by the support group at the United Nations Human Rights Commissions Working Group on Enforced or Involuntary Disappearances in Geneva.[78] The news of their arrest was immediately available on the Internet and was condemned by a variety of groups worldwide. The United States led a number of governments in calling for their immediate release, and a number of overseas scholars, dissidents in exile, and China watchers sent open letters to the Chinese president demanding the release of the three women.[79] In less than a week, all three were released by the Chinese government after "being admonished and showing repentance,"[80] the typical Chinese official face-saving explanation for its detention of dissidents. Compared with the fate of other dissenters who were jailed for years for lesser offenses, the official harassment of the Tiananmen Mothers was "lenient" indeed. The special status of this group of courageous women thus granted by the Chinese regime and the restraint the Chinese police showed in the handling of these women over the years were apparently due to international pressure from many fronts. Without the Internet, it stands to reason that the fate of the Tiananmen Mothers Campaign would have taken a totally different course.

The Falun Gong and the Tiananmen Mothers are by no means isolated events in present-day China. What we see is an emerging trend in which the Internet has changed the way dissidents, independent groups, and more importantly, average Chinese citizens, access information, communicate with each other, and organize social activities. More evidence is presented in later chapters in this regard.

Fragmented Authoritarianism, the Chinese Media, and Alternative Voices

To gain a better understanding of the changing nature of information control and media regulation in China, it is necessary to consider the current Chinese political system and its role in defining the triangular relationships of the media, the society, and the state in the country today. One useful perspective that may serve as a reference point is the "fragmented authoritarianism" model that is applicable to the conventional media as well as the Internet.

After the communist takeover of China in 1949, Mao Tse-tung established a unitary totalitarian state mechanism partly through his charisma and partly through his rule of terror. All policies were made by the top echelon of the power hierarchy controlled by a few political elites, and they were then implemented top-down with a high level of compliance from all levels of government. Lower level officials could only comply fully with the political priorities and orders set by the central elites and were not allowed to question or challenge in any way.

That monolithic totalitarian model in which the all-powerful, all-inclusive state could totally control all levels of government bureaucracies through a set of uniform policies is no longer true of today's political system in China. Through over two decades of China's economic reform and openness, what has been emerging is a "fragmented authoritarian" model in which the central authorities still maintain certain levers of state control while local authorities have successfully empowered themselves in securing their own spheres of influence. To facilitate the decision-making process in China's transition to a market-oriented economic system, local government authorities at the various levels and the various ministries have been given the power to develop their specific policy initiatives as long as they don't directly contradict the broad guidelines set by the central authority. The gradual decentralization of power is necessitated by the overriding objective of stimulating economic growth in all sectors set by the late paramount leader Deng Xiaoping because, pragmatically, an all-powerful central government that controls every aspect of policy-making is ineffectual in achieving economic development. As a result, interagency (such as interprovincial and interministerial) bargaining and maneuvering are common as each tries to promote its own interest (White, 1993). Therefore, in the place of a unified dictatorship, what we have is a diversified, multilayered, and multilevel interrelated network of authoritarian organizational structures.

> The fragmented authoritarianism model argues that the authority below the very peak of the Chinese political system is fragmented and disjointed. The fragmentation is structurally based and has been enhanced by reform policies regarding procedures. The fragmentation, moreover, grew increasingly pronounced under the reforms beginning in the late 1970s ... .
>
> (Lieberthal and Lampton, 1992: 8;
> see also Lieberthal and Oksenberg, 1988)

The most prominent change as a result of this fragmented authoritarianism is that many powers that were monopolized by the central government are gradually devolved to the lower levels of government agencies to facilitate decision-making and the functioning of the bureaucracy of the overall hierarchical structure.

In the process of turning the Chinese economy from the integrated, state-owned and state-controlled one of the Mao era to one that is market-based and export-oriented and dominated by foreign and private investment, a clear pattern started to emerge in the Chinese economic landscape with a patchwork of a few major "independent kingdoms" by the late 1980s and the early 1990s. Consequently, the power of the central government to ensure compliance from all local authorities has been declining, with the local governments having more edge in bargaining during the policy decision-making process (Lampton, 1992). Moreover, more economically advanced provinces or regions, such as Shanghai and Guangdong, clearly have more impact on national policy formation. Meanwhile, in the zero-sum game of power gouging and in the fierce competition for limited national and international resources in each region's economic initiative, the incentives for interagency cooperation between government organs are dwindling as middle and low echelons of the hierarchical structure gain more autonomy.

In a more recent effort to explain the fragmented nature of Chinese authoritarianism, Lieberthal notes:

> Despite the highly authoritarian nature of China's political system, actual authority is in most instances fragmented. There are numerous reporting lines throughout the system — through the party, through the government, to the territorial organs, and so forth ...
>
> The simple point is that the officials of any given office have a number of bosses in different places ... It becomes important in these circumstances to determine which of these bosses has priority over others. Typically, the Chinese cope with this in a minimal way by indicating that the primary leadership over a particular department resides either on the vertical line (*tiao*) or with the horizontal piece (*kuai*) ... The one with priority has what is termed a "leadership relationship" (*lingdao guanxi*) with the department in question, while the other one has a nonbinding "professional relationship" (*yewu guanxi*) with it.

(2004: 187)

Most fragmented authoritarianism literature has focused on its impact on economic decision making in the Chinese bureaucracy. Yet the transformation of Chinese politics from the full-scale totalitarian system to the fragmented authoritarianism model has significant implications for the understanding of Chinese mass media, too. In Mao's totalitarian China, mass media were first and foremost propaganda tools for the party, and all media were of one voice from a top-down mass propaganda approach in which orders from the central authority were uniformly followed by all; all media were tightly controlled by propaganda bureaus at the different levels of the government and no deviance was tolerated. Mass media got funded as part of the state-controlled economy, and media workers were ranked as government functionaries.

In the last decade or so of the reform era, fundamental changes have taken place in China's media industry. As the mass media have been increasingly commercialized, market forces, instead of party directives, have become the primary concern for media executives because circulation and advertising revenue constitute the lifeline for the media in this environment (e.g., Donald, Keane, and Hong, 2002; Zhao, 1998). The fundamental transformation in the Chinese media landscape from a traditional emphasis on state propaganda to a prominent role of the audience is no small matter in the contemporary Chinese media system. The state's practice of clinging to the old ideology of media control on one hand and introducing market mechanism in the media sector on the other has inevitably created contradictions that are not easy to tackle for all parties involved. As a result, the Chinese media are caught in a protracted tug-of-war between two masters, the Party and the audience (M. Chan, 1993; Polumbaum, 1990), and are facing the insurmountable task of pleasing both. Indeed, the "ambiguities and contradictions" (Lee, 1994) present as a consequence of this evolving relationship between state control and economic reform has been much of the focus of scholarship concerning China's media in the reform era. As a direct result of media commercialization and economic liberalization, audience weighs heavily as a crucial factor in the operation of media business, and the media can no longer afford to ignore public information demand and interest when eyeballs and circulation define the success and failure of a media enterprise.

At the same time, decades of marketization drive have also cultivated an emerging "professional culture" among media institutions and practicing journalists in search of new strategies to deal with state control and to supply information in accordance with audience interest (Pan, 2000; Polumbaum, 1990). A parallel development is that audience members in China "have liberated themselves from the yoke of the seemingly powerful medium of official propaganda television" and have creatively turned television use to meet individualized needs and desires (Zhong, 2003: 245). An emerging pattern in the reform era is that the government has been quite tolerant with programs that are not directly related to political news and do not challenge the authority of the party rule (Mu, 2004), and that "Chinese media producers have much greater latitude in subject matter and approach, and Chinese consumers face far broader informational choices and interpretive possibilities than ever before" (Polumbaum, 2001: 271). Lynch (1999) demonstrates that media reform has caused the Chinese state to lose a significant degree of control over thought work and the management of propagandistic communications in Chinese society. This changing nature of Chinese media is also noted by Li, who concludes that "the Chinese media have much more freedom and 'space' than before to pursue their professional goals and meet the needs of the audience. Unlike the previous role as a mere government mouthpiece, it can be argued that the media have now become the voice for both the party-government and the public" (Li, 2002: 29).

Another significant development in Chinese journalism is the rise of investigative journalism as "a product of the political necessity of the central party leadership facing mounting social pressures and a corrupt bureaucracy over which it no longer has effective control, the commercialized media's need for audience credibility and the commitment of reform-minded professional journalists" (Zhou [Zhao], 2000: 592). The most popular TV program that focuses on investigative report is *Jiaodian Fangtan* (Focal Points) on China Central Television (CCTV), China's only national television station, which broadcasts daily at prime time and attracts a daily audience of 300 million (Chan, 2002). The program exposes official corruption, discovers fake pharmaceuticals, criticizes bureaucratic inefficiency, and unearths all kinds of social ills that the average Chinese citizens hate. Top Chinese leaders are said to be regular viewers of this program and often demand official actions from local leaders to solve specific problems aired on the program (Chan, 2002; Li, 2002). As Zhan and Zhao (2002) point out, *Focal Points* is just one of many existing popular investigative programs that serve a supervisory role over government and society.

Granting more freedom and introducing a limited, or "friendly" competition mechanism does not mean that the Chinese government has given up its effort of media control. Although government orders or directives cannot be totally ignored by the media, administrative fragmentation and changing market conditions have caused the state to lose a significant degree of content control and day-to-day management of the mass media (Lynch, 1999). Fragmentation of the state authority allows more breathing room and more autonomy for the media, which can in turn vigorously pursue certain hot issues, especially nonpolitical ones that directly affect people's everyday life, or political issues that do not directly challenge the party's legitimacy and authority.

There is an unmistakable hierarchy in the structural relationships in China's media system. The CCP is the single monopolistic ruling party in the country, and runs the nation through controlling government agencies at the national and local levels. The Ministry of Propaganda is the powerful branch of the Chinese Communist Party that is in charge of ideological policymaking at the national level. Therefore, no media organization is allowed to challenge the legitimacy and the ideology of the Party. The Ministry of Propaganda, however, does not exercise direct control over provincial and local media organizations. Instead, execution of orders from the Ministry of Propaganda at the provincial and local media is supervised by the propaganda departments at these bureaucratic levels. The Ministry of Propaganda has its center of control with the national media, such as *People's Daily*, CCTV, and Xinhua News Agency. Thus publications that are further away from the Ministry, such as commercial press and metropolitan papers, may from time to time show more resilience with regard to resistance to party ideological lines than the Beijing-based national media.

This is contrary to Chen and Chan's assessment that "the degree of press freedom is negatively related to the distance between media and the center of political power. The further away media workers are from central political power, the greater their freedom" (1998: 6470). Because there is no hierarchical leadership connection between the national media and the various ministries and provinces, the national media have greater freedom to exercise their supervisory role over these bureaucracies for possible malpractices. This is exactly what the most popular television investigative program, *Focal Points* (*Jiaodian Fangtan*), has been doing over the years (Chan, 2002; Li, 2002; Zhou [Zhao], 2000). For this reason, reporters from the national media often command awe from local officials for fear that these reporters may dig something out that is not favorable to the officials and thus curtail their officialdom. It is not uncommon for local bureaucrats to bribe national reporters to hold off certain stories that do not project them in a favorable light. In this sense, national media have more, not less freedom, to expose official wrongdoing at the local level precisely because they are closer to the central authority and further away from the local bureaucracies, and there can be no direct retaliation from these officials. Therefore, it is more accurate to characterize this type of power relationship in this way: the closer the media outlets are to the specific center of power (either at the national or local level), the less freedom the media have to supervise that power. Conversely, the further away the media organizations stay from the center of power, the more freedom media workers enjoy in exercising their supervisory role. There is also a noticeable pattern with mass media at the provincial level. Because there is no leadership relationship between mass media in one province and the political administrative power in another, there are no qualms on the part of media professionals from one province to pursue sensitive issues in another province. The same is also true for reporters from provincial media when dealing with issues in relation to the local (subprovincial) level.

A typical example that testifies to the fragmented authoritarianism perspective is the 2004 media crusade against bogus or low-quality milk powder, which led to deaths and malnutrition problems among babies who drank the formula. Tenacious follow-ups by the Chinese media on this issue uncovered multiple cases involving numerous brands throughout the nation, which led to an official crackdown that resulted in the banning of sales of over 50 brands of infant formulas, the firing of local government officials, and prosecution of merchants that were directly involved in the production and distribution of the poisonous milk powder.[81] In cases like this one, the media clearly have assumed a watchdog role that alerts people to malpractice of business interests and negligence of local official duties. Because these incidents first involved the localities of Fuyang in Anhui Province and Zhuzhou in Hunan Province and then spread to other places, it was the media in Beijing, Shanghai, and Guangdong that took the leading role in uncovering a multitude of malpractices. The provincial media (mainly newspapers) of those provinces also vigorously followed leads in exposing official corruption at the subprovincial levels.[82]

The fragmented authoritarian press system also means that the media have fewer masters directly over them and that they can focus more on serving the audience. In the Chinese bureaucratic hierarchy, the propaganda bureau at each level of the CCP hierarchy is the most immediate official agency in charge of local media. Therefore, media in one province or city often have no hesitation in picking up negative news stories from another province or city that has no direct authority over them; and the few national media, such as CCTV and *People's Daily* as well as the official Xinhua News Agency, which directly report to the central government, have no qualms in exposing official corruption or incompetence at the local levels. Thus in a highly publicized case of 2003, Liu Yong, a ringleader in Shenyang, a major industrial city in

China's northeastern Liaoning Province, who was suspected of close connections with corrupt local officials, was retried by the Supreme People's Court and his sentence was changed from life imprisonment to death, largely due to aggressive coverage and investigation by media from Beijing and other parts of China as well as the Internet media, not the local media.[83] And when Huang Jing, a 21-year-old middle school teacher in Xiangtan city of Hunan province, died suspiciously in her dorm in early 2003 and the only suspect, her ex-boyfriend who was the son of a high-ranking local official, was exonerated by local law enforcement after crucial evidence had been tampered with, it was the national media as well as media from neighboring provinces, together with the online media, that kept the case alive by challenging authorities to pursue the investigation.[84] This pattern of media behavior in China is immediately noticeable in the coverage of many similar issues over the past decade in the country.

Two recent cases offer perfect support for the fragmented authoritarian perspective above. The first case involves the aggressive media exposure of a judicial blunder in Hunan province, which involved the mis-execution of Teng Xingshan by Mayang County law enforcement for an alleged murder. In 1987, pieces of a chopped-up woman's body was found in a river, and the victim was identified by police to be Shi Xiaorong, a former waitress for a local hotel in central Hunan Province. Teng, who was a butcher at the time, was arrested and was convicted by the Hunan Provincial Court for the murder, despite Teng's pleas of innocence and despite a signature campaign by Teng's villagers testifying to his innocence. Teng was executed by gunshot in 1989. However, it turned out that the "murder victim," Shi Xiaorong, was actually sold to another province to be somebody's wife in 1987. She returned to her hometown later and got married, and then got arrested along with her husband for drug trafficking. Teng's family and relatives learned of the news of Shi years later and appealed to a local lawyer for help in 2003. The news first broke on June 15, 2005, by *Jinri Nübao* (Women's News Today), a Hunan-based newspaper affiliated with the Hunan Daily Group, the biggest print corporation in the province. This story immediately made the headlines of major newspapers nationwide. An embarrassed Hunan provincial government told media in the province (including the major portal site in the province, Rednet.com.cn) to stop running stories in relation to this case, which they soon did. But media organizations at the national level and from other provinces tenaciously pursued the story and ran a series of in-depth reports that were extremely critical of the Hunan authorities.[85] The embattled Hunan provincial regime appealed to the Propaganda Ministry of the Central Committee of the Chinese Communist Party to stop the coverage of this case by the national media and media from other regions.[86] The behavior of the various media organizations involved in this case is highly congruent with analytical framework of fragmented authoritarianism.

The second case concerns a recent appeal from seventeen provincial and municipal governments to the central authority to ban cross-region supervision by Chinese media.[87] Each of those local governments is frustrated and infuriated by the blatant muckraking of official corruption, incompetence, and social ills in its jurisdiction by the national media or media from other regions. Yet the local regimes have no direct authority over these media organizations, and therefore remain helpless in controlling media outside of their own jurisdiction. Many of these local grievances are against national media or news organizations such as Xinhua News Agency, *People's Daily,* and China Central Television. In an apparent rebuff against these demands, Xinhua published a series of commentaries and reports calling for more, not less, media supervision of government work.[88] The central government has been quite tolerant of this cross-region media supervision because it works to its own advantage: After decades of economic reform, tensions between the central government and local authorities are rising as local officials continue to gain more autonomy in implementing policies on an expanding list of social and economic issues (e.g., Yang, 1997). In addition, rampant official corruption at the national and local levels poses a great threat to the legitimacy of the rule of the Chinese Communist Party. Under these circumstances, allowing media a certain level of freedom to supervise government work at the ministerial, provincial, and local levels helps the central government maintain its surveillance and control of local officials. Therefore, it is quite understandable that the central authority does not want to severely restrict media organizations in such behaviors — as long as this is not threatening the rule of the central regime or derailing its important agendas. As mentioned before, it is widely known that Chinese national leaders regularly watch investigative programs on television and read muckraking stories from the print media, and from time to time demand action from local leaders in redressing issues of public grievance. It is partly for this reason that the fragmented authoritarian press system finds fertile ground on Chinese soil under the current sociopolitical mechanism. Nonetheless, what this model suggests is that media supervision is minimal at the topmost level, making it impossible to demand accountability from the central authority.

Finally, let me end the discussion of this section by pointing out its relevance to Chinese civil society. It is the fragmentation of the authoritarian state that makes possible the birth of vibrant forces within Chinese civil society through significant cracks in the state mechanism and creates the opportunity for Chinese civil society to work with other segments of society, including the conventional and online media, to exercise limited supervision over the state sector and to induce desirable changes in China. This point should be clear from discussions in Chapters 6 and 7.

Chapter Summary

China's National Information Infrastructure initiative has been a dilemma in many aspects and on many levels. On the one hand, China has adopted a strategy of vigorously pursuing technological and economic advancement in its modernization drive; ICTs have figured prominently in China's national policymaking and have been an important segment in China's effort to increase the nation's competitive edge in a globalized economy. On the other hand, the authoritarian regime has been quite wary of the potentially destructive nature of a brand-new information environment brought about by ICTs and has aggressively put in place a set of regulatory measures to minimize any damaging effect from unwanted or undesirable information.

The ultimate goal of China's NII initiative is to maximize economic gains and to minimize political risks for the authoritarian regime. As communication tools, the Internet and other new emerging information technologies are no different from conventional media for the Chinese government; content that is politically incendiary or socially offensive should and can be checked. In this regard, China proves to be a direct contradiction to any optimistic proclamation of the Internet era as one of emancipation, empowerment, and transcendence of physical boundary; instead, it serves as a clear reminder that nation-states are as relevant as ever in the cyber age.

However, the long-term effect of China's Internet regulation remains to be seen. Although the state has been implementing severe restrictive measures on every kind of communicative activity on the Internet, ranging from access control to content filter, the ever-evolving information technologies may make it impossible for Chinese authorities to keep pace with information control on the Internet. Antiblocking software, proxy servers, mirror sites, remailers, and anonymous e-mail services have already helped many Chinese netizens successfully bypass official censors and have proved the vulnerability of the state regulatory mechanism. As Internet connectivity continues to penetrate into every sector of Chinese society, a fundamental transformation is already taking place in the injection of new blood to the life of the people of China.

The theoretical model of fragmented authoritarianism is particularly helpful in understanding the changing nature of the role of mass media in Chinese society and the implications for government control of information. Because the media have gained a substantial space of freedom as a result of the marketization effort in the reform era, mass media have become more responsive to the concerns of everyday citizens and may actively pursue hot issues. All this, however, happens within confined territories and within permitted terrains of a fragmented authoritarian network of relationships. While mass media have been vigorously conducting investigative reports to expose official corruption and social malpractices, this is done within well-orchestrated domains. Mass media rarely, if ever, challenge the powers that are directly above them, but they are relentlessly tenacious in uncovering negative stories in relation to bureaucracies that have no direct leadership relation with them. This dual nature of the Chinese press system is explained well by the fragmented authoritarianism model. The popularization of the Internet in China, in particular, has introduced a new glimmer of hope in weakening the government monopoly of information. Social movements, even those that are directly in opposition to official lines, such as the Falun Gong and the Tiananmen Mothers Campaigns, have obtained a new life in China because of the liberating effects of the Internet. The fact that these social groups that directly challenge the authority of the Chinese regime can sustain and interconnect not only among themselves but also with the outside world gives us reason to hope that the Internet is acting as a agent of change in a country with deep-rooted traditions of authoritarian governance. And that is where we see the prospect of new ICTs for Chinese civil society.

4

Historical Development of the Internet in China

During the past decade China has fostered an impressive telecommunications industry with the potential to become the world's leading communication market in both its user base and investment prospects. Leading the latest growth in China's telecommunications market have been the Internet and wireless communications (e.g., see Wong and Nah, 2001 for an overview). By the end of 2001, China surpassed the United States to become the world's biggest mobile telecom market, and as of the end of May 2002, mobile phone users in China reached 170 million, standing far ahead of any other country.[1] By the end of August 2005, mobile phone users rose to 372.8 million, according to the statistics released by the Ministry of Information Industry (MII).[2] But as a market report by USB AG, a Swiss investment bank, indicates, the official statistics may be inflated because there is an emerging business culture among Chinese entrepreneurs to have more than one cell phone, and the official statistic only reflects the actual number of cell phones in use, which may be higher than the number of cell phone users.[3] Nevertheless, that does not change the fact that the diffusion of cell phones has been on a fast track and that China boasts the most cell phone users in the world. Meanwhile, its fixed phone users totaled 190 million by the end of March 2002, roughly equaling the number of fixed phone population in the United States at the time.[4] As of August 2005, fixed line phone users rose to 342.3 million.[5]

As reviewed in the previous chapter, since officially joining the global Internet bandwagon in 1994, the Chinese government has carried out a series of important initiatives to openly embrace the Internet revolution; as a result, the Internet industry in China has witnessed exponential growth in the past few years, with a sharp rise in cash flows, a diversification of Web sites and portals, as well as an explosion in the netizen population. The latest statistics released on July 21, 2005, by the semiofficial China Internet Network Information Center (CNNIC) puts the number of Internet surfers at 103 million as of June 30, 2005, second only to that in the United States. Among the users, 53 million were connected to the Internet through broadband services (CNNIC 16th Statistical Survey Report on the Internet Development in China, 2005). The astounding growth rate (see later reports in this chapter) within the first few years of the twenty-first century is enough indication that the Internet is quickly becoming a significant force to be reckoned with in Chinese daily life.

China's ongoing Internet revolution has won enthusiastic support from the government, which sees it as a golden opportunity for another economic take-off for China in the new millennium. Jiang Zemin, the former Chinese president and party boss, called for a "vigorous" promotion of IT technology and said that e-mail, e-commerce, and other Internet services will transform the world's most populous nation. Jiang was quoted as saying in a widely publicized speech delivered at an international computer conference held in China in August 2000[6]:

> We should deeply recognize the tremendous power of information technology and vigorously promote its development. The speed and scope of its transmission have created a borderless information space around the world … The melding of the traditional economy and information technology will provide the engine for the development of the economy and society in the 21st century.

This was later echoed by Wu Jichuan, the Information Industry Minister, who, during the first China Internet Conference in November 2002, stressed that it is China's national policy to "give priority to the development of the information industry and apply IT in all areas of economic and social development."[7] Yet both Jiang and Wu were quick to call attention to the nature of the Internet as a possible double-edged sword, noting the challenge it poses to the communist regime and emphasizing the need to regulate and control the flow of the kind of information Jiang called the "flood of trash" on the Internet, which was defined to be "anti-science, false science, and information that is unhealthy to the point of being downright harmful."[8] This chapter, therefore, offers an overview of the development of the Internet in China and the government's effort to pursue the e-path of economic prosperity in an ocean of uncharted waters.

A History of the Internet in China

The dazzling pace of the Internet revolution worldwide has made it the fastest diffused communication medium history has ever seen. Since the invention of the World Wide Web in the early 1990s, the Internet has quickly established itself as a transforming force all over the globe by forever changing the economic, social, and political landscape of the world and by rippling through the lives of millions upon millions of people in every corner of the world like nothing before. This is also true with what now seems to be the unstoppable growth of the Internet as it further penetrates into every aspect of Chinese society.

The path of China's Internet expansion has much in common with that in the West because it has been closely tied to technological advances in Western nations where the Internet originated. At the same time, there have also been some unique twists and turns in China's Internet initiative. In their review of the status of Internet development and application in China, Wei Lu and colleagues (2002) mapped out two major phases. The first phase spanned 1987 to 1993 when Internet application was limited to e-mail transmission services among a selected few scientific research institutes; and the second phase, which started in 1994 and extends to the present, has been marked by the implementation of TCP/IP connections and the offering of full-scale Internet services. Yanli Qi (2000), on the other hand, sees the development of the Internet in China divided into three stages. Here are Qi's summaries:

1. 1987 to 1994: Using e-mail
   Since 1987, the e-mail system connecting the Internet by dial-up was put to use between the areas of Europe, North America, and China.
2. 1994 to 1995: Developing research and education networks
   In 1994, the Chinese Academy of Science provided connection to the Internet by a 64k bps log-in line. The National and Networking Facility of China (NCFC), which is currently known as China Science and Technology Network (CSTNET), connected hundreds of research institutes via the Internet. At the same time, the Chinese Committee of Education created its backbone network — China Education and Research Network (CERNET) — connecting many Chinese universities to the Internet. Both backbone networks are nonprofit and provide the communication services for their affiliated research institutes or colleges and universities. In this stage, China approached involvement in the world Internet community.
3. 1995 to present: Commercial use
   In June 1995, ChinaNet (China Net) was put into use for the public, and in September 1996, ChinaGBN (China Golden Bridge Network) was put into commercial use. Both of the commercial backbone networks (both belonged to the Chinese Department of Information Industry) came into operation and provided Internet connection services for Chinese Internet Service Providers (ISPs). In June 1998, ChinaNet provided a high-speed log-in line for connecting three other networks — the CERNET, ChinaGBN, and CSTNET — allowing Chinese users to access domestic Web sites in a local networking environment.

(Qi, 2000: 484–485)

Both Lu et al. and Qi see the jump from e-mail use to other applications of the Internet as a dividing line, and rightly so; however, they have ignored other important aspects in the evolution of the Internet in China's government, economy, and society. In addition, I find Qi's characterization of the year of 1995 as commercialization of the Internet in China to be both unsatisfactory and misleading. My assessment of the history of the Internet in China has led me to discern four distinctive stages, as elaborated in the following section. Each stage reflects a substantial change not only in technological progress and application, but also in the government's approach to and apparent perception of the Internet.

First, the period from 1986 to 1992 was the predawn era of the Internet age in China, when online application in the country was primarily limited to the use of e-mail and availability was extremely scarce. It was only accessible to a limited number of scholars in a few computer research labs and connection was made via some networks located in Western Europe and the United States. Internet application was purely a research initiative and was largely ignored by the government.

In the mid-1980s, at a time when it seemed that computer networking was gradually becoming something of a phenomenon in a handful of Western nations, China decided that it did not want to be left out of this ongoing revolution. Not unlike its Western counterparts, China's first computer networking undertakings centered upon research and educational activities. As a result, Chinese scientists at the Beijing Computer Application Technology Institute, in collaboration with their counterparts in Karlsruhe University in West Germany, started the CANet (China Academic Network) project. On September 20, 1987, Professor Qian Tianbai sent the first e-mail message from China to the German University network.[9] This message was delivered through a leased line from ITAPAC, the Italian part of the network, at a rate of 300 bps. The content of the first e-mail was fittingly phrased: "Cross the Great Wall and Connect to the World." This short message signified a giant step in China's Internet initiative; it told the world that China was officially plugged in. The international Internet community did not fail to notice this symbolic act — the NSF, CSNet, and BITNet, all from the United States and crucial players in the early days of the Internet, sent congratulatory notes to CANet to welcome it to the global family of the Internet (Chen Yan, 1999: 89).

In December 1988, the campus network of Tsinghua University in Beijing was linked to the University of British Columbia (UBC) via X.25 for e-mail exchange with the X400 protocol. In the same year, the Institute of High Energy Physics (IHEP) of the Chinese Academy of Sciences (CAS) connected its DECnet (which is a group of data communications products, including a protocol suite, developed and supported by Digital Equipment Corporation, and the first version of DECnet was released in 1975) to the central DECnet in Western Europe, thus making e-mail transmissions possible from China to Western Europe and North America. In May of 1990, it was upgraded to CNPac (X.25 with a speed of 4.8 kbps). Then in 1991, the decision was made by the Beijing Electron-Positron Spectrometer (BES) collaboration group to build an extensive communication network between IHEP and SLAC (Stanford Linear Accelerator Center), and three direct telephone lines with international dial-up access were set up at the IHEP computer center to provide login connectivity to the SLAC network (Cottrell et al., 1994).

In May 1989, the Chinese Research Network (CRN), with participants from research institutes and universities in five municipalities, was connected to the German research network DFN via CNPac, providing e-mail, file transmission, and limited Internet access services. A year later, in April 1990, a pilot initiative in building a local area network (LAN), the National Computing and Networking Facility of China (NCFC) project, was started with support from several ministries and participation of the Chinese Academy of Sciences, Beijing University, and Tsinghua University, the three most prestigious research institutions in the country. Financial support jointly came from the State Planning Commission and a loan from the World Bank. The original purpose of the project was to build a high-speed supercomputing center among these three units, but it later evolved into the Chinese Science and Technology Network (CSTNET), one of the four backbone network facilities in the nation.[10]

In October 1990, Professor Qian Tianbai, on behalf of China, officially registered China's top domain name as CN for Internet services from the Defense Data Network-Network Information Center (DDN-NIC), which was the predecessor of the Internet Network Information Center (INTERNIC) and then the official organization under ARPANET, which at that time was responsible for the distribution of domain and IP addresses. In 1992, the college network initiative under NCFC to connect Chinese college campuses, the Chinese Academy of Sciences Network (CASNET), was in full swing. CASNET originally linked thirty-plus research centers in the Zhongguancun area in Beijing and two local university campuses, the Tsinghua University Network (TUNET), and Peking University Network (PUNET). It extended to the whole nation in 1992 in an effort to connect major campuses over various regions. Because of the active involvement of research units and scientists from the Zhongguancun area, it quickly became the center of China's computer and networking industry and won the nickname "China's silicon valley."

Therefore, not unlike its counterparts in the West, China's first computer networks were started by research and educational institutions specializing in computer science. E-mail and file transfer were the major applications supported by these early networks, and bandwidth and cost were two major bottlenecks in popularizing these services to a critical mass. For example, the direct line between IHEP and SLAC cost about US$1 per minute for calls initiated from the U.S. side and US$3 per minute for calls made from the Chinese side. The Telebit T2500 modems providing connectivity could only effectively transfer data at a rate of 700 to 900 bps, very sluggish for interactive use; as a result, the typical monthly bill for IHEP was about $4000 (Cottrell et al., 1994), prohibitively high for any purpose other than experimental and research-oriented activities. In general, the early network services cost about RMB¥ 5 (approximately US$0.60) per kilobyte for the data received or sent. So the small number of technical professionals who had access to the online network were hesitant to publicize their personal accounts, and they asked their partners who knew their e-mail accounts to reserve their use for extremely necessary occasions (Chen Yan, 1999).

The second stage in China's Internet development started in 1992 and ended in 1995. Several factors contributed to China's official policy change from that of inattention to one of deliberation and search for a solution of its own to the emergence of a rapidly unfolding global network revolution during this period. First of all, what was taking place in the United States, China's long-time ideological and geopolitical rival, in the 1990s in its approach to the Internet, had caught the attention of the Chinese government and weighed in as an important factor in China's decision-making about important issues related to computer networking in China.

In the 1980s, the ARPANET, which originally started at the behest of government agencies, military contractors, and research and education institutions in the United States in the 1960s, could not meet many of the rising technical and operational challenges associated with the unanticipated growth of the network. By the mid-1980s, the Internet was already a well-established technology adopted by a broad community of not only researchers and developers but also other professional groups who used it for daily communication purposes. At this point, the National Science Foundation (NSF) began to take an active role in gradually taking over the task of managing the Internet from ARPANET. On June 1, 1990, ARPANET was officially decommissioned after 21 years of service, and the focus shifted to the NSF as spearheading the development of the Internet.[11]

In 1991, the High Performance of Computing Act of 1991 was passed into law by the U.S. Congress. The law called for the funding of a National Research and Education Network (NREN) to link educational institutions together. NREN was to be based on existing networks but was to operate at a much higher speed. Two years later, a new legislation, the National Information Infrastructure Act of 1993, set in stone many of the essential foundations for the subsequent commercialization of the Internet in the United States.[12]

The development of the Internet no doubt had benefited from the unwavering support of the Clinton Administration, which, with Vice President Al Gore as the adamant proponent, had made building a national "information superhighway" (a term that is rarely used today but was very popular at the time) a top priority. Alarmed by the technological gaps between China and the Western powers led by the United States, the Chinese leadership started to get worried that it might lag behind this global drive to modernize the international information infrastructure. Consequently, as mentioned in the previous chapter, there was a quick formation of a national official Chinese policy initiative for constructing China's own version of the "information superhighway."

Meanwhile, significant technological breakthroughs were made in the late 1980s and early 1990s that paved the way for the subsequent phenomenal growth of the Internet worldwide in the mid-1990s. In addition to a substantial increase of network bandwidth, an expanding critical mass of users, and a diversity of uses of Internet communication, two significant events had a direct impact on the diffusion process of the Internet: the invention of HTML by Tim Berners-Lee and the technological triumph of the World Wide Web (WWW) at the European nuclear research center CERN in 1989 to 1990, and an X-Windows interface for the WWW called Mosaic created by Mark Andreessen and his fellow developers at the U.S. National Center for Supercomputer Applications in late 1992. The Mosaic browser for different platforms was widely available for free downloading in 1993 and quickly popularized the WWW to the online community.

In the face of mounting external pressure and the gradual realization of the importance of a national computer network infrastructure for its information environment, the Chinese government during this period started to make an effort to formulate a long-term strategy in defining the place of informatization in China's process of industrialization and modernization (see the previous chapter for a detailed account). Its approach at the time was marked by an ambivalence between developing an independent national network of its own through self-reliance and joining the global community of the Internet.

One of the most important network projects in the historical landscape of China's internetwork is the Golden Bridge, which was first proposed by then Vice-Premier Zhu Rongji in March 1993. The original stated purpose of this initiative was to create a national information and communication network connecting all thirty provinces and major cities throughout the nation. In August of that year, then Premier Li Peng approved the use of the Premier Reserve in the amount of US$3 million for the initial phase of the Golden Bridge project. In addition to the initial Golden Bridge, two other projects were added to the informatization effort, Golden Card and Golden Customs (also translated as Golden Gate). In June 1993, Jiang Zemin, the Chinese president at that time, called for an acceleration of development of credit cards and electronic banking in China's major cities. This initiative was officially labeled the Golden Card Project. At the same time, China's then Vice Premier Li Lanqing proposed the Golden Customs Project, which would be a network of foreign trade information linking the Ministry of Foreign Economic Relations and Trade and the Customs Bureau. The three Golden Projects were soon formalized by the top Chinese bureaucracies into national information projects. In June the following year, the State Council, China's state department, issued the official directive in demanding cooperation from provincial governments in constructing the Three Golden Projects.

The purpose of the initial three Golden Projects was to build a national information superhighway backbone infrastructure that would pave the way for other important information networks. In Mueller and Tan's (1997: 52) summarization:

Golden Bridge is a satellite-based ISDN network that will serve as a "state public economic information network" linking government agencies, state enterprises, and the public. Golden Bridge will serve as an 'internet' connecting all of China's private data networks. Golden Customs is a specialized data network for the management of trade, tariff collection, import-export licenses, and exchange settlement. Golden Card is intended to provide the infrastructure for a public credit card system by linking banks, businesses, and consumers with adequate financial networks.

When the three projects were initially conceptualized by the top leadership, it should be noted that the original purpose was to construct an information network system within the Chinese boundary to streamline economic, financial, and trade information flow and central decision making. External connectivity, or linking to other regions in the world, was not of interest to the Chinese leaders. As Jeffrey (2000: 3) states:

In those early days, it's probably more accurate to say that these initiatives were establishing an Intranet within China, or a series of Intranets. The goal was internal connectivity, not an opening up. The wired world was seen as a tool to increase government control over the administration of economic development. It was also seen as a tool to pull the farthest reaches of the country closer to the center.

The Golden Bridge Project was enthusiastically backed by Zhu Rongji, the mastermind of many of China's official moves in imposing fiscal discipline upon China's chaotic banking systems in the late 1990s because Zhu believed the project could provide extensive and crucial up-to-date information for central decision making. Macro-level control of economic management has always been the dominant function of the Golden Projects as perceived by the central authorities. The importance of the Golden Projects in the official conceptualization, as Mueller and Tan (1997: 57) point out, was that they could "provide information about ongoing economic activities to central and local governments for planning and coordination purposes" and "foster the sharing of information resources throughout the economy." The Golden Projects were collectively called by Zhu "the national public economic information network," which unambiguously testifies to the expectation of the role the network could play in China's official economic management mechanism. Therefore, it is no wonder that the first three Golden Projects were online initiatives involving three major areas that could be pivotal for the national economy: communications, finance, and trade.

As the government anticipated, a series of other Golden Projects were soon added to the list. One of them was the Golden Sea Project, which started in 1994 to realize office automation in the two highest power organs in China — the CPC Central Committee and the State Council —was then quickly extended to government agencies at the local levels.[13] Networking information for internal sharing soon became part of the objective. Although not originally designed with the Internet in mind, the Golden Sea later evolved into the highly publicized "Digitizing Government Administration" (*dianzi zhengwu*) or "Government Online Project" (*zhengfu shangwang gongcheng*), which intended to make central, provincial, and local government information and services available on the Internet in the late 1990s.

In early 1995, at a time when the Internet revolution was gaining momentum worldwide, the Golden Projects were significantly expanded in witnessing several additions, as noted by Mueller and Tan (1997: 52–53):

Golden Taxation would computerize tax collection. Golden Enterprise would network supply and demand information between China's largest enterprises and government. Golden Agriculture would provide information about commodities and prices. The Golden Intellectual project would function as China's Internet and connect academic and research institutions. The Golden Macro-Economic Supporting System would provide strategic information for central planners.

Also at this time, as the Internet led by the emerging World Wide Web, became quickly diffused globally, the Chinese government came to the realization that the Internet was here to stay and could jumpstart China's domestic information environment, and officially made the decision to join the global Internet bandwagon. Subsequently, the various Golden Projects provided the foundation for the government's Internet initiatives in the years to come. In 1994, all the different Golden Bridge Projects were incorporated into one national network called the China Golden Bridge Network (CHINAGBN) and were connected to the global Internet via a 128 kbps international line. Thus the Golden Projects have evolved into online adventures that were not originally intended.

In addition to CHINAGBN, efforts were started in the implementation of other major national networks during this time. In October 1994, under the auspices of China's State Education Commission and modeled upon the U.S. NSF backbone project of the mid-1980s, the China Education and Research Network (CERNET) was inaugurated with funding from the State Planning Commission. CERNET encompassed the construction of networks at three levels — a national backbone, eight regional networks, and over a 1000 campus networks, all with international connectivity — and its goal was to link all universities and research institutes in China first and then to connect all high schools, elementary schools, and other educational units by the end of

2000. As of 2004, all colleges and universities in China are connected to the Internet; however, there is still a long way to go to incorporate the country's elementary and high schools into the Internet because only a small number of them (i.e., about 26,000 schools, or 4 percent of all schools in the country, as of early 2004) are hooked up to the Internet.[14]

In late August 1994, China Telecom, which was affiliated with the former Ministry of Post and Telecommunications (MPT), signed an agreement of international cooperation with the United States during then Commerce Secretary Ron Brown's visit to Beijing. According to the agreement, direct 64 kbps lines would be set up for China Telecom in two major Chinese cities, Beijing and Shanghai, by Sprint Communications, based in America, as China's international data gateways for global Internet connectivity.[15] This was the start of CHINANET, which quickly became the largest Internet network in China. CHINANET was open to the public in early 1995 as China Telecom established direct links to the global Internet. Another major national network, the China Science and Technology Network (CSTNET), was started in May 1994 as an extension of the aforementioned NCFC and CASNET to expand Internet connections to major academic units and research institutes throughout the nation. The initial stage of the CSTNET was completed by the end of 1995, and it has now evolved into the major academic network in China.

CHINAGBN, CERNET, CHINANET, and CSTNET form the four major national backbones in China's internetworking initiatives and have played important roles in its Internet development.[16] Thus by the mid-1990s, China had successfully put in place major national networks servicing the key areas of finance and trade (CHINAGBN, http://www.gb.co.cn), education (CERNET, http://www.cernet.edu.cn), academic research (CSTNET, http://www.cnc.ac.cn), and the general public (CHINANET, http://www.bta.net.cn) (see Chen Yan, 1999: 101–114 for detailed descriptions). Another significant development during this period was that China had made a series of important initiatives in fully embracing the Internet. China's first official contact with the global Internet community was made as early as 1992, when Qian Hualin, a CAS scientist, made the formal request at the International Networking Conference (INET' 92) hosted in Kobe, Japan, to the NSF to connect China to the Internet. NSF turned down China's request, saying that there was a lot of U.S. government information on the Internet and there were political barriers involved in connecting China to the Internet.[17] Because the Internet at the time was still largely a U.S. government project, it was a politically sensitive issue to decide who could be allowed connection to the network.

The following year, Chinese scientists repeated their request to be granted access to the global Internet community at INET' 93, San Francisco. The Coordinating Committee for Intercontinental Research Networks (CCIRN) held a special session to discuss China's request and most members approved linking China to the Internet. But there was still no formal commitment from the United States. A breakthrough was made at the Sino-US Joint Committee on Scientific and Technological Cooperation meeting in Washington, D.C. in April 1994 when China gained formal approval from the NSF to be fully connected to the Internet. Dedicated 64 kbps international lines were established on April 20, 1994, to directly link NCFC to the Internet. China formally became a member of the global Internet club. On May 15, 1994, the Institute of High Energy Physics (IHEP), affiliated with the CAS, set up the first WWW server and published the first Web page in China. The site, called "China Window" (http://www.china-window.com.cn/), was published in English. It featured information about the latest developments in China's high technology and there was a specific column called "Tour in China." Later it added news and sections introducing China's culture, economy, trade, and commerce, and became a major portal site for a variety of China-related information. Obviously, its intended audience was netizens in the West who are interested in China. Since then, the site has evolved into a portal serving Chinese as well as overseas audience, and it is published in simplified Chinese, traditional Chinese, and English.[18]

Therefore, during the second phase (1992 to 1995) of Internet development in China, the government made clear its determination to foster a national information network infrastructure that would accelerate China's economic expansion and increase its competitiveness. Initially, it was the goal of the government to construct several national networks within the Chinese boundary serving different purposes (i.e., more appropriately called a nationwide Intranet). However, as the global Internet fever caught on, a significant shift of focus started to occur in the mid-1990s to model China's network on the computer network that was already taking off in the West and to join the global Internet revolution. Substantial investments and research efforts were made during this phase in the early stages of the completion of major national network backbones. Unlike the first phase in which China had to rely on a third-party to pass on electronic information to the world, China had successfully built a few major network centers (or nodes) from which communication was directly established with the external world. Nonetheless, network use was very much limited. By July 1995, the IHEP network had approximately 500 e-mail accounts, and NCFC came in second with about 300 accounts (Jeffrey, 2000). Costs dropped substantially from the first phase but were still a major deterrent in discouraging the general populace from the e-world. A user had to pay RMB¥1100 (US$132) to open an e-mail account, in addition to a monthly server fee of RMB¥25 (US$3) and long distance and/or local phone charges (Jeffrey, 2000). At the time, computers were still not widely available for average Chinese citizens, and Internet connectivity was still primarily limited to work-related use among a selective group of scientists and researchers.

The third stage of China's Internet development lasts from 1995 to 1997, and was the pretakeoff era. Rapid growth was achieved in the information infrastructure and sustained expansion of a user base ensured that network economy was going to be an important part of China's national economic structure. Moreover, the government started to see the future of the modernization of its national communication networks in the Internet and had attached high expectations to the role of information technology in China's path to national development. Thus the Internet had become a top priority in the government's effort to upgrade the national telecommunications sector. Meanwhile, alarmed by the prospect of a changing information environment undermining the regime's powers of surveillance and censorship, the Chinese government started to implement a variety of technological and policy mechanisms to put the unfolding Internet industry under tight control.

At the start of this phase, the four major national network backbones, CHINAGBN, CERNET, CHINANET, and CSTNET, had been physically completed. Beginning from the mid-1990s, all four were in operation and started providing Internet-related services to their clients, which were mainly government agencies, financial institutions, colleges, universities, and a limited number of commercial institutions and individual users. CHINANET, under the protective umbrella of China Telecom, had an unusual edge over all other service companies because its official protégé, the Ministry of Posts and Telecommunications (MPT), had a complete monopolistic control of China's telephone industry. Therefore, it is no wonder that CHINANET was the first to offer commercial online services in 1995. The first commercial Internet service line by the Beijing Telegraph Bureau under MPT started trial operation in the Chinese capital in March 1995 and was opened to the public in June that year.

Encouraged by the rising interest in its online services, MPT came to two formal decisions in May 1995: the first was to construct a national backbone network that would connect all provincial capitals as an expansion of CHINANET specifically designed for offering public Internet connectivity services, and the second was to upgrade its Beijing Internet service station to be the center node of its national Internet network. MPT completed its national network in January 1996 and opened its commercial Internet services to residents in major Chinese cities soon after. In December 1996, MPT coordinated all its regional Internet public service programs into one entity and named it the China Public Multimedia Communications Network (or CHINFO 169). The user base was still very small at this point (i.e., a few thousand), and high cost was still a factor in making it difficult for the working class to get online.

At the same time, CERNET, which targeted the approximately 1100 institutions of higher learning and thousands of high schools and elementary schools, was also in service. Its first phase of construction, to connect 100 universities nationwide, was completed by the end of 1995. In January 1995, China's first online magazine *China Scholars Abroad* was published on the Internet via CERNET under the sponsorship of the State Education Commission. Its audience was Chinese students and scholars who were studying overseas, most of whom could access information on the Internet or contribute to the publication via the Internet. Shortly after, China's first BBS online, BBS.tsinghua.edu.cn, made its debut on the Internet through CERNET on August 8, 1995, mainly targeting a domestic audience located in major institutions of higher education.

Another major player in networking China, CHINAGBN, started to offer service to individual and institutional clients in September 1996 through its VSAT (very small aperture terminal) satellite communications backbone and microwave transmission devices. CSTNET, on the other hand, was the only nonprofit network whose purpose was to serve the scientific and technological community, and to fulfill some of the administrative roles of coordinating China's Internet activities. Since 1994, CSTNET has also been responsible for the management of China's top (.cn) domain name service (DNS). In June 1997, the government created an official body to oversee the day-to-day administration of the Internet in China (in the technical capacity, of course), the China Internet Network Information Center (CNNIC). CNNIC was set up as an umbrella agency of CSTNET and became the official National Internet Information Center in China. Another major accomplishment in 1997 was that the four major networks in China, CHINAGBN, CERNET, CHINANET, and CSTNET, were all interconnected to one another. Users of each network were no longer isolated from those from the others, and connectivity reached a new level.

As mentioned earlier, China's Ministry of Posts and Telecommunications (MPT) established direct links to the global Internet via international lines from Sprint Inc. in January 1995. Shortly after, the MPT made a milestone decision: access to the Internet went commercial. As it turned out, growth was exponential and soon exceeded official expectations: between March and July of 1995, Internet users jumped from 3,000 to 40,000.[19] Up to October 31, 1997, 620,000 people were logged onto the Internet, 299,000 computers were connected to the Internet, and the number of WWW sites published in China reached 1,500 (CNNIC 1st Statistical Survey Report on the Internet Development in China, 1997). Meanwhile, as public access to the Internet was open and user demand surged, major Internet service providers (ISPs) led by CHINANET made several important fee adjustments and reductions: by 1997, users only had to pay about RMB¥ 100 (approximately US$12) to open an Internet account and then were subject to an hourly connectivity fee of about RMB¥ 6 (less than US$1) (Chen Yan, 1999: 100). This was a sharp drop from the exorbitant charges just a few years earlier. Yet the proportion of Internet users compared with the national population of over a billion was still marginal at this stage, and the nature of the impact of the Internet on everyday life was hard to discern. But a few highly publicized cases in relation to the

Internet during this phase helped popularized the Internet as a novel technological invention and showed people its potential through the popular media.

Once people were exposed to the brand-new cyber information environment, the transformative power of the Internet in society started to assert
itself. As a demonstration of how China's borders were opened by the Internet,
Ms. Zhu Ling, a 21-year-old ailing Beijing University student suffering from
a mysterious disease (which her Chinese doctors suspect might be a nervous
system ailment called acute disseminated encephalomyelitis or a connective
tissue disorder called lupus erythematosus), got offers of help from hundreds
of doctors in the United States after her friends posted SOS messages on the
Internet in April 1995. The electronic plea for international medical assistance was posted on Sunday, April 21, 1995, and responses started coming in
from across the Pacific a few hours later. A group of ten doctors from Berkeley
even appointed a coordinator among themselves.[20] Moreover, a doctor in the
UCLA Medical Center set up a BBS column collecting information and updat-
ing progress on the treatment. After eight months in a coma, Zhu eventually
recovered, thanks to input from doctors worldwide (Chen Yan, 1999).

In another instance in April 1995, Ms. Li Lailai, a U.S.-trained sociolo-
gist and Director of the Institute of Environment and Development, a private
research unit intended to meet the growing popular demands for information about environmental protection and sustainable development, tried to
use the Internet to introduce a trove of global data about environmentally
safe technology and development ideas. Li got financial help from the Leadership for Environment and Development program, an international program
funded by the Rockefeller Foundation, and aimed to establish an electronic
link between Chinese environmental activists and the world community. Li
said that her service would help create "a cyber society where there are no borders, no political disputes, and people can talk about the issues freely."[21]

Information in the Chinese authoritarian tradition is not only something
to be desired but also something to be controlled. As China opened its door
to cyber information, its rulers started to get nervous about the messages that
might be accessible to Internet surfers in China. The potential challenge the
Internet posed to the regime that was used to a closed information environment was clearly at the top of its agenda in approaching the Internet. Immediately after China made commercial Internet services available in 1995, Mr. Wu
Jichuan, the Posts and Telecommunications Minister, told reporters that "as
a sovereign state, China will exercise control on the information" flowing to
China on the Internet, and he made no effort to hide the regime's intention to
regulate the Internet. "By linking to the Internet, we do not mean the absolute
freedom of information," he was quoted as saying.[22] Knowing Chinese authorities' long-time appetite for censoring content of any publication, Internet service companies eyeing the huge Chinese market made it their priority to sell a

special version of Internet to China: "no smut, no politics, no decadent Western culture — instead, just the gloriously capitalist language of commerce."[23]

The Chinese government wasted no time in issuing warnings to users of the Internet in China to bow to the Communist Party's dogma. In a joint statement from the Central Committee of the Communist Party and the State Council in the first week of January 1996, Chinese authorities acknowledged that pornography, political dissent, and other forms of "harmful materials" had entered China's cyberspace and vowed to "take effective measures" to deal with the situation. However, the official statement also made clear China's determination to earmark the IT sector as key areas of development in its ambitious modernization drive. "Good use of the Internet is of great importance to increase global information exchanges, promote economic construction and development science," the statement said.[24]

As early as February 18, 1994, China enacted its first law aimed at controlling computerized information. Titled "The Regulations of Safety Protection for Computer Information Systems in the People's Republic of China" (also called State Council Order Number 147), the ordinance forbids unauthorized distribution of computerized information that may threaten China's "national security," a term that has been subject to all kinds of interpretation at the whim of official agencies.[25] However, this law targeted computer information in general and the Internet was not yet its main focus. The first law that was specifically aimed at the Internet was the "Interim Regulations on International Interconnection of Computer Networks in the People's Republic of China" (also known as State Council Order Number 195) issued by the State Council on February 1, 1996, and later modified on May 20, 1997. It forbids use of the Internet to harm national security, disclose state secrets, damage national interests, endanger social stability, or produce, distribute, or consume pornographic information.[26] This directive became the foundation of a series of other laws in the years to follow that regulate the Internet and Internet use in China. It was clear to everyone from the early days of the Internet that China's promotion of the Internet was not without strings attached. This only marked the start of the government's effort to control information in the Internet age, as shown in Chapter 3.

In summary, during the third phase of China's Internet development (1995–1997), the Chinese government stepped up its effort to join the global Internet revolution in the hope that the Internet-led IT industry would yield significant economic benefits to the national economy. In doing that, the government successfully put in place a national telecommunications infrastructure that set the stage for fast-paced expansion of the Internet in the next phase. Meanwhile, Chinese authorities started to formulate and implement control mechanisms to keep undesirable information out of computer networks within China's border.

The fourth stage of China's state-led model of Internet development started in 1998 and continues to the present. The most noticeable feature during this stage is that the Internet has quickly reached a critical mass that makes the Internet's integration into Chinese society an unstoppable trend.

In a gesture to demonstrate to the world that China was determined to make IT a pillar of its national economy, the third plenum of the First Session of China's Ninth National People's Congress (NPC) approved on March 10, 1998, the proposal submitted by the State Council to restructure its institutional bureaucracies. A significant move in the proposal was the creation of the new Ministry of Information Industry (MII) based on the former Ministry of Posts and Telecommunications (MPT) and Ministry of Electronics Industry (MEI). The new MII was also to take over some of the government functions in the areas of telecommunications from the eliminated Ministry of Broadcast, Film and Television (MBFT) (which was replaced by the newly installed State Administration of Radio, Film and Television), China Aerospace Industry Corporation (in charge of satellite communications), and China Aviation Industry Corporation (in charge of air traffic control).[27] MII would be responsible for policy making, regulation, and licensing in the information industry (and also for negotiating China's entry into World Trade Organization (WTO), one task at the top of the government's agenda).

Prior to the founding of MII, no single ministry had been designated as the official bureaucracy for managing the emerging Internet sector because government policymaking and regulation of the Internet industry had been spread over different organizations under different ministries, especially MPT and MEI; as a result, there had been tensions between MPT and MEI, the two most powerful players in the information industry. MPT traditionally maintained control of the telecommunications service sector and was slow to change. It was generally protected from foreign competition. MEI, on the other hand, was the major manufacturer of IT products and entered the service sector in the late 1980s. In the face of growing domestic and foreign competitions, MEI slowly favored deploying state-of-the-art technologies and introducing competition into the telecommunications market (Foster and Goodman, 2000: 13–14). For a long time, MPT had a monopolistic control over the basic telecommunications sector. Because the basic telecommunications service sector includes local, long-distance, and wireless phone services and involves lucrative business operations, it naturally became the chief battle ground for MPT and MEI. By successfully lobbying the State Council, MEI was able to establish China Unicom under its own tutelage to offer local and long-distance phone services in some areas in China (Foster and Goodman, 2000). Here the perspective of fragmented authoritarianism mentioned in Chapter 3 may be helpful to explain this lack of interministerial cooperation. As two independent government bureaucracies, MPT and MEI had little incentive to work together unless their superiors (in this case, the State Council) intervened. As a result, the infighting between MPT and MEI sometimes created confusion for companies in the information industry and led to chaos in business practices. Undoubtedly, this kind of official mechanism caused resentment and was not conducive to entrepreneurial innovations in the Internet age.

The birth of the superministry was predicted to be good news for the fledging Internet industry because it was expected to provide more flexible, clear, and streamlined strategic policies toward the Internet. "In the past, no ministry was defined as the administrator to tend to the detailed issues in the Internet service sector. But things are expected to improve, since the Ministry of Information Industry will cover the whole industry," commented Wan Pingguo, president of ChinaNet Infortech Co. Ltd in response to the official decision.[28]

Since 1998, Chinese entrepreneurs and the government started to tap enthusiastically into what they consider a "gold mine" of online business opportunities. For one thing, e-commerce became the buzzword in the West at the time, with popular sites such as Yahoo.com, Amazon.com, and eBay. com producing millionaires at dazzling rates, and everybody was putting up Web sites to sell everything. E-commerce caught on in China overnight in 1998 — at least conceptually. 1998 was named the "Year of E-Commerce" in China (Jeffrey, 2000), which witnessed the birth and rise of major portal sites such as Sina.com, Sohu.com, and Netease.com. Meanwhile, two events highly publicized by the Chinese media that year topped Chinese business headlines. One was the founding of an online trading place of Chinese commodities, www.chinamarket.com.cn, which attracted 46.25 million visits from around the globe within the first four months after its debut. It was widely believed to be the business model of the future and earned the name "China's Never-Ending Fair." The other event was the textile quota online bidding hosted by the government, once in October and once in November of that year, which was open to all businesses in China in the spirit of "equality, fairness, and openness."[29] Because countries in the West issued quotas on Chinese textile products every year, the Chinese government had been involved in distributing the quotas among Chinese enterprises to engage in these exports.

Up until the early 1990s, China's focus on upgrading its outdated business transaction infrastructure was on Electronic Data Interchange (EDI) systems. The Golden Bridge Projects were originally conceptualized and operationalized as a significant technological breakthrough for the national EDI network. However, EDI technologies were costly to implement because they needed not only dedicated lines between the nodes of communication but also identical communicating devices among the parties involved so that messages from the originator could be rendered properly by the other end. Therefore, as the Internet established itself as the technology of the future, a strategic shift of emphasis occurred on the part of the Chinese government to make the Internet a national priority.

Rise of E-Commerce in China

As e-commerce brought about by Internet technologies stepped up the transformation of production, exchange, distribution, and consumption of products and services in the United States in the mid-1990s, the Chinese authorities decided to make a strong case for the power of e-commerce as an engine for its own economic growth. While China lagged a few decades behind the United States in development of traditional retail and wholesale industries, the Chinese leadership believed that it could close the gap between China and the United States in e-commerce. Former Chinese President Jiang Zemin noted at the APEC Leaders Informal Meeting of November 1998 that e-commerce represents the direction of future development of trade and the application and promotion of e-commerce will bring more trade opportunities.[30] Shi Guangsheng, former Minister of Foreign Trade and Economic Cooperation of China (MOFTEC), pointed out in 2001 that e-commerce is an important part of China's national informatization policy that will "realize a frog-leaping development of social productive forces" in China.[31] Governments at various levels have even been actively involved in initiating and promoting e-commerce projects themselves. As early as 1988, local governments in Beijing, Shanghai, and a few other big cities invested in "exemplary e-commerce projects" of their own to jump-start online business opportunities in their administrative regions (China E-Commerce Yearbook, 2002: 13).

On March 6, 1998, the first e-commerce transaction was arguably completed by the Beijing Century Intercom Technology Company and the Bank of China.[32] This is, however, disputed by Chen Yan (1999), who claimed that as early as 1996 and 1997, a few Web sites specializing in tourism, air travel, and hotel reservations started to offer online services and had attracted clients from worldwide. Additionally, in 1997, a handful of Web sites in a few big cities in China also started to sell books to local customers. This dispute depends to a large extent on how one defines e-commerce and how one understands the transaction processes in China. The few instances given by Chen Yan (1999) were not exactly e-transactions since they still very much depended on the conventional face-to-face mode to complete. In the travel reservation case, an individual expressed the intent to book a room or an airline ticket, but the transaction was not complete until that person went to a designated physical place to make the payment. The main reason was that there was not a sophisticated online payment system in place in China, and credit cards were not widely used by Chinese consumers. But since then, e-commerce sites have mushroomed and expanded to include a variety of products and services. Regardless of their targeted market, these early e-commerce initiatives were very limited in scope of services and restricted in approaches. Most of them were designed to advertise their services and products to attract offline businesses rather than to complete transactions online.

Some heavy-weight players came onto the stage in 1999. On March 10, Alibaba.com, the first B to B (Business to Business) Web site in China, went online amid much fanfare. In less than a year, it made a big splash in China's emerging e-commerce market. Jack Ma, the founder of Alibaba.com, was featured on the cover of the July issue of *Forbes*, the first time a Chinese entrepreneur had ever had this honor;[33] moreover, for two consecutive years (2000 and 2001), Alibaba.com was named the "Best of the Web: B 2 B." Also in 1999, another big player in China's e-commerce market, 8848.com, the first major B to C (Business to Customer) online mall, went into operation on May 18. Within the same year, 8848 quickly became the most influential B2C online entity (China E-Commerce Yearbook 2002: 13).

These two were soon joined by other big names, such as Ease.com, Sohu.com, Yabuy.com, and EachNet.com, in China's online business arena. A 2000 CCINnet survey by the China Center for Information Industry Development under the Ministry of Information Industry (MII) indicated that as of 1999, there were about 600 Web sites carrying out e-commerce activities of one kind or another, and the number increased to 1,100 Web sites (out of 16,000 total Web sites in China) in 2000. Of these sites, 800 were online shopping, 100 online auction, 180 online remote educational, and 20 online medical care sites. Out of the 800 online shopping sites, one third was engaged in traditional retail operations while two thirds offered online services exclusively.[34] The latest statistics show that as of 2004, the number of Web sites specializing in e-commerce in China has risen to 4000, and China's Internet Data Center (IDC) estimates that domestic revenue from e-commerce amounted to US$60 billion in 2003.[35] Just two years ago, China's e-commerce market was still valued at US$5.6 billion.[36]

This staggering growth rate, in all likelihood, is to continue in the years to come. At least, this belief was shared by most of the about 1000 big players of Chinese e-commerce, who met in Hangzhou to attend China's first Network Merchant Convention from June 12 to 13, 2004. They proclaimed China to be entering the "era of network merchants," with over 6 million Chinese netizens having attempted commercial activities online, and 22 percent of China's 1.1 million medium and small enterprises being engaged in online commerce.[37] In May 2004, Alibaba.com, a primary business-to-business Chinese Web site, announced that it had 3.5 million members, with an addition of 9000 newcomers every day.[38] The explosive trend of online commerce was also corroborated by the latest CNNIC semiannual surveys of China's Internet development. Its 16th Statistical Survey Report released in July 2005 put the number of Chinese individuals who had made purchases online at 20 million, or about 20 percent of the total Internet population (CNNIC 16th Statistical Survey Report on the Internet Development in China, 2005). As the latest government effort to create a favorable legal framework for China's booming e-commerce, the National People's Congress, China's top legislature, passed the Law on Electronic Signature, which legalizes electronic signatures and grants contracts signed on the Internet the same legal authority as paper contracts.[39]

However, China's e-commerce development is still in infancy stages; the e-market remains immature because both consumers and enterprises still look at online transactions with a suspicious eye and prefer traditional business transaction modes in most cases.[40] The great potential in the huge Chinese market opened up by e-commerce has been limited by several crucial factors, as many have noted (e.g., Chen Yan, 1999; China E-Commerce Yearbook, 2002: 15–19; Chvaja, Mokudai, and Efendic, 2001; Jeffrey, 2000; Makawat-sakul et al., 2001; Wong and Nah, 2001). In addition to the comparatively low penetration of the Internet in the nation (about 7.9 percent of China's 1.3 billion people had access to the Internet as of June 2005), there are several major hindrances to the spread of e-commerce in China: first, the country still lacks a sophisticated nationwide credit card or electronic payment system; second, a dependable delivery system has not been established so most online sites only serve local customers; third, customer service for most online service providers remains unsatisfactory and slow in responding to customer requests; fourth, a legal framework for protecting online consumers is lacking; fifth, most Chinese still don't trust the novel e-environment and prefer to conduct business face-to-face or rely on personal relationships or connections.

A recent article about China's current e-commerce status summarized the major formidable challenges faced by Internet firms in China this way: "poor payment systems, inefficient infrastructure and consumer reluctance to shop online."[41] Additionally, China's currency, the RMB, is still not freely convertible to other major global currencies, which stops China's e-commerce activities from being truly transnational in nature. China's entry into the WTO has not had any significant impact on the solution of these problems as of now; in the long term, however, its entry into the WTO may help promote an overall e-commerce-friendly environment. Nonetheless, these issues have caught the attention of the government bureaucracies, which have vowed to find solutions so as to build a brighter future for China's e-business.

Globalization of China's Internet Sector

One commonly held expectation is that, with the further integration of China's Internet industry with the world market, significant changes may be inevitable in the long run because if Chinese online businesses are to survive, they have to adopt standardized global business practices (e.g., management, financing, accountability to investors or stockholders) in the globalized Internet market, especially in the context of increasing cash inflow from overseas investors. As an integral part of its economic liberalization plan, the Chinese government has made a sustained effort to promote the development and use of information technologies in all industries and professions across the nation, and it has been keen to boost China's global profile politically and economically in its national Internet strategy. The government is well aware that this is the only way to win recognition and cooperation, and attract urgently needed foreign investments.

On July 12, 1999, when China's Internet was still at an early developing stage, China.com, the Hong Kong-based Internet company, which has a prominent presence in China's Internet market, became the first Chinese Internet business to list on the technology-driven NASDAQ in the United States (NASDAQ: CHINA). China.com, called the "Chinese answer to America Online," is a leading pan-Asian Internet company offering web solutions, portal and online advertising services, and a full range of Internet services around the Asia Pacific region. Its portal site in the mainland, www.china.com, has been the most successful of its all Web initiatives; it offers news, entertainment, free e-mail, chat rooms, online shopping, and many other services. Its mainland hit led the BBC to call it "China's Cultural Revolution on the Web."[42] Driven by its success in mainland China and the prospect of the forthcoming growth of the Internet in China, China.com's initial public offering at NASDAQ was a roaring success; its opening price of $20 rose to a high of $66 on its first day of trading.[43]

Nearly a year later, encouraged by China.com's NASDAQ success, the Chinese government gave permission to three of the top mainland-based Internet companies in their NASDAQ listings to raise capital. On April 13, 2000, the first "pure" China-concept Internet public offering, Sina.com, was listed on NASDAQ after a lot of fanfare (NASDAQ: SINA). Sina.com was (and remains) a leading Internet media and services company for Chinese communities worldwide, offering online news, entertainment, and community and e-commerce services, and it was the most visited online destination in China. Set at $17 a share, its stock price rose almost 22 percent at $20.69 on its first trading day on a stock market recently shaken by deep losses with NASDAQ stock index slipping from over 5000 in March to 3676 in mid-April of 2000.[44]

On June 30, 2000, Netease.com, which was the second most popular Web site in China at the time, averaging 20 million page views a day, made its debut on NASDAQ at US$15.05 a share (NASDAQ: NTES). Netease.com began in 1997 as a community site, bringing together users through chat rooms, online auctions, e-mail, and instant messaging. However, the market did not bode well for Netease.com, with its stock price closing at $12.125 on its first day of trading, a drop of nearly 22 percent — sending shivers down the spines of young Internet entrepreneurs who saw an overseas listing as their only hope of survival.[45] That had to do to a great extent with the timing, because the Internet bubble on Wall Street was already on a downward turn at the time.

About two weeks later, on July 12, 2000, Sohu.com, a Beijing-based premier online portal attracting the third largest traffic in China, became the fourth China-concept Internet entity to be listed on NASDAQ (NASDAQ: SOHU). Sohu.com, founded by MIT-educated Charles Zhang in 1996, offers a variety of news and information, commerce, and community services. It opened at US$13.031 and ended at US$13.062 on its first day of trading.[46]

Unlike China.com whose IPO occurred at a time when the global Internet fever was still on the rise, the timing for the Internet gold trough of Sina.com, Sohu.com, and Netease.com was not ideal. Externally, it was the start of souring sentiment toward dot-com companies on NASDAQ after months of the Internet bubble, and public confidence in the future of dot-com enterprises was mixed. Internally, it was a time when the Chinese authorities had taken a series of intensified measures to tighten their control of the Internet, which dampened the international speculation of whether the predicted blossoming of China's Internet market would materialize.

When the Internet bubble burst and the dot-com myth was gone, the China Internet concept stocks were among the victims. In mid-2001, all NASDAQ trading prices of three China-based Internet companies, Sina.com, Netease.com, and Sohu.com, fell below the $1 mark and faced the uncertainty of being removed from the NASDAQ list. Eventually, all three hung on, and as the market started to recover, they gradually rebounded to the double digit level in late 2002. In 2003, profits and revenue were reported as increasing rapidly for all three, with Netease.com taking the lead.[47] Their ups and downs on NASDAQ are a clear reminder that China's Internet economy is not immune to the fluctuations in the world market.

Another landmark event that will not only speed up China's implementation of a Western-style market economy but also fundamentally transform China's Internet landscape is China's membership in the WTO. On November 15, 1999, after 15 years of arduous, on-and-off negotiations, China and the United States signed a bilateral agreement on China's accession to the WTO; on May 19, 2000, China completed its WTO talks with the European Union. China's bilateral negotiations with all WTO members were concluded on September 13, 2001, after reaching agreement with the last country, Mexico. The WTO Ministerial Conference approved China's terms of membership on November 11, 2001, in Doha, Qatar, and China officially became a member on December 11, 2001.[48]

Telecommunications, including the Internet, had been a major area of negotiation in the process of China's WTO bid. In the China–U.S. accord concerning the WTO deal, the Chinese government will allow 49 percent foreign ownership in telecommunications companies immediately after accession into the WTO, followed by 50 percent after two years; with the Internet, foreign firms will be allowed to invest in Internet content providers, such as Sohu.com and Sina.com, and international companies will be allowed to buy 49 percent of Chinese Internet firms starting when China entered the WTO, then 50 percent in two years.[49] China's concessions in allowing foreign investment in the telecommunications industry would set off a new round of rapid Internet growth after Beijing's entry into the WTO, Charles Zhang, CEO of

Sohu.com predicted, because major hurdles in attracting foreign capital to China's Internet companies would be removed.[50] Recent commercial moves by Internet giants Yahoo.com, Amazon.com, and eBay.com have demonstrated the attraction of the enormous potential of the Chinese Internet market to Western Internet businesses.

China's WTO membership paved the way for the next phase of its Internet development, which will witness more presence of Western investments in the Chinese Internet market. On June 12, 2003, eBay, the biggest global online auction company based in the United States, announced that it had acquired a two-thirds share of the Shanghai-based auction site EachNet.com for about US$150 million. EachNet is the largest online auction business in China and boasted 2 million active users as of June, 2003. Since eBay had already bought one third of EachNet.com for US$30 million earlier, the new deal means that eBay becomes the sole owner of EachNet.com. A spokesman from eBay said that the potential of the huge Chinese market and eBay's business model were the driving reasons for the acquisition.[51] In early 2004, EachNet started the process of integrating its transaction platform with that of the U.S.-based eBay with which EachNet's users can register as eBay users and through which China's 5.5 million registered users on EachNet can trade with eBay's 104.8 million registered users in 27 countries and regions (as of March 2004). Shao YiBo, founder and CEO of EachNet, noticed an ongoing but accelerating improvement with China's transportation and banking systems, which have reduced delivery time and greatly facilitated money transfers.[52]

At the same time, other leading international companies are vigorously promoting their presence in the Chinese Internet market. On June 15, 2004, Baidu.com, the leader in China's search engine market, received US$10 million from the global leader in the market, Google. A few days later, Google's archrival, Yahoo launched a search engine portal Yisou.com dedicated to Internet searches in China, the first time that the U.S. company had registered a new Web site for its search engine service outside the United States.[53] Multinationals from other countries did not delay in following U.S. companies in grabbing a slice of the expanding pie of the Chinese Internet market. Rakuten Inc., a Japan-based Internet retailer, became the second largest stakeholder in Cstrip.com by acquiring a 20.4 percent share in its stocks with US$110 million in June 2004, and NHN Corp., a South Korean portal Web site, signed a cooperative agreement with SeaRainbow Holding Corp., the largest online game portal in China, to invest up to US$100 million to establish a 50–50 joint venture in the country.[54] In a recent development, the global online retailer giant Amazon.com Inc. announced on August 19, 2004, that it acquired China's first business-to-commerce (B2C) company Joyo.com Ltd. for US$75 million.[55]

There is also surging interest among Chinese Internet businesses to realize their NASDAQ dreams. In early 2004, a dozen more Chinese Internet companies were considering IPO filings on NASDAQ to raise more dollars. Among them were eLong (a travel site), 51job.com (an Internet recruitment group), The9 (an online gaming company), Shanda Networks (an Internet game producer), Tencent (an instant messaging provider), Mtone (also an instant messaging provider), Harbor Networks (an Internet equipment maker), Alibaba. com (a portal site), and Hurray (a mobile messaging provider).[56] On December 9, 2003, Ctrip, a Chinese travel Web site, went public on NASDAQ and received a warm welcome from investors, with its share price rising 89 percent on the first day.[57] Meanwhile, more Chinese Internet companies succeeded in their bids for listings on NASDAQ. Linktone, a Shanghai-based company that provides ring tones, games, and other services to mobile phone users, made its debut on March 4, 2004, on NASDAQ, and its shares rose 30.71 percent on its first day of trading, allowing the company to raise US$85.96 million for business expansion in China.[58] On March 11, 2004, Tom Online, a leading mobile Internet company in China, opened its trading on NASDAQ and had a surprisingly low performance of 6.7 percent below the issuing price.[59] On May 13, 2004, Shanghai-based Shanda Interactive Entertainment Limited, China's biggest online games operator, raised US$154.2million through its initial public offering on NASDAQ.[60] Although Shanda did not have a glowing performance in the first days after its debut, it quickly gained full steam a few months later. In late August 2004, Shanda overtook all Chinese Internet stocks on NASDAQ to become the leader because of its astounding performance in the second quarter of 2004, as its sales reached RMB¥302 million (approximately US$37.7 million) by the end of June 2004.[61]

Clearly, during the fourth phase of Internet development in China, the road map has been created for the fast growth of the Internet and the role it will play in social and economic life as China continues its ambitious long march to digitization. The top Chinese leadership hopes that the Internet revolution will help upgrade China's business environment as China braces for the new millennium. Meanwhile, this is also a time when the Chinese authorities realize the potential challenges they face in regulating the flow of information in the untested waters of cyberspace, and the government started to implement a series of legal and technical frameworks to bring the World Wide Web under its control, as reviewed in the previous chapter.

This is also a time for Chinese Internet companies to reach beyond the Chinese border to curry favor with foreign investors. As the Internet market expands, Chinese businesses have an uphill battle to raise capital crucially needed for investment. Because of the limitations of the Chinese financial market, their natural target becomes foreign capital and stock markets. On the other hand, lured by the great potential of China's Internet sector, multinationals in the West are also stepping up their efforts to establish their presence in the Chinese market. As the Internet becomes fully integrated into the economic, political, and cultural life of mainstream Chinese society, the Chinese leadership will soon find out what is the inevitable next stage: China's

Internet can only survive and prosper by being part of, not being separated from, the globalized market. As has been the case with China's traditional industry, Chinese entrepreneurs of online businesses can only prosper with Western hard currency.

The marketization and the flow of foreign cash into the Chinese Internet industry naturally spell good news for Chinese businesses because the whole process brings in much-needed capital as well as Western models and ideas of management and operation. At the same time, this also brings new hopes for Chinese civil society. Survival and prosperity of businesses in a market-oriented environment can only be achieved by meeting the needs of consumers and by following the flow of the market. Consumer demands, instead of government ordinances, on most occasions, have become the driving force of change as quarterly reports and profit margins get reflected immediately in the stock market. The following incident may shed some light on the pressures that Chinese Internet companies face in the new era.

Starting in July 1998, the China Internet Network Information Center (CNNIC) added a new item in its semiannual survey of China's Internet development: it asked users to rank top Web sites and then released the information in its "Investigative Report of China's Most Influential Internet Websites." The Web sites that received more popular votes were given higher ranks, and the results undoubtedly put them in a more advantageous position to attract advertisers, to promote themselves to the users, and to become the favorite son of venture capital firms. Because there was an intense pressure for the major Web sites to perform well in the surveys, many of them engaged in irregular vote-chasing campaigns, such as carpet advertising for votes, asking users to vote multiple times, linking user votes to special online services, and even bribing users, friends, and relatives to cast votes. At the end of 2000, widespread corruption and cheating forced the CNNIC to discontinue its practice of ranking Web sites and to look for a "more scientific" way to survey users on this issue in the future.[62]

As is mentioned in Chapter 2, economic liberalization in China in the reform era has created social conditions favorable to Chinese civil society. Likewise, the opening of China's Internet sector will inevitably produce similar effects. The Internet will even play a much more significant role in the growth of Chinese civil society because, unlike economic reform whose focus is on turning bankrupt state-run enterprises into profit-making private undertakings, the Internet directly introduces a brand-new information environment of its own and creates a social space for citizens to access information and to communicate with one another. It is here that we see the liberating and revolutionizing effect of the Internet in Chinese society. We see in Chapter 3 that despite the government's all-out effort to control information flow on the Internet, Chinese individuals and social groups have successfully waged different campaigns on the Internet — sometimes in direct challenge to the regime's heavy-handed suppression and mistreatment of dissenting individuals or groups. More discussion of this emerging trend is provided in succeeding chapters.

Patterns of Internet Growth in China

The unstoppable trend of the Internet in China as it takes a great leap forward in the new century is best illustrated by actual figures of growth in the past few years. In a short period of less than a decade, the Internet has become a strong presence in many aspects of Chinese society. The entry of China as a major Net player in the cyberworld is now beyond doubt in any measure. This section maps out a path of growth in the diffusion of the Internet in China by relying on a series of survey reports from the China Internet Network Information Center (CNNIC).

Authorized by the State Council Information Work Leading Group and operated and managed by the Computer Network Information Centre under the Chinese Academy of Sciences, CNNIC was inaugurated on June 3, 1997, as the only organization providing realm name registration and automatic system signal allotment services to Internet users in China.[63] In November 1997, CNNIC released its first "Statistical Survey Report on the Internet Development in China," including information (as of October 1997) about the number of Internet users in China and their demographics, number of networked computers, amount of available bandwidth, and a host of other important online resources. Since 1998, CNNIC has continued to produce semiannual survey reports on the status quo of China's Internet. These reports constitute the most comprehensive, up-to-date, and authoritative information about the growth of China's Internet.

According to the 16th Statistical Survey Report on the Internet Development in China released by CNNIC on July 20, 2005, China had 103 million net surfers as of June 2005, making it the second largest online population in the world, trailing only behind the United States. The netizens accounted for about 7.9 percent of China's overall population, and Chinese surfers made up 10.8 percent of the estimated global users of 957.8 million (estimation by World Internet Stats as of September 2005) at the time.[64] However, compared with the penetration rate of the Internet of about 70 percent in the United States, China still has a long way to go to make the Internet an omnipresent tool in the everyday life of average citizens.

Figure 4.1 reports the growth pattern of Internet use in China from 1994 to mid-2005. In 1994, when the Internet was still a novelty in China, only 1,600 people used the Internet at all. That number increased to 80,000 in late 1997, but that still constituted a negligible fraction of over a billion Chinese citizens. There was a significant jump in 1998, which, as pointed out earlier in this chapter, was a dividing year for China's Internet expansion. By June 1998, there were 620,000 people connected to the Internet, which represented a 675

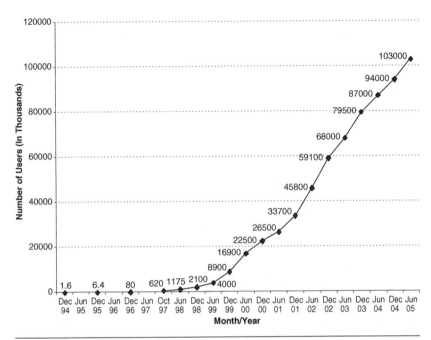

Figure 4.1 Growth of Internet users in China (1994–2005). From CNNIC Semi-Annual Statistical Survey Report on the Internet Development in China (1994–2005).

percent increase in eight months. Clearly, 1998 was a takeoff year for China's Internet growth. The skyrocketing trend of growth since then is obvious from the figure. By the end of 2002, China's 59.1 million Internet users represented 9 percent of the estimated global users of 655 million then,[65] and the percentage of Chinese netizens in the total world Internet population rose to 10.8 percent in mid-2005. This indicates that the growth rate of the Internet in China surpasses the general global growth rate during this period.

Figure 4.2 describes the growth of the number of computers connected to the Internet from 1997 to mid-2004. As of June 30, 2005, there were 45.6 million computers that were Internet accessible. Of those, 15 percent were connected to the Internet through dedicated lines, 45.4 percent had phone dial-up connections, while the rest were connected via other means (such as xDSL, cable modem, ISDN), indicating that telephone line dial-up was still the most popular means of Internet connectivity. From 299,000 networked computers in October 1997 to 45.6 million in June 2005, Internet connectivity has truly experienced a giant leap forward in merely eight years. It can be seen that the growth pattern of Internet-accessible computers and that of Internet surfers have followed quite similar paths of expansion during this period.

An important indicator of the flow of online traffic is the available bandwidth that serves as gateways to the global networks. As shown in Figure 4.3,

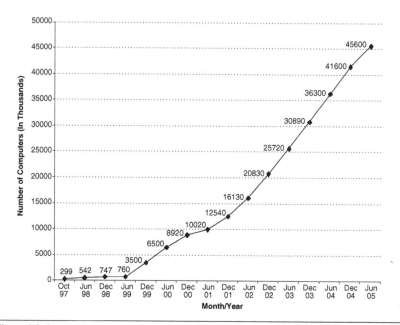

Figure 4.2 Growth of Internet-connected computers (1997–2005). From CNNIC Semi-Annual Statistical Survey Report on the Internet Development in China (1997–2005).

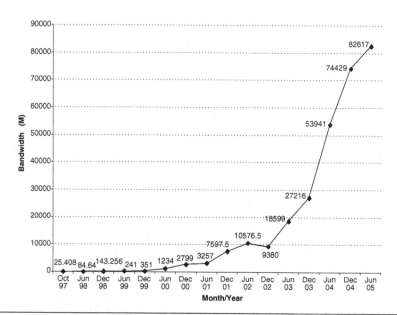

Figure 4.3 Internet bandwidth growth (1997–2005). From CNNIC Semi-Annual Statistical Survey Report on the Internet Development in China (1997–2005).

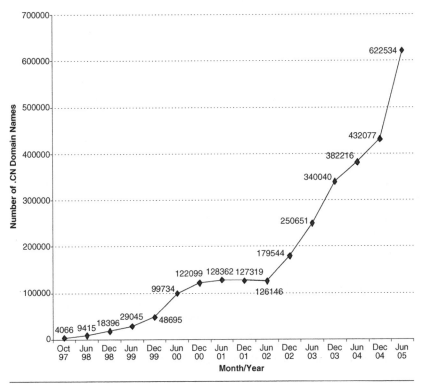

Figure 4.4 Growth of registered domain names in China (1997–2005) (excluding .edu domain names). From CNNIC Semi-Annual Statistical Survey Report on the Internet Development in China (1997–2005).

from 25 Mbps in October 1997 to 82.617 Mbps in June 2005, network traffic has been growing more than exponentially. The rate of bandwidth growth has noticeably surpassed the rate for the growth in such areas as the Internet population, connected computers, and domain names. It is also worth noting that major growth has occurred in the new millennium, which indicates that heavy government investment in network infrastructure has paid off.

The next two figures, Figure 4.4 and Figure 4.5, reflect the growth in the number of domain names registered under .cn and the growth in Web sites published in China from October 1997 to June 2005, respectively. There was a flattened period for both from the start of 2001 to mid-2002, a time of deepened downturn in the global IT market. The explosion of Internet bubbles worldwide clearly had had an impact on China's Internet growth, an indication that China's Internet market is not immune to the ups and downs of the industrialized nations.

A Chinese "digital divide" is observable among Internet users. As has been the case in the United States and other countries where the Internet is highly

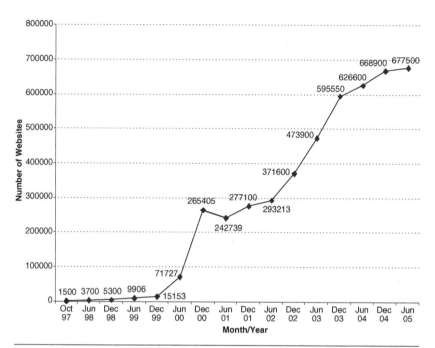

Figure 4.5 Growth in the number of Web sites (1997–2005). From CNNIC Semi-Annual Statistical Survey Report on the Internet Development in China (1997–2005).

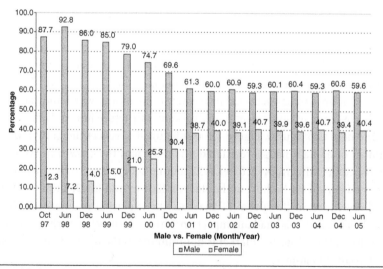

Figure 4.6 Growth patterns in gender distribution (1997–2005). From CNNIC Semi-Annual Statistical Survey Report on the Internet Development in China (1997–2005).

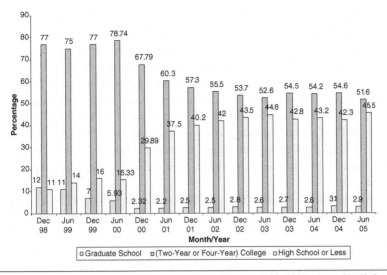

Figure 4.7 Growth pattern in users' educational background (1998–2005). From CNNIC Semi-Annual Statistical Survey Report.

diffused, a clear gender difference existed in the early days of China's Internet use. As observed in Figure 4.6, in the early years, the Internet was very much a male-dominated domain of activity. In October 1997, when the Internet was still at the takeoff stage in China, 87.7 percent of the Chinese netizens were male and only 12.3 percent were female. However, as time went by, more and more females joined the Internet bandwagon, and the gender gap gradually narrowed. In June 2005, 59.6 percent of China's Internet surfers were male, and 40.4 percent were female. So there has been an unmistakable trend toward equalizing gender differences.

Figure 4.7 reports the change in Internet users' educational background over the years. Because comparable questions were not included in the two surveys conducted prior to December 1998, the figure excludes the first two CNNIC semiannual survey reports. As the figure indicates, in the earlier years of China's Internet diffusion, Internet use remained the privilege of the well-educated — those who received a college degree or better. Noticeably, in December 1998 and June 1999, users who possessed a graduate degree (master's or doctorate) made up 12 and 11 percent of the total cohort of the Internet population. As the years went by, we see a general trend of a gradual increase in the number of netizens who only possessed a high school education or less; meanwhile, the proportion of graduate school and college degree holders in the online population display a trend of decrease. As of June 2005, we can see that the majority of Chinese netizens possessed a college degree (51.6 percent); yet there was also a large proportion of the netizens who were high school graduates (31.3 percent) or had less education (14.2 percent). It should be pointed out that of those whose education level was categorized as below high school, many were still high school students.

A comparison with the structure of the population makeup during this period may illustrate the elite nature of China's online population. The data from three recent China's official population censuses show that in 1990, only 1.42 percent of the Chinese population (age 15 and older) had completed a college education or graduate school (China Population Statistical Yearbook, 1990); in 1997 and 2000, that percentage increased to 2.53 and 3.61, respectively (China Population Statistical Yearbook, 1997 and 2000). Therefore, Chinese netizens are overall much better educated than the general populace over the years.

China's Internet surfers are typically not only well-educated, but young as well. In CNNIC's first Survey Report on China's Internet Development conducted in late 1997, it was found that young people aged 21 to 35 dominated China's net surfers (78.5 percent), followed by the 36 to 50 age group (11.1 percent) and the 20 or below group (5.6 percent). Figure 4.8 reports the change in age distribution in China's Internet population. Because comparable questions are only available from CNNIC's semiannual survey reports released in January 2000 and later, a longitudinal examination of the data for this period is reported in Figure 4.8. It can be seen that over the years, the 18 to 24 age group has been leading China's net population, followed by the 25 to 30 group. In particular, there was an abrupt growth in the adolescent group in the second half of 2000, with an over 10 percent increase in the overall makeup of the net population. The growth pattern has been stabilized since then. In general, Chinese cyberspace is still dominated by the younger generation; people in their 40s are not totally invisible on the Internet, while those who are 51 or older are more inclined to shy away from the cyberworld.

There also have been regional differences in Internet use and available online resources. Year-by-year analysis show a persistent pattern of differences among the various Chinese geographic regions, and this pattern shows substantial change in the fourteen CNNIC survey reports. To better understand the nature of regional differences in the diffusion of the Internet in China, I have incorporated into my analysis the recent results of China's modernization studies conducted by the China Modernization Strategy Research Group and the China Modernization Research Center of the Chinese Academy of Sciences, which summarize their findings in a recently published book titled *China Modernization Report 2004*. In the book, the Chinese researchers developed a comprehensive modernization index based on indicators in the areas of economic and industrial developments, quality of life, and knowledge production and dissemination to describe the current levels of modernization in China's three regions, which are further divided into eight areas (see Table 4.1). The studies conclude that as of 2001, three Chinese metropolises, Beijing, Shanghai, and Tianjin, had already entered a moderately developed

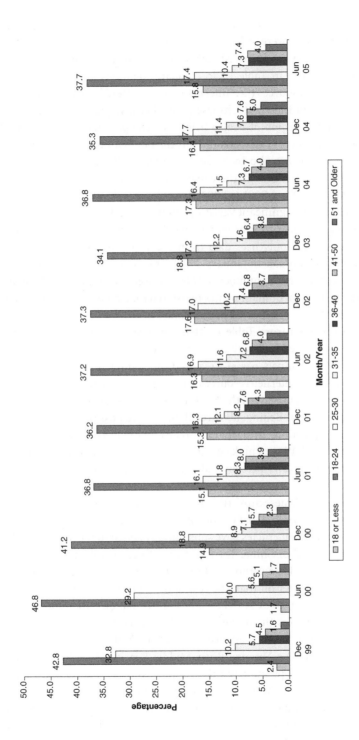

Figure 4.8 Change in age distribution of China's Internet population (1999–2005). From CNNIC Semi-Annual Statistical Survey Report on the Internet Development in China (1999–2005) on the Internet Development in China (1998–2005).

stage, while eleven provinces were at the initially developed stage, and seventeen provinces were still underdeveloped (China Modernization Strategy Research Group & China Modernization Research Center, 2004). I have included the data in Table 4.1 to compare the levels of modernization with their Internet resources (i.e., Internet users, registered .cn domain names, and WWW sites) in the eight Chinese areas. Because population density varies from region to region, it is also helpful to compare these domains with the actual population of each region. Thus the population distribution data from the 2002 census are also included in the table (China Population Statistical Yearbook, 2002). Although there may have been some slight fluctuations from region to region from 2001 to 2003, these changes should be negligible enough to not cause any significant variations in the overall patterns.

Because the year-to-year pattern has been very consistent over the years, my analysis here only uses data from the 15th CNNIC semiannual survey report (made available in January 2005). The three areas of Internet resources compared here are the number of Internet users, the number of WWW sites, and the number of domain names registered under .cn (excluding .edu) by the end of 2004. All are reported in percentages.

It can be seen from Table 4.1 that the three areas whose modernization indexes are ranked higher than the national average — the Northern Coastal Area, the East China Coastal Area, and the South China Coastal Area — all enjoy a level of Internet resources that is proportionately higher than their population percentages. In the Northern Coastal Area, led by the cultural and political capital of Beijing, all three domains are positively out of proportion with the population. In particular, registered Chinese .cn Internet domain names and WWW sites make up an unusually large proportion of all domain names in China (27.9 percent and 26.2 percent against a population base of 14.2 percent).

Because all Chinese ministries and central government agencies are located in Beijing, it is expected that various Web sites and domain names sponsored by these official bureaucracies have substantially added to the number of domain names registered in China. The East China Coastal Area led by Shanghai has been the economic powerhouse of the nation, and in general, people there are economically better off than the rest of the country, as indicated by the level of modernization index (45, the highest in the nation). Therefore, we see that this region achieves the highest ratio of Internet users versus its population base ($17.4/10.6 = 1.64$) as against those of the Yellow River Middle Reaches Area (0.62) and the Yangtze River Middle Reaches Area (0.67). About one tenth of China's population in this area possess over one fifth of the registered domain names and one quarter of the number of Web sites in the country. The South China Coastal Area comes third in terms of Internet resources it owns. Guangdong Province, which has been a window to China's economic reform

Table 4.1 Regional differences in socio-economic development and Internet resources

Region	Area	Provinces	Modernization Index[a]	Population (%)[b]	Internet Population (%)	.cn Domain (%)[c]	WWW Sites (%)
Northern	Northeast Area	Liaoning, Jilin, Heilongjiang	37	8.3	8.2	5.4	4.9
	Northern Coastal Area	Beijing, Tianjin, Hebei, Shandong	44	14.2	19.5	27.9	26.2
	Yellow River Middle Reaches Area	Henan, Shanxi, Shannxi, Inner Mongolia	31	14.8	9.2	4.1	3.9
Southern	East China Coastal Area	Shanghai, Jiangsu, Zhejiang	45	10.6	17.4	23.0	27.7
	South China Coastal Area	Fujian, Guangdong, Guangxi, Hainan	33	13.2	19.6	19.5	25.5
	Yangtze River Middle Reaches Area	Hubei, Hunan, Jiangxi, Anhui	30	18.0	12.2	5.2	6.3
Western	Southwest Area	Chongqing, Sichuan, Guizhou, Yunnan, Tibet	27	15.7	10.8	4.8	4.5
	Northwest Area	Gansu, Qinghai, Ningxia, Xinjinang	29	4.4	3.1	1.3	1.0
Total			31[d]	99.2[e]	100	91.2[e]	100

Notes: Data about the modernization index come from "China Modernization Report 2004" (China Modernization Strategy Research Group & China Modernization Research Center of the Chinese Academy of Sciences: 2004). Data about Internet population, domain names, and number of Chinese Web sites are from CNNIC's 15th Statistical Survey Report on the Internet Development in China (released in January 2005).

a The modernization index is a comprehensive index taking into account factors involving industrialization, informational infrastructure, knowledge creation, knowledge distribution, quality of life, and economic development. The index data are based on statistics for the year 2001.

b Percentage of the national population is based on China Census Bureau data for the year 2002.

c Excluding edu.cn domain names.

d This is the national average for the year 2001.

e Totals for these two categories do not add up to 100 because the CNNIC report also includes information from Hong Kong and Macao.

and has led all other provinces in its high speed of economic growth in the reform era, is the leader in this area.

Among the areas that register a level of modernization index higher than the national average, the Northeast Area is the only exception in this pattern. While the percentage of its Internet population roughly matches that of its overall population (8.2 percent vs. 8.3 percent), its registered domain names and the Web sites published in this area are lower than its population level. The reason for this deviation from the general pattern is that the three provinces here, Liaoning, Jilin, and Heilongjiang, are all traditional industrial bases for the country. They had a glorious history in the early phase of China's industrialization effort up to the reform era. In the past two decades, the advantages of these three provinces have been gradually dwindling as China's pace of privatizing its ill-managed and money-losing state enterprises has accelerated. These state enterprises make up the mainstay of the area's industry. China's Northeast Area has been a hotbed for workers' protests and demonstrations in the last decade as more and more workers have lost their jobs and retirees have been unable to get their pensions from bankrupt enterprises. However, a sophisticated industrial infrastructure and a well-trained work force remain potential advantages for this area in its future development. It is precisely for this reason that China's new administration has declared the revitalization of the Northeast Area to be a national strategy.[66]

The four areas whose modernization indexes are on or below the national average are all geographically inland and economically backward provinces, and they lag behind the coastal areas in economic achievement. As a result, they are disproportionately undeveloped in the availability of Internet resources; they are truly China's wild west waiting to be explored in cyberspace. The reasons are manifold: first of all, all the provinces in these four areas with the exception of Chongqing are China's traditional agricultural production bases, and they are economically underprivileged as compared with other parts of China, as they significantly trail the coastal provinces in terms of foreign investment, productivity, and annual GDP output; secondly, most provinces in these areas are mainly mountainous areas where the telecommunications infrastructure has been weak; thirdly, there is a large proportion of rural population in these areas and illiteracy rates are high.

The imbalance in regional Internet development is graphically represented in Figure 4.9, which presents data about the percentage of the population as well as the available Internet resources for the eight Chinese areas. Figure 4.10 illustrates the possession of digital resources by the top six provinces and provincial administrative metropolises in terms of economic development. For decades they have been leaders among the 30-plus provinces and centrally administered metropolises in their economic productivity, per capita income, and disposable expenses, and are far ahead of other regions in Internet development as well. These six provincial areas leading China's modernization drive

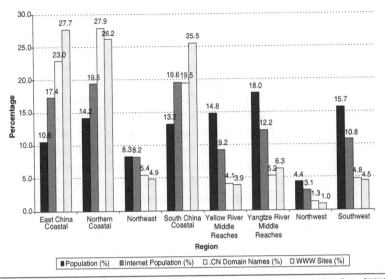

Figure 4.9 Regional distribution of Internet resources versus population (as of 2004). From CNNIC's 15th Statistical Survey Report on the Internet Development in China (released in January 2005).

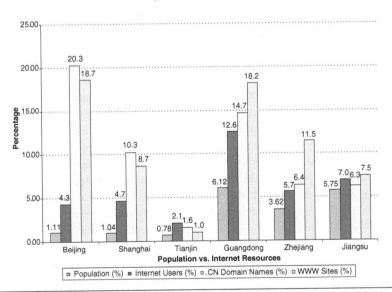

Figure 4.10 Leading provinces and metropolises in China's Internet development (as of 2004). Population data come from the 2002 census, and the Internet resources statistics are from the CNNIC semiannual Statistical Survey Report on the Internet Development in China released in January 2005, which covers data as of December 2004. These five provinces and metropolises are ordered by their levels of modernization index developed by the China Modernization Strategy Research Group and the China Modernization Research Center (2004).

were also leaders in China's Internet development. Although their aggregate population only accounted for about 18 percent of the national total, their available Internet resources as of December 2004 were all significantly above that percentage. The percentage of Internet users in these provinces more than doubled that of their population out of the national total, while registered .cn domain names and active WWW sites more than tripled their population proportion. When we compare the percentage of Internet users with the percentage of the population for each province, we can see that the level of modernization is the most important determinant of Internet use: Beijing has a modernization index of 67, and the ratio of its online population against the population base is 3.87, in Shanghai, which has a modernization index of 63, the ratio is 4.52, whereas Tianjin (modernization index of 50), Guangdong (modernization index of 39), Zhejiang (modernization index of 37), and Jiangsu (modernization index of 36) achieve a ratio of 2.69, 2.06, 1.57 and 1.22, respectively. In other words, in provinces where people are better off, there is a larger proportion of people connecting to the Internet. There is solid support for the relationship between development level and Internet use in each of the provinces and metropolises. As of December 2004, the proportion of Internet users in the overall population for the five leading provinces was: 27.6 percent for Beijing, 25.8 percent for Shanghai, 19.1 percent for Tianjin, 12.6 percent for Guangdong, 11.4 percent in Zhejiang, and 8.9 percent in Jiangsu (CNNIC's 15th Statistical Survey Report on the Internet Development in China, 2005), correlating perfectly to the order of their modernization indexes.

In a 2005 survey of Chinese citizens aged 16 to 65 in five Chinese cities conducted by CASS Social Development Research Center of the Chinese Academy of Social Sciences as part of the UCLA World Internet Project, respondents (Internet users as well as nonusers) were asked whether they think the Internet should be regulated and controlled, 36.8 percent of them agreed that it is very necessary to do so, and 45.6 percent concurred that it is somewhat necessary to do so. Whether one used the Internet is not a significant factor in determining responses to the question (CASS Social Development Research Center, 2005). But when asked to indicate the level of control they would like to see on different types of content, there is a substantial variation: 85 percent of the respondents agreed that online pornography is subject to regulation (very necessary or somewhat necessary), followed by violence on the Internet (73 percent), junk e-mail (62 percent), online advertising (33 percent), and Internet games (16 percent). However, the vast majority of them did not like to see any regulation or control over political content or online chatting, while only 8 percent agreed that it is very necessary or somewhat necessary to do so. Apparently, the general public in China is much more tolerant of political ideas than the Chinese regime is.

There is one significant point to be made about the current status of the diffusion of the Internet in China. As was mentioned before, the sixteenth

CNNIC semiannual survey puts China's net population at 103 million as of June 2005, which makes up roughly 7.9 percent of total Chinese population of 1.3 billion. This apparently indicates a very low penetration rate of Internet use in the country overall. However, China's Internet diffusion must be cast in the broad context of the particularities of China's national development. Here it is relevant to mention that the majority of China's population still lives in the rural areas where the telecommunication infrastructure is rather under-developed and illiteracy rate is still high. For the rural residents whose life depends very much on land farming, there is not much of a need for Inter-net connections, and commercial Internet service providers have no reason to invest in this portion of the Chinese population. More and more urban residents, by contrast, have the economic resources and need to go online, and they will be dominating China's Internet development for decades to come. Therefore, the priority of China's Internet strategy has been focused on the urban areas exclusively. According to China's National Bureau of Statistics, the Chinese urban population is about 389 million.[67] If all or most of the 103 million Internet users of 2005 were in the cities, this would put the rate of Internet penetration at approximately 26.5 percent, which provides a more realistic scenario to understand the Internet's diffusion in China.

The preceding description is highly consistent with the result from the CASS Social Development Research Center survey of residents in twelve Chi-nese cities in 2003, which shows that about 25 percent of the urban population in these cities was already online as of January 2003 (CASS Social Develop-ment Research Center, 2003). A follow-up survey of residents in five large Chi-nese cities in 2005 indicates that 49 percent of residents in these cities were Internet accessible (CASS Social Development Research Center, 2005). The large gap between the results from 2003 and 2005 are most likely attributable to two factors: first, the overall Internet population throughout the country has been growing fast during this period; second, the selection of specific cit-ies has contributed to the large difference between 2003 and 2005 surveys. The 2003 CASS survey includes three mega cities, four large provincial capitals, and five small cities, whereas the 2005 survey is based on three mega cities and two provincial capitals. Under most circumstances, the Internet in large cities is much more accessible than in small cities because of differences in infra-structure, residents' disposable income, as well as their information needs.

Finally, it is also worth mentioning the role of Internet cafés in the promo-tion of Internet services in China. In the CASS survey of Internet use of 2005, 29.7 percent of Internet users reported mostly accessing the Internet at public Internet cafés. CNNIC's sixteenth survey report shows slight variations, with the percentages of the respondents reporting often accessing the Internet at Web Internet cafés being 25.2 percent, and the majority of them connecting to the Internet at home (68.5 percent). The 2004 Morgan Stanley report projects the number of Internet cafés in China to be around 200,000 (as of the end of 2003), which connected about 5 million PCs to the Internet. Affordability of Internet cafés makes them popular. As the Morgan Stanley report notes, some Internet cafés in Chongqing charge only RMB¥0.30 (US$0.03 to 0.04) per hour, making them accessible to just about anyone who intends to surf. That the Internet is generally affordable in China is further supported by the CNNIC survey reports over the last few years. Its survey released in July 2005 found that the primary reason for people not to use the Internet had little to do with monetary issues, but lack of technical skills and perceived need. About 47 percent of the nonusers said they did not use the Internet because they lacked the necessary skills; 15.5 percent of them indicated that they opted not to go online because there was no need or use for them to do so, while only 7.5 percent said they did not connect to the Internet for economic reasons.

Chapter Summary

The Chinese government has displayed an unusual level of enthusiasm in embracing the Internet since the mid-1990s. The government has taken a series of important steps in laying the groundwork for the Internet revolution in China by investing heavily in the infrastructure and in promoting Internet use among its government agencies, businesses, and citizens. Meanwhile, China's Internet sector has achieved a staggering growth rate over the last decade by incorporating cutting-edge technologies from the West and by luring foreign venture capital into the exploding Chinese market. As of year-end 2003, China was the leader in three of the five core areas in technology, media, and telecommunications (TMT) markets: telephone lines, mobile phones, cable subscriptions. The United States took the lead in the other two areas: installed PC and Internet users. China is projected to be the leader of all five core areas within the next ten years (Morgan Stanley China Internet Report: 2003). All these five areas continue to experience spectacular growth in the new millennium.

From the analysis in this chapter, it can be seen that the general path of China's Internet development is not markedly different from that in the United States (UCLA Internet Report 2000; 2001; 2003; see also various Pew Internet Project Reports 2000 through 2003) and for that matter, most other nations that have embraced the Internet: education, income, age, and gender have played significant roles in determining who was likely to be online in the early stages of Internet diffusion, but there is a general equalizing trend in the long run as the Internet penetrates further into society. However, a digital divide, which is discernible among Internet users in all nations, has some particular Chinese twists: significant gaps in Internet connectivity exist among the different regions in China because of variations in economic development, telecommunications infrastructure, and available resources; mega and big cities enjoy many more resources in Internet connectivity. In addition, there has been a traditional, almost unbridgeable gap between the urban areas and vast rural regions in almost every aspect of life, telecommunications being no exception.

As Karsten Giese (2003) argues, the economic and social potential of the Internet has thus far been seriously limited by the fundamental disparities between regions; yet the government has shown neither the political will nor the financial resources needed to bridge the divide and to realize its self-acclaimed ambition of mobilizing the Internet to help alleviate poverty and close regional gaps. If the current policy of following the commercial interests generated by the Internet economy continues, there is no realistic hope of speeding up development in the backward areas and expanding Internet connectivity to the peripheral and marginalized segments of the Chinese population. There is a long, long way to go before China can bring the cyber-world to the majority of the rural population. On the other hand, it is the urban population that has been the most active in leading China's social and political revolutions in modern Chinese history. Therefore, it is with the urban population that we see the hope of the Internet for the revitalization of Chinese civil society in the Internet era. Evidence from the latest surveys of Chinese Internet users has shown us unequivocally that the Internet has become an important part of Chinese social life in terms of information access and expansion of communicative space.

5

Communication, Empowerment, and the Emergence of Network Public Opinion in Chinese Cyberspace

Fueled by the explosive development of the Internet and related technologies in the past decade or so, interest in their economic, social, cultural, and political dimensions has grown exponentially among people with a wide spectrum of backgrounds and training. As computer-mediated communication systems, with the Internet at its lead, are "slouching toward the ordinary," as Susan Herring (2004) put it, we are witnessing a fundamental transformation that is led by the "mainstreaming of new media," to use Lievrouw's words (2004), as evidenced from various sources of survey data over the years (e.g., Rainie and Bell, 2004). As a result, "users' expectations about them have become more expansive and more routine" (Lievrouw, 2004: 11) because the new media have become ingrained in people's everyday life.

In 1996 Newhagen and Rafaefi made the observation that all forms of content and all sorts of people are congregating on the Net, and as a result, new modes of communication are born and reborn all the time. As the Internet passes the novelty stage and moves into all aspects of people's ordinary life (e.g., Wellman and Haythorthwaite, 2002), we are witnessing a ubiquitousness and "banalization" of the Internet and related technologies in society (Graham, 2004). What is needed from the research community is a set of new theoretical and methodological approaches to understand the cyberworld as a social space and how this new space fosters brand-new social relations and possibilities. Yet all this has to be accomplished on the premise that Internet communication is not isolated nor is it detached from the material life, but rather it is deeply rooted in existing social, political, and cultural practices. As Graham (2004: 20) suggests, all virtual domains and worlds are actually "physically embedded and located in real places." But on the other hand, the "technospaces" appropriated by new media technologies empower users to create dynamic, relevant, contingent, and contested spaces that are redefining the previous concepts of spatiality (Munt, 2001). It can be more theoretically and methodologically productive, as Walther, Gay, and Hancock (2005) appropriately point out, to study the Internet as media rather than as a medium. In other words, the Internet represents a rich terrain of human communicative activities and should not be conceptualized as a monolithic medium. Along that line, the examination of new forms of sociability, multifaceted uses of Internet-related technologies, and emerging trends of online engagement among individuals and social groups can lead to revealing perspectives on the revolutionizing effect of the Internet. Specifically, in studying the ongoing interaction of Chinese civil society and the Internet, we need to scrutinize how the Internet is redefining existing social relationships and fostering new ones under different social settings. This is where we see the greatest hope for the Internet as an empowering tool for Chinese civil society.

This chapter starts with the theoretical proposition that the Internet be approached as a brand-new social space, which I call the fourth place, to differentiate cyberspace from all previous communication technologies. Next I review current scholarship on the democratization potential of the Internet and how the Internet contributes to the formation of a particular type of Habermasian public sphere. The chapter then includes an analysis of the communicative and socializing power of the Internet in China, and ends with a discussion of the emergence of network public opinion in Chinese cyberspace.

The Internet as the Fourth Place

One area that is key to understanding the revolutionary impact of the Internet on individuals, social groups, organizations, and society at large concerns the fundamental differences between the Internet and conventional media in both the processes and results of communicative activities. Although there have been efforts to solicit public participation in their programs, communication via conventional mass media remains to a great extent one-way: audience members are largely left out in the communication process because the noninteractive and nonparticipative nature of conventional media, despite sustained efforts on the part of media professionals to increase public participation through live questions, phone call-ins, and on-site interactions. Raymond Williams, for example, suggests that broadcast technology, along with automobiles, actually fostered interactional density among members of society and led middle-class families to withdraw from public spaces of association and sociability to the seclusion of their private homes (Williams, 1974). Similarly, Mark Poster observes that "[c]ontemporary social relations seem to be devoid of a basic level of interactive practice which, in the past, was the matrix of democratizing politics" and that "the media, especially television but also other forms of electronic communication isolate citizens from one another and substitute themselves for older spaces of politics" (Poster, 1997; 217).

The Internet, on the other hand, marks a dramatic departure from all previous communication models: it not only enhances the conventional one-to-many communication but also fosters brand-new types of communication in which users' messages can be sent by a heterogeneous user base to a heterogeneous audience. In Internet-mediated communication, everyone is potentially a consumer as well as creator of information.

> What the Internet offers is a flexible communicative space that can be constructed and bent in an infinite number of ways by sufficiently moti-vated groups of people. The implications and significance of what these groups build depends on the shape that they give to the space they cre-ate, and the relationships produced within it.
>
> (Feenberg and Bakardjieva, 2004: 39)

The nature of the Internet as a social space marks such a contrast to con-ventional mass media and makes it imminently relevant to the research of civil society in the new era. And this is where we see the greatest potential of the Internet — as a liberating force in civil society, especially in repressive regimes like China. As Chinese netizens become actively involved in the com-munication process, this fundamentally changes the platform of public com-munication, which used to be monopolized by officially sanctioned media as the sole source of information.

Thus traditional mass communication theories are inadequate to address the two-wayness of Internet connectivity and the interactiveness of computer communication systems (Shaw, Hamm, and Knott, 2000); and the dominat-ing research paradigm that simply treats users as audience(s) is questionable when looking at Internet use (e.g., Green and Adam, 2001). Because two of the most prominent properties of digital media are interactivity (in the technical sense, which creates a technological platform for users to interact with each other) and interaction (in the social sense, which refers to actual instances of users building relationships or forming ties in the digital world), it is no wonder that they also lie at the center of new media design and use. As Fornäs et al. note,

> Some recent digital technologies have radically enhanced these kinds of interactivity by explicitly emphasizing the user's response and active assistance in the formation of the media text itself and by developing par-ticular tools to facilitate this. The whole "cyber"-metaphors … stresses individual steering by the media-user, and thus puts interactivity at the core of reception … Recent digital techniques are thus not the only inter-active ones, but it is true that their particularly great potential of induc-ing interactive uses has further problematized some habitual boundaries in media research which have long deserved to be questioned.
>
> (2002: 23–24)

Therefore, in the new media environment, there is a particular need to rein-vigorate the dual aspects of audience research — reception and consumption — because the concept of "active audience" takes on a new meaning

(Livingstone, 2004). Caplan (2001) argues that computer-mediated communication has spawned a set of entirely new and radically different communication phenomena, which he terms "hyperpersonal communication systems," in addition to extant mass and interpersonal systems. These hyperpersonal communication systems resist classification within existing interpersonal or mass communication systems, and current theoretical perspectives in either interpersonal or mass communication constrain, rather than enlighten, our understanding of their nature and consequences.

In this regard, Bolter and Grusin's (1999) idea of remediation is worth noting. As an apparent effort to revise Marshall McLuhan's seminal work *Understanding Media* (1964) in the new media environment, they propose the idea of remediation in demythicizing new media forms. "Remediation," according to Bolter and Grusin, is "the formal logic by which new media technologies refashion prior media forms" (p. 273), and is a "defining characteristic of the new digital media" (p. 45). Every new digital medium pays homage to, and re-represents its predecessor; computer networks, however, have the power to remediate all previous media forms into one platform:

> As a digital network, cyberspace remediates the electric communications networks of the past 150 years, the telegraph and the telephone; as virtual reality, it remediates the visual space of painting, film, and television; and as social space, it remediates such historical places as cities and parks and such "nonplaces" as theme parks and shopping malls. Like other contemporary telemediated spaces, cyberspace refashions and extends earlier media, which are themselves embedded in material and social environments.
>
> (Bolter and Grusin, 1999: 183)

Bolter and Grusin's discussion focuses a lot on digital visual technologies, such as computer graphics, photography, video games, and film, and it does not delineate much about the textual representational aspects of the Internet. To this date, the Internet still remains largely dominated by a text-based interactive communication medium, although other emerging video and graphic capabilities may open up a lot of new opportunities in the future. This is testified to by Howard Rheingold's (1993) groundbreaking book and three popular readers edited by Steve Jones (1995; 1997; 1998) on virtual community and cybersociety, all of which focus almost exclusively on text-based communication systems over the Internet. Moreover, the Internet as a new media format not only remediates existing media forms, but it also radically transforms existing media types and brings in new potentials in fostering social relationships and connections in many cases. This is an area that warrants close scrutiny as new forms and technologies continue to unfold.

Feenberg and Bakardjieva summarized the general findings of research on the socializing effect of the Internet into "two durable results":

> First, studies of the origin and functions of online groups demonstrate the remarkable power of the medium to enable new forms of sociability. Second, studies that inquire into the motives for joining and contributing to these groups demonstrate consistently that online participation offers unique opportunities for actively and interactively pursuing identity-related projects that used to be impossible, and even inconceivable.
>
> (Feenberg and Bakardjieva, 2004: 40)

Because "[u]sers approach the medium [the Internet] ... from a variety of situational motivations, needs and ideologies" and in so doing "they generate a rich repertory of use genres, each of which needs careful consideration and evaluation on its own merits," what is needed in researching Internet use, Bakardjieva argues, is "discerning, recognizing and articulating the empowering aspects of the technology as they arise out of the everyday lives of real people in particular situations" (2003: 310–311). Studying the empowering aspects of the Internet and other new communication technologies in the everyday lives of civil society groups accomplishes precisely this purpose.

Although the Internet serves for most of its users and on many occasions as a venue for information (e.g., news, entertainment, commercial messages), much of its transformative power lies in its ability to act as a social space where people gather, interact, gossip, banter, play games, and do many, many more things that groups do. As Roger Slack and Robin Williams (2000: 330) conclude in studying a community information service, "the space of flows enters into a dialectic with the space of places, articulating a novel mode of representation tied to neither but trading on the potentialities afforded by both."

Therefore, to better capture the socializing effect and the uniqueness of the Internet, I here propose a more radical view to understand cyberspace as the fourth place. My theoretical proposition is primarily inspired by Ray Oldenburg's (1997) discussion of the third place, the "Great Good place" where people hang out for the pleasure of good company and lively conversation, and where community, citizenship, and grass-roots democracy come to life. This is how Oldenburg describes the third place, which provides "the core settings of the informal public life":

> The third place is a generic designation for a great variety of public places that host the regular, voluntary, informal, and happily anticipated gatherings of individuals beyond the realms of home and work ... It is neutral, brief, and facile. It underscores the significance of the tripod and the relative importance of its three legs. Thus, the first place is the home — the most important place of all. It is the first regular and predictable environment of the growing child and the one that will have

greater effect upon his or her development. It will harbor individuals long before the workplace is interested in them and well after the world of work casts them aside. The second place is the work setting, which reduces the individual to a single, productive role. It fosters competition and motivates people to rise above their fellow creatures. But it also provides the means to a living, improves the material quality of life, and structures endless hours of time for a majority who could not structure it on their own.

(Oldenburg, 1997: 16)

The ranking of the three places (home, work, and the third place) is appropriate, Oldenburg argues, because it corresponds with individual dependence on them. This ranking, he further contends, also correlates with the demands of time and attention in an individual's life.

Third places, such as the German beer garden, Main Street, the English pub, the French café, the American tavern, and the Chinese teahouse, all share a set of common features that are summarized by Oldenburg thus:

Third places exist on neutral ground and serve to level their guests to a condition of social equality. Within these places, conversation is the primary activity and the main vehicle for the display and appreciation of human personality and individuality. Third places are taken for granted and most have a low profile. Since the formal institutions of society make stronger claims on the individual, third places are normally open in the off hours, as well as at other times. The character of a third place is determined most of all by its regular clientele and is marked by a playful mood, which contrasts with people's more serious involvement in other spheres. Though a radically different kind of setting from the home, the third place is remarkably similar to a good home in the psychological comfort and support that it extends.

(Oldenburg, 1997: 42)

Third places are where people are most themselves and where participation and exit are voluntary. As a home-away-from-home, the third place plays a crucial role in a quality community life. Freedom of association and assembly lie at the heart of third places, and that is why they are so essential to the political process of a democracy. One cannot find a better example than the fact that the American Revolution had its origins in the local taverns of the colonial era, Oldenburg notes. He points out that it is because of the political potential of the third places that totalitarian regimes have been so unfriendly to them throughout history. Yet, just as Robert Putnam bemoans the steady decline of social capital in America in the past decades, Oldenburg decries the deterioration of the third place in American life as more and more people withdraw from the collective experience in the community and opt to the confined space of private life. The restoration of public life, Oldenburg argues, requires a spawning of third places in the everyday life of average Americans.

The emerging cyberspace on the Internet has been characterized by many scholars as primarily a social place, as mentioned previously, mainly due to the radical departure of the Internet from all previous types of communication technologies. As Mark Poster notes,

> [W]hat the Internet technology imposes is a dematerialization of communication and, in many of its aspects, a transformation of the subject position of the individual who engages within it. The Internet resists the basic conditions for asking the question of the effects of technology. It installs a new regime of relations between humans and matter, and between matter and non-matter, reconfiguring the relation of technology to culture and thereby undermining the standpoint from within which, in the past, a discourse developed — one which appeared to be natural — about the effects of technology.

> (Poster, 1997: 215–216)

To put it another way, Poster explains,

> [T]he Internet is more like a social space than a thing so that its effects are more like those of Germany than those of hammers. The effects of Germany on the people within it is to make them Germans (at least for the most part); the effects of hammers is not to make people hammers … but to force metal spikes into wood … The problem is that modern perspectives tend to reduce the Internet to a hammer. In this grand narrative of modernity, the Internet is an efficient tool of communication, advancing the goals of its users who are understood as preconstituted instrumental identities.

> (Poster, 1997: 216)

The power of the Internet as a social space, it goes without saying, arises out of it connecting users from diversified backgrounds and it being used as a socializing tool. The empowerment of the Internet lies in its ability to allow different types of communication to take place — users are not only recipients but also participants in the communication process, and they can be informed, be entertained, maintain contact with old friends or make new friends, and interact with other users under different circumstances. Ball-Rokeach and Reardon (1988) have classified new media communication as "telelogic communication" in comparison with the "monologic communication" via traditional mass media and "dialogic" interpersonal communication. They have identified three types of telelogic communication relationships: (1) exchange telelogue (i.e., exchange of services or goods), (2) associational telelogue (i.e., the creation and maintenance of personal relations), and (3) debate telelogue (i.e., the expression of personal opinions).

In Oldenburg's third place "lively, scintillating, colorful, and engaging" conversation is "the cardinal and sustaining activity" (1997: 26). Likewise, Internet-mediated communication may take on the characteristics of conversational discussions among different user groups whose interests may extend to anything that exists in real life. For example, in his structural analysis of ongoing discussions in a Usenet newsgroup, Steven Schneider (1996) concludes that computer-mediated communication creates "the conversational arena" where discussions run their own course.

Yet social interaction in cyberspace is more than conversation. Oldenburg has listed a variety of activities and features of the third places in the physical world:

They are a "mixer" in that they draw different people together from the neighborhood.

They serve as "ports of entry" through which newcomers and old occupants meet each other.

They are located on "neutral ground" (so no one is burdened by the role of host or guest) where people feel at ease to associate with others, where cost of entry is minimal, and where participants can come and go as they please.

They also serve as "sorting areas" in that visitors to third places are exposed to others who may share their interests or who have totally different interests.

They are places where people seek entertainment and joy, yet they may also engage in serious debates on political and other issues whenever the occasions arise.

They are also places where people can accomplish things or organize actions to support themselves or others.

We see all of these activities and features manifest in social groups on the Internet. Therefore, there are striking similarities between third places in real life and the social space on the Internet. It is for this reason that some have classified cyberspace as a new type of third place (e.g., Rheingold, 1993; Schuler, 1996) or virtual "third place" (e.g., Horrigan and Rainie, 2001).

It is true that the social space that has been created on the Internet bears a lot of similarities to real-life communication prototypes and many online community-oriented projects have been modeled on real-life entities. However, to treat cyberspace as just another type of third place does not give us a good understanding of the uniqueness and specificity of Internet-mediated communication, which has stood out as a distinctive mode of socially transformative force in the new millennium. Kathleen Olson, for example, bemoans the limitations of treating cyberspace as a place (that is, a space in the normal sense of the word) and calls for "a more appropriate metaphor"

(2005: 17). Therefore, I propose to understand cyberspace as the fourth place for the following reasons.

First of all, as I have argued earlier in the chapter, the Internet has created a brand-new social space that is unlike anything in the history of human communication. It is then more appropriate and more fruitful to study the Internet as such rather than just view it as an extension of third places in the physical world. As argued earlier, computer-mediated communication spawns new communicative possibilities and cultivates new social relationships because it is fundamentally different from all other media types. As I pointed out in Chapter 1, Robert Putnam has blamed television for being partially responsible for the decline of social capital in America. Oldenburg agrees with Putnam and further extends his castigation to all media types for exerting a harmful and alien influence on third places in the United States. The heavy dependence on the mass media today, Oldenburg argues, alienates citizens from the informal public life in the community and downplays the socializing effect of third places. The Internet, however, is not only informational, but also participational. It brings people together and invites the participation of anyone who cares to participate.

Secondly, as mentioned at the start of the chapter, although Internet-based communication is deeply rooted in the existing material world, it extends beyond relations in the physical world and redefines them. Putnam, for example, sees the primary value of the Internet as a social force to broaden and strengthen existing physical communities (Putnam and Feldstein, 2003). Oldenburg, meanwhile, has displayed unmistakably strong neo-Luddite tendencies in his popular book and has specifically pinpointed such modern communication technologies as the telephone and television as part of the cause for the dwindling of third places in the life of average citizens today. Nowhere in his book did he mention the computer or the Internet or any type of computer-mediated communication. And I seriously doubt that Oldenburg will agree with those who equate gathering places in cyberspace with the third places he advocates.

Harold Innis argues that the impact of a communication medium has to be evaluated in terms of its emphasis on the idea of time or space:

> A medium of communication has an important influence on the dissemination of knowledge over space and over time and it becomes necessary to study its characteristics in order to appraise its influence in its cultural setting. According to its characteristics it may be better suited to the dissemination of knowledge over time than over space, particularly if the medium is heavy and durable and not suited to transportation, or to the dissemination of knowledge over space than over time, particularly if the medium is light and easily transported. The relative emphasis

on time or space will imply a bias of significance to the culture in which it is imbedded.

(Innis, 1951: 33)

Innis's emphasis on the aspects of time and/or space is particularly applicable to the understanding of the Internet as a social space because that is where the Internet drastically departs from all other types of media formats. In his analysis of the role that mass media play in controlling consciousness, organizations, and cultural expectations, Innis divides communication media into two types based on the biases they display in engendering social institutions and cultures: time-binding media (e.g., manuscripts and oral communication that are limited in distribution and that favor traditional authority) and space-binding media (e.g., print and electronic media that facilitate control over space and that favor the establishment of commercialism, empire, and technocracy). The World Wide Web was invented as a tool to break away from the constraints of time and space, as Tim Berners-Lee, the inventor of the Web, notes (Berners-Lee, 1999). The biggest breakthrough of the Internet, however, is that it not only binds time and space in a fashion that is unsurpassed by any of the previous media types, but it also tilts significant control from the establishment to individuals. Admittedly, big corporate powers and "big brothers" are as present as ever in cyberspace, but it must also be recognized that the Internet has brought about a level of empowerment for individual users that was unthinkable in the pre-Internet age.

Thirdly, and perhaps most important of all, the Internet as a social space has generated potential that no previous media form was able to achieve. When Tim Berners-Lee first conceptualized the World Wide Web, his primary interest was to make it a space that would not be bound by time or geographic space in terms of information sharing. What has been happening since the birth of the Web, however, is that it is increasingly used as a space for social interaction. The innovative use of cyberspace and the ties, social relations, and activities it engenders are what has revolutionized the Internet as a social arena. And more important, this is just the start of a future that is beyond anyone's imagination or design at this point.

In warning against falling into the extremist, one-sided traps of the "dystopian nightmares and utopian daydreams," James Katz and Ronald Rice propose the idea of syntopia and have provided empirical support through survey results and user studies over recent years (i.e., 1995–2000). They come to the conclusion that:

> [T]he Internet is a part of syntopia, a together place that allows people to pursue their interests but that is also a continuity with other aspects of their lives, including their technology of communication, such as mobile phones. At the same time, the Internet is not only a political

phenomenon but an expressive one as well. The same processes that draw people on the Internet and into social relationships can, in many cases, create new intellectual and artistic terrain for themselves and others to enjoy. We have argued that syntopia includes both individual and collective levels and that by looking at the total communication picture, not just one modality called the Internet, we can understand more accurately the social processes involving and revolving around the Internet.

(Katz and Rice, 2002: 352)

The last point is an important one because one can find evidence for any kind of argument for or against any perspective of the Internet. The Internet is not a monolithic object or tool for its users, and it is fair to say no two persons' experiences on the Internet are exactly alike. Only by looking at the collective experience and the emerging patterns can one gain a fuller understanding of the Internet. Katz and Rice have also demonstrated that, contrary to fears by some, the Internet is not anathema to social capital accumulation; rather, it contributes to social capital and enables new forms of social capital. Likewise, Jennifer Light (1999) argues that the Internet presents exciting opportunities to reinvigorate civic engagement in new ways. I pursue this point in greater detail in the following section.

Finally, to understand the Internet as the fourth place not only recognizes the distinctiveness of the Internet as a communication tool, it also calls attention to the uniqueness of the nature of the social space on the Internet. Online relationships often are borne out of, and complement, offline connections, but they are not exact duplicates of each other and cannot replace each other. In some cases, cyberspace leads to brand-new relationships that would not be possible in the offline world; and in other cases, online interactions strengthen offline ties. In all cases, the Internet is an alternative platform for the third places to form social relations and interactions. Especially in totalitarian regimes like China, the Internet has created possibilities that would otherwise not be possible in the physical third places by bringing people together and by allowing people to express themselves in various ways.

The Socializing Effect and Communicative Power of Internet Use in China

While the Internet has experienced staggering growth in China in recent years, it is also important to know what the users actually do online. I present an overview of online behavior among Chinese surfers by relying primarily on five recent survey reports: the CNNIC 14th and 16th Statistical Survey Reports on the Internet Development in China (released in July 2004 and July 2005, respectively) (hereafter referred to as the CNNIC 14th Report and the CNNIC 16th Report), the Survey of the Usage and Impact of the Internet in Twelve Chinese Cities conducted by the Research Center for Social Development of the Chinese Academy of Social Sciences and published in October

2003 (thereafter referred to as the CASS Internet Report of 2003), and a follow-up survey by the same center in five Chinese cities in 2005 (referred as the CASS Internet Report of 2005), and Morgan Stanley's The China Internet Report published in April 2004 (thereafter referred to as the Morgan Stanley Internet Report of 2004).

It should come as no surprise that reading online news, searching for information, sending and receiving e-mails, and navigating Web sites and homepages on the Internet are popular activities among Chinese Internet users. After all, the Internet is an ocean of information for anyone. However, it should be noted that socializing and community building also get most of the Chinese netizens online. As Morgan Stanley's The China Internet Report summarizes, "[t]he usage patterns [a large number of Chinese Internet users flock to chat rooms, BBS, and online forums] suggest the Internet has opened up venues for increased interaction in a culture where self-expression and interaction have not been hallmarks" (p. 14).

In the CASS Internet Reports of 2003 and 2005, Chinese respondents were asked to associate their perceptions of the Internet with one or more of the following metaphors: post office, shopping center, library, school, entertainment place, meeting place, and bank. The percentages of Internet users that viewed the Internet as a library were 59.4 percent (2003) and 39.9 percent (2005) respectively; some users also compared the Internet to a meeting place (48.2 percent vs. 41.1 percent), an entertainment place (47.8 percent vs. 41.5 percent), a school (31.9 percent vs. 23.5 percent), a shopping center (28.7 percent vs. 25.2 percent), a post office (14.8 percent vs. 14.5 percent). Only a very small proportion of China's Internet population viewed the Internet as a bank (6.6 percent vs. 8.6 percent), apparently because online banking is still at its early stage in the country. In the CASS survey of 2005, two more metaphors were added: to compare the Internet to an information center and a news medium. Chinese netizens mostly agreed with these two analogies: 60.2 percent regarded the Internet as a news platform and 84.5 percent considered the Internet to be an information center.

In Table 5.1 and Table 5.2, I have summarized the findings from the CNNIC's 14th and 16th survey reports and the CASS Internet Reports of 2003 and 2005 regarding the types of online activities Chinese Internet users perform. While the data were collected by two different organizations under totally different circumstances, the results are consistent enough to provide a glimpse of the Chinese Internet population: the Internet offers a venue for information, news, socialization, and entertainment, whereas only a small proportion of them engage in online shopping or banking. The discrepancies between the findings in the two reports may be due to two factors. First, the two sources gathered data from two different sample pools. CNNIC's reports used national samples from all over the country with both online and offline data gathering, while the CASS Internet Reports relied on probability

Table 5.1 Popular online activities among Chinese Internet users (June 2004 and June 2005)

Online Services	% of Survey Respondents (June 2004)	% of Survey Respondents (June 2005)
E-mail	84.3	91.3
Search engine	64.6	64.5
News	62.1	79.2
Navigation of Web sites or Web pages (nonnews)	47.8	57.2
Real-time chatting or instant messaging	40.2	44.9
Downloading and uploading (nonmusic)	38.2	25.8
BBS and community forums	21.3	40.6
Online games	15.9	23.4
School/classmate BBS	13.7	28.5
Online purchasing	7.3	19.6
Online education	5.8	10.6
Online banking	4.9	14.1
Personal Web site hosting	4.4	16.6
Stock trading	3.9	4.5
E-magazine	3.5	9.6
Job search	3.4	12.2
Short message service (SMS)	2.9	4.6

Source: CNNIC 14th and 16th Statistical Survey Reports on the Internet Development in China released Report on China's Internet Development (released in July 2004 and July 2005, respectively).

samples of users from a few Chinese cities. Secondly, the original questions were worded slightly differently in the two surveys. In the CNNIC survey, users were asked to choose as many items as applicable from a list of online functionalities that they used on a regular basis, and the two CASS Internet surveys asked respondents how often they used each of the online applications on a five-point Likert scale. Additionally, there were slight variations in the categories used in the two surveys.

From the findings of Table 5.1 and Table 5.2, it can be observed that online communicative actions are quite popular activities in addition to information and news services. In both the CNNIC reports and the CASS surveys, a substantial proportion of Chinese net surfers indicated that they went online to use chat rooms, bulletin board services (BBS), or community forums. In particular, QQ/ICQ/QICQ, an instant messenger service for finding online pals and getting together with friends on the Internet, is a popular application among China's Internet population. Although online banking and online shopping activities are not as popular as in most developed nations, there is an unmistakable trend of rapid growth during the last two or three years. The potential of the Internet as a socializing tool in China is confirmed by the findings from the World Internet Project study coordinated by UCLA Center for Communication Policy with participation from researchers in 14 countries. The findings show that China ranked number one among all the 14 countries

Table 5.2 Popular Internet applications among Chinese Internet users in twelve cities (2003 and 2005)

Internet Applications	% of Respondents (Often or Always) N = 2457 (2003)	% of Respondents (Often or Always) N = 1169 (2005)
Browsing Web sites	57.7	65.2
Reading news	56.8	65.9
E-mail	51.4	44.8
Listening to or downloading music	49.1	56.5
Searching entertainment information	44.2	52.5
QQ/ICQ/QICQ	36.0	44.1
Online discussions or chat groups (IRC)	34.5	41.1
Playing games	33.6	62.2
Downloading tools or antivirus software	30.8	46.3
BBS	17.7	23.8
Online study or study for a degree	13.3	30.5
Searching medical information	9.6	24.0
Conducting stock business or searching stock information	8.9	16.4
Online shopping	5.3	15.6
Online professional training	4.2	12.6
Banking or online payments	2.6	12.2
Checking personal bank account	2.5	11.2

Source: Research Center for Social Development, Chinese Academy of Social Sciences: Surveying Internet Usage and Impact in Twelve Chinese Cities (2003) and Research Report on Internet Use and its Impact in Five Chinese Cities (2005). The twelve Chinese cities included in the 2003 survey are Beijing, Chengdu, Changsha, Xi'an, Shenyang, Shanghai, Guangzhou, Nanhai, Yima, Jimo, Guangshui, and Fengnai. In the 2005 survey, five cities were selected due to budget constraints: Beijing, Shanghai, Guangzhou, Chengdu, and Changsha.

for the number of friends Internet users have met online but not in person (an average of 7.7, more than twice as many as any other surveyed country, and the number in the United States was 2.6).[1]

Meanwhile, a relatively high proportion of Chinese Internet users frequently visit chat rooms or BBS. It is useful to compare the online behavior of Chinese netizens with that of those in other countries. Table 5.3 reports results from surveys in different nations in recent years concerning popular net surfing activities. It can be seen that Chinese netizens are the most likely to visit online forums, BBS, and newsgroup sites; they are also more inclined to use Internet relay chat as a communication platform (only after Italian netizens among the six countries included in the table). This indicates that user-generated content (UGC) plays a particular important role in Chinese cyberspace, and most UGC tends to reflect a user's personal opinion on particular issues. In line with the popular use of online chat rooms and BBS in China, Chinese netizens show some willingness to believe some of the information they obtain from chat rooms or BBS services. In CASS's 2003 survey of Internet use in twelve Chinese cities, when asked how much of the information they got

Table 5.3 Cross-national comparison of popular Internet activities.

Activities	China (2005)	U.S. (2004-5)	Germany (2002)	Japan (2003)	Hungary (2002)	Italy (2002)
E-mail	91.3	91	72.7	N/A[b]	49	89.9
Surfing (news)	79.3	72	36.2	60.3	N/A[b]	66.4
Search engines	64.5	84	20	N/A	N/A[b]	N/A[b]
Surfing (nonnews/entertainment)	57.2	66	35.4	75.5	N/A[b]	62.5
Forum/BBS/Newsgroup	40.6	17[a]	N/A[b]	17.1	20	14.3
IRC (Chat)	20.7		10.5	9.2	20	24.4

Data sources for each of the countries listed: China (CNNIC, 2005), Germany (European Institute for the Media, 2002), Japan (Mikami, 2003), Hungary (Information Society and Trend Research Institute and Social Research Centre Inc., 2002), Italy (SDA Bocconi, 2002). Survey results for the United States come from various projects associated with the Pew Internet and American Life Project survey results from 2004 to 2005. See the report at http://www.pewinternet.org/trends/Internet_Activities_8.05.05.htm (Retrieved June 2005). Results are the percentage of users who reported that they were engaged in those activities.

[a] The two questions were combined into one in the Pew survey project, which asked how often Internet users participated in chatting or online discussions.

[b] Result was not available for this question in the survey.

from the different sources was credible, 23.9 percent of the respondents said most of the information from BBS was credible, and 47.8 percent said some of the information from BBS was credible. In chat rooms, the perceived credibility of the information there was slightly lower: 13.6 percent said that most information from the chat rooms was credible, and 38.9 percent said some of the information was credible (CASS Research Center for Social Development, 2003). The willingness of Chinese netizens to give a certain level of credibility to information from BBS or chat rooms on the Internet explains why these often serve an alternative source of information other than the news Web sites on some particular occasions, as is discussed in Chapters 6 and 7.

In CASS's 2005 survey of Internet use in five Chinese cities, the penetration rates of some main media formats were investigated. As would be expected, television was leading all other media in its reach, with 97 percent of the respondents reporting using television on a regular basis. Newspapers came second on the list with a penetration rate of 86 percent. The Internet was quickly rising in its popularity, and it was used regularly by 49 percent of the respondents surveyed, lagging slightly behind books (56 percent) and magazines (53 percent). Noticeably, the Internet was more popular than the radio (38 percent penetration rate). Users have also developed a dependency relationship with the Internet, as 78.4 percent of the Internet adopters reported that the Internet was a major source of information for them, surpassing the role of television and newspaper as an information source (73.7 percent indicated TV was a major information source, and 71.4 percent chose newspa-

Table 5.4 Informational and socializing use of the Internet (2005)

Importance of Role Played by the Media in Meeting Need.
(Users vs. Nonusers of the Internet)

Need	Internet	TV	Newspaper	Radio	Magazine	Books
Understanding domestic/ foreign news	67.0	81.4	67.3	16.5	15.0	8.9
	13.4	90.8	76.8	22.5	12.0	7.2
Getting everyday information	62.4	43.7	46.4	7.3	28.3	14.8
	12.5	59.8	60.3	14.1	18.6	10.9
Getting study- and job-related information	60.4	26.6	36.1	5.2	21.2	51.7
	11.5	43.9	50.3	10.4	20.3	36.7
Entertainment or personal hobbies	72.0	46.0	20.0	14.0	17.0	11.0
	15.0	63.0	29.0	19.0	12.0	7.0
Expressing personal opinions and views, and publishing one's works	63.4	10.2	17.7	3.2	12.9	7.7
	15.2	15.8	25.7	4.9	10.7	6.6
Exchanging opinions and information with others	74.6	9.3	13.3	3.3	7.0	5.6
	20.2	14.5	20.4	5.1	7.0	4.5
Participating in social events	45.5	16.1	17.9	4.0	8.7	3.9
	11.9	22.6	20.6	6.6	5.8	3.5
Enhancing and improving personal relationships	70.2	8.5	10.8	3.3	7.9	6.5
	18.5	13.3	17.2	4.6	5.9	4.6

Source: CASS (Chinese Academy of Social Sciences Research Center for Social Development) *2005 Survey Report on Internet Use and Impact in Five Chinese Cities.*

pers). Nonusers of the Internet, by contrast, relied mainly on television (84.4 percent) and newspapers (78.5 percent) as major sources of information.

The Internet is a multifaceted communication platform where a variety of tasks can be completed. In the 2005 CASS survey, respondents were asked how important a role each of six common media types plays in meeting a set of everyday needs in their life. The six media types are the Internet, television, newspaper, radio, magazine, and books. The survey covered eight aspects of everyday needs in people's life: (1) understanding domestic and foreign news, (2) getting everyday information, (3) getting study- or job-related information, (4) entertainment or personal hobbies; (5) expressing personal opinions (views) or publishing one's works; (6) exchanging opinions or information with others; (7) participating in social events, and (8) enhancing or improving personal relationships. The results from the survey are summarized in Table 5.4.

This set of eight needs in life falls into two general categories: informational needs (1–4) and socializing needs (5–8). It can be seen that the Internet is playing a significant role in both categories of needs among Chinese netizens. Except for the first question (understanding domestic and foreign news) in which both Internet users and nonusers agreed that television plays the most important role in spreading the news, Internet users display the heaviest dependence on the Internet for all other informational and social needs.

In particular, the role of the Internet overshadows all other media types in meeting users' socializing needs. Internet users agreed that the Internet has enabled them to express their views and opinions and to build up personal relationships. It is a clear indication that the Internet has become an important part of Chinese netizens' social life in addition to providing much-needed information in everyday life.

The Internet, Democracy, and the Public Sphere

Since its early days, the Internet has been envisioned by some politicians, social scientists, and communication practitioners, among others, as a potentially liberating and democratizing force in an emerging realm of civil society. The U.S. government under the Clinton Administration, a big fan of the Internet, made a sustained effort through the National Information Infrastructure Program to promote access to information for all Americans, in the hope that would "transform the lives of all American people — ameliorating the constraints of geography, disability, and economic status — giving all Americans a fair opportunity to go as far as their talents and ambitions will take them" (quoted in Streck 1998, 22).

The rise of the Internet paralleled an era when public participation and deliberation in the political process in Western democratic polities were steadily declining, as noted in Chapter 1. So it should be no surprise that the popularization of the Internet would win the open embrace of a group of technological determinists who claim to have found the solution for the revival of democratic politics in the Internet. Long before the Internet had become a mass communication tool, Amitai Etzioni spent a third of a million dollars of an NSF grant to work out a plan for an electronic town hall conducted over (broadcast and cable) television, radio, and telephone based on the assumption that "reasoned, informed, broadly shared position requires dialoguing" (1972: 458). Two decades later he renewed his call for "technologically enhanced national 'town meetings' " to revitalize participatory democracy in American politics (Etzioni, 1993).

Since the 1980s, futurists and utopianists have been making various prognostications about the impact of new interactive communication technologies, such as cable TV and computer networks, on democracy and development (e.g., Barber, 1984; Naisbitt, 1982; Toffler, 1983). The instantaneous popularization of the Internet in the 1990s quickly shifted the focus to online democracy. Susan Herring summarizes the prevalent democratization claim of computer-mediated communication technologies into two essential components: "access to a means of communication, and the right to communicate equally, free from status constraints" (1993). In contrast to the unidimensional, centralized, pyramidal, and hierarchical system created by traditional media, Hanson and Narula (1990) argue that the Internet introduces a multidimensional environment and fosters decentralization, pluralism, and democracy.

Along similar lines, Grossman coined the term "keypad democracy" to talk about the birth of an electronic republic in which Internet-based communication makes possible civic participation of the public in the policy-making process. In Grossman's (1995: 248) words, "through interactive technologies, new opportunities are becoming available to get members of the public engaged in resolving the issues that directly affect them." Poster claims that the decentralized nature of the Internet provides an opportunity to move away from the established structure of political communication centered on broadcasting media to a new type of "cyborg politics" that instantiates a fundamental reversibility of status, authority, and power (Poster, 1997). John Pavlik (1994) contends that geographic barriers have been removed on the Internet and that diasporic communities can be reinvented online.

In summarizing prevalent rhetoric and practices concerning the Internet, Lincoln Dahlberg identifies three dominant camps:

> First, a communitarian camp, which stresses the possibility of the Internet enhancing communal spirit and values. Second, a liberal individualist camp, which sees the Internet as assisting the expression of individual interests. Third, a deliberative camp, which promotes the Internet as the means for an expansion of the public sphere of rational-critical citizen discourse autonomous from state and corporate power through which public opinion may be formed that can hold official decision makers accountable.
>
> (Dahlberg, 2001a: 616; see also Dahlberg, 2001b)

The third camp is particularly relevant to the role of civil society in the democratic process.

Meanwhile, there has also been increasing attention to the building of social capital on the Internet, as mentioned in the previous section. Howard Rheingold (1993), in his pioneering book on virtual communities, contends that online communities contribute to the formation of three types of collective goods: social network capital, knowledge capital, and communion. Hans Pruijt (2002) cites evidence that socialization online generates public good as well as private good, and hence spawns social capital, and comes to the conclusion that "[s]ocial capital is the spirit of the Internet and also the direction in which its equalizing potentials can be found." However, he also points to the current deficiency of the Internet infrastructure and cautions that "continuing investment in Internet social capital at all levels is needed" (p. 113).

In examining the Pew survey results of online surfers in the United States, Pippa Norris found evidence that "those Americans who are most active in online groups feel that the internet widens their experience of community (by helping them to connect with others who have different beliefs or backgrounds)" and "they feel that it [surfing online] deepens their experience (by reinforcing and strengthening existing social networks)" (2004, 40), which,

Norris argues, points to the bridging and bonding functions of online groups. However, Norris also found that the effect of the two functions is not universal among all online groups and their strength varies significantly depending on the nature of the groups.

One of the most vocal proponents for social capital in modern society, Robert Putnam, on the other hand, along with Lewis Feldstein, argues that new communication technologies, the Internet in particular, are the most important "as support and stimulus for long-standing forms of community, rather than as instigators of radically new 'virtual communities'" and Putnam further suggests that "[c]omputer-based technology matters not because it can create some new and separate form of virtual community, but because it can broaden and deepen and strengthen our physical communities" (Putnam and Feldstein, 2003: 239). However, as I have argued repeatedly in the book, one's understanding of the role of the Internet in empowering civil society should not be limited to its function in strengthening existing physical communities only; its greater potential may rest with its capability to create brand-new forms of community or social ties on the Internet that may or can not exist in real-life communities, such as diasporic communities on the Internet mentioned later in the chapter.

There has also been sustained effort to experiment with real-life Internet projects in the hope of revitalizing democratic practices among citizens from many parties in different geographic areas. Some of the well-publicized and well-researched cases are DNet (dnet.org), Project Vote Smart (vote-smart.org), the California Online Voter Guide (Doctor and Dutton, 1999), Santa Monica's Public Electronic Network (PEN) (Doctor and Dutton, 1998), the Missouri Express project (Pigg, 2001), and the Minnesota E-Democracy movement (e-democracy.org) (Dahlberg, 2001a). All those projects have been tied closely to existing political communities and have been designed to increase public participation and deliberation in the political process. After reviewing current norms and practices of e-democracy and e-government worldwide, Andrew Chadwick summarizes them into four converging areas: "online consultations integrating civil societal groups with bureaucracies and parliaments, the internal democratization of the public sector itself, the involvement of users in the design and delivery of public services, and the diffusion of open-source collaboration in public organizations" (2003: 453).

Not everyone, however, is enthusiastic about the prospects of cyberdemocracy. Peter Levine (2002), for one, categorizes the assumption of the myth of e-democracy into four premises: "Convenience is the key to participation; We need more information; The Internet is a massive town meeting; and Democracy will flourish when the 'power brokers' are gone" (pp. 122–128). And he contends that none of them is defensible. Instead, Levine concludes that "the odds favor an increasingly privatized and commercialized cyberspace" (2002: 137). Wilhelm studied some popular political newsgroups and found no evidence that the online political forums "do not provide viable sounding boards for signaling and thematising issues to be processed by the political system" and deliberation and critical debate are not yet the norm among these newsgroups (1999: 175).

In perhaps one of the most radical criticisms of the utopian view of cyberdemocracy, Margolis and Resnick contend that instead of inspiring democratic politics and mass civic participation, the Internet has created "politics as usual" by reflecting and reinforcing patterns of behavior and the sociopolitical structure of the real world:

> What has occurred is the normalization of cyberspace. Cyberspace has not become the locus of a new politics that spills out of the computer screen and revitalizes citizenship and democracy. If anything, ordinary politics and commercial activity, in all their complexity and vitality, have invaded and captured cyberspace. Virtual reality has grown to resemble the real world.
>
> (Margolis and Resnick, 2000: 2)

Notwithstanding their rebuttal of some popular claims for the revolutionizing effects of online democracy, Margolis and Resnick agree that the most powerful effect of the Internet on democracy will be its capability to bring information to people in a speedy and bountiful manner. Information means power, one has to agree, and this is what I call the "democratization of information" on the Internet, which has particular implications for citizens living in authoritarian states like China.

Robert McChesney paints a similarly gloomy picture about the prospect of Internet democracy:

> Aside from the question of access, bulletin boards, and the information highway more generally, do not have the power to produce political culture when it does not exist in the society at large. Given the dominant patterns of global capitalism, it is far more likely that the Internet and the new technologies will adapt themselves to the existing political culture rather than create a new one. Thus, it seems a great stretch to think the Internet will politicize people; it may just as well keep them depoliticized.
>
> (McChesney, 1995)

One can indeed find indisputable evidence that the Internet culture has been penetrated by the capitalist mode of production and has become the battleground of different commercial interest groups. However, the Internet was invented as a project to defy information control on the network, and thus to distribute the power of control to all. There has already been enough evidence that the Internet has been successfully used to circumvent information monopoly by either the capitalist or government powers, and I am optimistic that we will see more of this in the future. So, instead of viewing the democratic potential of Internet-mediated communication from the extremist perspectives of either the utopianists or the pessimists, it may be more productive to abandon this all-or-nothing approach and to look at the whole issue of cyberdemocracy on a continuum. The question posed by Chadwick (2003: 444) is an important one:

> Is an all-or-nothing approach helpful in describing and explaining changes that are occurring under the weight of new uses of Internet technology, or does it risk becoming blind to a number of recent developments, many of which point to an inevitably more complicated, messy, and contingent future in which the practices and norms of e-government and those of e-democracy become interwined?

Rather than asking whether the Internet democratizes communication in general, we should ask in what areas certain Internet-based forms of communications are democratizing public communication under what circumstances, and in what context this has not happened, and more importantly why. Furthermore, we should also examine some emerging trends of online communication and study their social, political, and economic implications. After all, the Internet is still in its infancy, and so is our knowledge about its potential as a brand communication medium.

This point is particularly relevant to the case of China. Because the Chinese government has long enjoyed a monopolistic control of information in the country through conventional media outlets and its other propaganda machines, the anticontrol nature of the Internet brings the hope of democratizing information production and dissemination to the Chinese people as more and more information gets spread to a larger user base in ways that were not possible before. In the meantime, we must bear in mind that although cyberspace has created a social space of its own, it cannot be totally detached from the physical world. Human communication on the Internet is deeply rooted in real life; meanwhile, it also modifies or changes real life situations. As Diana Saco (2002: 211) acknowledges, "As a disembodied space for the liberal unencumbered self … cyberspace promises a utopian ecstasy (a 'bodiless exultation') on which it ultimately cannot deliver because cyberspace is not a space we can inhabit completely … It is, rather, a point of passage, an obligatory one, but a passage nonetheless." A key issue, of course, is to what exit does this passage lead — Will it lead to more official surveillance, or more corporate power, or more civil society thrust? Will there be a universal pattern or will it differ from society to society? Research in this book can provide answers to some of these important questions.

Rhetoric about the Internet has also centered on its power to extend the role of the public in conducting rational-critical political debates in cyberspace and hence the possibility that the Internet will open avenues for a brand-new public sphere. What lies at the heart of the public sphere is that the public needs equal and unfettered access to sources of information and equal opportunities to participate in public debates about public policies. In Habermas' conception of the public sphere, the media are central to the function of the viable public sphere because they deliver the essential information to the public for it to make an informed decision and they provide an independent forum of public debate (Habermas, 1989). Therefore, the media, the fourth estate of the state as some call it, are the principal institutions of the public sphere (e.g. Dahlgren and Sparks, 1991; Verstraeten, 1996). Neil Postman (1985), for example, argues that the print media played a pivotal role in bringing about the public sphere of eighteenth-century America by spreading literacy among the working class and encouraging rational and ordered thinking as well as popular participation in important debates of the day. Television was a revolutionary medium of public communication in the twentieth century because of its ability to broadcast information to the general public in a timely manner with massive reach (Dahlgren, 1995).

This is particularly so in today's society with its ever-increasing media presence. Indeed, the media have often been credited with the functioning, or blamed for malfunctioning, of modern society. Habermas, together with a group of modern critical scholars (e.g., Brandts, Hermes, and van Zoonen, 1998; Livingstone and Lunt, 1994; McGuigan, 1996), is highly critical of the role of modern mass media because its domination by the government and the corporate realm inevitably compromise the public sphere they help create. Moreover, there is no lack of media theories providing prescriptions for organizing the media based on the public sphere model (e.g., J. Thompson, 1995).

Not surprisingly, the emergence of the Internet and the role it plays in public communication have triggered public debates about its role in the public sphere. As pointed out previously, there has been much attention paid to the differences between conventional mass media, which are primarily informational, and the Internet, which is both informational and interactive. Zappen, Gurak, and Doheny-Farina (1997) contend that the new computer-mediated communication environments on the Net have the potential to become public forums or places where local communities and individuals can engage in dialogue and discussion. Dahlberg (2001a; 2001b), Fernback (1999), Jones (1999), and Poster (1997), among others, have proposed that the Internet be approached and studied as a public sphere.

To view the Internet as a public sphere is not merely a modification or change of a designation; it involves some fundamental theoretical and methodological paradigm shifts in examining the Net. Also, it can have significant implications for policy making concerning the Internet. The computer nowadays should not be only regarded as a tool for fast and accurate calculation; more importantly, it is "an evocative object that causes old boundaries to be renegotiated" (Turkle, 1995: 22).

In a critical review of current debates on the Internet as public sphere, Papacharissi (2004: 12) notes three broad aspects of contention: "the ability of the internet to carry and transport information, its potential to bring people from diverse backgrounds together, and its future in a capitalist era." Evidence from extant research, Papacharissi argues, has been not positive toward any of the three aspects: first, "access to the internet does not guarantee increased political activity or enlightened political discourse" (p. 13); second, "[g]reater participation in political discussion [from people with diverse backgrounds] does not automatically result in discussion that promotes democratic ideals" (p. 16); and third, as a medium constructed in the capitalist era, the Internet "is susceptible to the same forces that ... originally transformed the public sphere [created by conventional mass media such as radio and television]" (p. 18). So overall, Papacharissi concludes, the view of the virtual sphere as a public sphere remains "a vision, but not yet a reality. As a vision, it inspires, but has not yet managed to transform political and social structures" (p. 23).

However, in the place of the common all-or-nothing approach, I argue that it may be methodologically and theoretically more productive to consider the Internet as an imperfect Habermasian public sphere in the twenty-first century, just as Blumler (1992) and Garnham (1986; 1990), among others, have argued that broadcasting is an imperfect twentieth-century equivalent of Habermas's eighteenth-century bourgeois public sphere. Although it is true that access to the Internet is not egalitarian, universal, and unfettered (one wonders if any medium has ever achieved that status in human history — even Habermas' ideal type of public sphere as embodied in clubs, cafés, newspapers, journals, libraries, and museums was only accessible to the bourgeoisie and excluded women, slaves, and menials), and rational debates have not become the norm on the Net, there is no denying that the Internet has already transformed the traditional communication landscape by making information available to a variety of social groups that otherwise would be off limits without the Internet; and the Internet has become a gathering place for like-minded netizens to socialize with each other and to talk about issues of common interest, as evidenced from the foregoing discussion in this chapter. Wilhelm (2000: 9) nicely summarizes the role of the Internet in the political process when he observes that the Internet "represents the vital channels in civil society in which individuals and groups can become informed about issues, discuss and debate these issues autonomously, and ultimately have an impact on policy agenda." As the reach of the Internet continues to expand to a larger population, we can only expect that these trends will continue in the future. In all fairness, aren't we putting too much onus on the Internet when we expect it, still in its infancy, to transform the social and political arena that no other communication medium has ever accomplished? The Internet alone cannot solve many of the persisting problems in representative democracies, or in any society, for that matter. In the case of China, I repeat a point that I made earlier: the important question to ask is not whether the Internet will democratize China, but rather in what ways the Internet is democratizing (or will democratize) communication in China.

Quite a few scholars have proposed a model of multiplicity of publics and hence multiple public spheres (see, for example, Calhoun, 1995; Dahlgren, 1991) to help us better understand the nature of the public sphere today. These scholars question the existence of a single, unified public in the Habermasian model and argue that it is necessary to examine the existence of multiple, intersecting, heterogeneous public spheres. Nancy Fraser (1992) points out that Habermas fails to address other, nonbourgeois, competing public spheres that coexist with the liberal, idealized public sphere of Habermas's focus, and she further presents her postbourgeois concept of the public sphere in modern societies in which a host of "counterpublics" or "subaltern publics" compete with and offset the unjust participatory privileges enjoyed by, and exclusionary norms established by, dominant social groups in stratified societies. According to Fraser, counterpublics are "parallel discursive arenas where members of subordinated social groups invent and circulate counter-discourses to formulate oppositional interpretations of their identities, interests and needs" (1992: 123); moreover, "... subaltern counterpublics have a dual character. On the one hand, they function as spaces of withdrawal and regroupment; on the other hand, they also function as bases and training grounds for agitational activities directed toward wider publics. It is precisely in the dialectic between these two functions that their emancipatory potential resides ..." (1992, 124).

This conception of the public sphere as a multiplicity, which "has been spurred by recognition of social complexity and sociocultural diversity" (Asen, 2000: 425), has found echoes in Benhabib's (1996) "plurality of modes of association," in which adults participate in multiple arenas of opinion formation through free and spontaneous processes of communication within and across interlocking and overlapping networks; it is also reminiscent of Lash and Urry's "neo-tribes" that, facilitated by new communication technologies, achieve self-sufficiency and need not participate in the larger arenas of public discourse. Similar views can also be found in Lievrouw's (2001) "pluralization of life-worlds," which affords a special role of new media technologies, and Taylor's "nested public spheres," wherein smaller public spheres nested within larger ones find a niche in the parameter of a national public sphere. The fragmentation of the public sphere, however, may be counterproductive to the democratic process, as Fraser argues, "the proliferation of a multiplicity of publics represents a departure from, rather than an advance toward, democracy" (1992: 122). Likewise, Seligman (1992) contends that the organization of interest groups along particular lines, such as ethnic or racial criteria, leads to a breakdown of civil society.

The conceptual model of multiple public spheres will be particularly helpful for understanding the Internet users and Internet use. Keane (2000) claims that the Internet is most promising in contributing to the growth of macropublic spheres that connect netizens on a global or local level, whereas Dahlgren (2001) sees the Internet as fostering the emergence of multiple microspheres that create a deliberative space for politically engaged people to exchange views or ideas. People may use the Net as a social technology, looking for affiliation, support, and a sense of community (Sproull and Faraj, 1997; Wellman, 1997), sharing common interests and sustaining relationships (Baym, 1997), and forming "diasporic communities" (Boczkowski, 1999; Pavlik, 1994) or what some call "diasporic public spheres" (Appadurai, 1996; Stubbs, 2001) linking ethnic and/or linguistic groups across different geographic regions. But these are more like special interest groups, and these "national and global special-interest forums on the net operate like global talk radio, only participants don't have to speed-redial for an hour to get through" (Doheny-Farina, 1996: 79). Obviously, as has already happened with other media of mass communication, like television, radio and magazines, the audience on the Internet, new as it is, is rapidly transforming into segments of special interest groups and special communities. In this sense, the idealized single general public in Habermas's public sphere model does not exist on the Internet. It may be more appropriate to use the idea of multiple publics or multipliers of publics to describe patterns of Internet usage.

Last but not least, examination of the social and political effects of the Internet worldwide will not be complete without systematic exploration of the transformative effect of the Internet on civil society forces that intervene between the state and individual interests. Sassi's view (1996) is typical of the dominant school of social scholars whose understanding of civil society and democracy is deeply grounded in the vitality of conventional social groups and organizational powers:

> If in recent history there were civil societies without any means of communication of their own, there now are networked public spheres without any significant social organizations and citizen activities — or put another way, there is a tiny civic body that has developed an enormous public head. The heterogeneous and fragmenting nature of these public spheres constitutes another problem of politics.

In other words, any impact of the Internet on civil society should be assessed by how it affects civic virtues, political participation, and involvement in voluntary and other social groups in the bricks and mortar world. In China, as I demonstrated in Chapter 3, despite heavy government control and surveillance, the Internet has already proved to be an alternative form of information and communication, and dissident groups, such as the Tiananmen Mothers and the Falun Gong, are also able to establish their presence on the Internet to circumvent official persecution and to win support both at the domestic and global levels.

This is, Ester and Vinken (2003) contend , exactly where current debate concerning civic virtues on the Internet is out of tune with "the signs of time" in the new millennium. They point out that a main weakness in mainstream sociological research is "the lack of sensitivity in civil society studies to new, alternative and innovative forms of solidarity, connectedness and civic, and political engagement, particularly those facilitated by the Internet" (Ester and Vinken, 2003: 660). The long-held view that community life and civil society are in serious trouble in the United States, they further argue, may be off the mark because "[n]ot being engaged in traditional forms of advancing the common good is not equal to refraining from any civic engagement" (p. 674) and because "the Internet is likely to be the ultimate tool for particularly younger generations to gain and advance social capital, to build and take part in communities, and to contribute to the common good and their personal identity" (p. 675). Nonetheless, one cannot totally scrap the physical world and exclusively focus on the cyberworld in examining any effect of the Internet because any netizen may be able to cultivate his or her own cyberactivity space on the Internet, yet he or she inevitably also has a mundane life to live. The biggest challenge for researchers, I think, is how to strike a balance between virtual life and real life while not being constrained by the limits of any single mode in looking at the opportunities opened up on the Internet.

Castells (1996) concurs that the Internet provides an alternative to classic forms of civic engagement and allows people to both create their own civil society online and produce their own reality of civil society. Norris (2001) offers empirical evidence to support Castells's prognostication in her study of the presence of civic society formed by transnational advocacy networks, grassroots political organizations, and the independent media institutions around the world. Baber (2002b) and Gomez (2002) demonstrate that the Internet opens up possibilities for the expansion of civil society and the emergence of a robust public sphere, albeit without its limitations, in an authoritarian political culture in Singapore. This is a promising line of research that needs to be continued by expanding to various online settings within different social, cultural, and political contexts among different online groups in different regions of the world.

The Rise of Online Public Opinion in China

In Habermas's conception, public opinion is very essential to the function of a viable and healthy public sphere. The public sphere is where public opinion is formed and expressed, although the specific nature of public opinion has varied at different historical times. In the bourgeois public sphere, public opinion, which stood in opposition to state power and special interests that were to shape bourgeois society, was formed by reasoned debate and consensus, in public, on the issues of common concern and the practices of the state. The transformation of the bourgeois public sphere to today's "welfare state capitalism and mass democracy," however, has degraded the function of public opinion, limiting public discourse to themes approved and administered by political, economic, and media elites who turn the public sphere into a venue of representation for their private interests (Habermas, 1989; 1992). In its ideal formulation, the production of public opinion in the public sphere serves to legitimate authority in a democratic society, and the corruption of public opinion as well as the role of mass media in shaping public opinion in contemporary society is also noted by Rutherford (2000: 274–275):

> The [public] sphere remains a site for the production of public opinion that is given concrete form by surveys and polls which, to a degree, actually fashion the opinion through the process of asking certain questions (and not asking others). Because of an excess of goods and risks competing for attention, the sphere continues to be a contested arena; however, much of the excess is manufactured by people and institutions with money, moral clout, or other forms of power. The mass media play out a double role here, both as the vehicle for competitive spectacles and as the source of news, a different kind of discourse, though again a monologue and now contaminated by the ubiquity of publicity.

Notwithstanding the Habermasian normative perspective of public opinion formation and its critics, there has been a well-established line of research about the impact of public opinion on political governance (e.g., Heith, 2004; Manxa, Cook, and Page, 2002; Sharp, 1999) and the theory and practice of accurately gauging public opinion (see Ferguson, 2000 for an overview) as well as the role of mass media in shaping public opinion (e.g., Perse, 2001). It is only natural that the quick popularization of the Internet as a communication phenomenon in the past decade or so has led academics to ask what the Internet has brought to the current public opinion landscape. As a result, two general camps of scholarship have emerged: the first camp focuses on how the Internet may transform the practice of public opinion production and the second camp is principally interested in exploring how the Internet can be used to assess public opinion.

Among the first camp, Norris points out that there are two hypotheses concerning how the Internet in society can influence mass public opinion in different ways:

> [T]he participation hypothesis holds that the opportunities for information, networking, and communication via digital technologies might affect patterns of civic engagement, either *reinforcing* those citizens who are already most active through traditional channels, or *mobilizing* new participants who are currently disengaged from the political process. Alternatively, the *cultural* hypothesis ... holds that the rise of the Internet will influence the predominant values and attitudes within society

... If politics on the Internet affects both new groups *and* new values, then this has the potential for the greatest transformation of public opinion ... .

(Norris, 2001: 195-196, italics original)

Wheeler, likewise, contends that "the new media decentralize the production of knowledge and democratize opinion formation through interactivity. Through such decentralization technologies check dominant authorities from managing the flow of information" (1997: 222); and Savigny concurs that

[T]he internet represents a countervailing power against the traditional media's agenda-setting ability, and the attempts by the state, political parties and the traditional media to define and defend the status quo. Communication via the internet can be top-down and bottom-up, horizontal and vertical; a dynamic interactive two-way process. It is a medium as yet unharnessed and undistorted by competing interest of the media and political parties, both of which are, as yet, unable to set the agenda or control the parameters of debate.

(2002: 5)

These points are particularly relevant to the Internet and civil society in China. As I demonstrate later in this chapter and in the two succeeding chapters, the Internet has transformed the arena of public opinion in Chinese society in at least three ways: first, it creates a new platform that was not available before for Chinese netizens to express their opinions online on just about anything; secondly, it produces a steady, core cohort of opinion leaders that constantly sway public opinion in China's cyberspace; thirdly, the Internet allows an ever-increasing number of Chinese Net surfers to be exposed to the pulse of their Net pals' opinions. From time to time, the Chinese media may cover the barometer of netizens' opinions on selective issues, and the government may decide to respond to these opinions in its policies or approaches to issues of common concern to the Chinese public.

From the second camp, the interest in online surveys as a method is justified by the mushrooming of different types of Web surveys by various administrators on almost any kind of topic in recent years. The availability of cheap, easy-to-use Web-design techniques has broken down the monopoly of social surveys by a limited number of governmental, industrial, or professional survey organizations that lie at the power center of society, and it has made it possible for almost anyone who occupies a Web space to conduct a large-scale survey online; on the other hand, with the proliferation of online surveys comes a multitude of new problems that cast a shadow on the bombardment of survey reports in cyberspace — one hardly knows how much trust to place in those surveys because of wide variations in survey procedures. In a review of current Web survey practices, Couper (2000: 490) comes to this conclusion:

> The Internet has truly democratized the survey-taking process. However, one outcome of this process is that the quality of surveys on the Internet varies widely, from a simple act of questions intended to entertain to full probability-based designs intended to describe the general population. The need to educate consumers of surveys (whether sponsors/clients or the general public) regarding quality indicators is already apparent. To dismiss all Web surveys because of the overenthusiastic claims of the few is a mistake. Similarly, to assume that no major embarrassments will occur as the method matures is unrealistic.

Contrary to the this assessment, I would not put Web surveys with serious flaws in "the few"; rather, I think good surveys on the Web are few and far between because of technical problems in the design, sample, and report procedures of most surveys conducted online. Martinson demonstrates how a popular news Web site, through the use of nonsystematic, nonrepresentative, and self-selected survey design, misconstrued public opinion in the reporting of online survey results, and he concludes that, "despite the fact that sophisticated survey techniques and technology have raised the likelihood that public opinion polls can be representative and accurate, technology can also be used in ways that distort and misrepresent the public pulse" (2002: 70). Some of the persistent problems in current Web surveys have been low response rates, self-selectivity of Internet users, nonrepresentative samples, and noncoverage errors, all of which cast serious doubt on the credibility of results from these surveys (e.g., Cook, Heath, and Thompson, 2000; Sills and Song, 2002). Nonetheless, there has also been sustained effort to take advantage of the available Internet technologies and to improve the quality of online surveys (e.g., Heerwegh and Loosveldt, 2002; Kaplowitz, Hadlock, and Levine, 2004; Trouteaud, 2004).

The foregoing discussion about the theory and practice of public opinion, however, has been heavily grounded in the Western democratic polity. In the West, a free and independent press is considered to be vital for the formation of public opinion from rational, critical debates, while in the Chinese system, the Communist Party holds tight control on the mass media, which serve as mass mobilization tools to "guide public opinion" to support Party policies, and to conduct positive propaganda for Party ideologies (Dai, 1999). Mass media in the state-controlled Chinese context play a totally different set of roles in shaping and reflecting public opinion than their counterparts in the Western free press systems.

After its takeover of China in 1949, the Chinese Communist Party, under the supreme command of Mao Tze-tung, put in place a totalitarian government ruled by a single party. Mass media were used "as agitator, propagandist, organizer" (Siebert, Peterson, and Schramm, 1956) for ideological campaigns and mass movements, and all forms of communication, such as radio and newspapers, banner posters, posted announcements, study groups, street lecturers, and other channels, were mobilized to indoctrinate the Chinese people in cities, towns, and the remote countryside in an effort to solidify rule of the country by the Communist Party (Markham, 1967; for Mao Tze-tung's theoretical deliberation about the role of mass media in the communist system, see Mao, 2000). As a result, any opposing voice and dissension was not tolerated and the media were simply propaganda tools to unify public opinion in support of whatever the Party said or did.

The Great Proletarian Cultural Revolution (1966–1976), which was staged on the direct order of Mao to purge dissenting members (or the so-called Rightists) in the Party and bureaucracy, and to strengthen Mao's absolute hold on power, wreaked havoc in the country and caused disastrous consequences for the already feeble civil society. Millions of intellectuals, Party members, and common Chinese citizens were persecuted for their opinions and beliefs, and public opinion was highly unified into one — that of the highest authority (i.e., Mao himself) in China. Mass media became Mao's mass mobilization machine to organize zealous "Red Guards" into mob violence and factious fights throughout the nation, and civil society groups were marginalized and sidelined in the social structure.

Mao's death in 1976 put Deng Xiaoping at the helm of China's new generation of leadership, who immediately shifted the Party's strategic focus from political campaigns to economic reform and openness. The process of transformation in the Chinese media landscape has accelerated since the mid-1990s. This is summarized by Yuezhi Zhao (2000: 21–22):

> The commercialization of the press opened some spaces, enabled a degree of organizational autonomy, and conferred limited sovereignty to its consumers. In this sense, it has helped to liberate the press from the state … The other side of this transformation, though, is the institutionalization of new control mechanisms in the forms of advertising pressure, bias toward affluent consumers in the urban and coastal areas, clientelist relationship with business and political sources, and a new regime of labor discipline in the newsrooms.

Commercialization of the media, as well as liberalization of the economic sector, as I pointed out in Chapter 2, works to the advantage of Chinese civil society because the general public has more input in the news production and dissemination process. Consequently, audience interest weighs as an important factor, and public opinion can no longer be totally ignored by the press.

The Chinese authority, nonetheless, has never intended to give up its control of the media. As Weber points out, "the Government's reluctance to open the door to foreign and cross-media ownership and the maintenance of its strong regulatory line on foreign programming and thus management of culture, continue to perpetuate the control and propaganda modalities — albeit cloaked in the rhetoric of a competitive domestic structure" (2002: 75). The subtle change in the government's approach in effecting control over the media is characterized by Chan as a pragmatic shift "from propaganda to hegemony," which resorts to "leadership, not dictatorship," or "the moral and intellectual leadership of the Party" to produce people's consent (2002: 50).

China's economic reform policy has not only transformed the media landscape but also witnessed the change of the role in public opinion in its national policymaking. China under Mao's tyrannical rule largely followed the Soviet Bolshevik theory of public communication built upon the revolutionary ideas of Lenin and Stalin. Contrary to the common belief that Bolshevik (Communist) policy operates without regard to the state of public opinion, Inkeles (1950: 24) points out,

> Bolshevik theory does not disregard public opinion. Its emphasis, however, more or less completely rejects following public opinion and stresses the prime need to shape and mold it. This implies that one studies public opinion primarily to determine the pace and speed of his own actions. The goal is not to cater to public opinion but to move it along with you as rapidly as possible without undermining your popular support.

But public opinion in Mao's era was only legitimate as long as it served the overall purpose of Party ideology. Indeed, propaganda machines within the Party mechanism worked not only to shape and mold public opinion but to create public opinion that was needed for Mao's social revolutions as well.

Reform in both the economic sector and the mass media has also triggered the need for the assessment of public opinion on issues that are directly related to the reform process. Change in the international geopolitical environment, especially since the collapse of communism in Eastern Europe and the former Soviet blocks, has created a sense of urgency among the Chinese leadership to find legitimacy for the Communist Party to hold on to power in China. This means the regime may show some limited responsiveness to the terrain of public opinion. Meanwhile, the more liberalized environment in academia has led to an expansion of interest in the theory and research of public opinion among Chinese social scientists. As a result, the Western tradition of survey research was introduced to Chinese social scientists along with the revival of the social sciences in China in general in the early 1980s: popular textbooks and academic works in survey research in the West were translated into Chinese and published, courses on survey and public opinion were offered in Chinese universities, and public opinion and survey centers were founded in the Chinese Academy of Social Sciences (CASS) (which itself was founded in 1977 after the death of Mao) and some universities, and publications on survey methods and results were on the rise (Rosen and Chu, 1987). The development of survey research in China underwent a two-stage process, as Rosen (1989: 157; see also Rosen, 1987) notes:

> If a decentralized, methodologically unsophisticated survey research grew out of the early years of post-Mao reform, the development of far more sophisticated public opinion studies in which scientific sampling methods are employed on a national scale can be traced to the mid-1980s, when the reform program faced a series of problems, the solution to which required a comprehensive understanding of the state of society.

In the early 1980s, in addition to serving propaganda-related purposes, as would be expected in all authoritarian or communist systems, survey research was used by different emerging social and political forces, such as academic institutions, semiofficial research organizations, and government policy research agencies at the central and local levels, to pursue policy agendas and to influence government policy decisions. However, as reform deepened, the Chinese authorities quickly learned that public opinion is a double-edged sword: while in the early years of the 1980s, popular enthusiasm and support for the reform policy remained high, public resentment and dissatisfaction rose as the reform policy disrupted the old social structure, produced social inequalities, and led to widespread inflation — all of which was well reflected in surveys at different times during this period (Rosen, 1989). Nonetheless, the regime was largely successful in its uphill battle in "seeking to unify public opinion and harmonize interests, politically and ideologically, at a time when economic and social forces are pulling society *away* from the state" (Rosen, 1989: 169. Emphasis original). That is, until public grievances came to light as epitomized in the 1989 massive student protest in Tiananmen Square in the heart of Beijing.

China's reform suffered a setback after the crackdown of the 1989 student movement — but only temporarily. The emergence of conservative forces within the Party led to Deng Xiaoping's widely publicized Southern Inspection Tour in 1992, which aimed to push forward China's path of reform. The collapse of communism in Eastern Europe and the former Soviet blocks sent a clear warning to the Chinese regime: change or face demise. The Party decided to initiate a series of changes to maintain its hold on power in the most populous nation in the world — a "repackaging" to move the Communist Party "from a revolutionary party to a political party" and stress of pragmatism over the traditional Marxist–Leninist–Maoist ideology. As a result, "the outward symbol and the all-important name brand CCP© remain, but the content and meaning of the party's activities have changed significantly" (Brady, 2002: 563). While the goals of uniting public opinion under the auspices of the Party remain basically the same as the Mao era, the specific strategic approaches to achieving these goals have become more subtle. The regime has opted to take advantage of the persuasive, rather than the coercive, power of the mass media in building a national consensus to lend legitimacy to its rule, and in rebuilding and reinventing the image of the Communist Party in the changing environment; public opinion polls, Western-style public relations, and advertising campaigns have been employed by the government in "regimenting the public mind" (Brady, 2002).

Within this context, waves of national surveys have been conducted by various research or government institutions that attempt to feel the public pulse about important social, economic, and political issues (e.g., Wang, Rees, and Andreosso-O'Callaghan, 2004). One of the most well-known survey projects is the annual survey of social trends conducted by the flagship government-sponsored research institution, CASS, whose recent survey results reveal the rising public resentment toward some of the prominent social problems facing Chinese authorities today: "creating jobs for those entering the workforce, building an effective social safety net, resolving the income gap between the rural areas and the cities, reducing corruption, carrying out political reform at least in a limited sense, and so forth" (Fewsmith, 2002: 63). However, government involvement in the research process means that the government can control the overall direction of the survey and set the general rules of the game, and surveys can only be conducted within the parameters granted by the authorities.

To set the tone for government work under the new leadership, Chinese President Hu Jintao, at a recent national propaganda and ideological work conference, called for all propaganda agencies[2] within the country to "take command of the propaganda and ideological work, and provide scientific theoretical guidance and powerful public opinion for building a well-off society in an all-round way." In Hu's keynote speech, the section on journalistic work said "we should firmly adhere to a correct orientation in guiding public opinion; uphold the principle of unity, stability, boosting morale, and mainly positive propaganda; play up the theme of the times; and cultivate and develop a positive and healthy mainstream public opinion throughout society."[3] Meanwhile, Premier Wen Jiabao recently reiterated his cabinet's pledge to "consult public opinion on major issues involving economic and social development, to make decisions in a scientific way, in accordance with law, and under democratic supervision" at a State Council consultation meeting with top economists in the nation.[4]

Foreign polling organizations have played an indispensable role in promoting the use of polls and surveys in China. While their operation is primarily driven by commercial interests and they often work for business clients on market- or consumer-related topics, these professional organizations may also occasionally enter the area of public opinion on social and political issues. By mid-2001, it was reported that there were already about 1000 research institutions specializing in polling in China, with 50 of them focusing on social issues. Many of the institutions were affiliated with the National Bureau of

Statistics or had connections with research universities in the country, and improvements in the scientific procedures and rigor had added credibility to the results.[5] Well-known polling organizations, such as Gallup and AC Nielsen, have established their presence in China. For example, Gallup China, a subsidiary of the U.S.-based Gallup organization, has thus far conducted three large-scale, longitudinal national surveys in China investigating consumer attitudes and lifestyle trends among Chinese consumers: one was completed in 1994,[6] one in 1997,[7] and one in 1999.[8] Another big name, AC Nielsen, has also gained a foothold in China by doing what it does best, such as finding out where Chinese consumers like to shop,[9] what foreign brands are favored by the Chinese,[10] what television and cable channels[11] and programs they watch,[12] or which city lands highest in terms of private car possession.[13]

From time to time, these polling organizations also beat the drum for Chinese government efforts by polling Chinese citizens on hot issues of the day by working hand in hand with the authorities. To put this in the Chinese perspective, survey results that may please the authorities help these foreign polling organizations in two ways: to promote and make known their presence among the general Chinese citizens and to curry favor with the authorities so as to build good connections (or *guanxi*) with the government that will benefit these business organizations in the long run. As an example, early in 2001, in the height of China's effort to bid for the 2008 Summer Olympic Games, a Gallup poll of Beijing residents, much to the pleasure of the authorities, showed that 94.9 percent of the people backed Beijing's Olympic bid and 94 percent wanted to become Olympic volunteers.[14] In an effort to expand its business scope, Gallup formed a partnership with CCIDnet.com in 2000, a Chinese domestic company specializing in online polling, to provide both online and offline market research services to Chinese and overseas clients.[15] Granted, in the strict sense, surveys and polls by most of the foreign professional polling companies focus on consumer attitudes and lifestyle issues and do not fall in the domain of public opinion. But they play a positive role in transforming the Chinese public in that they promote the idea that people's opinions matter and that you can develop a systematic way to figure them out. That in and of itself is a significant step forward.

The growth of the survey practice as an industry and as an academic endeavor in China brings more than just information about the latest public opinion on certain issues or trends; more importantly, it brings in the idea that public opinion can be assessed and analyzed, and can serve a purpose — in the eyes of the authorities the purpose of lending legitimacy to state policy initiatives and thus of managing public opinion to expand state power. Of course, the practice of managing and controlling public opinion in favor of the state is nothing new — either in authoritarian regimes or democratic polities. As Benjamin Ginsberg argues, domestication and manipulation of mass opinion became a well-established practice among Western regimes in their efforts to continuously expand the size and power of the state. As they began to take account of public opinion in the twentieth century, Ginsberg contends, Western governments did not become subservient to public sentiments; instead, they "began what was to become a protracted effort to reshape the character and political content of their subjects' views" (1986: 32). He notes four key components in this transformation of the character of public opinion:

> First, western regimes altered the manner in which mass beliefs were formed. While earlier such beliefs were formulated through social processes, now state agencies were involved in their creation. Second, western governments changed the social basis of public opinion from class to market, thereby converting lower social classes from producers to consumers of opinion. Third, governments restructured the political foundation of mass opinion, changing the central political perspective underlying popular attitudes from an adversary to a proprietary view of the state. Fourth, governments recast the expression of mass opinion from a spontaneous, citizen-initiated act, into a formal and routine public function.
>
> (Ginsberg, 1986: 32-33)

For Ginsberg, the latest Iraqi war is a perfect textbook example of how the U.S. government created and manipulated the force of public opinion in going to war with Iraq.

As Michael Guo, general manager of the Gallup Poll China pointed out during an interview with CNN, "A lot of information is flowing, so government cannot make any random decisions or one-sided decisions without considering the opinions of its people."[16] "Opinion polling, along with the news media and other government channels, enable ordinary Chinese to express their views and address their grievances," Victor Yuan, chairman of Horizon, one of the leading private polling organizations in China was quoted as saying.[17]

Naturally, the Chinese authorities would not like to be left out in the decisions on what topics can be surveyed and what cannot. In a set of regulations that took effect on August 15, 1999, the government decided that "[a]ll survey activities undertaken by foreign institutions or domestic agencies employed by foreigners must first be approved by provincial statistical bureaus or the NBS [National Bureau of Statistics]. Overseas organizations or foreign individuals may not conduct surveys in China without authorization. They must commission qualified organizations to do surveys."[18] These regulations came at a moment when the Chinese government noticed that some polling agencies had overstepped permissible boundaries by conducting surveys about politically sensitive topics in the country, such as the ranking of local leaders and local government agencies and issues that touched the nerve of the political system (e.g., rule of the Communist Party in China, political reforms). These regulations were part of the government effort to tighten control in directing public opinion to its own advantage within its overall propaganda apparatus.

Pollsters in China still find themselves very much at the whim of the Chinese authorities. On January 6, 2003, the Propaganda Ministry of the CCP Central Committee issued a notice entitled "On Work to Strictly Control What Is to Be Chosen Through Public Appraisals and Public Opinion Polls" to propaganda, information, culture, education, and publication departments of party and government organizations at the prefectural and provincial levels with the order that they "must not conduct activities to choose through public appraisal major domestic and international events in 2002, man of 2002 in China, and man of 2002 of the world and must not openly or privately conduct activities to choose through public appraisal or through public opinion polls party, government and military leaders."[19] This official notice was in response to the move led by a Guangzhou-based newspaper, *Nanfang Zhoumo* (Southern Weekend), among other local papers and Web sites, to poll audiences on issues, events, and people of the past year, and was believed to have been orchestrated by Zeng Qinghong, a Politburo member (who later became the Chinese vice president in the spring of 2003) and a protégé of Jiang Zemin. Zeng suggested that results from public opinion polls on those issues can be used by "foreign hostile forces and hostile media to create political incidents, sow discord, and instigate various social strata to intensify contradictions and social turmoil."[20] Zeng may be right in that people do indeed express their likes and dislikes in choosing (or not choosing) domestic and global issues or people of the year, and the results may end up making the regime look bad.

As was mentioned earlier, the manipulation of public opinion for political gains is nothing new for either democratic governments or authoritarian regimes. But control of public opinion is more direct and blatant with the latter. While China under Mao's rule allowed no opportunity for individuals to express their opinions (and even if given the opportunity, people would balk at the very idea of speaking their minds in public), more and more people in China's reform era are willing to express themselves on public issues, political or otherwise. After all, economic openness has significantly decreased individuals' dependency on the state for housing, livelihood (jobs), and mobility (where to live, work, and socialize). Expanding independence, on the other hand, means fewer reservations on the part of the individual citizens to say what they think. At the same time, the disruptive effects of the reform era have been increasingly felt in the life of the ordinary Chinese citizens — rampant official corruption, widening gap between the rich and the poor, deteriorating environment, rising crime rate, widespread unemployment, not to mention an enlarging base of political dissidents within and outside of the country. These factors in combination have created the social conditions that foment complaints, protests, and calls for change. Display of true mass sentiments, in those cases, may be embarrassing and damaging to the ruling authorities, yet resorting to the heavy-handed approach of Mao's era to silence public voices is not highly desirable in consideration of the changing social environment. Therefore, instead of shutting down all individual voices (talking to any individual Chinese citizen on the street today will lead to a bellyful of complaints and grievances against political power), the official strategy in the new era is to focus on the control of the media outlets and direct them on what to highlight and what not to publicize.[21] Thus, suppression of public opinion by the authorities on certain politically or socially sensitive topics in the coverage of mainstream media makes it impossible to accurately gauge the public pulse on some key issues of the day. Under these circumstances, the Internet has created a viable alternative as a barometer for public feelings, in spite of all its imperfections. Notwithstanding all the official regulations and attempts to control the Internet, it is the only public space where grievances, resentment, and criticism of the government can be openly expressed and often be heard by a vast number of people in China because of its widespread availability and accessibility. In an effort to increase traffic flow and expand their user base, all major Chinese news or portal sites have special forum sections that allow registered users to comment on hot news or major events of the day. But once the users have the opportunity to speak, there is no guarantee that they will follow the official line. Indeed, most of the comments and opinions in the online forums are negative. As shown in the Introduction and in the cases discussed in Chapters 6 and 7, the flood of online public opinion concerning breaking events or major issues may prompt the government to respond to public sentiments and take actions to redress popular grievances. But on other occasions, as the cases discussed in Chapter 3 demonstrated, the government may choose to selectively punish those who openly challenge its rule. In all cases, there is mounting evidence that the Internet has provided an alternative platform for organized or unorganized individuals in Chinese civil society to vent their opinions, and occasionally to demand official accountability.

Access to information is essential for the formulation of independent opinion. Therefore, the first step toward the successful control of public opinion is the control of information. In Mao's era, the government was able to mobilize its propaganda machines to filter unwanted information and to let through to the masses the portion of information allowed by the government. The Internet, however, has reduced people's reliance on conventional media for information and has diminished the government's ability to set the agenda for its people. This "democratization of information," a term I used earlier, or "decentralization of information," as some may want to say, occurs as a result of the multiplication of competing sources of information on the Internet. As Li Xiguang observes, the Internet creates a communication environment in China where "multiple sources of information" have replaced the "single-source news" age of the pre-Internet days when the only news available came from government-sanctioned media.[22] Up to the 1980s, the traditional media had observed a formula set in the Mao era that prescribed that all media must follow the official Xinhua News Agency in the coverage of sensitive stories. This practice led to the saying in Chinese journalism of "a thousand newspapers with the same face." Major Chinese news portal sites are updated on a 24-hour basis, and online editors of official-sanctioned news or portal sites often take the liberty to step into the gray areas of the official line in publishing news stories from multiple providers under contract to diversify their sources of news and to compete for audience share.

Up to this point, the Chinese authorities have adopted a supportive policy toward online media, which affords Internet news sites a more preferential treatment than traditional media. As Qian Xiaoqian, head of the Internet Bureau of the State Council Information Office, openly admitted, "We plan to adopt policies towards Internet media that are preferential and more lenient than those for traditional media. There is a great difference between traditional media and Internet media, so it's not possible to apply the past methods of managing traditional media to the Internet."[23] To a certain extent, this allows Internet media to adopt a more aggressive approach in covering major news events.

The Internet has gradually eased its way into the Chinese political process. In March each year, delegates to the National People's Congress, China's legislative body, meet in the Chinese capital of Beijing to discuss important issues in Chinese politics. During the last few years, in one noticeable difference from the past, more and more delegates came to the meeting with laptops. Zhou Hongyu, from Wuhan city of Hubei Province, was the first NPC delegate to have a personal Web site, www.hongyu-online.com, which is mainly used to solicit proposals and opinions from Chinese netizens. Just before the NPC annual session in 2004, Zhou Hongyu also set up a special section at the Strong Nation Forum of the official Web site of the *People's Daily* (www.people.com.cn), which he said would openly "accept and forward suggestions from netizens." From late February to mid-March, there were 201 postings and 55 follow-ups, 10 of which were written by Zhou himself in response to the postings. Most of the postings had focused on issues in the areas of education, official corruption, laid-off workers, poverty, and agriculture.[24] According to Zhou, "Netizens are a special group of constituency who can express their will at ease on the Internet, and their activities will facilitate to some extent the development of democracy in China."[25] Another delegate, Chen Yiheng, from Shaanxi province, said that he got hundreds of e-mail contacts expressing a variety of opinions on social issues from the public every year, which helped him draft and finalize motions to the NPC sessions.[26] An example at the local level took place during the 2005 local People's Congress in Hangzhou, the capital city of Zhejiang province, when representatives actively solicited ideas and suggestions from citizens via the Internet as well as hotlines through arrangements by hangzhou.com.cn, a portal site mainly serving local residents.[27] Rather than an isolated occurrence, the practice of making an online presence through Internet connectivity represents an emerging trend that has been followed by an increasing number of delegates to people's congresses throughout major administrative districts in China. The People's Congress at the national and local levels, China's legislative body for national and local affairs and for long dubbed China's rubber stamp, have in recent years become more aggressive and more involved in the political process. But unlike their Western counterparts who have regular offices and staff members and where the channels of communication to their constituents are readily available, Chinese representatives to the People's Congress lack an effective means of assessing opinions of the constituents they are supposed to represent. The Internet fills in the void as an emerging public venue connecting Chinese citizens and their lawmakers. Granted, there is much room for improvement and the biggest problem is that access to the Internet is still very limited; yet this latest development represents an expanded public space for Chinese society to have some input — limited as it is — in the political process.

This "network supervision" of government work has gotten a lot of publicity in both national and local politics in recent years. *Hongwang*, or *Red Net*, a portal site specializing in local affairs in Hunan province with a reported 4 million daily hits, actively solicited opinions from its registered users during the 2004 local People's Congress session in January and forwarded these opinions to the delegates. Over a dozen delegates interviewed during the session indicated that they avidly looked for input and suggestions from Internet surfers for political ideas, and sometimes criticisms of the local government.[28] In another development, on March 25, 2005, the Shanghai People's Congress founded the "Delegate Online Discussion Day," which features online meetings once every month between delegates and netizens on issues of public concern; similar efforts have been in place in other localities in major cities in China.[29]

There are also indications that local governments are using the Internet as a new outlet of public communication. At the end of 2003, Beijing municipal authorities decided to conduct an online survey on the dissatisfaction (or satisfaction) rate of its government bureaucracies, and Internet surfers were asked how satisfied they were with the services from a list of the city-level government agencies. Within less than a month, 110,000 people had responded, and the three most unpopular local government bodies were found to be the Transportation Commission (86 percent disapproval rate), Urban Planning Commission (75 percent), and the Tax Bureau (62 percent).[30] This move was hailed by the English-language newspaper, *China Daily*, as signaling the municipal government's intention to create a "more transparent" environment and to "open new channels of communication with the public."[31] In another instance, in April 2004, a draft regulation by the Beijing municipal government was stopped for the first time because of public opposition after it was posted on the government's Web site to solicit citizens' input. The draft proposal, which was about the supervision and management of non-Beijing construction enterprises that were engaged in construction contracts in Beijing, stipulated that harsher punishments be imposed on violations of relevant regulations by those enterprises. Eight people who read the draft on the Internet strongly opposed it and posted their reactions to the proposed regulation on the ground that it would constitute discriminatory treatment of nonlocal enterprises.[32] Although the opposition only came from a small number of people, the fact that their views were taken seriously by local government authorities was a symbolic posture that the government may on occasions respect public opinion from the Internet and respond in a limited manner to public sentiments on the Internet. In a related development in the coastal city of Qingdao, suggestions from citizens' postings on Qingdaonews.com have been regularly picked and printed to be read by local government functionaries.[33]

Political Efficacy and Participation on the Internet

It was mentioned previously that Chinese netizens are more inclined to visit online forums and BBS, and use Internet chat rooms. A more important point for understanding the role of the Internet in the Chinese political arena is Chinese Internet users' political behavior online. The preceding section suggests that online public opinion has been gradually woven into China's political process, limited as it is. An exploration of why online behavior among Chinese Net surfers differs from that of users in other countries will help us better understand the political impact of the Internet in China.

Of particular interest are Chinese netizens' opinions concerning the Internet, politics, and government. As part of the UCLA World Internet Project, a survey of Chinese Internet users by CASS's Social Development Research Center in 2003 included four questions on the impact of the Internet on government and politics (CASS Research Center for Social Development, 2003):

1. By using the Internet, people can better express their political views.
2. By using the Internet, people have more say in what the government does.
3. By using the Internet, people can better understand politics.
4. By using the Internet, government officials can better learn people's views.

In their responses to the 2003 survey, Chinese Internet surfers generally agreed that the Internet had allowed them more opportunities to express their personal views on government affairs and political issues: 71.8 percent of the Internet users surveyed agreed or strongly agreed with the first statement (better express political views), 60.8 percent of them agreed or strongly agreed with the second statement (have more say in what the government does), 79.2 percent of the surveyed netizens agreed or strongly agreed that the Internet contributes to their knowledge in politics, and 72.3 percent agreed or strongly agreed that the Internet makes it possible for government officials to learn people's opinion. There was no significant variation with responses to any of the statements in terms of age, income, education, and marriage status, indicating a high level of consensus among users of all spectrums (CASS, 2003).

In CASS's follow-up study of Chinese Internet users in 2005, the same four questions led to similarly positive responses: 54.2 percent of Chinese netizens surveyed agreed or strongly agreed with the statement "By using the Internet, people can better express their political views," 45.1 percent agreed or strongly agreed with the statement "By using the Internet, people have more say in what the government does," 62.8 percent agreed or strongly agreed with the statement "By using the Internet, people can better understand politics," and 60.4 percent agreed or strongly agreed with the statement "By using the Internet, government officials can better learn people's views." The 2005 survey also included an additional question "By using the Internet, the government can better serve the people," with which 55.3 percent of the respondents agreed or strongly agreed (CASS, 2005).

It is helpful here to compare responses from Chinese Internet users with those in other countries. In the UCLA World Internet Project (WIP), Internet users from different countries were asked similar questions about the impact of the Internet on politics and government. Table 5.5 reports responses to two questions by netizens from ten countries. Since not all of the four questions asked in CASS's Internet survey in China were included in surveys conducted in other countries, comparison is possible only for the two questions listed in the table. Only the 2003 CASS survey result was included in the comparison because of proximity in time. As Table 5.5 demonstrates, Chinese netizens offered the most positive assessment to both statements "Do you think by using the Internet, people like you can have more say about what the government does" and "Do you think by using the Internet, people like you can better understand politics?" A substantially higher percentage of Chinese Internet users agreed or strongly agreed with the two statements than their counterparts in other countries.

The differences in perceptions of the Internet's power in the political process between Chinese Internet users and users in other countries are astounding. Why do Internet surfers in China lead users in all other nations in believing that Internet can empower them in the political process? This, I believe, can be best explained by the general information environment in China. For historical as well as political reasons, information has been highly controlled in China by the authorities. Since the Communist Party came to power in 1949, it has implemented a highly regulative media control mechanism to realize its mission of bombarding the masses with propagandist messages. The audience has been treated merely as passive recipients of government-sanctioned information and has had no say in the message production and dissemination

Table 5.5 Cross-national comparison of self-perceived competence on the Internet (all respondents 18 and above)

Country	Percentage Agreeing with "More Say"[a]	Percentage Agreeing with "Better Understand"[b]	Year of Survey
China	60.8	75.2	2003
Chile	18.1	20.4	2003
Hungary	8.6	23.1	2001
Italy	37.1	33.4	2002
Japan	24.2	30.5	2002
Korea	25.7	18.9	2001
Singapore	19.2	20.0	2001
Spain	25.2	20.2	2003
Sweden	10.1	11.0	2002
USA	20.0	42.5	2002

[a] "Do you think by using the Internet, people like you can have more say about what the government does?"
[b] "Do you think by using the Internet, people like you can better understand politics?"
Source: Chinese Academy of Social Sciences Research Center for Social Development (2003); UCLA Center for Communication Policy (2004).

process. The Internet, however, has disrupted that traditional landscape of mediated communication and has enabled average Chinese citizens to create, deliver, and receive all sorts of information in ways that were unimaginable before. While the Chinese government shows no indication that it will relent in its censorship and surveillance of the Internet, it cannot fundamentally change the nature of the Internet as a user-centered communication tool that has shifted much of the power from the conventional media and government propaganda agencies to individual users and social groups. It is partly for this reason that, as the Morgan Stanley China Internet Report has noted, user-generated content (UGC), such as web postings, online forums, and online feedback, is becoming so prevalent and so valued in China's cyberspace (Morgan Stanley, 2004). It should not be underestimated how much this new found self-expressive power means to the Chinese people, who had been cut off from the information flow process prior to the Internet era. On the other hand, in such democratic polities as the United States, people have many more options — which in many cases may be more effective and immediate — to effect change in the political process, and the Internet, therefore, is not ranked very high by users in those countries as a political tool. It should come as no surprise, then, that the Internet should give the most self-perceived communicative power to netizens in the country with the lowest level of conventional freedom in the ten countries listed in Table 5.5.

It is useful here to borrow the important concept of political efficacy in the studies of political attitudes and behaviors to further the argument above. Political efficacy is generally defined to be "the feeling that individual political action does have, or can have, an impact upon the political process ... It is the feeling that political and social change is possible, and that the individual citizen can play a part in bringing this change" (Campbell, Gurin, and Miller, 1954: 187). Measurement of political efficacy as a theoretical construct was first proposed by the Survey Research Center (SRC) at the University of Michigan by four agree–disagree questionnaire items (Campbell, Gurin, and Miller, 1954: 187–188):

1. People like me don't have any say about what the government does.
2. Voting is the only way that people like me can have any say about how the government runs things.
3. Sometimes politics and government seem so complicated that a person like me can't really understand what's going on.
4. I don't think public officials care much what people like me think.

The treatment of political efficacy as a unidimensional construct was, however, subsequently challenged by many. Theoretical considerations and empirical evidence have led scholars to develop the concept into two related but separate dimensions: (1) internal efficacy, which is "the individual's belief that means of influence are available to him," and (2) external efficacy, which is "the belief that the authorities or regime are responsive to influence attempts" (Balch, 1974: 24; see also Converse, 1974; Niemi, Craig, and Mattei, 1991). This suggested distinction has been adopted by the Survey Research Center in its subsequent national election studies, and accordingly two more items have been added to the original four questions to construct indices of internal and external efficacy by the following list of items (Miller, Miller, and Schneider, 1980):

Internal efficacy is measured by these three items:

1. People like me don't have any say about what the government does.
2. Voting is the only way that people like me can have any say about how the government runs things.
3. Sometimes politics and government seem so complicated that a person like me can't really understand what's going on.

External efficacy is measured by the following three items:
1. I don't think public officials care much what people like me think.
2. Generally speaking those we elect to Congress in Washington lose touch with the people pretty quickly.
3. Parties are only interested in people's votes but not in their opinions.

Over the years, although some analysts have attempted to develop alternatives to measure efficacy (e.g., Acock, Clarke, and Steward, 1985; Miller, Erbring, and Goldernberg, 1979; Morrell, 2003; Niemi, Craig, and Mattei, 1991), the preceding items have been adopted by many scholars as measurements of individual political efficacy. An item of major contention is the statement "Voting is the only way that people like me can have any say about how the government runs things," which has been argued to be invalid (e.g., Acock, Clarke, and Steward, 1985; Converse, 1972; Wright, 1976) and has been dropped in SRC's National Election Studies since 1980 (Miller and Traugott, 1989).

In accordance with the above indices, the two statements, listed in Table 5.5, of the World Internet Project cross-national surveys clearly measure some aspects of the respondents' individual internal political efficacy online, which can be defined here as the self-perceived accessibility and availability of online resources and channels to them in understanding politics and participating in the political process via the Internet. Table 5.5 clearly shows that Chinese netizens display the highest level of internal efficacy online among the ten countries listed. As explained previously, because offline channels of political participation are much more limited to Chinese netizens, it is reasonable to expect that they are more likely to seek alternative opportunities to influence the political process.

Two of the five questions asked in the CASS 2005 survey, "By using the Internet, government officials can better learn people's views" and "By using the Internet, the government can better serve the people," obviously concern some aspects of external political efficacy online, which is defined here as the perceived level of responsiveness from government and political institutions to netizens' interests and demands online as well as one's perceived ability to successfully influence that responsiveness. As reported previously, 60.4 percent of of Chinese respondents agreed or strongly agreed with the first statement, while 55.3 percent of them agreed or strongly agreed with the second, pointing to a high level of external efficacy among Chinese netizens. Because similar questions were not asked in most of the other WIP surveys, no cross-national comparison can be made. However, the results are suggestive that Chinese netizens also possess a higher level of external efficacy, although this claim needs empirical support in future cross-national research.

It is logical to expect that those with a higher level of efficacy tend to be more active in a variety of related activities. Primary support can be found in Bandura's study of self-efficacy — defined as "beliefs in one's capability to organize and execute the courses of action required to manage prospective situations" (1997: 2) — which suggests that stronger beliefs will translate into more active relevant behaviors (see also Bandura, 1977). Therefore, the high level of political efficacy online among Chinese netizens is most likely to result in active political participation in online forums, BBS, chat rooms, and online protests among Chinese netizens. This is consistent with the results in Table 5.1, Table 5.2, Table 5.3, and Table 5.4; it is also congruent with Chinese netizens' online behavior in the multiple cases mentioned in this and later chapters.

Chapter Summary

Since its inception, the Internet has been acclaimed to be a revolutionary force in changing existing social relationships and in fostering brand-new ones. The very nature of the Internet as a decentralized and interactive platform of human communication calls for fresh perspectives in understanding the new capabilities in cyberspace. To look at the Internet and its impact on society within established frameworks that have worked well with conventional media may blind us to the full potential of the Internet. This chapter suggests that the Internet be approached as the fourth place, which maintains its connectedness to the physical world but is meanwhile situated in emerging social relations that can only find full expression in the cyberworld. Tim Jordan's characterization of cyberspace is relevant here: "The fundamental power of the metaphor of the frontier is to take as protean a form of communication as cyberspace and conceive it as space. This is, perhaps, the reason why the metaphor of the frontier is the foundation metaphor for cyberspace because it conceives virtual life fundamentally as a place, and nearly all other metaphors for cyberspace follow this conception" (Jordan, 1999: 176). For Jordan, "the totality of cyberpower" lies in its ability to mingle three levels of interrelated regions: the individual, the social, and the imaginary.

Because public opinion on sensitive issues or topics in China may not be readily available or may not even be possible to assess from alternative sources elsewhere, the Internet has created the opportunity to allow Chinese netizens to express their opinions on important issues of interest and has thus become a barometer for politicians, government functionaries, and lawmakers, among others, to gauge public opinion and to consider actions thereafter. One can certainly make the argument that availability of public opinion on the Internet does not mean that it is going to have an impact on anything in any noticeable way. That the government is starting to take these online opinions seriously is a significant move in and of itself in Chinese politics. As has been demonstrated in this chapter, responses and opinions from Chinese netizens are increasingly becoming an important factor in China's political arena. So much so that in March 2005, in the press conference after the annual sessions of the National People's Congress (NPC) and the Chinese People's Political Consultative Conference (CPPCC) in the People's Hall of Beijing, Premier Wen Jiabao started by remarking that he was deeply touched by hundreds of questions Chinese netizens posted on the official Xinhua Net (Xinhuanet.com), and promised that he and other government officials would look into many worthy suggestions.[34] The Chinese premier is also reported to be a regular reader of a bulletin produced by staff members of the State Council through collecting online information on hot issues, and to demand action from local bureaucrats.[35] On the other hand, the Chinese regime understands well that network public opinion is a double-edged sword. Chinese society is much more open than it used to be, and heavy-handed suppression of public opinion off- or online may backfire and may not be the most desirable approach. Therefore, wherever possible, swimming with the tide of network public opinion, rather than against it, may win over popular support for the regime. In addition, it is a growing trend for authorities at various levels to resort to a more subtle approach to controling online public opinion by recruiting undercover online commentators to spread opinions favorable to them on cyberforums and BBS.[36]

The quick rise of the Internet as a popular tool of public communication in China has essentially turned Chinese cyberspace into a Habermasian public sphere of the twenty-first century, imperfect as it is — important issues are debated and public opinion gets formed. Political efficacy is an important predictor of public participation in politics, and results from surveys across nations indicate that Chinese netizens display an unusually higher level of political efficacy online than their counterparts in other countries, which is highly consistent with Chinese surfers' use pattern on the Internet. The controlled political environment offline turns Chinese citizens to seek alternative participation channels online to make their voice heard by the authorities.

In many ways, China cannot be isolated from the global trend of the changing dynamics of Internet politics. As Castells observes,

> In fact, freedom is never a given. It is a constant struggle: it is the ability to redefine autonomy and enact democracy in each social and technological context. The Internet offers extraordinary potential for the expression of citizen rights, and for the communication of human values. Certainly, it cannot substitute for social change or political reform. However, by relatively leveling the ground of symbolic manipulation, and by broadening the sources of communication, it does contribute to democratization. The Internet brings people into contact in a public agora, to voice their concerns and share their hopes. This is why people's control of this public agora is perhaps the most fundamental political issue raised by the development of the Internet.
>
> (Castells, 2001: 164–165)

The key issue is that once people are given the freedom, limited as it is in China, their creative use of the Internet can initiate social change in ways that have not been designed, envisioned, or desired by the political elites. Wacker's assertion is worth quoting here:

> … freedom of expression has expanded considerably since the end of the late 1970s due to the overall policy of "reform and opening" initiated by Deng Xiaoping, despite intermittent phases of contraction. Thus, what can be said of the Internet can be said of other media in China as well, namely that the limits of toleration are constantly being tested and

re-negotiated. The common practice of conducting activities under the cloak of pseudonames in Chinese cyberspace and the relative weakness of "virtual" sanctions might still make the Internet more of a catalyst of social change than other media, but it is more likely to play a significant role if a social or political movement emerges in the non-virtual world. It is then that, along with fax machines, mobile phones, and mails via mobile phones, the Internet's ability to distribute news and facilitate organisation could play a decisive role.

(Wacker, 2003: 73)

So one should not expect the Internet alone to be the sole agent of change; it is the use of the Internet by real people and civil society groups, such as the Tiananmen Mothers and the Falun Gong activists, that can bring the hope of change. However, I believe the biggest potential does not merely lie in one or a limited few social movements; rather it rests with the Internet being ingrained in the everyday life of the ordinary citizens so that it becomes a way of life. That will be the most revolutionizing effect of the Internet on Chinese civil society — which has not fully occurred yet, but there are cumulative signs that things are going in that direction.

6

A School Explosion, a Fatal Virus, and the Internet Factor

While the Internet is still in its early stage of development in China, there are already unfolding promises that it is becoming an important force in Chinese society. As an information and communication network, it has already started to rejuvenate public participation, leading self-organizing individuals and social groups to relentlessly pursue information, entertainment, and self-expression. In a society that is deeply entrenched in authoritarian rule and information control, the Internet brings in the newest hope of transforming a country in which popular participation in political and social life has not been the hallmark. To understand the nature of this transformation, this chapter and the following one offer a critical analysis of the role of the Internet in the revival of Chinese civil society through close examination of a few prominent cases in which the Internet has played a significant role in shaping the course of development of key events. This chapter starts with a review of the case study method, and then presents studies of two cases in which the Internet disrupted the official network of information manipulation and circulation by devolving the abilities to communicate to grass-roots individuals.

The Case Study Method

As controversial as it has been, the case study research method has been widely used by social researchers across a variety of disciplines in the past, and has recently become increasingly popular in many areas of social inquiry (e.g., Hammnersley and Gomm, 2000). Robert K. Yin defines the case study method as an empirical inquiry that "investigates a contemporary phenomenon within its real-life context, especially when the boundaries between phenomenon and context are not clearly evident" (1994: 13). And as a "comprehensive research strategy" in its data collection and data analysis strategies, which are driven by "prior development of theoretical propositions," case study research "copes with the technically distinctive situation in which there will be many more variables of interest than data points," and "relies on multiple sources of evidence, with data needing to converge in a triangulating fashion" (Yin, 1994: 13).

Over the years, critics of the case study method have argued that the study of a small number of cases (or one case on many occasions) can offer no justifications for establishing reliability or generalizability of findings. Current debates on the issue of generalizability in social research has been very much influenced by Campbell and Stanley (1963) in their groundbreaking chapter in the *Handbook of Research on Teaching*, in which they explored four specific threats to external validity: the interaction of testing and the experimental treatment, the interaction of selection and treatment, reactive arrangements, and the interference of multiple treatments with one another. After pointing out that external validity directly deals with the issue of generalizability, Campbell and Stanley argue that social research must be designed such that abstract generalizations from the specific findings are made possible. In relation to the issue of generalizability, Campbell and Stanley dispelled the usefulness of the "one-shot case study" approach in concluding that the research displays "such a total absence of control as to be of almost no scientific value" and they further asserted that "(a)ny appearance of absolute knowledge, or intrinsic knowledge about singular isolated objects, is found to be illusory upon analysis" (Campbell and Stanley, 1963: 176).

Some years later, in a startling reversal of his earlier position, Campbell wrote:

> In past writings [dating from 1961 to 1970] I have spoken harshly of the single-occasion, single-setting (one shot) case study, not on the grounds of its qualitative nature, but because it combined such a fewness of points of observation, and such a plethora of available causal concepts, that a spuriously perfect fit was almost certain. Recently, in a quixotic and ambivalent article, "Degrees of Freedom" (1975), I have recanted, reminding myself that such studies regularly contradict the prior expectations of the authors, and are convincing and informative to sceptics [sic] like me to a degree which my simple-minded rejection does not allow for.

(Campbell, [1978]1988b: 373)

In his well-known 1975 "Degrees of Freedom" paper, Campbell suggested that there might be some merit in "the intensive study of a single foreign setting by an outsider for whom this is the only intensively experienced foreign culture" (Campbell [1975]1988a: 377). However, he was also quick to point out:

> This is not to say that such commonsense naturalistic observation is objective, dependable, or unbiased. But it is all that we have. It is the only route to knowledge – noisy, fallible and biased though it be. We should be aware of its weaknesses, but must still be willing to trust it if we are to go about the process of comparative (or monocultural) social science at all.

(Campbell, [1975]1988a: 377)

As "an extreme oscillation away from my earlier dogmatic disparagement of case studies" (p. 388), Campbell makes this acknowledgement in defense of case studies:

> In a case study done by an alert social scientist who has thorough local acquaintance, the theory he uses to explain the focal difference also generates predictions or expectations on dozens of other aspects of the culture, and he does not retain the theory unless most of these are also confirmed. In some sense, he has tested the theory with degrees of freedom coming from the multiple implications of any one theory. The process is a kind of pattern-matching in which there are many aspects of the pattern demanded by theory that are available for matching with his observations on the local setting.
>
> (1975/1988: 380)

Hamel (1993) sees the merit of the case study method in three keywords: describing, understanding, and explaining. This is accomplished through establishing the "relationships and forces that link the parts in the form of the whole" in the analysis of the singularity of the case under investigation (Hamel, 1993: 39); the general applicability of the methodological qualities of a case study is manifested in making the transformation from the local to the global.

While many advocates of the case study method have recognized the importance of dealing with the issue of generalizability, they agree that the classical view of external validity as propagated principally by quantitative researchers needs to be adapted to the specific nature of case study research. Robert E. Stake, for example, proposed a process of "naturalistic generalization," which is "arrived at by recognizing the similarities of objects and issues in and out of context and by sensing the natural covariations of happenings" (2000a: 22), to apply the findings of the study of one case to the understanding of similar situations.

Lincoln and Guba (2000) suggest that the concept of generalizability be replaced with "fittingness," which is defined as "the degree of congruence between sending and receiving contexts" (p. 40). Therefore, the extent to which results from one qualitative study are transferable to another situation, which is called "transferability" by Lincoln and Guba, is "a direct function of the *similarity* between the two contexts" (2000: 40; emphasis original). Thus fittingness, Lincoln and Guba argue, is a more practical and workable approach than the classical concept of generalizability. However, adoption of the concept of fittingness would put the onus on the readers to determine the degree of congruence between cases before they can make the decision as to the transferability of findings across cases.

To expand the applicability of results from qualitative research to other situations, Goetz and LeCompte (1984) call for researchers to specifically address two important issues: "comparability" and "translatability." They write:

> ...comparability refers to the degree to which the components of a study — including the units of analysis, concepts generated, population characteristics, and setting — are sufficiently well described and defined that other researchers can use the results of the study as a basis for comparison with other studies addressing related issues. Establishing the comparability of a study makes it scientifically useful. Translatability ... refers to the degree to which the researcher uses theoretical frames, definitions, and research techniques that are accessible to or understood by other researchers in the same or related disciplines. A study is of little use to other researchers if its theoretical basis or the constructs around which it is organized are so idiosyncratic that they are understood only by the person who executed the study. The lack of comparability and translatability reduces the usefulness of a study to interesting, but unscientific, reading.

(Goetz and LeCompte, 1984: 228)

Thus researchers need to clearly identify and describe the typical characteristics of a phenomenon that are comparable with other types so as to ensure applicability of results across sites and disciplines.

In a key text on the case study method, Robert Yin (1994) makes the distinction between two types of generalizations: "statistical generalization" and "analytic generalization." In the former, "an inference is made about a population (or universe) on the basis of empirical data collected about a sample" (p. 30), and "is commonly recognized because research investigators have ready access to formulas for determining the confidence with which generalizations can be made, depending mostly upon the size and internal variation within the universe and sample" (p. 31). In the latter, "a previously developed theory is used as a template with which to compare the empirical results to the case study" (Yin, 1994: 31). A fatal flaw in doing and understanding case study research, Yin argues, is that some researchers try to aim toward statistical generalization when the right choice should be analytical generalization.

J. Clyde Mitchell makes the distinction between two types of inferences commonly practiced in social research: statistical inference, and logical or causal (or scientific) inference. Statistical inference is "the process by which the analyst draws conclusions about the existence of two or more characteristics in some wider population from some sample of that population to which the observer has access," while logical, causal, or scientific inference is "the process by which the analyst draws conclusions about the essential linkage between two or more characteristics in terms of some systematic explanatory schema — some set of theoretical propositions" (Mitchell, 1983: 176). The process of inference associated with case studies, Mitchell argues, is purely logical or causal, and not statistical in any way, and hence the "validity of the extrapolation depends not on the typicality or representativeness of the case but upon the cogency of the theoretical reasoning" (p. 183). However, Mitchell's use of terminology here is bewildering: Why is the process of logical analysis typically associated with qualitative research, not the statistical inferential procedure that is most often identified with the quantitative tradition, only denominated "scientific?" What is the "unscientific" aspect of statistical inference? He does not make any attempt to clarify his position on this point.

Another dichotomy that is closely related to the conceptualization of statistical versus causal inference is the distinction that Florian Znaniecki made in *The Method of Sociology* (1934) between enumerative and analytic induction that has influenced the practice of conducting case studies in the social sciences for decades. The general presuppositions of enumerative induction were described by Znaniecki as follows:

> It is dominated by that conception of knowledge which regards truth as the final and unshakable result of research past and done with .... Induction from this point of view is an attempt to discover some final truths about a certain class of empirical data, circumscribed in advance, by studying a number of cases belonging to this class. Originally and fundamentally, the truths sought for are to be characters common to all the data of the given class and only to these. Such a problem, however, if real, is insoluble; and, if soluble, is fictitious.
>
> (Znaniecki, 1934: 222)

The flaw with this approach, Znaniecki argued, is that if you circumscribe a class by a set of common and distinctive characters that are already known to exist with the data of this class, your discoveries "will consist at best in making explicit what was already implicit in the definition" (p. 223), because all data in such a class are essentially similar among themselves and different from all the data of all other classes, just as you already knew in advance. On the other hand, if you define a class of data based on an unknown set of common and distinctive characteristics, then "you may be sure there are no such characters" and therefore "your class is scientifically worthless" (p. 222). The use of such common-sense categories breaks no new ground, Znaniecki concluded. Understandably, many researchers following the quantitative tradition will take issue with Znaniecki's extremist positions here.

By contrast, in analytic induction, the approach favored by Znaniecki,

> ... certain particular objects are determined by intensive study, and the problem is to define the logical classes which they represent. No definition of the class precedes in analytic induction the selection of data to be

studied as representative of this class. The analysis of data is all done before any general formulations; and if well done, there is nothing more of importance to be learned about the class which these data represent by any subsequent investigation of more data of the same class.

(Znaniecki, 1934: 247)

In comparing the two approaches, Znaniecki wrote:

While both forms of induction tend to reach general and abstract truths concerning particular and concrete data, enumerative induction abstracts by generalization, whereas analytic induction generalizes by abstracting. The former looks in many cases for characters that are similar and abstracts them conceptually because of their generality, presuming that they must be essential to each particular case; the latter abstracts from the given concrete case characters that are essential to it and generalizes them, presuming that in so far as essential, they must be similar in many cases.

(Znaniecki, 1934: 250-251)

Znaniecki has set a high standard that few can attain in analytical induction because it is rare that any research will leave "nothing of more importance to be learned" about a class. Although he acknowledged the role of discovering new knowledge in subsequent studies, Znaniecki claimed that "the new knowledge does not by the investigation of similar concrete instances merely supplement preexisting knowledge about the class previously defined: it is supposed to be knowledge about *some new class* somehow related to the class already known" (p. 250. Emphasis added). Znaniecki's conceptualization of analytic induction has greatly shaped the theoretical debates as well as the practice of case study research (see, for example, two volumes on case study research edited by Gomm, Hammersley, and Foster, 2000; and Ragin and Becker, 1992).

A point that is of particular importance to the research in this chapter is the distinction made by Yin between the single-case and the multiple-case design. Yin argues that the treatment of multiple-case studies as a design distinctive from the so-called classic (or single-case studies) approach is misguided and must be avoided because both single- and multiple-case designs are grounded in the same methodological framework. However, the decision whether to use the single- or multiple-case studies design largely depends on what one aims to accomplish: the single-case method is typically used to confirm or challenge a theory, and is most likely to involve the unique, the extreme, the rare or the unusual, the critical, or the revelatory case, whereas the "evidence from multiple cases is often considered more compelling, and the overall study is therefore regarded as more robust" (Yin, 1994: 45).

The single-case design can be embedded (i.e., attention is also paid to the subunit or subunits in the case under investigation) and holistic (i.e., focus is on the global nature of the case), and requires careful investigation to minimize any chance of misrepresentation and to maximize the investigator's access to the case evidence. Multiple-case studies, on the other hand, follow a replication logic that is akin to that used in multiple experiments and serve to strengthen results by replicating pattern matching among the cases selected for investigation. Yin cautions researchers not to confuse the replication logic of multiple-case research with the sampling logic commonly used in surveys, which strives to get a number of respondents or subjects that are representative of a larger pool of respondents or subjects of interest. Finally, Yin makes the case that the generalization of results from case studies, be it single-case or multiple-case designs, are made to the specific theoretical framework adopted in the study, not the population at large as typical survey research designs.

Thus the case study is a method that can help us learn about complex instances through extensive description and in-depth contextual analysis. Indeed, in certain complex situations, it is only possible to generate in-depth understanding through focusing on particular instances or cases, hence leading to the "paradox of case study" as called by Helen Simons — "by focusing in depth and from a holistic perspective, a case study can generate both unique and universal understandings" (Simons, 1996: 225).

The two cases discussed in this chapter plus the two additional cases in the following chapter examine the interplay between the Internet and civil society in China and provide in essence a multiple-case design as proposed by Yin (1994), or a collective case study as identified by Robert Stake in which "a researcher may jointly study a number of cases in order to investigate a phenomenon, population, or general condition" (Stake, 2000b: 437). This is also in line with the approach of multisite studies advocated by Herriott and Firestone (1983), which, by focusing on the same issue in a number of settings, can avoid the "radical particularism" as called by Firestone and Herriot (1986) and thus enhance the generalizability and the relevance of the findings from these studies. The study of the four cases in China in the two chapters, which have taken place under different settings and involve different parties, may add to our cumulative knowledge about the use of the Internet by Chinese civil society in the new era.

Each of the cases chosen for close examination can be considered a "functioning specificity" or "bounded system" as described by Stake (1995) because each case is studied as an object that may be intrinsically revealing, and through examining the common as well as the particular about each case, it is expected that some persistent patterns may emerge. Although these cases may not be representative or even typical of what is happening on the Internet in China with regular online surfers on a daily basis, each instance is an *instrumental case* as defined by Stake in that "it facilitates our understanding of something else" (Stake, 2000b: 437) — here it advances our understanding of the role of the Internet in the changing landscape of Chinese civil society. Because the Internet is still very much in the middle of an evolving revolution in breeding a brand-new information environment in China, these cases offer us a chance of "studying the 'leading edge' of change," as suggested by Schofield (2000), who maps out three targets for generalization in designing case studies: *what is* (studying the typical, the common, or the ordinary), *what may be* (studying the most likely issues or trend for the future) and *what could be* (locating situations that are expected to be ideal or exceptional). Certainly all these cases represent an ongoing social situation, yet they may not be the most typical of the online world in China as of yet. However, one can make the case that these cases do represent unmistakable opportunities and challenges that are likely to play pivotal roles in shaping Chinese civil society in the years to come.

The SARS Epidemic of 2003: From a Regional Health Crisis to a National Political Disaster

In the spring of 2003, a mysterious and lethal virus, called atypical pneumonia in China and defined by the World Health Organization as Severe Acute Respiratory Syndrome (SARS), first broke out in China's southern Guangdong province and then spread to Beijing and other regions in the country before it quickly grew into a global epidemic crisis. From the time when WHO officials were first notified of an outbreak of atypical pneumonia with unknown cause by the Chinese authorities on February 11 (CDSR, 2003) to July 3, when the World Health Organization pronounced it contained, the total cumulative number of confirmed or probable cases reported worldwide reached 8456 and the number of deaths amounted to 812; the five nations or regions that were hit the most were China (5327 reported cases and 348 deaths), Hong Kong (1755 reported cases and 298 deaths), Taiwan (682 reported cases and 84 deaths), Singapore (206 reported cases and 32 deaths), and Canada (251 reported cases and 39 deaths), and the total number of nations reporting SARS infections reached 36.[1]

An Overview

The SARS outbreak put the spotlight on the inequitable and inefficient public health care system in China, a system that has been largely out of tune with the country's economic reform policy in the past decades because of lack of government support and investment since the country embarked on a course of economic reform and openness in the late 1970s (e.g., Huang, 2004). On a deeper level, however, the evolution of SARS from a regional epidemic to a medical crisis to a political debacle for the Chinese leadership reflects a failing bureaucratic and malfunctioning Chinese political system that cannot deal adequately with a crisis of such magnitude. As Sautedâe (2003: 21) summarizes, the SARS crisis "highlights all the contradictions of the Chinese development model, the inequality if has generated, and the obsolescence of a certain mode of government that is ferociously monopolistic within a context of extraordinary diversification." In retrospect, what the SARS case highlights is also the expanding space of civil society and the increasing role it plays in Chinese society and politics.

SARS also points to the lack of transparency and public accountability in the Chinese polity (e.g., Thiers, 2003), which accounts for the official unresponsiveness in the early stages of the crisis. For decades, the official strategy in dealing with epidemics and contagious diseases has been heavy-handed cover-up, blunt denial, and all-out information control. This approach had worked successfully in most instances, as most viruses and epidemics would eventually die out or be brought under control without causing much public outcry other than among those directly affected. However, after more than two decades of breakneck economic prosperity since its reform and opening initiative, the Chinese government has learned both the promise and peril of the consequences of opening up the society to the world at large: the changing information environment brought about by new communication technologies and increased contact with the outside world and the rising public consciousness as a result of exposure to this information environment. These create the social conditions that empower different elements in Chinese civil society at times of crisis or uncertainty. The Internet has been a particularly important factor in this whole process.

Other than SARS, another high-profile case that illustrates this inevitable contradiction between the dysfunctional political system and the social and economic structure in Chinese society is the HIV–AIDS problem. After years of denial and cover-up, the Chinese Health Minister made the official acknowledgment at the United Nations General Assembly Special Session on HIV–AIDS in June 2001 that as many as 600,000 cases of HIV existed in China, although the UN AIDS program (UNAIDS) estimated that there were more than 1 million people infected with HIV in China at the end of 2001.[2] The province hit the hardest is Henan, the second most populous province in China, largely owing to an unsafe blood collection system through which many poor peasants got infected while selling their blood for money. AIDS campaigners believed that there might be 500,000 HIV cases in Henan province alone as of June 2001.[3] Like SARS, the HIV problem was only openly acknowledged by the Chinese officials when it had reached an alarming enormity and when multiple channels of information were readily available from foreign media and the Internet (for a description of the HIV situation in China, see Gill, Chang, and Palmer, 2002; Kellogg, 2002). A story from the China News Agency reported that UNAIDS officials, with cooperation from the Chinese government, were scheduled to be engaged in online chats with Chinese netizens about HIV–AIDS on May 23, 2004.[4]

The Internet has played an increasingly prominent role in the dissemination of information about HIV in China — both from inside China to the outside world and vice versa, especially when access to information at the local level was scarce or limited. Persistent efforts by international media, individual Chinese activists, and international and domestic groups to gather and publish AIDS-related information have built up enough pressure to force an attitude change on the part of the Chinese government from denial to cover-up to open acknowledgment. For years up to 2002, in response to the lack of sufficient information and supportive resources from the Chinese government, Chinese activists organized themselves into self-support groups and resorted to the Internet to spread information, to recruit members, and to solicit donations worldwide. One of the most popular Web sites focusing on AIDS issues in China, http://www.aizhi.org/, was launched by Wan Yanhai, one of the most prominent AIDS and homosexual activists in China. It publishes news, forums, ongoing projects intended to help Chinese AIDS patients, and educational information for the general public. Wan, who used to work for the Health Ministry, played a key role in exposing a scandal in Henan province in the mid-1990s in which thousand of rural residents were infected with HIV during blood transfusion because of failures of government-sponsored clinics to sanitize needles. Revealing this scandal cost him his job in the Ministry in 1993. In 2002, he was detained by security police in Beijing for "releasing state secrets," which was information about the AIDS epidemic in China that was sent to friends, media outlets, and Internet sources. He was freed four weeks later.[5]

In another example, one of the popular Chinese Web sites, called "the sky of hope," available at http://aidscare.netsh.net/ and publicized by the official Xinhua News Agency,[6] was started by Xiao Cai, an AIDS sufferer, around 2000; it quickly evolved into an online support group for Chinese AIDS patients. On the Web site, visitors, who mainly come from China as indicated by the postings, can post all kinds of questions and information in relation to the disease, organize online and offline activities, and leave contact information or contact others. As of September 2004, there were 201 pages of user-posted messages on the forums.[7]

The paradoxes of the Chinese political, social, and economic systems as reflected by the SARS crisis are summarized by Jacques DeLisle in this way:

> SARS illustrates the interdependence of China's health, both economic and public, with that of its neighbors and the wider world. It highlights the Chinese regime's increased but limited transparency and amenability to international pressure, as well as the challenges the Chinese leadership faces stemming from the country's uneven development and partial reform. The regime's conflicting approaches to SARS indicate

growing responsiveness and responsibility but also the persistence of pre-reform-style attitudes.

(DeLisle, 2003: 587)

These paradoxes are deeply rooted in the "glocalized" nature of present-day Chinese society: unlike Mao's China in the prereform days, when the whole country was a self-contained and self-sustaining entity, today's China has been intricately integrated with the world after decades of Deng Xiaoping's policy of economic reform. This reality is indicated by the spread of SARS to so many countries within such a short period. It is also shown by the Chinese leadership's responsiveness and resolute action that came only in the face of mounting international pressure after the world community had learned the calamity and severity of the epidemic through neighboring regions such as Hong Kong, Taiwan, and Singapore as well as rising domestic demand for more transparency in the wake of more and more individual efforts to break the official chain of information control of SARS-related information.

There has been much speculation about the potential impact of SARS on China's sociopolitical structure and the future path of China's reform. Some have argued that the SARS episode was likely to be "China's Chernobyl"[8] and would lead to fundamental political changes at the institutional level and might even spark democratization. Others claim this occasion was tantamount to China's "glasnost moment"[9] because it would convince the Chinese leadership that openness and transparency were the only solution to SARS and similar problems.

At the other end of the spectrum are those who predicted that the SARS epidemic would have a minimum impact on China's political system because the current leadership would have all the resources to put the epidemic under control and life would soon return to normal after the crisis. This view is best expressed by Hu Angang, director of the Center for China Study, Tsinghua University (Beijing), who claimed SARS was a "benign crisis" on May 11, 2003, because "the government has the political and organizational advantages to mobilize and organize social forces and resources, and eventually control, settle and dismantle the crisis" and he envisioned a nation more united as a result of confronting this crisis.[10]

DeLisle made the same kind of prediction in concluding that SARS would only have a minimal effect on Chinese politics — but toward a different direction. DeLisle sees the root of the crisis in the institutional failure of a paradoxical system in Chinese polity:

If SARS returns, or when the next crisis strikes China, the same paradoxical tendencies toward liberalization and authoritarian institution-strengthening, openness and opacity and obstreperousness, can be expected to recur. SARS has underscored the importance of learning how to navigate the resulting turbulence in and around China, where seemingly irresistible forces of globalization and reform press against intractable obstacles rooted in China's hypertrophic notion of sovereignty, residually Leninist institutions, destabilizing social cleavages, and weakly institutional politics.

(DeLisle, 2003: 604)

Because any change is unlikely in the nature of the Chinese political system in the near future, DeLisle believes that the same pattern will persist in the next similar crisis. I disagree with DeLisle here, because I think that the SARS crisis and its ramifications will extend beyond the case itself. It will definitely make the central and local government officials think twice in the handling of similar cases in the future, although its impact on the political system is less certain.

It is beyond the scope of this chapter to speculate on how the SARS crisis will shape the future course of China's political agenda. But the impact will be twofold: the short term and the long term. The short-term impact will be the investment of more tangible resources by the state in the public health sector throughout China, which has proved to be ill-prepared for a large-scale national epidemic because of decades of neglect and underfunding. As the SARS case clearly shows, a public health crisis can easily turn into a human security threat and endanger the stability and prosperity of not only a single state, but a whole region (Curley and Thomas, 2004). In the long run, we should expect to see some change in the bureaucratic response mechanism in the institutional structure at both the state and the local level. One lesson from the SARS fallout is that lack of coordination and communication between the central leadership and the local authorities exacerbated the crisis in the early phase of the outbreak (Huang, 2004). Because of the increasing interdependence of China's economy and the world market, the Chinese leadership is very wary of the possibility of infectious diseases like SARS dampening people's interest or confidence in conducting business in China. So it is essential for the Chinese government to work out an effective system for controlling future epidemics. However, one should not overestimate the impact of SARS on political changes in the current system — especially in the short run. To what extent an unhealthy political system can work to maintain public health in the face of widespread epidemics in the long run still remains a question.

The immediate impact of SARS on the Chinese government's approach to similar situations was soon felt. As a direct result of the lessons learned from the handling of the SARS case in 2003, China's candor and resoluteness in dealing with the deadly bird flu virus that was spreading through Asia in early 2004[11] and in confronting the recurrence of SARS in April 2004[12] mark a sharp contrast with its initial failure in the SARS outbreak. The results, however, were also totally different: once both the bird flu virus and SARS were quickly put under control in China, citizens' confidence in their government was restored and China was internationally praised for its handling of the outbreak.[13] Granted, there are still areas that need much improvement, but the change in the Chinese government's approach clearly indicates that it has learned something from the SARS crisis of 2003.

The SARS epidemic is not only a lesson for the Chinese authorities, however; it will also have some far-reaching effect on Chinese citizens and civil society. As I show later, there had also been enormous pressure from within the country for the government to come clean as the crisis deepened. As more and more individuals stood up to challenge the official cover-ups, the government had either to tell the truth or face the possibility of losing credibility among its own citizens. The lesson for Chinese civil society is that it can make an impact on government policy making in a crisis like this.

Background: The Chinese Politics of Power Succession

As noted previously, much of the delay, confusion, and miscommunication in the early phase of the SARS crisis is attributable to the dysfunctional institutional politics of the authoritarian Chinese regime. There has already been much debate about the institutional ailments in Chinese politics in the SARS case, as exemplified by Huang's remarks below:

> The pattern of the Chinese government's response to SARS was shaped by the institutional dynamics of the country's political system. A deeply ingrained authoritarian impulse to maintain secrecy, in conjunction with a performance based legitimacy and an obsession with development and stability during political succession, contributed to China's initial failure to publicize the outbreak. Meanwhile, an upwardly directed system of accountability, a fragmented bureaucracy, and an oligarchic political structure hampered any effective government response to the outbreak.
>
> (Huang, 2004: 130)

In addition to these institutional issues, another relevant situation was the unsettling condition of the political transition that coincided with the SARS outbreak from November 2002 to April 2003. The ambivalence and conflicting information that came from the Chinese leadership in the first few months of the SARS outbreak apparently reflected a regime suddenly caught up in an uncertain transition of power at the top.

The power transition from the third-generation to the fourth-generation leaders formally began in the Sixteenth Party Congress held in Beijing from November 8 to November 15, 2002, when Hu Jintao, handpicked by the late Deng Xiaoping to succeed Jiang Zemin, was inaugurated as the new General Secretary of the powerful Central Committee of the Communist Party of China (CPC).[14] As noted by many, this was the first smooth and orderly transition of power in modern Chinese history. Naturally, all state-controlled media and propaganda machines were exclusively focusing on the coverage of this major event, and no one dared to rock the boat by reporting negative news or stories that were outside the official boundaries.

The leadership change in Beijing was the focus of not only Chinese domestic media, but also a large group of international press corps because this power shift has significant implications for China's future direction. Nonetheless, even though Hu had the top job in China, it was widely believed that, for some time, he would not be his own man because his predecessor, Jiang Zemin, still remained as the chairman of China's Central Military Commission and Jiang's protégés made up a formidable force in the new leadership.[15] Hu had survived in Chinese politics over the years through maintaining a low-key approach in not directly confronting Jiang or promoting himself; and he was expected to continue doing so to strengthen his power before departing from Jiang's old policy. For the officials that were caught between the two political camps, this meant that they had two masters to serve, and this delicate situation would inevitably impede the decision-making process.

After the completion of the power transition at the national level came the selection of party bosses at the provincial levels from mid-November to early December of 2002. So the top priority for local leaders was to maintain stability while engaging in calculated power struggles. There was no incentive for any local authority to break disturbing news like epidemics or social disturbances if they did not have to.

While the convocation of the Sixteenth National Congress of the Communist Party of China witnessed the power transition within the Communist Party, the First Session of the Tenth National People's Congress from March 5 to March 18 of 2003 concluded the change in the leadership of the state and government. At the end of this session, Hu Jintao took over as the new head of the state from Jiang Zemin[16] with Wen Jiaobao anointed as the new premier.[17] Thus the leadership transition at the level of the Party, the state, and the government was slowly finalized from November 2002 to March 2003. It was at this moment that the new lines of authority were clear to the Chinese bureaucracies at the state and local levels.

After the Party Congress of November 2002, Hu carefully tried to step out of the shadow of his predecessor Jiang Zemin and made an effort to craft his image as "man of the people" who was in touch with the ups and downs of the common people, the poor and underprivileged in particular.[18] So in a series of symbolic postures, in early December Hu visited the holy revolutionary base of Xibaipo, which served as the army headquarters in the early years of the Communist Party, and stressed the importance of "plain living and hard struggle"[19]; in early January of 2003, Hu was pictured side by side with herders and farmers in subzero Inner Mongolia, one of the poorest regions in China;[20] and he paid visits to policeman, office clerks, workers, and other ordinary commoners around the Chinese Lunar New Year of 2003.[21] All this was aimed toward cultivation of a new image of the new leadership to distance Hu from Jiang who was more associated with the coastal cities and the elites; and this effort to shift image was done in preparation for Hu's inauguration as the Chinese president in March 2003.

The first public news report of a mystery pneumonialike infectious virus in Guangdong appeared in the Chinese media on February 11,[22] and the first official report of Premier Wen Jiabao and his predecessor Zhu Rongji expressing personal concern about the epidemic situation when the National People's Congress was still in session was made known on March 26 by the Hong Kong–based pro-China *Wen Wei Po*.[23] However, the first indication of this issue being taken seriously by the top leadership came on April 2, when China's cabinet members listened to a report delivered by the Ministry of Health and discussed the issue of atypical pneumonia at a meeting presided over by Premier Wen Jiabao.[24] At the time, the epidemic was already getting out of control in Hong Kong, and China's handling of the case was already incurring heavy criticism from the world and WHO.[25] But in retrospect, perhaps it is no surprise that the new Chinese leadership could confront the reality of SARS first in early April and come up with a consistent strategy in managing the crisis in mid-April once they were well-entrenched in the power transition.

Inattention to the outbreak of the SARS epidemic on the part of the central authority and the failure of the central government to tackle the disease at the beginning means that the state was not a dependable source of information and support for the ordinary citizens while the crisis deepened. So at the early stages, civil society took the lead in breaking the news and in offering advice to the general public in relation to the epidemic, as is seen later. Yet the official cover-up effort complicated the situation and quickly led to widespread panic in major Chinese cities in late March and early April. Control of the disease was only possible when the government and civil society made a concerted effort in the face of this enormous crisis.

The SARS Outbreak: From Full Cover-up to Full Disclosure

In testifying at a hearing on the impact of SARS in June 2003 by the U.S.–China Economic and Security Review Commission, a group that advises Congress on national security implications of U.S. trade with China, Xiao Qiang, director of China Internet Studies Program at University of California Berkeley, divided the information flow about SARS in China into three periods: first, from November 2002, when the first known SARS case appeared in the southern province of Guangdong, until February of 2003 is the "rumor period," and official information on SARS was scarce; second, from early February until April 20 is the "cover-up period" during which information about SARS was strictly monitored and censored; third, from April 20 onward was the "recognition period," and the government decided to enforce a policy of transparency in covering SARS largely due to international pressure (Xiao, 2003).

Xiao's characterization is generally accurate but does not quite capture the full scale of the outbreak. To more accurately review the nature of the information flow during the SARS crisis, I divide the information flow about SARS into four phases: the mystery phase (from November 2002 to February 11, 2003), the cover-up phase (from February 11, 2003 to April 2, 2003), initial response phase (from April 2, 2003 to April 20, 2003), transparency and mass mobilization phase (from April 20 to late June). The remaining section discusses the chronological development of the SARS epidemic in these four phases. Discussion of the role of the Internet and short messaging services in the communication about SARS and the role of Chinese civil society throughout this whole crisis appears in the next section.

Phase one starts on November 16, 2002, when the first known SARS case occurred in Foshan, Guangdong province (CDSR, 2003), and ends on February 11, 2003, when Guangdong health officials broke the silence by holding the first press conference in China about the mysterious disease called atypical pneumonia and declared that the epidemic was under control.[26] It was also on February 11 that WHO was notified by the Chinese Ministry of Health of an outbreak of acute respiratory syndrome with 305 cases and 5 deaths in Guangdong Province (CDSR, 2003). During this time, as will be clear in the next section, news, rumors, gossip, and backchannel information were already available through verbal communication, circles of friends or relatives, and Internet chat rooms in a few big cities in Guangzhou. The official response was apparently intended to quell public panic and maintain order in the southern province of Guangdong.

During this period, because of the unknown nature of the disease, there was a lot of confusion and ambivalence among both hospital workers and local government officials. In mid-December, the virus spread to Heyuan city about 140 miles from the provincial capital of Guangzhou, and patients quickly spread the virus to hospital workers. Then the virus hitchhiked to Zhongshan city with a patient transferred from Heyuan in early January.[27] Quickly, rumors of a murderous flu were circulating among hospital workers and circles of friends and family members in both cities; desperate citizens that got the information were flooding pharmacies seeking antibiotics. Phone calls, wireless text messages, and word-of-mouth were the main channels of information at this stage.[28] Soon Guangzhou was contaminated with the virus, and widespread panic on the street alarmed local officials who feared that this might lead to instability during a time of festivities as the Lunar Chinese New Year was approaching.

The first news from the local media about the virus seems to have appeared on January 3, in a local paper in Heyuan[29] and in Guangzhou-based *Yangcheng Evening News* (Congressional Executive Commission on China, 2003), a widely read newspaper in Southern China. The story said that an unknown virus that was highly contagious had been found in Zhongshan and Guangzhou but was under control. In mid-January, more people were alerted about the virus as more and more hospital workers and citizens were infected. Panicking crowds in major cities in Guangdong raised concerns among local officials that the situation might get out of control, and officials ordered all local media to stop carrying stories about the virus until further notice.

Contrary to what many have believed, local officials were rather quick in taking action. After being alerted about the ongoing virus, the provincial health department sent a team of health experts to Heyuan to investigate the cause of the epidemic on January 2, and the team concluded that the disease was a result of infection by an unknown virus.[30] Local health officials were also pretty quick in reporting to their superiors, because a team of experts from the Health Ministry and the province was formed and then dispatched to the infected areas for further investigation in mid-January.[31] The team turned in a completed report labeled "top secret" that detailed the highly contagious virus to the Guangdong provincial health department on January 27.[32] But the report sat sealed for three days because officials with sufficient security clearance to open it were away on vacation. It was only three days later that the report was read and local hospitals were alerted about the dangerous virus.[33] By that time, valuable time had been wasted and more people, many of them medical professionals, had become infected.

This points to a crucial loose link in China's political hierarchy noted earlier. Chinese laws stipulate that any occurrence of infectious diseases should be classified as a state secret and must be handled by the Ministry of Health. Any public disclosure of such information must also directly come from the Ministry of Health (Wang, 2003a). The legal framework naturally added to the disincentives and perhaps even provided excuses for local authorities not to release information about epidemics. Moreover, SARS, or atypical pneumonia as it was called in Chinese, was a new strain of virus that was excluded from the list of infectious diseases according to existing laws. Local authorities, then, had no legal obligation to report the disease to the Ministry of Health. This was acknowledged as the main reason the Guangdong provincial government had not reported the disease to the public and to the Ministry of Health in time by the Guangdong Provincial health bureau chief at the February 11 press conference.[34] The legal loophole was the focus of a May 2003 *China Daily* news analysis, which pointed out that provincial authorities only had limited empowerment to deal with SARS prior to the direct intervention in April by the central government because existing laws give the State Council and the Ministry of Health the authority to classify and publicize a new contagious disease.[35] So the Guangdong provincial government was not able to take effective measures to deal with the disease, even when the epidemic was reaching national proportions in March.

To make things worse, after decades of economic reform, the Ministry of Health and health officials have been somewhat sidelined in the official bureaucracy because focus has been on economic growth and development. Additionally, the Ministry of Health has no direct authority over provincial leaders, who appoint all officials to the health department at the local level. Therefore, in Chinese officialdom, local health officials are more likely to follow orders from direct authority (the provincial regime) rather than those from the Ministry of Health whenever potential conflicts exist.

On the other hand, the Propaganda Ministry of the Central Party Committee, together with the local propaganda departments, is directly in charge of media control at the national and local levels. Lack of interdepartmental coordination and communication within the political establishment clearly exacerbated the situation. In early January 2003, a directive from the Propaganda Ministry was sent to all media outlets in China, instructing all reporters and editors to disregard stories on the spread of a pneumonialike virus that had killed several people in Guangdong.[36] The Guangdong provincial propaganda department issued similar orders in late February to the local media (Huang, 2004).

In looking at the SARS crisis, it is trendy for many to put the blame on local authorities, as typified by an editorial in China Daily: "Initially, local authorities failed to inform the public of the situation. In the absence of an official voice, people's worries were heightened by rumours ... But once the provincial government issued detailed reports on the virus, people gradually calmed down and the disease was put under control."[37] What is often ignored is the system factor, the institutional deficiencies that impeded the information flow process during this whole period. This apparently has caught the attention of the Chinese government, which quickly passed new laws to correct some of the problems in the hierarchy (Wang, 2003b). But how far the government can go in the future still remains unclear.

During this initial stage, informal networks of communication played a pivotal role in spreading information about the virus because of the unavailability of information from the official media and the nonresponsiveness of the government. Telephone, text messaging, and word-of-mouth were the primary channels as more and more concerned individuals and citizen groups took an active role in getting the information out; the Internet only played a limited role largely due to the localness of the epidemic at this point (see the following section for more discussion).

The second phase, the cover-up phase, lasts from the first press conferences held by Guangdong health officials on February 11 to April 2, 2003, when the SARS epidemic caught the serious attention of the Chinese bureaucracy at the highest level. During this period, the ambiguity and uncertainty about whether a deadly virus spreading in Guangzhou were removed with the official acknowledgment from the provincial officials. This official admission was forced by the widespread panic and the circulation of a variety of rumors in connection to the epidemic through informal networks of communication (see Zhou Xiaohong, 2003 for the spread of rumors concerning SARS). The severity, or the level, of scare caused by the epidemic at this point could be demonstrated by two press conferences held on February 11, one by the Guangzhou city government in the morning, and the other by the provincial health officials in the afternoon.[38] At both conferences, government officials claimed that the disease was under effective control. There is also indication that the central government had knowledge of this development because the Vice Health Minister was sent to Guangzhou to assist in the investigation of the virus in early February.[39]

After the press conferences, the news media started to run stories about the ongoing epidemic from time to time. Although the mainstream media strictly toed the official line, some of the so-called fringe media outlets, which are not so tightly controlled, maintain more autonomy from the government, and are more dependent on circulation, took a more brazen approach in covering the virus (Sun, 2003). The availability of information about the disease at first worked as expected: public panic and anxiety were temporarily assuaged — people went out into the streets again without masks, previously emptied pharmacies were restocked, and the price for white vinegar, which was rumored to kill the virus, went back to normal.[40] An editorial in the *Southern Weekend* at the time best reflects the general feeling at that moment: "People Calm Down Once Told the Truth."[41]

However, people were not told the whole truth about the virus. The theme propagated by the official media at the instruction of the government was that everything was under control and there was nothing to worry about, when the fact was that the cause of the virus and how it spread was still unknown and the epidemic was still spreading quickly. Most people trusted the official information and relaxed their vigilance, and the virus was soon spreading with vengeance.

The provincial government certainly did not want to create the impression that public health was in danger for fear of derailing its top priority of promoting economic growth and attracting foreign investment. Therefore, the government instructed the media to avoid any move that might undermine social stability and banned the release of SARS-related stories from mid-February until March.[42] The next focus in the propaganda war would inevitably be the forthcoming National People's Congress in Beijing in March, where all top-level provincial bureaucrats would make an appearance for the next round of political jockeying. Politicization of SARS-related information in Guangdong province led to deadly consequences not only in the southern Chinese province in the months to follow, but also in more localities as the virus quickly spread to other parts of China (including Hong Kong) and other countries.

While the mainstream media largely toed the official line by remaining silent at this stage, some fringe publications saw this as a great opportunity and rose to the occasion. Among them was *Caijing* (Finance and Economy), a Beijing-based publication that was very popular among business professionals and known for its coverage of malpractice and wrongdoing in corporate and government circles. The fringe media, unlike the mainstream publications that are closely watched and controlled by Party and government officials, have gained relatively more space in their news coverage. Because the fringe media cannot get any financial support from the government and are totally dependent on the market, they have to be more responsive to audience demands and interests to survive in the increasingly competitive Chinese media environment. When SARS-related news was seldom mentioned in the mainstream media in early February, *Caijing* editors apparently saw the potential of a great human interest event and decided to follow the developing story closely. In March, four reporters were sent to cover SARS stories in Guangdong, and the number quickly increased to ten as the crisis deepened. In April, *Caijing* published four weekly special issues devoted to the SARS epidemic in addition to its normal publication. While the mainstream media closely kept within the spheres of Party and government organizations shackled themselves with government orders, *Caijing*'s aggressive approach earned respect from readers and colleagues. Its managing editor, Ms. Hu Shuli, was named World Press Review's International Editor of the Year for 2003 for her courage and leadership in covering the SARS crisis.[43]

An internal power struggle within the Chinese regime at the national and provincial levels took a toll in the prompt handling of the SARS crisis. Because the National People's Congress (due to open on March 5), which was to decide China's new leadership, was approaching, no one understandably wanted to be the bearer of bad tidings at a politically sensitive moment. In the central government, the ultimate line of order was not clear, so the best thing for the Chinese bureaucrats to do was to wait. At the local level in Guangdong province, this led to ambivalence and conflicting signals from the provincial government. The February 11 press conferences were said to be held on direct orders from the governor, Huang Huahua, a close ally of president-to-be Hu Jintao; bans were quickly imposed on the media against covering SARS stories by the party secretary in Guangdong, Zhang Dejiang, a protégé of Jiang Zemin, who was still China's president until the end of the Congress in March.[44] The news blackout was in place until late in March, when external pressure, in combination with rising domestic discontent, took the situation on a new unexpected course.

While the Chinese government officials were bogged down by inaction, the virus quickly found its way to more localities. On March 2, the first SARS patient recorded in Beijing, who returned from a recent trip to Guangzhou, was admitted to 301 Military Hospital. Without much clue about the cause of the illness, doctors first treated her for a serious cold and then transferred her to the 302 Military Hospital, which specializes in contagious diseases, for further treatment.[45] In mid-March, the epidemic traveled to more cities in China, with recorded cases in such remote provinces as Inner Mongolia and Shanxi.[46]

However, it was not until the outbreak of SARS in Hong Kong and other parts of Southeast Asia in mid- and late March that global media attention started to focus on China. Signs of respiratory tract infections quickly progressing to pneumonia were first reported in Hong Kong on March 7, and the number of SARS-infected patients grew fast in mid-March (CDSR, 2003). Soon it was determined that the "index patient" of Hong Kong's infection was a Chinese doctor who stayed in a Hong Kong hotel from February 21 to 22 after treating SARS patients in Guangzhou.[47] Visitors to the hotel subsequently carried the virus to Vietnam, Canada, and Singapore.[48] As a global tourism and financial center in Asia, Hong Kong quickly caught the attention of the world community. Following more cases in Hanoi and Hong Kong, WHO issued a global alert about SARS on March 12 and issued a travel advisory, declaring SARS "a worldwide health threat" on March 15 (CDSR, 2003). But the Propaganda Ministry instructed Chinese media not to report this news.[49] Nonetheless, public panic on the street was a clear indication to the average person in major cities in China that the epidemic was being taken seriously by the public. Many people by now had access to nonofficial channels of information about the disease and were desperately searching for more news.

"Hong Kong took the heat of being the epicenter of SARS not because it started there but because it was the disease's first outbreak in a place with a free press," noted Cunningham (2003: 53). Unlike China's government-controlled media, the media in Hong Kong responded well to reporting the epidemic. Meanwhile, a large group of media professionals stationed in Hong Kong spread the news to the world in no time. While all indications led to the epidemic in Guangzhou as the origin of SARS patients worldwide, Chinese government officials were still stonewalling and denying. WHO officials sent to investigate SARS were given a cold reception in Beijing in March, and their requests to visit Guangzhou met with no response from the Chinese government (Cunningham, 2003).

In the early part of March, two types of news dominated the Chinese media: the National People's Congress in Beijing in domestic news, and the U.S invasion of Iraq in world news. However, in late March, the severity of SARS worldwide had reached a level that made it impossible for Chinese authorities to ignore the disease any longer. News from Hong Kong and other parts of SARS-infected areas bounced back to China through the Chinese media, calling people's attention to the situation in their own backyard. On March 28, on the day that WHO listed China as one of the world's SARS-infected areas, the official Xinhua News Agency reported 792 cases with 31 deaths in

Guangdong and 10 and 4 cases in Beijing and Shanxi, respectively, with 3 deaths in Beijing.[50]

If public panic and rumor-mongering combined had triggered the official response on February 11, mounting international pressure had forced the Chinese government to take action because the whole SARS issue had evolved into a crisis for the newly installed Chinese leadership. On April 2, 2003, Premier Wen Jiabao presided over the first State Council executive meeting to discuss the prevention and control of SARS in China. It was decided at the meeting that control of the disease was the "first priority" and a national "emergency response mechanism" was set up to deal with sudden outbreaks of public health events and an interministerial committee was formed to coordinate activities from different government agencies; the decision was also made to keep WHO informed and involved in the epidemic situation.[51] This marks the start of the initial response phase, when the media were no longer banned from covering the disease. On the same day, the Health Minister appeared on CCTV, the national television network in China, to talk about SARS, followed by an hour-long program on SARS prevention in prime time.[52] SARS and the State Council meeting were front-page stories in the nation's media the next day.

The State Council meeting marked a clear shift of strategy in that government officials started to communicate with the public as well as the world through various media outlets. At the same time, WHO officials were finally granted permission one day after the meeting to travel to Guangdong to find out the cause of SARS, on April 3.[53] But the theme in all official responses during this period was that, although there had been an epidemic, things were under control; government officials were also vehemently dismissing accusations from the international media that they had lied or covered up the SARS epidemic in China.

On April 3, Health Minister Zhang Wenkang held a press conference to brief the media on the SARS situation in China. By the end of March, there were 1190 infections and 46 deaths, with most of them in Guangdong, Zhang claimed. Zhang also said that it was safe to live, work, and travel in China, and added that "I say to you here, as minister of public health, that the epidemic of atypical pneumonia has been put under effective control."[54]

In the next few days, high-level Chinese officials repeatedly assured the public that the government was taking effective measures to control the disease. Vice Premier Wu Yi, known as the iron-lady in Chinese politics and who would later take over as the interim Health Minister, visited the Chinese Center for Disease Control and stressed the importance of building a national emergency mechanism in response to epidemics. Wu said that fighting SARS was the first priority for China's health work.[55] Premier Wen Jiabao visited the same center on April 7, again announcing that SARS was under control, and assured the world that "the Chinese government is completely capable of controlling atypical pneumonia."[56] On April 14 at a national conference on SARS, in a clear shift from his early optimistic assessment, Premier Wen Jiabao said that "the overall situation [concerning SARS] remains grave," as the number of infections was reported to have grown.[57] On the same day during a visit to a hospital in the hardest-hit province of Guangdong, President Hu Jintao said "I feel very worried. I feel anxious for the masses" in front of members of the national media.[58] The sense of urgency and gravity was clear now, with the top leadership expressing concerns to the world.

Although the gravity of the situation in the nation gradually sank in on the government level, high-level officials continued their defense of how the government had responded throughout the epidemic and insisted that there had been no attempt to falsify SARS statistics or to cover up the situation.[59] However, many people in China had access to SARS information via multiple sources and started to question the credibility of Chinese officials as well as the Chinese media. From mid-March to early April, media in the Western world and Hong Kong were filled with SARS stories about the spread of the disease worldwide and included clear indications that the virus most likely originated from Guangdong. Chinese netizens started to flock to overseas online sources for more information about the disease, and information then got circulated via BBS, wireless text messages, and informal networks. At this stage, the Internet quickly became a major alternative source of information for some Chinese citizens, some of whom in turn became messengers themselves in the communication chain during this period. This change in the role of the Internet was largely prompted by the globalization of the virus, which led to a diversification of information sources on the network and an explosion of interest among users worldwide.

Jitters and concerns were spreading among residents in big cities despite reassurances from the official media.[60] The veil of truth was finally lifted by an insider — Jiang Yanyong, a 72-year-old retired surgeon and former director of the 301 Military Hospital. After watching the Health Minister's press conference on television on the evening news of April 3, Jiang was infuriated by the blatant lie from the official side and concerned that public health might be in danger if people were not given enough information; he decided to contest the official statistics from his first-hand knowledge in treating patients at the hospital. Jiang e-mailed a letter to *CCTV-4* in Beijing and *Phoenix TV* in Hong Kong the next day, saying that at 309 PLA Hospital alone, doctors had admitted sixty patients showing signs of SARS symptoms and seven had already died, contradicting the official figures at the time of twelve infections and three deaths. He also described in the letter how and when several patients were infected and how hospital workers were ordered by superiors to keep everything secret. At the end of the letter, Jiang left his full name and contact phone number, contrary to most whistle-blowers in China. The content of the letter, however, was not run by the two stations; it was instead published in *Time Online* on April 8, 2003.[61] Jiang Yanyong suddenly became the focus of world media in the next few days, and his three phone lines were busy all day with requests for interviews from *Time*, the *Wall Street Journal*, Associated Press, Deutsche Presse-Agentur, and Agence France Presse, among others. His letter published in English in *Time Online* was translated into Chinese and posted online in BBS, on portals, and was circulated among Chinese netizens via e-mail within China.[62]

The whirlwind created by Jiang's letter was catastrophic for the credibility of the Chinese authorities. John MacKenzie, head of WHO investigation team, apparently pressured by Jiang's letter, announced that WHO would investigate the claims that Chinese officials falsified SARS statistics and warned that the official tally might be just "the tip of the iceberg."[63] An official rebuttal of Jiang's revelation came on April 13 from Meng Xuenong, then the Mayor of Beijing, who in a special interview denied that there were sixty SARS cases in the military hospital and insisted that SARS was under control in the capital city.[64] The public at this point, however, was more willing to place their trust with the nonofficial side, as more and more hospital workers volunteered information to contest the official figures from what they had witnessed.[65] Meng's interview would soon cost him his job as Mayor of Beijing. The more liberal information environment that resulted from decades of economic reform and openness has made Chinese civil society more resistant to the old style of propaganda and information control; more and more Chinese citizens are willing to stand up to challenge the authorities when the citizens perceive truth is at stake. The brand-new public sphere brought about by the Internet and new information technologies undoubtedly gives these citizens more power to do this.

A turning point came in the official strategy on April 17 at an emergency meeting of the nine-member Politburo Standing Committee of the Communist Party, the highest decision-making body in Chinese politics. The meeting, chaired by President Hu Jintao, explicitly warned against covering up SARS cases and demanded accurate, timely, and honest reporting of the SARS situation at all levels of government, and members at the meeting decided to establish a responsibility monitoring system within the communist hierarchy.[66] Noticeably, the call on government officials to be honest and open in reporting SARS information from the Politburo was tantamount to acknowledging lying and cover-up practices within its bureaucracy in the Chinese way. Realizing the institutional barriers to interdepartmental coordination and communication, the meeting also set up a special task force headed by Liu Qi, Beijing's party boss and a Politburo member, to smooth the information flow and optimize the allocation of resources in the government's much belated crusade against SARS.[67]

Something more extraordinary was needed to turn the tide and to restore the Chinese government's credibility. The milestone moment came at a scheduled press conference on April 20, when Vice Health Minister Gao Qiang, not the Health Minister as originally arranged, appeared to address the press. First, Gao announced a nearly 10-fold increase in the number of SARS patients in the capital, soaring from the previous announced 37 infections to 346. Second, Gao announced the official decision to cancel a nationwide week-long holiday for International Workers' Day in May to contain the spread of SARS by encouraging people to stay home. And third, in the first public admission, Gao acknowledged "major weaknesses" in his Ministry in handling the reporting of SARS cases and promised that China would start daily reports of SARS cases in line with WHO recommendations, and those found hiding cases intentionally would be severely punished.[68] Shortly after the conference, in a surprising move that was rarely seen in Chinese politics, the official Xinhua News Agency made the startling revelation that Health Minister Zhang Wenkang and Beijing's mayor had been stripped of their posts within the Communist Party for their mishandling of the crisis, a clear indication of their inevitable dismissal from government functions.[69]

The "first sign of political innovation by China's new leadership," the firing of two top officials, was noted by the *Economist*: "It almost looks like the way that politics works in a democratic, accountable country. Chinese people might start to get a taste for it."[70] Similarly, a *South China Morning Post* editorial commented: "The SARS crisis may be one of the greatest to hit China for years but that does not mean the outlook is all bleak. It may have brought a new energy and need to take the economic openness of recent years into a wider arena."[71] So the April 20 press conference together with the sacking of the Health Minister and Beijing mayor marks the start of a phase in which the Chinese authority unmistakably showed the world its intention of becoming transparent and coming clean in its handling of the SARS crisis.

As another part of the government strategy in crisis management, Liu Qi, the party boss of Beijing, in another scene rarely seen in Chinese politics, issued an apology at a publicized meeting of senior officials on April 21 over the "inaccurate and late disclosure of facts on the disease's spread," "poor management systems for tackling the virus," and a "failure to abide by the policy of 'early discovery, early reporting, early isolation (of SARS sufferers) and early treatment.' "[72] The unprecedented level of accountability was "likely to have been prompted by concern about losing international kudos as much as a desire to communicate more openly" and could foreshadow a "new openness and transparency" in the way the Chinese government works, Chinese commentators were quick to point out.[73] At the same time, the central government started a highly publicized national campaign to improve its image and to ensure that the directives from Beijing were implemented by local officials; as many as 120 officials had been fired or reprimanded for dereliction of duties as of May 8.[74] In Henan Province alone, 891 people were disciplined for incompetence in fighting SARS as of May 16, the Henan Provincial Discipline Inspection Commission disclosed.[75] This was unheard of in the history of the

Chinese Communist Party, and it demonstrates the seriousness as well as the desperation of the entrenched Chinese government in searching for ways to weather the SARS storm.

In a related move to assure the world of its resolution, the Chinese government announced on April 23 the creation of a national fund of RMB¥2 billion (US$243 million) for SARS prevention and control as well as a special task force to coordinate national efforts to combat SARS.[76] On April 25, Vice Premier Wu Yi announced China's decision to invest RMB¥3.5 billion (US$421.7 million) in establishing a nationwide public health network within the year.[77]

The dramatic increase in the acknowledged number of SARS infections in China after April 20 led to some public panic within the next two or three weeks because citizens felt betrayed by their government and desperately sought to take things into their own hands. In late April, for example, furious residents of a rural town in Tianjin ransacked the interior of a four-story building at a local school after rumors spread that it would be turned into a ward for urban SARS patients. Self-organized rural residents in the town and surrounding areas confronted local officials directly and protested the practice of treating rural residents as "second-class citizens" by relocating SARS-infected urban residents to their precinct.[78] In other instances, rural farmers in Beijing acted together by barricading roads and setting up 24-hour checkpoints to keep Beijing visitors away from their villages for fear of being contaminated by SARS[79]; riots among villagers in rural central and eastern China also occurred, resulting in buildings being destroyed, officials being beaten, and rioters being arrested.[80] Nervous residents in Beijing (as well as other cities) began to stockpile basic goods, and people flocked to railway and bus stations to leave Beijing in late April, disregarding official orders to stay put.[81] Most of the riots took place because residents believed they were betrayed by local officials, who lied to them and were not able to provide reliable protection for them. This is a strong indication that more and more social groups in Chinese civil society, especially those that are weak and have been traditionally neglected by the state, are willing to work together in protecting their own interests, even if this means direct confrontation with the authorities.

Starting in late April, with closures of schools, cafes, cinemas, and many other public facilities, the Chinese government launched a massive nationwide "People's War" against SARS, as called for by President Hu Jintao.[82] The mass media were also mobilized in full gear, urging a patriotic campaign in waging a People's War in combating the disease[83] and in turning a health campaign into a massive political movement, as neighborhood committees and street organizations developed "community watch" surveillance networks in detecting and reporting SARS cases.[84] Meanwhile, people showing any signs of respiratory illness were isolated and monitored, temperatures were checked at bus and railway stations and airports, and tens of thousands of people were quarantined. By the end of May, 29,000 people were quarantined in Shanghai,[85] and the number of quarantines in Beijing reached 29,768.[86]

Following the April 20 press conference where an honest and open approach in reporting SARS was promised, the Chinese media began a period of vibrant activities covering the disease as daily briefings of SARS statistics, many of them televised live,[87] became available from central and local governments. Substantial progress had been made in containing the virus by late May, and life was gradually back to normal in the cities,[88] as public panic subsided when more accurate SARS-related information became available from the media on a daily basis. On June 24, 2003, Beijing became the last city in China to be removed from WHO's SARS-infected areas and to have the travel advisory against the city lifted, marking a milestone in the global war against SARS.[89] The Chinese government survived its biggest crisis since the 1989 Tiananmen Massacre.

The Chinese media also showed a high level of resilience during the SARS epidemic and demonstrated that they do not always willingly collaborate with the government as just a mouthpiece of the state machine. Led by fringe publications, many of the media were highly critical of the official practice of cover-ups and nonresponsiveness at the time of the SARS crisis. In the process of covering SARS, many of the media in Guangdong had repeatedly called for a more transparent approach to dealing with SARS news, maintaining that the only way to stop rumors or public panic was to respect the "public right to know" and to keep the public updated with the truth.[90] An overview of the SARS-related news stories by *Caijing* (Beijing), *Sanlian Life Weekly* (Shanghai), *21st Century Economic Report* (Bejing), and *News Weekly* (Beijing) in early April 2003 indicates that most information sources were dependent on overseas media outlets (which were most of the time unfriendly to Chinese authorities), leading to the phenomenon of "exported news about domestic affairs."[91] Three of the mentioned news publications are fringe media, with the exception of *News Weekly*, which is owned by the official Xinhua News Agency. The reliance on overseas news sources in early April may be due to two reasons: first, because the government attitude was ambivalent at this stage, use of foreign news sources could be a self-protective measure for the Chinese media because the consequences would be more serious than sending their own reporters to uncover the stories; second, not a lot of reporters were sent to cover the SARS stories, so information was still limited for the Chinese media.

On May 30, 2003, at a press conference, Deputy Health Minister Gao Qiang openly denied that former Health Minister Zhang Wenkang was dismissed because of covering up the SARS epidemic situation.[92] In early June, *Economic News Watch* (Jingji guancha bao), a Beijing-based fringe newspaper, published an opinion essay titled "Being Fired for Covering Up: No Question There," apparently in response to the comment by Gao Qiang. It bluntly pointed out, "in the face of life and death, crime and punishment brought about the SARS disease, any act or speech of frivolity or irresponsibility cannot be tolerated."[93]

Internet, Short Message Services (SMS), and Alternative Information Flow

Many people have noted the role of the Internet and SMS as an alternative, and in some cases, the main source of information for people in China, especially in the early phase of the SARS outbreak.[94] Unlike the 1989 Tiananmen Student Democracy Movement, which relied heavily on shortwave radio broadcasts from the West, fax machines, and international phone lines, information about the SARS epidemic unfolded in a vastly different information environment led by the emergence of the Internet and mobile phones as increasingly popular communication tools.

When SARS first broke out in November 2002, there was no media coverage at all, and no one knew anything about the disease, so no information was available about it either from the public or private sources. Even when the first news story appeared in early January of 2003 in local newspapers, there was not much public attention to the issue. It was only in late January when the disease spread to more cities and infected more patients that rumors about a fatal flu got disseminated by word of mouth and by a new popular means of communication called Short Message Service (SMS).

In a short period of three years, the number of messages by SMS subscribers to the two biggest telecomm service providers in China, China Mobile and China Liangtong, rose from 0.5 billion messages in 2000 to 19 billion in 2001 and 90 billion in 2002 (Jiang, 2003). Its popularity and its rising role in people's life have earned it the name "the fifth medium,"[95] and the economic potential of SMS to the Chinese telecommunications market is referred to as the "economy of the thumb."[96] Its immediacy, flexibility, portability, and most of all, its affordability (about US$0.01 per message in China) make it the more preferable medium over e-mail for many people. As a result, SMS quickly became a popular way of communication outside of the official domain.

On February 8, 2003, residents in Guangzhou, who were just back to work from a weeklong Chinese New Year holiday, were flooded with the same message: "a fatal flu is spreading in Guangzhou." On the same day, 40 million SMS messages were sent; on February 9, 41 million messages; and on February 10, 45 million messages.[97] Most messages were about a mysterious virus that had even killed doctors who were supposed to treat patients, and people started to panic.

But people tend not to trust most messages like this easily; they know all too well that there are always those who take fun in creating mischievous notes of this nature. So for many people, the initial response was to seek confirmation (or disconfirmation) from others about the truthfulness of the messages — via phone calls, word of mouth, or informal, personal networks.[98] In popular Internet chat rooms, the same kind of messages got disseminated. But there had been no confirmation from any official source, so all kinds of rumors started to emerge on the street (see Zhou Xiaohong, 2003). The widespread rumors and other kinds of informal information created a public alarm that pressured the government to respond. That resulted in the two press conferences on February 11, 2003, by both the provincial and city governments. At this stage, SMS in combination with informal networks of communication (e.g., e-mail, chat rooms, BBS) built up a fermenting pressure on the government from within civil society.

During the early stage of the SARS outbreak, the Internet only played a marginal role in communicating information about the disease. It was the SMS that played the major role in breaking the news to local residents. However, SMS alone did not constitute a credible source for most people; it was when people were able to cross-validate the information from multiple sources that they started to take the disease seriously. The Internet was not a major factor for people's source of information at this stage largely because the epidemic was still regional in scope, affecting a few cities in Guangdong province only. Under this circumstance, SMS and informal networks were more effective in spreading the message to a local audience.

The Internet played a much more important role at the next stage, when the epidemic spread to more areas, especially when it was spread to neighboring Hong Kong. Starting in mid-February of 2003, information about an outbreak of an unknown epidemic got spread to other parts of the country via Internet chat rooms, SMS, and word of mouth; media in Guangzhou got inquiries from colleagues around the nation, and they did not know how to respond.[99] Meanwhile, some online postings from self-proclaimed experts started to attribute the cause of this illness to anthrax, mouse virus, or biotech tests.[100] But the credibility of these claims remained very low, and very few actually believed those statements.[101] Uncertainty about the cause of the disease and about how it spread created the natural breeding ground for rumors during this phase.

That situation started to change when the epidemic reached Hong Kong from early to mid-March. Unlike their counterparts in Guangzhou, the Hong Kong media responded in no time to the virus, and WHO got involved from the very start. More and more information started to become available in March from WHO and its Web site (which is accessible in China), including the global alert on March 12, the announcement of atypical pneumonia as a "global health threat," and the travel advisory on March 15, and Guangzhou as the originator of the disease (CDSR, 2003). At this point, people began to turn to the Internet to search for more information, especially Web sites in Hong Kong, Singapore, and Taiwan, most of which were not banned in China. Meanwhile, many surfers who got hold of fragments of information were already posting on the BBS of major portal sites in China.[102] The Internet created a venue of public communication that was not available before in the face of such a major crisis for Chinese civil society.

At this point, people who were more vigilant already knew that there was a problem in China, and started to pay attention to SARS-related information from Internet sources, as disclosed by one computer professional: "I first started getting information on SARS through the grapevine in February, mostly on the BBS (bulletin board) of commercial portals."[103] The availability of the amount of information about SARS accelerated as international pressure built for the Chinese authorities to change their approach to dealing with SARS in early April.

The government was certainly aware of the spread of information on the Internet at this time because Web site managers had secured government directives to remove "negative" postings about deadly diseases, and they had been warned that violators could face fines or punishment.[104] But this proved to be a mission impossible for anyone because there are hundreds of thousands of registered users on any of the major portal sites, and tens of thousands are engaged in online chatting on a typical day.[105] At first, major portal sites were closely following government orders in filtering "undesirable" postings; however, as time went by and as the epidemic spread to more localities, many content managers did not remove SARS-related postings,[106] whether out of their own conscience or out of negligence. When faced with the choice of siding with the government or civil society, some unwilling censors had opted to align with the latter in a time of a major public health crisis.

For those who had been exposed to the Internet or overseas media on the situation of SARS in China, it was Health Minister Zhang Wenkang's well-publicized press conference that turned them off. Although they had no specific clue as to the exact scope of this disaster, they were sure that what the minister said at the conference was only half-truth. "We already knew it was much worse [than what the government told us] from reading about it on the Internet," university student Cecilia Hu told reporters; her view was shared by her classmates and friends.[107] A young man who was constantly online was quoted as saying:

> The turning point came for me in early April. I felt the media were lying, and that they were intentionally suppressing news about SARS. I saw the April 7 press conference by Health Minister Zhang Wenkang, and I thought his lies were really outrageous ... Because we work with the Internet, we have long felt that news in mainstream media is routinely manipulated. They just tell you what they want you to think.[108]

This clearly shows the insurmountable difficulty in controlling information on the Internet by the Chinese authorities, and that is why the Internet should be considered an empowerment tool for Chinese civil society, especially when the traditional media are still under strict surveillance.

Starting in early April, news about SARS was no longer banned by the government; however, most official media were strictly following the government line in assuring the public that the disease was under control. Most online postings begged to differ. In a well-circulated posting in BBS among major portal Chinese sites that originated from a message posted on the BBS at Sina.com on April 6, 2003, one of the three major Chinese news sites, the author named Xiao Han (most chatters use pen names instead of their true names while authoring messages) started with the opinion that the coverage of atypical pneumonia by the Chinese media should be listed as one of the major fiascos in mass communication textbooks, and he then blasted the media for covering up important news stories in the process. The author seems to be a very well-informed person, since a lot of citations from WHO statistics and foreign media were used in the discussion. At the end, the author concluded that in the information age, it is impossible to block news from the public, and what is needed is the courage to face truth and to be responsible to the people.[109] This opinion was shared by another popular posting at the time, in which the author cited multiple sources to prove that life was not normal any more and that SARS was having a significant negative effect on people's life.[110] Postings like these are popular reading on the Internet among Chinese netizens, and they get circulated very quickly while it is common for surfers to repost messages they like on other popular forums or BBS. It was mentioned in Chapter 5 that chatting or posting messages on Internet forums was a popular activity among Chinese netizens (approximately 40 percent of Internet users regularly engage in these activities). Therefore, these popular postings have a significant reach among Net surfers in the country.

Many college students, the most likely Internet adopters in China, were glued to the Internet because of hunger for information about SARS. Most college campuses set up special BBS sections for students to exchange information with one another. Students not only posted news about the situation of SARS infections on their campuses,[111] but they also condemned the government for lack of transparency in handling the crisis.[112] In one popular commentary titled "Broad Reflections on Atypical Pneumonia," which had been read thousands of times and posted on the Beijing University online forum and forwarded to many other forums, the author first pointed out that the outbreak of atypical pneumonia was not a sudden event, as the government had argued, but an incremental disaster resulting from official negligence. The author then analyzed the institutional flaws in the Chinese political system that had caused the crisis. Finally, the author called for political reform to change China from an official-centered society to a civilian-centered one to eliminate system barriers.[113] The heavy reliance on the Internet as an information source about SARS explains why college students were leading all other groups in fleeing the capital in April.[114]

From early April until April 20, therefore, as more information became available from official media, Chinese netizens desperately sought alternative information from online media. Many of them posted their findings on BBS to counter the official side of the story. Most Web site administrators, meanwhile, adopted a more tolerant attitude toward messages posted in chat rooms and on BBS. The event that catalyzed this online behavior was, of course, the letter from Dr. Jiang Yanyong, which had been well circulated and well read by mid-April. Encouraged by Jiang's bravery, many doctors, nurses, and others followed Jiang's example in exposing government lies by telling the truth about what had been happening in local hospitals.[115] Voluntary actions from members of civil society add to their power at times of national crisis like the SARS epidemic to negotiate with, or force changes from, the government.

Then came the government order for a "full disclosure" on April 20. This was the breeze of freedom that the media had been praying for. There was an explosion of SARS-related stories and all kinds of columns about SARS prevention, a 180-degree shift from the earlier approach to the disease. However, contrary to what might be expected, the initial response from the general public to this "full disclosure" was a nationwide panic, mainly caused by this sudden turn from too little to too much information about the disease. This led to the critique by some media scholars in China of a media "overreaction" to SARS after being unleashed from official control.[116] But soon the public calmed down as people got information closer to the truth, and they quickly joined the government campaign in conquering the disease.

In response to the "full disclosure" order, major Chinese portals were also immediately in full gear as more people went online for information. "We've been recording 100 million page views a day, and we've had to increase the capacity of our servers by 40 percent," the head of the news center at the NAS-DAQ-listed Sohu.com said in an interview.[117] Special coverage, daily statistics, exclusives, emergency measures — anything and everything in relation to SARS became hot items for the portal sites.

In a telephone survey of residents of five cities (Beijing, Shanghai, Chongqing, Guangzhou, and Nanjing) in China from May 23 to May 25, 2003, it was found that over 40 percent of the respondents first heard about SARS through sources other than the mainstream media; in Guangzhou where the epidemic first broke out, the percentage was as high as 60 percent. In terms of the specific channels through which people first got the news about SARS, people mainly said that they heard it from others (56.7 percent), got the information from talking to others (such as on the phone) (19.4 percent), or from the Internet (14.2 percent).[118] For lack of details about the exact wording of the questions, it is assumed that the first category, "heard from others," includes SMS and being passively exposed to the information. Several points are worth mentioning here. First, the survey was conducted over a month after the government began a "full disclosure" policy, and by this point all kinds of information was already readily available from all media sources; second, the survey did not ask people *when* they heard the news, but instead focused on how. It is reasonable to assume that most of those who said they heard the news from nonmainstream media most likely learned of the disease early; had efforts been made to determine the origin of the sources of information (i.e., the network of informant-informed relationships), the Internet would likely be named as a main source of SARS-related information for the early informants at a time when most official media were silent about the issue. In any case, the role of the Internet in the information flow process of the early stages of the SARS outbreak should not be underestimated. Popularization of the Internet has led to its inevitable emergence as a powerful tool for civil society in China.

Whether they monitored the Internet for public opinion or for other purposes, top Chinese government officials were not shy about acknowledging that they were connected to the cyber world. President Hu Jintao, during an inspection of doctors fighting SARS in May, told a doctor: "Your suggestion is very good. I have seen it on the Internet." On another occasion, Premier Wen Jiabao said to a group of college students during his pep-talk visit to Beijing University on April 26, "I am deeply moved by some online postings from the students. Your confidence in the government is rising."[119]

It did not take long for the Chinese government to realize the potential of the Internet as a propaganda tool. In late April, in typical style of Chinese propaganda campaigns, over a dozen major portals in China called on all the Web sites throughout the country as well as the broad masses of Web users to join hands to:

> fully develop the role of the Internet media to fight the sudden outbreak of atypical pneumonia, with courage and confidence and under the staunch leadership of the CPC Central Committee and the State Council, and to steadfastly join together with medical workers who are battling the disease in the forefront and with the broad masses of people in waging a resolute struggle shoulder to shoulder, with one heart and one mind, and with concerted efforts, aim at defeating the disease.[120]

As part of this effort, a new Web site was created with the URL http://wenming.cycnet.com/ to join the government's "People's War" effort.

Voluntary Support Groups Online

Most attention to the role of the Internet during the SARS crisis has been on its function as an alternative source of information in the face of a government cover-up. However, that is only part of the big picture. As the SARS epidemic evolved, the Internet emerged as an arena that has changed the role of civil society and its members in more than one way.

The Chinese government also used the Internet as an effective mass mobilization tool to organize various social groups to join its efforts in winning its war against SARS. In Hangzhou, the capital city of Zhejiang Province, for example, local government officials organized community groups to make phone calls, send flowers and groceries, and deliver books and even phone cards to residents confined to quarantined buildings to boost their morale; officials also set up BBS where more people could leave messages or express their best wishes for those quarantined. Among the people who left messages on the BBS was the provincial Party Secretary, whose note read: "The sacrifices you have made in the fight against SARS heighten our optimism further that we can surmount all types of difficulties."[121]

An unusual level of national cohesion can be achieved at catastrophic times, and the SARS crisis is no exception. The government capitalized on the patriotism of the Chinese people during the SARS crisis in waging a "People's War" against the epidemic, part of which involved the organization and coordination of hundreds of thousands of volunteers from all walks of life. Here, the Internet again played an important role. Starting in late April, the Internet was used to recruit volunteer groups from schools, technical and professional groups, community activists, and other affiliations in such activities as blood donation, sanitation of public places, monitoring of neighborhoods and key places, promotion of public understanding and prevention of SARS, and publication and dissemination of SARS-related information.[122] The Internet worked particularly well on this occasion because it was able to reach a great number of people within a short period when SARS kept people from public places and public gatherings.

In the SARS case, we see quite well the dual nature of civil society in its relationship with the state. It was a relatively effective tool for overcoming the government's information control effort in circulating news and challenging the state's monopoly on information; on the other hand, when civil society perceived the advantage of working with the state in conquering a fatal virus, it displayed an unusual level of willingness to cooperate with the state. Either civil society or the state alone could not wage a successful war against a national disaster of such magnitude.

Indeed, the vibrant civil society demonstrated such an unprecedented level of enthusiasm and support for the Chinese government during the nationwide SARS campaign that the Ministry of Civil Affairs, the main official government agency that is in charge of coordinating government activities with nongovernmental organizations, held an awards meeting at the end of July 2003. Special recognition was given to the important contribution of civil groups and organizations to the government victory in containing SARS.[123]

Lessons from the SARS Case

SARS as a fatal virus obviously was a serious public health threat, yet nonresponsiveness from the Chinese government and the tightly controlled official media at the initial stages created a high level of ambiguity and uncertainty among the public. When information was officially sanctioned and viable functional alternatives were not readily available from conventional media, many individuals became information producers and disseminators themselves to create an alternative form of information exchange. SMS played an important role in the initial outbreak stage by making people aware of the disease. However, SMS alone did not constitute a credible source; people actively sought cross-validation from other sources for confirmation at this stage.

As the epidemic spread from Guangdong to more areas first in China, then to other countries, the Chinese government continued to cover up information about the virus. At this stage, the Internet, in collaboration with foreign media, became a more stable and diversified source of information for Chinese citizens. The Internet became an especially empowering tool for individuals and voluntary groups to create communication channels of their own; many netizens took matters in their own hands and actively engaged in information production and dissemination on the platform created by Internet chat rooms, BBS, and forums. Some openly stood up to challenge official claims and volunteered eyewitness stories of their own. Voluntary actions by individuals and independent groups within China, along with growing pressure from the international community, pressured a dramatic shift in the Chinese government strategy from cover-up and open denials to a "full disclosure" of SARS-related information. The SARS case clearly demonstrates that in today's globalized information society, it is impossible for any government to keep its people in the dark. Pressure from the international community, led by the global media, and from the internal force of civil society was crucial in holding the Chinese authority accountable to its own citizens and the world at large. Obviously, two indispensable factors have shaped the course of events during the epidemic: the availability of the Internet and other related new information technologies, and the existence of self-organizing individuals and voluntary groups in Chinese civil society that were willing to challenge authoritarian manipulation of SARS-related information.

Although the long-term impact of the SARS crisis on the Chinese political arena is hard to predict, its immediate effect is obvious — it has taught Chinese authorities the price of information cover-up and the benefits of transparency. The clearest indication of a change is that shortly after a Chinese submarine sank on a training mission in the Yellow Sea killing all seventy crew members aboard, the Chinese government publicly released information about the accident.[124] This was the first time that the Chinese authorities went public with a military accident, which had hitherto been classified as top state secret. Although how much and to what extent the SARS aftereffect can have in the future transformation of China's political system remains to be seen, there is no doubt that the Internet has opened a potentially expanding space for Chinese civil society to take root and to grow. Partly as fallout from the SARS outbreak, the Ministry of Civil Affairs and the National Security Bureau jointly announced on September 12, 2005, that casualties in relation to natural disasters, such as earthquakes, floods, and epidemics are no longer classified as state secrets and can thus be freely reported by the media.[125]

School Explosion in Jiangxi in 2001: From Premier's Denial to Apology

On March 6, 2001, the National People's Congress, China's legislature, was in the middle of a meeting in Beijing for the annual session of the Congress to exercise its role in a Chinese-styled orchestrated political juggling match. As an annual event at which all the political elite in China make an appearance and from which some glimpses can be gained into different kinds of delicate moves in Chinese politics, it attracts a large presence of domestic and overseas reporters every year. However, the focus of the press corps and China's legislators at this event soon shifted from Beijing to a small village some 900 miles south of the capital.

At around 11:10 am, a two-story building of Fanglin village school in Wanzai county of China's southeast province of Jiangxi, suddenly collapsed after a loud explosion, trapping about 200 third-, fourth- and fifth-grade students as well as a few teachers in the debris. By late evening that day, the blast had caused forty-one deaths and twenty-seven injuries. Among the dead were thirty-six elementary school students, four teachers and one villager. A pregnant teacher was among those killed. Rescue workers, ambulances, police, and reporters as well as bereaved parents stormed the accident site within hours of the explosion. By mid-afternoon, the breaking news was reported by major national media in China as more reporters flocked to the site.

Initial investigations by many reporters claimed that students were installing fuses into firecrackers at the time of the blast. The headmaster of the school, villagers told reporters, had signed a contract with a local fireworks factory to earn money for the cash-strapped school. Students at the school were asked to produce fireworks, and those who refused were punished with a fine; meanwhile, teachers whose students were involved in fireworks manufacturing were offered kickbacks as incentives. It was also reported that the first floor of the school was rented out to a fireworks factory while the second floor was used as the classroom. Other villagers said they had seen a man carry two heavy bags into the school shortly before the explosion.[126]

There were also eyewitness accounts from surviving students that they were having classes when the fatal explosion occurred. Blackboards with Chinese characters used to teach the students were also found in the wreckage. A government spokesman told the press that "Most probably it is because of firecrackers, but a final result will come out after investigators convene."[127]

Wanzai county has been known as an important base for fireworks production in the impoverished Jiangxi province, and fireworks manufacturers and dealers can be found everywhere along both sides of the highway throughout the county. However, because of the primitive working conditions of these fireworks factories, accidents are common. Prior to the elementary school blast, several major explosions involving fireworks factories in Jiangxi and Guangdong had caused over a hundred casualties altogether, which led the provincial governments to call for a safer working environment.[128] The calls were largely ignored by local officials, who were more interested in increasing production than safety. But none of the previous fatal accidents had involved school-age children.

A policy factor that indirectly contributed to this disaster is that, for many decades, the Chinese authorities had been advocating a practice of "work-for-study" (*qingong jianxue*) for China's elementary to high school students. Because the central and local governments lack enough funds to support Chinese schools, individual schools are encouraged to find their own ways of subsidizing the underfunded school system. So it is common for schools to get involved in money-making enterprises, called "school-affiliated factories" (*xiaoban gongchang*), which enjoy tax-reduction incentives from local governments. In the curriculum approved by the Ministry of Education for students from elementary to high schools, at least one class period should be devoted to work-study — the so-called labor class in Chinese schools. Some students told reporters after the Fangli school blast that they had been manufacturing fireworks during their weekly "labor class."[129]

The shock caused by this accident went beyond the Chinese border. Delegates to the National People's Congress from Jiangxi province as well as other parts of China expressed their outrage at the disaster and called for laws protecting school safety and sought compensation for student deaths and injuries.[130] On March 8, the United Nations Children's Fund expressed outrage at the tragedy and at the report that children were working, and called on the Chinese government to enforce laws to end child labor.[131] "Exploitative child labor of any form is morally unacceptable and a violation of children's rights and of international law ... What is even more appalling is that the children killed were engaged in particularly hazardous work at a place that should be safe haven: their school."[132] The accident was understandably an embarrassment to the Chinese authorities both at national and local levels.

Response from the Chinese media to the tragic incident was prompt. Within hours of the explosion, reporters from a few newspapers in Jiangxi province as well as neighboring provinces began to file stories about the event, and more reporters were on the way to the site. Meanwhile, the school blast, not the Chinese legislature, immediately became the focus of attention for the international press corps in Beijing. On March 9, in response to a reporter's question during a television interview to Hong Kong reporters about whether the tragedy happened because the school was asking students to make fireworks, Premier Zhu Rongji said:

> This is the case that worries me the most. Originally, I also suspected that this primary school had rented out school premises as storage for

raw materials for making firecrackers in strings, in order to create a revenue stream. Later, it was found out that it was not the case at all, because the raw materials for fireworks and firecrackers were moved in afterward. The person suspected of having ignited the raw materials was also killed in the blast. Initial findings indicate that the suspect did it intentionally. His wife was divorcing him. He was vindictive and had a mental problem, so he moved the raw materials for fireworks and fire-crackers outside the building and the explosion also killed himself.[133]

Meanwhile, Xinhua News Agency reported the result of the official inves-tigation on the previous day,[134] apparently on which Zhu's "madman theory" was based, and soon afterward released the "official" version of the story by two of its reporters investigating the case.[135] However, even after Premier Zhu's public interview, Xinhua's investigation was disputed by reporters from regional media, such as local newspapers from Shijiazhuang of Hebei prov-ince, Guangzhou of Guangdong province, and Chengdu of Sichuan prov-ince, which decided to run their versions of the accident.[136] That local media were willing to venture against the established practice of relying on Xinhua for major events indicates their intentional shift from the national center of media control.

Not long after the explosion, paramilitary personnel and police dispatched by local authorities blocked all entrances to the village and forbade all villag-ers from talking to the media. Dozens of domestic and overseas reporters were kept miles away from the site of the explosion while local officials enforced a "man-on-man" strategy by which each villager was followed by paramilitary officers. Those reporters who were lucky enough to infiltrate the village and got close to the villagers had difficulties in getting their notes or videotapes out.[137] At the same time, bulldozers sent by the local government leveled the blast site and thus eliminated any possible remaining evidence that might reveal the cause of the disaster.[138] Nonetheless, grieving parents were able to talk to both domestic and overseas media by telephone or in person, and angry Chi-nese reporters volunteered information to their overseas counterparts during the coverage of the blast for fear that the Chinese media might not run their stories, and overseas media were quite successful in getting the stories out to challenge the government version of the cause of the explosion.[139] Specifically, Western reporters from the Associated Press, Reuters, the BBC, and Agence France-Presse reported a lot of information through telephone interviews with villagers via random number dialing, when their physical presence at the vil-lage was not possible because of blockades by the local police.[140] On March 13, an angry Foreign Ministry spokesman characterized the coverage of the blast by foreign media as "absurd and erroneous" in a routine press conference.[141]

The Chinese premier was well aware of the long tradition of local offi-cials falsifying or covering up and keeping information from their superiors for fear that negative news might ruin their future path to promotion. Zhu noticed the discrepancy between what he was told by Xinhua and the official investigators and the coverage of this blast by overseas media, especially the Hong Kong newspapers (which are openly accessible in major cities of mainland China), which Zhu read regularly. Zhu grew suspicious that he might be kept in the dark about the truth of this incident. So Zhu secretly ordered the Minister of Pubic Security to send an undercover team of investigators to find out the truth.[142]

On March 15, 2001, in a televised press conference at the end of the legislative session, Premier Zhu Rongji made an apology to the Chinese people and the families of the victims of the Jiangxi school explosion for which he said the State Council and he "bear an unshirkable responsibility."[143] Zhu's act broke with a tradition in Chinese politics that top leaders rarely publicly acknowledge any kind of mistake. After his earlier comments about the cause of the explosion, Zhu said, he noted that overseas media, including the Hong Kong media, all said the explosion was caused by production of fireworks at the school; to find out what really had happened, he instructed the Minister of Public Security to send an expert investigation team of six persons in plainclothes to the village. Zhu admitted that the findings did indicate that the school children had previously been making fireworks, which contradicted his early denial of any such activity at the school. However, Zhu stressed again that there was no evidence of firework production at the site at the time of the explosion. Furthermore, Zhu vowed to continue the investigation until the "full truth" was out.[144] On April 3, 2001, the party secretary and the governor of Jiangxi province were both removed from office,[145] apparently in connection to the school blast.

Looking at this manmade disaster in hindsight with all the details available from the various media now suggests that students likely were not engaged in fireworks manufacturing at the time of the explosion because all later eyewitness accounts from surviving students and teachers indicated that they were having classes. All claims that students were producing fireworks at the time came from parents or relatives who later came to the rescue after the explosion. However, it must also have been true that there was a large stockpile of explosive material at the site, and the school had been used for fireworks production (probably by a third party that rented the school property); the students had been asked to assemble fireworks as part of the school policy to subsidize its routine expenses. Undoubtedly, local officials at the township and county levels had tried various ways to cover up after the school blast. Some reporters from the foreign as well as domestic media got some facts wrong from the start about the blast. But that people were willing to question any "truth" from the government reflects the ongoing credibility crisis of the Chinese regime with both its own people and the overseas media. When the official version of the "truth" is perceived to be questionable, members and organizations from civil society, including the media, either try to supply information or actively seek information from alternative sources. The Internet is an important facilitator in that process.

The Internet as an Alternative Information Source

As has been true with major disasters, the first response from the local authorities was to block information and downplay the severity of the school blast incident. In the Chinese system of official promotion and punishment, government officials only need to be accountable to their superiors, not the subjects they govern, since only officials who occupy a higher position in the hierarchy can decide the fate of officialdom. But the changing information environment brought about by modern communication technologies led by telephones and the Internet has greatly affected the course of the development of this whole event. No longer can the official media maintain their monopoly on the circulation of information because more and more elements of civil society vigorously take part in getting the information out to the public.

Within hours of the school blast, major Chinese portal sites started to run stories as breaking news. This change in the speed of information propagation created an immediacy that put great pressure on each major news site to keep up with developing stories to win in an increasingly competitive environment. In addition to free e-mails, free games, and other free services, the quantity as well as quality of information becomes a crucial determinant in winning over users.

In addition to speed, another aspect that is new to China's Internet age is the scope of information dissemination. Traditional media are limited in that they can only cover a certain geographic area, and therefore their impact is limited only to the audience within reach. This geographic barrier is no longer true with Internet media because anyone anywhere with access to the Internet can process information from any of the Chinese news sites online. In the old days before the Internet, domestic issues in China could only gain national attention when they were covered by a few of the powerful national media, such as Xinhua or CCTV (and hence the elite status of the Chinese national media in Chinese journalism). The Internet has ended that monopolistic control of information by the few elite national media, both because of the diversity it brings from multiple sources and the interactive participation it gets from the audience.

As pointed out in Chapter 3, all online publishers that intend to get involved in the online news business must be licensed by the state. Therefore, all major Chinese portal sites have partnered with both local and national media organizations in sharing information and resources. This means that news stories by a regional newspaper can be used by any news site within the network of information-sharing partners. Indeed, any of the major regional portal sites, such as Dongfang Wang (Eastern Net), Dongbei Wang (Northeastern

Net), Xibei (Northwestern Net), Nangfang Wang (Southern Net), as well as the three national portal sites (i.e., Sina, Netease, and Sohu), all have signed agreements with newspapers from all parts of China in sharing resources. In practice, cross-listing and cross-referencing among Chinese portal sites are the norm. Soon after the blast, most portal sites created special coverage sections on the Internet to update readers about the latest development of the story. Thus the Internet revolutionized the spread of information in the case of the Jiangxi blast both in terms of the speed of delivery and the scope of reach that would be unimaginable in China's media landscape before. As John Schauble, the China correspondent for *The Age* noted in covering the explosion, "The Internet ... and more aggressive media coverage has resulted in the spread of news stories to a larger audience"[146] — and at a greater speed for that matter. Audience interest and media coverage in this case were a reciprocal process — timely coverage of the breaking event captivated people's interest, and mounting audience interest not only built up the pressure for a more aggressive coverage from the media, but also triggered citizen participation in volunteering information. These are the necessary conditions for the growth of civil society in the country.

In addition, the Internet became an important alternative source of information for the audience in the process of covering this event. The Internet provided an abundance of information in relation to the tragedy by offering users access to different sources, which led a large number of netizens to challenge the official version of the story. After Premier Zhu's March 9 public comment about the "one madman" causing the blast, all Chinese media were instructed by Chinese authorities to stick to the official version of the story from Xinhua. However, the official Web site of the *People's Daily* (known as *Renmin Wang*, or People's Net), the other main official mouthpiece, still left untouched a news report from Nanjing-based *Yangtze Daily* that claimed that the students were putting fuses in the firecrackers just before the explosion.[147] In an investigative story by its own reporters posted on *Renmin Wang* on March 10, although the reporters agreed with the official verdict about the "madman" exploding the school, they cited eyewitness accounts confirming that students had previously engaged in fireworks production at the school site,[148] directly contradicting the Premier's denial about any such previous activity at the school. On March 11, *Remnin Wang* still featured a link to stories by a local newspaper Web site in Jiangxi that continued to talk about the exploitation of child labor among Jiangxi grade schools.[149]

Of the three best-known portal sites in the wake of Zhu's verdict, Sina. com classified the blast as a "man-made" explosion, and Netease.com left the issue open by saying that available evidence was inconclusive, and the official statement of criminal activity was a possibility, while Netease.com displayed a strong tendency toward blaming firecrackers as the cause of the blast by featuring many links to similar stories from various media outlets.[150] Tactically, none of the three portal sites directly confronted the official verdict while all tried to avoid leaving the impression that the official story was unchallengeable. Some portal sites affiliated with local media organizations, such as Shanghai's East.com and Sichuan's Newssc.org, and the Beijing-based Qianlong.com, adopted similar approaches to leave room for linking the blast to firecrackers.[151] The online media showed much more resilience in covering the school blast than conventional media. These are indications of significant cracks in the state's control of information in the Internet age.

The media were not the only sources of information; Chinese netizens were actively involved in the dissemination of information about the disaster throughout the coverage of the blast. The most common practice for spreading word about the blast was for people to post breaking news or the latest update on the BBS and in chat rooms of popular portal and news sites. Among the most popular news stories being reposted were eyewitness accounts by Chinese as well as overseas reporters of how reporters were interfered with in their reporting and in some cases blocked by local authorities from talking to local residents.[152] Another way that people contributed to the information flow is that they posted first-hand accounts from themselves, eyewitnesses, or parents. For example, surfers from Wanzai, the county where the explosion occurred, posted background information about prevalent practices among local schools and other local sites where fireworks were manufactured.[153] Members within Chinese civil society thus created an open venue of public communication that proved to be a viable alternative channel of information.

Above all, public sentiments as reflected in popular online chat rooms and on bulletin boards created direct pressure on Chinese authorities to respond to rising public outrage and disbelief. As noted in Chapter 5, because the Chinese regime lacks a reliable and systematic mechanism to tap into public opinion on major issues, online discussions provide one ready avenue for government officials to gauge public opinion. Immediately after news broke about the school blast, most major Chinese portal sites created special chat-room sessions for online users to share their views on this event, and angry Chinese netizens stormed online forums from popular portal and news sites to vent their disbelief and disgust at the tragedy. From the date of explosion to the date of Premier Zhu's public interview with the Hong Kong press on March 9, more than 1000 netizens had posted on Sina.com's online forum alone;[154] a much greater number of people had read these postings by the same time. Many people expressed their dissatisfaction with the government's inability to fund basic education in China while at the same time spending billions of dollars for the 2008 Beijing Olympic bid and many more billions of dollars on its military every year; others directly attributed the root cause of accidents like this to official corruption; still others called for the resignation of the governor of Jiangxi and the Minister of Education (who was Ms. Chen Zhili at the time, a protégé of Jiang Zemin). The most brazen message questioned why children had to make money through producing fireworks while their president could spend more than US$100 million to purchase a Boeing aircraft for himself.[155]

Public anger online peaked on March 9 after Premier Zhu's announcement of the cause of the explosion. The vast majority of netizens expressed their disbelief at the official verdict and condemned what they thought was the official effort to cover things up.[156] One thoughtful piece posted on Sina.com's BBS said: "The government conclusion may be truthful. But why so many people don't believe it? It seems that our government's credibility among the public is reduced to nil, which is the most pitiful."[157] Indeed, as this case shows, social issues often evolve into political ones through discussions because they are so interwoven with each other.

In fact, the Sina.com's chat room was so flooded with comments criticizing the government that Sina.com decided to shut down its chat room specifically devoted to the discussion of the school blast on March 9 "in order to abide by China's Internet laws." One Sina.com official said: "The net citizens can raise questions over issues but they can't criticize the government."[158] Whether Sina.com did this for self-protection or to comply with directives from the government is unknown. Another popular discussion site, the *Strong Country Forum* on Renmin Wang, did not completely close down its forums but monitored closely its postings and deleted any message that might prove offensive to the government.[159] However, many chat-room visitors on both Renmin Wang's *Strong Country Forum*[160] and Sina.com's other chat rooms that remained open[161] still found ways to outwit the censors by playing word games to continue posting messages in relation to the blast without using sensitive words. This again shows that the state does not want to be kept out of the sight of Chinese netizens. Yet the fact that Chinese authorities cannot totally eliminate alternative or opposing voices in cyberspace signifies the new challenge for the state as well as a new opportunity for civil society in the cyber age.

Lessons from the Jiangxi School Blast

Information flow was greatly affected by the presence of a large overseas press corps scheduled to cover the Chinese parliamentary session in Beijing in the spring of 2001 when the school explosion occurred. Compelling interest in the blast at the very start built a formidable pressure on the Chinese government to respond to the media's request for information on the cause of the disaster. However, in this case, the Chinese media worked hand in hand with overseas media, and on some occasions took the lead in excavating information and in bypassing local officials' blockades to get at the truth. State control of conventional media is not as suffocating as it used to be, especially at times of calamities such as this one involving lives of innocent children. Information that was once localized in the pre-Internet days became national, and in some cases, global, once regional media released their stories on the Internet. The reach of the Internet undoubtedly changed the arena of news coverage of such a compelling story.

The Internet played an indispensable role in bringing immediacy and diversity to the news made available to a national audience. An unusually high level of audience interest, on the other hand, contributed to aggressive coverage of this tragedy. Mounting audience anger, as expressed in online chat rooms and on bulletin boards and as reflected in coverage by the conventional media, led to a certain level of public accountability on the part of the Chinese government that had been rarely seen in Chinese politics in the pre-Internet age. Voluntary participation from a wide spectrum of online groups and individuals in the news gathering and dissemination process built up the pressure from the mass media as well as authorities at various levels to present the public with more credible information. First-hand accounts, eyewitness stories, and telephone interviews from the conventional media as well as nonmedia professionals that were suppressed by official publications became available on the Internet to counter the official side of the story. The interplay between the Internet and Chinese civil society provides a fresh platform for citizen participation that was impossible before.

Chapter Summary

The two cases studied here are among a growing number of high-profile events in recent years where the Internet has played a significant role in pressuring the authorities for responsiveness and accountability. In both cases, the Internet created a public platform that did not exist before for spreading news and generating vigorous discussion, and more importantly, public participation from a variety of self-organizing and self-supporting individuals and social groups. It has also been crucial in providing an alternative channel of information when information was either not available from the mainstream media or sanctioned by the state. This brand-new information environment has provided a fertile ground for the growth of Chinese civil society and its involvement in state affairs at various levels.

The events in these two cases took place in different settings and involved different players. In the SARS case, while SMS and networks of informal communication were the major channels of information when the epidemic was mainly local and in the early stage, the Internet became the essential tool to both get information out to the national and international community about the severity of the virus and bring to the Chinese netizens news from overseas media sources. In the Jiangxi school explosion, the Internet played an indispensable role in circulating the news to the domestic audience about the tragedy and in challenging the official version of the story; domestic and overseas media worked hand in hand in excavating the gruesome details of the story, which were then communicated via the Internet. In both cases, there was a high level of public fervor in demanding updated information from fellow netizens and in supplying requested information to Net pals. Online BBS, forums, and chat rooms spawned a spontaneous outpouring of public opinion that was hard for the authorities to ignore.

The perspective of fragmented authoritarianism mentioned in Chapter 3 is useful to understand the dynamics in the processes of the two cases. That explains why, in the early stages of the SARS crisis, interagency cooperation among provincial authorities and the Ministry of Public Health was hard to achieve; it was only later with the direct intervention from the central authority that different agencies from different levels came together to coordinate efforts and resources in gaining an upper hand over the disease. Fragmented authoritarianism also explains why Chinese media from different localities (and mostly outside of Jiangxi province) actively pursued the school explosion in Jiangxi. Authorities in one province generally do not have jurisdiction over media in other provinces because the local media tend to be more responsive to orders from local authorities. Meanwhile, although the central government still maintains control over the media in the country, its control has been significantly weakened by the marketization effort. The Internet, on the other hand, can cut across the line of command more easily because it can present information from multiple sources and it serves audiences from no single central location.

From the two cases, it should be clear that a pattern is unmistakably emerging in which the Internet plays a more and more significant role in mobilizing different social forces in China to create moments of change in Chinese civil society. These should not be considered isolated, rare events; rather, they point to a trend that in all likelihood is going to continue in the future. However, as it stands today, the Internet has not yet become a fully powered democratizing force in China; the authoritarian state will continue its long-time effort to control information in the country — either online or offline, and the regime will keep selectively punishing a few who dare to violate its dicta. But the tug of war between the state and various segments of civil society, along with the new possibilities brought about by the Internet and other emerging new communication technologies, will determine the future course of Chinese society. We already see the potential of the Internet as an empowering tool for Chinese civil society to organize action, to express itself, and to induce change in the country. With the increasing popularization of the Internet as a communication tool among ordinary Chinese citizens in the years to come, there is reason to hope that the expanding social space on the Internet will contribute to the formation of a sizable civil society force in negotiating for further change with the power of the state.

Online Activism, Internet Protest, and Social Movements in Cyber China

The Internet not only facilitates the creation and dissemination of information from a rising number of individuals and social groups whose access to conventional media channels is limited, but it also transforms the global arena of social movements by building networks of activism that are disorganized and dispersed in the physical world. Given the lack of physicality in cyberspace, social movements have been rejuvenated by the Internet and other new media technologies in many significant ways when traditional geographic barriers have been crossed and nation–state borders have been bypassed in interconnecting scattered individuals and social groups into a common base of action. This is an especially promising line of development for Chinese civil society because Chinese cyberspace is dominated by people in their twenties and thirties (a popular term in Chinese to refer to this particular group is *fenqing*, or angry youth), the staple force of social movement and collective action, and because serious restrictions exist for collective action in the offline arena. This chapter, after a general overview of Internet activism, presents two case studies in which network activism significantly changed the course of events: one is the Internet-based protest over the death of Sun Zhigang in 2003, and the other is the online petition against Japan's bid for a permanent seat in the United Nations Security Council in 2005.

Activism and the Internet

Throughout human history, social movements have been precursors of social change. In the nineteenth century, women's rights activists, abolitionists, and other activist groups resorted to magazine and newspaper publishing as their weapon to induce and effect change in American society (e.g., Kessler, 1984; Streitmatter, 2001). The twentieth century witnessed the rise of first radio (e.g., Lasar, 1999; Walker, 2004), and then television (e.g., Gitlin, 1980), as influential channels for informing the public and organizing individuals and groups into action. The success of collective action, which is "joint action in pursuit of common ends" (e.g., a protest, a revolt, an uprising, a strike), to a great extent depends on resource mobilization (i.e., the amount of resources under the collective control of the group) (Tilly, 1978: 84). Mass media, which controls so much of our information resources today, apparently weighs in as a crucial factor in determining the success or failure of a social campaign. The press and activist groups have developed some kind of symbiotic relationship: the latter are potential sources of headlines for the former under particular circumstances, while the former influences public perception of the latter by its specific coverage (and sometimes lack of coverage) and framing of news and issues in relation to the latter (e.g., Ryan, 1991; Wolfsfeld, 1984). However, because activist groups typically dwell outside of established social and political institutions, they are largely shoved away from the spotlight of routine media operations. Therefore, the relationship is asymmetrical in nature, and is called by Gadi Wolfsfeld (1991) to be a "competitive symbiosis." As a result, media strategies have been an essential part of many marginal groups in society in their daily operations (e.g., Rucht, 2004).

Social movements that are intended to challenge the dominant social and political institutions and the prevalent ideologies strive for access to media of public communication for at least three reasons: mobilization, validation, and scope enlargement (Gamson and Wolfsfeld, 1993). First, "[m]edia discourse remains indispensable for most movements because most of the people they wish to reach are part of the mass media gallery, while many are missed by movement-oriented outlets" (p. 116). Second, "[r]eceiving standing in the media is often a necessary condition before targets of influence will grant a movement recognition and deal with its claims and demands" (p. 116). Third, coverage by the mainstream media is a vehicle for broadening the scope of conflict in the efforts of a social movement to alter the balance of power by winning the alliance of sympathetic third parties. It is for this reason that social and political activists almost invariably seek the power of mainstream media to publicize their voices, to mobilize and recruit, and more importantly, to redefine their position in the established power structure. Accordingly, social movement groups have had a long tradition of establishing their own media outlets once desired access to the mainstream media is denied or when they feel they have been betrayed or disappointed by existing media portrayals (Downing, 2001). Therefore, during the 1989 Tiananmen Movement, because official media was sanctioned and coverage of this event was controlled by the regime, the Chinese students desperately sought access to international media via fax machines and telephone calls, and set up their alternative channels of communication to Chinese citizens through temporary radio stations, pamphlets, newsletters, and brochures.

The ascendancy of the Internet as a global platform of public communication parallels an era of declining political activism and discourse. It comes as no surprise, then, that the Internet and miscellaneous new information and communication technologies (ICTs) would become the next promising opportunity for global social and political activism in the new century. Although we must be cautious not to idealize and exaggerate the potential effect of the Internet and new ICTs on the spheres of political and democratic participation, Peter Dahlgren (2004: xiii) observes, what we have seen over the years is that

> a good deal of civic discussion takes place on the internet, not only in explicit public forums and within varieties of online journalism, but also within the vast networks of activist organizations and social movements ... the internet helps promote what are called alternative or counter public spheres that can offer a new, empowering sense of what it means to be a citizen.

Moreover, "[i]n the context of social movements and activist networks, this is taken one step further via mobilization and the various forms of political practices that they embody."

In offering their preliminary observations on the impact of new ICTs on social movements, van de Donk and colleagues (2004: 18) conclude that "some movements, and some groups within movements, are more inclined than others to introduce and use some applications of ICTs." In addition, van de Donk et al. also point out that the Internet allows for immediate global organization and serves as a tool for information that tends to be suppressed by the established media. The Internet, however, is not likely to replace traditional forms of protest (such as rallies, demonstrations, and collection of signatures), although it may facilitate them, van de Donk et al. contend. Finally, "the use of the Internet affects the *internal structure* of social movement organizations, above all the density and direction of their links ... there is ample evidence that ICTs are conducive to forging (temporary) alliances and coalitions, both vertical and horizontal, across different movements" (van de Donk et al., 2004: 19. Emphasis original).

The above characterization, to a large extent, summarizes well recent developments in online activism and social movements, but it fails to give sufficient attention to emerging lines of formations that can only be realized in cyberspace. While the Internet and new ICTs have indeed reinvigorated traditional forms of social movements, there are also promising signs that they have spawned brand-new forms of cyberactivism that would have not been possible before (e.g., McCaughey and Ayers, 2003). For example, in her study of two of the earliest Internet-based (and text-oriented for that matter) protests, the cases of Lotus MarketPlace (which was designed by Lotus in 1990 to be a direct mail marketing database for commercial interests) and the Clipper chip (a U.S. federal encryption standard implemented in a chip proposed in 1993 and officially adopted in 1994 by the Clinton Administration), Laura Gurak (1997) concludes that "mobilization exigency" in the form of online discussions, debates, protests, form letters, and signatures can come together quickly — typically in a matter of days or even hours — and that the Internet's nonhierarchical structure makes it possible for individuals to bypass "standard procedure" to allow information to circulate both to a widespread user base and to specifically targeted individuals (e.g., the CEO of Lotus and the U.S. president). The speed and reach of these protests created by "computer populism" over the Internet would have been impossible in pre-Internet days.

As another form of online activism, the Independent Media Center (IMC) has become a transnational force against global dominance of corporate media giants by aligning individual and group activists from multiple fronts based mainly in North America and Europe. The most noticeable, and most effective, presence of IMC is its official Web site, indymedia.org, which links over sixty autonomously operated and jointly coordinated Web sites across North America, Europe, and other parts of the world (Kidd, 2003). The IMC is a textbook example of how local and global media activists, independent media producers, independent journalists, and international media organizations collaborate and share resources on the cyberplatform, thereby galvanizing activists from a wide spectrum of backgrounds into collective action on the global stage. While the Internet in this case has not totally substituted for offline protests or movements, it has certainly uplifted them to a brand-new level.

While some forms of Internet activism provide an extended arm of, and are therefore deeply rooted in, offline campaigns, other formations of online activism are the reverse. An example of the latter is the Electronic Frontier Foundation (EFF), a nonprofit watchdog organization founded in 1990 with the stated goal of protecting free speech, civil liberties, and privacy in the digital age. Whereas EFF also engages in conventional types of offline campaigns such as funding court cases, its main base and chief battlefield is online, with its official Web site at www.eff.org acting as the meeting and mobilization center for its over 50,000 members dispersed mainly in North America (Godwin, 2003; Rheingold, 1993; Sterling, 1993). Here we see an instance in which an entity establishes its presence primarily online and is complemented by offline activities. A more recent example in this category is MoveOn.org, which, as an Internet-based grassroots advocacy group involving more than three million activists in the United States, has established its presence in U.S. politics through its mass mobilization and massive participation in a variety of issues in the political process.

It has been mentioned in Chapter 5 that the defining feature of the Internet and new ICTs as empowerment tools is their two-wayness (or multiwayness) in shifting the power of communication from traditional media institutions to individual participants. In that regard, the new communication environment has made possible certain types of human actions in a virtual world that were not available before. It is in this sense that Howard Rheingold (2003: xii) concludes that the new information infrastructure creates "smart mobs," which "consist of people who are able to act in concert even if they don't know each other." The result is, Rheingold goes on to point out, that "[g]roups of people using these tools [mobile communications and pervasive computing technologies] will gain new forms of social power, new ways to organize their interactions and exchanges just in time and just in place" (2003: xii–xiii). Wireless communication devices and mobile Internet-accessing gadgets, Rheingold contends, amplify human cooperative capabilities.

In examining various forms of Internet activism, Graham Meikle (2002) describes how each type of online behavior — among them, cultural jamming (sabotaging cultural signs and symbols to call attention to particular issues), adbusters (an anticonsumerism campaign), electronic civil disobedience (or hacktivism), and virtual sit-ins — is accomplished differently and subsequently serves to redefine boundaries in the media environment of the cyberage. The main point from Meikle's book is, I think, that ingenuity and creativeness can lead Net activists to a whole new terrain of potentialities.

To sum up, although the Internet and new ICTs have not drastically disrupted the basic constellation of power relations in society, they have fundamentally reinvented grassroots social and political activism by breathing new life into networks of individuals and groups in cyberspace. Four constant themes emerge from current research literature on global Internet activism. First, some traditional forms of collection action have been energized by cybernetworks; second, new forms of Internet activism have spread to the offline world and have gained a life in the material world; third, we have also seen creative forms of activism that are solely or primarily based on the Internet; fourth, activism has become globalized in nature, and the Internet intensifies that trend in the new millennium. The entwining of networks of activists online and offline is likely to be the dominating theme in the years to come for global Internet activism.

In the case of China, these points are particularly relevant. The decentralized nature of cyberspace has tilted the power into the hands of the individuals and marginal social groups in a lot of ways, thus presenting opportunities for activists to form into networks of collective action that would not be possible otherwise. Because protests, demonstrations, and other types of collective action that do not fall within the official line are highly controlled and heavily monitored in China, and because Chinese laws require that any public gathering of social activism be held with official permission (applying for which is a harassing process in most cases), cybergatherings of like-minded individuals and cyberprotests may become the more desirable alternative, as demonstrated by the following cases.

Sun Zhigang: The Death of One Man, Protest of Many, and the Change of China's Vagrancy Law

On the night of March 17, 2003, 27-year-old Sun Zhigang, a native of Wuhan city of Hubei Province and a college graduate of central China's Wuhan Technical College, who at the time was working as a graphic designer for a clothes factory in Guangzhou, went out to a nearby Internet café for some online surfing, a popular activity for young people in major cities who are away from home. He was stopped halfway by the police who were randomly checking residency permits among passersby on the street. Unfortunately for Sun, he had not obtained his permit yet because he had just moved to Guangzhou to his new job about twenty days earlier from Shenzhen, a city adjacent to Hong Kong, and he had not found the time to apply for a temporary residency permit. This was a mistake that Sun would pay for with his life. Sun was taken to a local detention center for beggars and vagrants on suspicion that he was one of them.

Starting in the 1960s, the Chinese government put in place a custody and repatriation system to stop large numbers of rural vagrants entering the cities because those homeless and jobless migrants were a major threat to the country's social welfare and public security in the cities. A huge gap between urban and rural areas that continues to this date proves to be a big attraction for poor people to migrate to the urban areas to seek better lives. But many of these vagrants became a main source of criminal activities and social instability and were headaches for local police. So the official policy was to repatriate these people to their place of origin once they were identified. A national custody and repatriation network was also put in place that was in charge of processing these cases.

The situation started to worsen after Deng's reform and open policy initiated in the late 1970s. Economic development that centered in the cities had opened up a lot of opportunities for all kinds of people and substantially added to the incentives that attracted vagrants to the cities: some found a living by begging, others sought temporary employment, and still others wanted to evade the family planning policy and made the city the shelter for more babies. The increasing floating population in all major cities quickly turned into a big social problem nationwide, which resulted in the "Measures for Internment and Deportation of Urban Vagrants and Beggars" promulgated by the State Council in May 1982. This policy stipulated that nonnative people living on the street and without reliable means of self-support are subject to being collected and returned to their home of origin in the care of local authorities.[1] These people were classified as "Three Have-Nots" — no regular home, no stable income, and no legal ID.

These broadly stated, guideline-type measures, however, had not worked effectively to reduce the number of migrating rural people who wanted to make a living in the cities. Instead, they created a source of revenue for local police enforcement, who would detain the vagrants and then issue a fine. Those who paid the fines were often let off on the street again — until they were caught next time and faced another fine. Local police had no motivation to send the detainees to their native place because this incurred cost in money and time. So returning vagrants to their homes of origin was often the last alternative local police chose. Issuing temporary residency permit was the way for local authorities to differentiate between legitimate workers employed from outside the city and the floating vagrant population that often proved to be a headache for law enforcement.

Abuse of police power is nothing new in any Chinese city, and people generally don't pay much attention unless it directly involves them, especially when it is about vagrants (whose number can vary from several thousand to hundreds of thousands depending on the size and location of the city), who are typically associated with hooligans and good-for-nothings and who are despised by urban residents. Therefore, when Sun Zhigang was taken to the detention center without being given any chance to explain, police found nothing unusual that distinguished him from the rest of the 110 people who were detained that night. However, one key characteristic differentiated Sun from other people who frequented the custody and repatriation centers — Sun was a college graduate. That would turn out to be a major factor that led this incident toward an unexpected direction.

After he was detained by the police, Sun contacted two of his friends in Guangzhou, who came immediately to the police station and told the police officers on duty that Sun was a local employee and volunteered to be his "guarantors." The friends also promised that they would help Sun get his residency permit the next day with the help of his employer. The police officers, however, turned down all the requests and told them that "there was no need to check these claims (about Sun's identity)." The reason, one of Sun's friends later revealed to reporters, might have been that Sun had had some verbal argument with the police there, which might have infuriated the officers in charge. Sun repeated his story several times to different police officers and asked the officers to check his identity with his employer, all to no avail.

The next day, on March 18, Sun told the police that he was not feeling well, and he was then transferred to a clinic that night. The clinic, protected by iron gates and high walls, was specifically set up for patients from various custody and repatriation centers in the Guangzhou metropolitan area, and it was ill equipped. All four doctors there were once psychotherapists who had treated mentally ill patients; assisting the doctors were a dozen nurses and nursing workers. The nursing workers had no background in nursing and were actually security guards in the clinic. They were classified as nursing workers because all institutions that wanted to hire security workers had to register with, and pay, the local police station. The use of the term "nursing workers" allowed the clinic to get away without paying the fee. So, instead of treating patients in the clinic, these nursing workers were often involved in beating them for any kind of misbehavior or disobedience. In the investigation of Sun's death, it was found later that from March 16 to March 19, prior to the death of Sun, three died, with two from some type of illness and one from internal bleeding in the head. In the last quarter of the previous year, forty-six patients died in this clinic.

When Sun Zhigang arrived at the clinic, one nursing worker took an instant dislike for him and instructed the inmates to "teach him a lesson." The lesson was too much for Sun to endure. After being kicked, punched, and slapped for several hours while his numerous pleas for help and mercy were ignored, Sun was taken to his cement bed in the cell after midnight. A motionless Sun was found by one nurse the next morning, March 20, 2003, and Sun was taken to the emergency room, where he was pronounced dead ten minutes later. A postmortem indicated that Sun died from "wound-induced shock caused by extensive soft tissue damage."[2]

Sun Zhigang's friends were notified that Sun had died of a "heart attack" when they tried to contact him at noon on March 20. After learning of Sun's death, his family members, relatives, and friends tried to contact local police, the clinic, and other official agencies to demand an explanation, but they received no definite answers of any kind for days. No lawyer in Guangzhou dared to take up the case for fear of offending the local authorities.

Everything started to change when Sun's friends and family contacted a local reporter almost a month after Sun's death. In the wake of the marketization of the Chinese media in recent decades, reporters have been more willing to take up cases like this because human interest stories involving police brutality draw more audience interest than dull political news. The reporter was infuriated and did a thorough investigation of what happened to Sun Zhigang from his detention to his death at the clinic, and the story was published in the April 25 issue of Guangzhou-based *Nanfang Dushi Bao* (Southern Metropolitan Daily), and became available on *Nanfang Wang* (Southern Net) on the same day.[3] The atrocity of this incident immediately caught public attention and led to public outrage. Starting on the second day after the publication of the news story, Sun's family members were contacted by different government agencies that had been previously nonresponsive to their requests, and on April 26, officials from the district police bureau and the civil affairs bureau visited Sun's family members in person and promised a quick reply to their request for an official investigation. At the same time, the officials asked Sun's family not to appeal to higher authorities, and offered RMB¥2000 (US$250) "comfort money," which was turned down by the family.[4]

In Chinese politics, it has been a long tradition since ancient times for citizens to seek justice by appealing to higher authorities to exert pressure on the lower officials who otherwise would not be responsive. Since officials are only accountable to their superiors at the higher levels who control their promotion and reward in the official hierarchy, they naturally want to cover up negative news and glamorize positive stories to curry favor with the higher officials. Discontented citizens, then, may be successful in redressing social injustices by airing their grievances to the higher authorities who may in turn force lower authorities to take action. At each level of the Chinese bureaucracy from the township to the central (national) government, one official branch is specifically in charge of dealing with complaints from the public.

Fortunately for Sun's family, they did not have to appeal to higher authorities themselves; public outcries as a result of the media coverage of Sun's death were swift and overwhelming. Pressures from online communities, social groups, and the central government prompted the provincial authorities to quick action. In early May, a special joint team led by the provincial chief of the Public Security Bureau was formed to investigate Sun's death; all thirteen suspects involved in beating Sun were caught by the police in mid-May.[5] From June 5 to June 9, 2003, a highly publicized trial was conducted in Guangzhou, and twelve were pronounced guilty at the end of the trial on June 9, 2003. Of the twelve found guilty, one was sentenced to death and another to death with suspension, and the remaining were sentenced to prison terms. Meanwhile, six hospital workers were sentenced to two- or three-year prison terms for dereliction of duty.[6] Twenty-three government officials and police officers faced Party or administrative disciplinary punishment for their roles in this case.[7]

Sun's family was reported to have been compensated RMB¥440,000 (approx. US$55,000), many times more than the normal amount for similar cases.[8] Most surprising of all, as a result of a heated national debate and subsequent uproar about the Chinese deportation system directly stirred by Sun Zhigang's death, the State Council decided at a conference chaired by Premier Wen Jiabao on June 18, 2003, to terminate the 1982 Measures on the custody and repatriation of urban vagrants and enforce a new set of management methods for such people.[9] Thus Sun Zhigang's blood ended a 21-year-old government policy concerning the lowest class of people whose voice had been ignored for so long.

The Role of the Internet in the Public Debate Triggered by Sun's Death

Like in the Jiangxi school explosion case studied in the previous chapter, the Internet played a pivotal role in the timely dissemination of the news to a national audience. From the moment the first story about Sun's tragic death from *Southern Metropolitan Daily* was published online on April 25, 2003, major Chinese portal sites posted the story without delay and spread the news to a large group of online citizens in no time. The portal sites also quickly set up special hot topic sections for this event where all related stories were posted and related stories from similar pages were cross-linked. For example, on the special coverage page of the Web site of *Renmin Ribao* (*People's Daily*), the arch propaganda mouthpiece of the Chinese Communist Party, titled "Death of Sun Zhigang Challenges the Custody and Repatriation System," sections were devoted to the latest updates, follow-ups, comments and analysis, and audience messages.[10] Other portal and news sites took a similar approach and started to provide a variety of in-depth news and analysis about the incident.[11]

On the day that the story about Sun Zhigang broke online, an online memorial page was established for Sun by an enraged software engineer in Hangzhou, and it attracted over 3000 visitors within the first two hours. The initial title of the page was "Sun Zhigang: You Are Swallowed by the Dark" and, as a clear indication of protest about the government's policy toward vagrants, it was changed to "Heaven Does Not Require Temporary Residency Permits" the next day. The number of Web page hits passed 10,000 in two days, and the number reached 20,000 at the end of the third day. On the morning of May 14, 2003, the number of hits came to 100,000, and the number doubled on June 6 on the second day of the public trial.[12] Visitors came from those who knew or did not know the victim, and people left messages, wishes, comments, and some made donations to the family. Many of the messages criticized police brutality and the official policy of treating rural residents as lower class citizens.

The print media was also quick to pick up the issue and do in-depth coverage of Sun's death. Because the government abolished the old subsidization system with the conventional media through which media used to gain financial support from the government over a decade ago, the mass media in China have since been pushed in the market to compete with one another for market share and advertising support. Therefore, Chinese media are becoming more aggressive in identifying selling points among audience members, and reporters are willing to take on a watchdog role in exposing social injustices and malpractices — to the extent that they can avoid sensitive political issues and don't question the leadership of the Communist Party. The Internet becomes a useful tool for the reporters to find what interests people and then to do their own exclusive stories. After all, although online citizens make up only a small proportion of the Chinese population, what interests them will probably also interest the general audience. In the Sun Zhigang case, the instant online hullabaloo it created meant that it was worth pursuing further. So the national media and news organizations, such as *People's Daily* and Xinhua News Agency, together with a handful of regional newspapers, immediately sent their own reporters to Guangzhou to cover this story. Those reporters also contributed to a number of exclusively online stories for major news and portal sites.

The most important impact of the Internet in this case was audience feedback in terms of online postings in chat rooms, blog entries, and commentaries. On the first day that the story from *Southern Metropolitan News* was published on a major portal site, reader responses in relation to the story reached 10,000 within the first few hours, it was reported. Soon after, a search in Google with the key words "Sun Zhigang" yielded over 40,000 items.[13] After Sohu.com published the Sun Zhigang news on its front page as the lead story on April 25, 2003, readers posted over 37,000 messages in response to the incident as of the end of the year, revealed Charles Zhang, the founder and CEO of

Sohu.com.[14] Most messages that flooded the Internet from netizens demanded a thorough investigation of Sun's death and called for an immediate halt to the deportation system,[15] both of which were quickly pursued by the authorities.

In another example, on June 18, 2003, it was reported on the BBS of Sina. com that focused on this issue that the government decided to terminate the current deportation system by the end of that year. At that time there had been altogether over 156 pages of postings and the total number of messages exceeded 9000.[16] Most of the messages were overwhelmingly positive about the quick government move in ending this discriminatory policy against migrant workers, and an unusually large number of netizens expressed their approval of the performance of the new government led by Premier Wen Jiabao.

This kind of explosive, spontaneous outpouring of opinions on the Internet creates a platform that is hard for the regime to ignore. As a professor from a Beijing university commented, "To a certain extent, the Internet has filled in the place of overseas polling organizations in China, especially in the area of politics."[17] Admittedly, that function is only allowed within a certain parameter; the Chinese regime has no qualms about trying to shut down the voice that is sensed to be a direct threat to its rule. Nonetheless, the interaction between the Internet and civil society has created a platform of participation and debate that may force a certain degree of change and responsiveness on the part of the authorities, as this case clearly demonstrates.

To solicit audience input and participation on its Web site on the one hand, and to feel the pulse of public opinion on the other, *People's Daily* took the initiative to selectively publish netizens' comments and feedback on major issues of interest or big stories of the day posted on its official Web site, *Renmin Wang*.[18] The publication of feedback from online visitors about the newspaper serves the purpose of showing that the newspaper is not detached from the online community, and so it can substantially increase the reach of these views to a different audience base. This practice of *People's Daily* is not unique, for many reporters for the print media in China often search for new perspectives on a story by browsing online feedback. In relation to the Sun Zhigang case, an insider familiar with the official investigation process revealed to reporters from the *Southern Weekend* that an online commentary titled "The Sun Zhigang Case: Who Is Playing Deaf,"[19] which criticized the evasive approach of local government officials in the case and later appeared in the print edition of *People's Daily*, added to the determination of the investigative team to find out the truth. It was further admitted that the overwhelming coverage of the story by the online media created great pressure for the investigative team to uncover the truth about the incident.[20] So the Internet, under some circumstances, can play a leading role in the coverage of news events and has the potential to become a revolutionary medium of communication. The leading force, without question, are Chinese netizens and online activist groups.

Sun Zhigang's death met with furious protests from people online and offline, partly because his status as a college graduate made him different from the typical vagrant population found in major Chinese cities. One Chinese reporter aptly noted, "Such is the hypocrisy of Chinese society that when a vagrant is abused, no one protests, but few people can stomach the idea of a college graduate being victimized."[21] An unusually large group of people responded to Sun's fate because, like Sun, most online citizens are young and have a college degree and can more easily empathize with Sun. And indeed, a common feeling that could be observed in many chat rooms was that people did not want to see another Sun Zhigang because the next one might be one of them.[22]

The explosion of online rage and public outcry also quickly mobilized other sectors of civil society to join hands in promoting change in the current system. Before the publicity of Sun's death on April 25, his parents could not even find a lawyer for help; within hours of the publication of the story, they were contacted by a few famous local lawyers who volunteered free legal services.[23] Many more posted free legal advice or suggestions on how to pursue the case and engaged in discussions on the legal implications of Sun's death.[24] Ai Xiaming, a professor at Guangzhou-based Zhongshan University, published a well-circulated open letter online on May 2, 2003, blasting the inhumanity of the current deportation system and the prevalent abuse of power by police in connection to Sun Zhigang's death and similar tragedies.[25] Another open letter addressed to the Supreme People's Court and the Supreme People's Procuratorate in China by Lü Bolin, which called for a thorough investigation into all culprits, was a popular posting on major Web sites and attracted many hits.[26]

Public anger about Sun Zhigang's death also quickly evolved into an online signature and online protest movement against police brutality and abuse of power. The first online protest letter, addressed to the National People's Congress, was started by Dongfang Yixiao on April 26, 2003, and called for the abolition of the current custody and repatriation system, and it soon gathered over 200 signatures.[27] Another similar online protest letter, addressed to the Supreme People's Procuratorate, was started by Yang Zhizhu on May 29, 2003, and urged an end to the deportation system as well as calling for an investigation into Sun's death by an independent civilian team; it had 270 signatures by June 3, 2003.[28] Open letters and public protests on the Internet have become a popular expression of discontent in China, partly because of the unavailability of similar forms of expressive activities offline. Open letters stand little chance of being published by the Chinese media, and protests in physical places are tightly controlled by public security police. So the Internet has become not only the alternative, but in many cases the only possible popular platform for Chinese civil society to protest or express its disapproval of government policy or action.

In the meantime, on May 14, 2003, three young law scholars, who were all 30 years old and all held doctorate degrees from Beijing University, seized upon Sun's case to file a petition to the Legal Work Committee of the National People's Congress Standing Committee for a review of the constitutionality of the current custody and repatriation measures. The motivation, they said, was the death of a young man of their age by an out-of-date administrative directive from the State Council.[29] The petition was echoed by five renowned legal experts led by He Weiwang of Beijing University Law School, who called for a special investigation procedure by the National People's Congress into the death of Sun Zhigang and into the current practice of China's repatriation system.[30] The news about the two petitions was first reported by *China Youth Daily* and immediately picked up by other major Chinese media, and it appeared on most Chinese news and portal sites. It also triggered a fierce debate among scholars as well as legislators about the existing deportation measures and the implications for China's legal reform.[31] All these efforts turned a new page in citizen participation in reforming China's legal system, and it substantially sped up the termination of the 1984 deportation directive by the State Council in the wake of Sun's tragedy.[32]

Lessons from the Sun Zhigang Case

In the Sun Zhigang case, nonresponsiveness and evasion from the local authorities in the initial stage were quickly replaced by swift, decisive actions in investigating, arresting, and trying those responsible after the story came to public light through the conventional media and the Internet. The online media took a more aggressive approach in covering the case and in soliciting audience feedback; the conventional media, on the other hand, worked hand in hand with the online media not only in supplying information but also in sensing the pulse of public feelings from cyberspace and acting accordingly. Spontaneous outbursts of disgust and outrage on the Internet created a public pressure that could hardly be ignored by the authorities.

The government took a more lenient approach to the online and conventional media in their pursuit of this story because a story of this nature did not pose a direct threat to the regime rule. The media showed no hesitation in investigating and publishing information in connection to the case. Public opinion as reflected in online chat rooms, on bulletin boards and feedback to specific news, in conjunction with online and offline petitions, prompted timely action from the Guangdong provincial government to investigate and prosecute the case and from the national government to end a 21-year-old deportation policy.

The Internet infinitely fanned the flames of public anger, and facilitated debate and protest over the brutality of Sun's death; it became the center of public meeting, open discourse, and collective action from a wide spectrum of individuals, journalists, legal experts, and social activists. The scale and scope of outpouring of public sentiments in cyberspace from Chinese civil society built up enormous pressure on the Guangzhou authorities and the national government to respond immediately and decisively. In the pre-Internet days, a movement of this magnitude would have been impossible in China mainly for three reasons. First, circulation of this story would have been extremely limited, perhaps primarily to a local audience; second, coverage of this story would not have involved so many reporters from such a large number of media organizations from different parts of the country because it would not have been possible to assess the degree of audience interest displayed over the Internet; third, it would have been impossible for self-organizing networks of activists in Chinese civil society to form so quikly. Therefore, we see the empowering potential of the Internet at its full display in the course of the Sun Zhigang case.

Japan's Bid for a UN Security Council Permanent Seat: Online Protests, Internet Petition, and Offline Rallies

Reform in the United Nations, the G-4 Proposal, and Japan's UN Ambitions

The United Nations (UN), officially founded on October 24, 1945, after World War II, has played a pivotal role in the maintenance of international peace and global order. The predecessor of today's United Nations was the League of Nations, an international organization conceived during World War I and established soon after its end in 1919 under the Treaty of Versailles. Its goal was to "to promote international cooperation and to achieve peace and security" through disbarment, negotiation, and diplomacy.[33] Forty-four states signed the Charter of the League of Nations. The outbreak of World War II in 1939 proved that the League failed in its primary purpose of preventing future world wars and signaled its official demise.

But the idea of having a global association of governments that would work toward the "collective security" of all members was kept alive, and the need for such a transnational body to facilitate intergovernmental cooperation was urgently felt during World War II. The name "United Nations" was coined by U.S. President Franklin D. Roosevelt, and was first used in the "Declaration by United Nations," signed by representatives of twenty-six nations on January 1, 1942, which pledged their governments to mobilize all their resources in the war against the Axis Powers (i.e., Germany, Italy, and Japan).

In April 1945, delegates from fifty nations gathered in San Francisco to hammer out the United Nations Charter, which was completed and signed by all fifty nations on June 25, 1945 (hence the name for this event, the San Francisco Conference). Poland, which was one of the original signatories of the "Declaration of the United Nations" but did not have an officially recognized government at the time, was left a space for signature on the Charter. China, the first victim of aggression by an Axis Power (i.e., Japan), was given the honor of being the first to sign the Charter. Because the Charter had to be approved by the parliaments or congresses of many countries, participating countries at the Conference agreed that the Charter would come into effect when the governments of China, France, Great Britain, the Soviet Union, the United States and a majority of the other signatory states had ratified it, which took place on October 24, 1945. The UN Charter, or its constitution, is a constituent treaty, and all member nations have to agree to and be bound by its articles. Since then, UN member nations have expanded from the original 51 signatories to 191 (as of October 2005).

The United Nations fulfills its functions through its regular meetings and the activities of its administrative bodies. The most powerful organ at the United Nations is the Security Council, which has the power to make decisions that all member nations must follow under the UN Charter. The Security Council currently has fifteen members, five of them permanent and ten elected for a two-year term. The five permanent members (the "P-5") are China, France, Russia, the United Kingdom, and the United States, the five victorious powers of World War II, each of which holds veto power over any Security Council resolution. The makeup of the Security Council continues to reflect the power relations of 1945 when it was founded and fails to represent the post-WWII global geopolitical structure. Additionally, the Security Council works heavily in favor of industrialized nations, with only one of the five members coming from the developing nations, which constitute the vast majority of the member nations. Therefore, criticisms have been mounted over the years by virtually all parties over the inadequacy of representation in the international organization, yet there has been little consensus as to the specific steps of reform in this gigantic bureaucracy.

Thus, a constant theme that has been dominating UN debates in recent years is the need for reform and restructuring in realignment with changing post–cold war global circumstances. Soon after UN Secretary-General Kofi Annan started his first term on January 1, 1997, he initiated a broad UN reform program that was intended to make the organization more transparent, accountable, efficient, and democratic. As the most important part of this initiative, reform of the Security Council has been on top of Annan's agenda. The 2003 Iraq war, in which the United States acted unilaterally in the invasion of Iraq to topple the regime of Saddam Hussein without approval from the Security Council, gave a fresh sense of urgency to the UN reform efforts. At the UN General Assembly of 2003, UN Secretary-General Kofi Annan harshly criticized the U.S. doctrine of preemptive and unilateral military action, which, according to Annan, brought the UN to "a fork in the road." Recognizing the need for sweeping reform at the United Nations, Annan announced that he would establish a "high-level panel of eminent personalities" to examine current challenges to peace and security and to recommend fundamental reforms to the world body, including an expansion of the Security Council and the restructuring of other UN institutions.[34]

On December 2, 2004, the high-level panel of sixteen eminent persons appointed by Annan released their recommendations on UN reforms in a report titled "A More Secure World: Our Shared Responsibility" (United Nations General Assembly, 2004). The report first calls for a new collective security consensus among UN member nations, then maps out a list of major challenges the United Nations faces in the twenty-first century — poverty, infectious disease, and environmental degradation; inter- and between-state conflict; nuclear, radiological, chemical, and biological weapons; terrorism; and transnational organized crime — and offers specific recommendations to the United Nations for meeting these challenges. Among its 101 recommendations for sweeping UN reforms, the most attention grabbing, and perhaps the most controversial, are the two models proposed for revamping the Security Council. Model A would create six more permanent seats (with no veto power), and three new two-year nonpermanent seats to expand from its current fifteen members (five permanent and ten 2-year elected members) to twenty-four members, with six from each of these regions: Americas, Africa, Asia, and Europe. Model B would provide for no new permanent seats but instead create a new category of eight 4-year renewable-term (semipermanent) seats and one new two-year nonpermanent (and nonrenewable) seat, with six from each of the same four regions (United Nations General Assembly, 2004).

In particular, the report proposes two specific principles for overhauling the Security Council: first, it should "increase the involvement in decision-making of those who contribute most to the United Nations financially, militarily and diplomatically — specifically in terms of contributions to United Nations assessed budgets, participation in mandated peace operations, contributions to voluntary activities of the United Nations in the areas of security and development, and diplomatic activities in support of United Nations objectives and mandates;" and second, it should "bring into the decision-making process countries more representative of the broader membership, especially of the developing world" (United Nations General Assembly, 2004: 93).

The significance of the Security Council reform is highlighted by Kofi Annan, the UN General Secretary, who remarked in response to the need for reform after the official release of the report, "I do not believe that anyone will consider the UN reform complete without security council reform, bringing it into line with today's realities."[35]

The first criterion particularly spells good news for Japan, which is assessed 19.6 percent of the total UN regular annual budget, second only to the United States (which pays 22 percent of the total assessments). Germany is the third in terms of annual assessment to the United Nations (about 9.8 percent).[36] The first recommended principle works particularly to the favor of Japan in gaining a permanent seat in the reformed Security Council, and indeed, this has been the primary argument that Japan has been making in lobbying the United Nations and its member nations for such a privileged status in recent years. For Japan, the second largest economic entity in the world, representation at the UN Security Council as a permanent member can achieve its long-time ambition of boosting its political status at the global stage. In addition to Japan, seven other regional powers — Germany, Brazil, India, Nigeria, South Africa, Egypt, and Indonesia — all explicitly indicated their willingness to compete for new permanent seats in an expanded Security Council.[37] Together with Japan, leading the campaigns for new Security Council permanent seats are Brazil, Germany, and India (called the "Group of Four" or G-4), which have regularly held minisummits to coordinate their efforts. In March 2005, Annan formally presented his proposals to the General Assembly for sweeping changes to the UN, among them were the two suggested formulas for change in the Security Council.[38] Everything started to look right for Japan in its bid for a permanent seat in the Security Council.

Internet Populism, Online Protest, and Network of Global
Activism Against Japan's UN Security Council Bid

The release in late 2004 of the UN report on reforming its structures set the stage for new rounds of debates among UN member nations, and possibly, as expected, some key voting during the forthcoming General Assembly in September 2005, when leaders of all these nations would address the Assembly. Indeed, as an indication of both Japan's confidence and eagerness for its Security Council bid, Kenzo Oshima, Japan's ambassador to the United Nations, announced publicly in March 2005 that he would call on UN members to adopt a resolution on Security Council reform before the 2005 September UN summit.[39] Kofi Annan's speech on various occasions also called attention to the urgency of the task of UN reform. Therefore, Japan had stepped up its efforts in waging a full-fledged campaign for a permanent Security Council seat by mobilizing all its diplomatic resources and even appointing a special envoy.[40]

Before any reform can proceed, a broad consensus must be reached among the majority of the members to amend the UN Charter. Any Charter amendment, as specified in the Charter itself, needs approval from two thirds of the members plus no opposition from any of the five current standing members of the Security Council. Because the veto-bearing permanent members of the Security Council are enviable objects of courtship in international diplomacy, it is understandable that none of the existing permanent members intends to have its power or status weakened. Therefore, the Security Council reform involves a power redistribution process that will have a lasting impact on all member nations. However, while significant debates on the specific procedures and direction of the UN reform had barely got off the ground among the UN member states and organizations, a global campaign led by diasporic

Chinese communities and Chinese netizens against Japan's Security Council bid went into full swing.

The protest against Japan's UN Security Council bid was not the first large-scale public online campaign among Chinese netizens in the new millennium; rather, it started at a moment when dust had not even fully settled in the wake of a nationwide online petition against Japanese participation in an unprecedented railway upgrade project linking Beijing and Shanghai in China. As part of its sustained effort to upgrade the national railway network to meet increasing demands of human and cargo transportation, the Chinese government proposed in as early as 1994 that a 1300-kilometer-long (800 miles) high-speed railway link be constructed between Beijing and Shanghai (called the Beijing–Shanghai High-Speed Railway Project).[41] In 2001, the Chinese government completed the feasibility study for the proposed project and estimated the cost to be RMB¥100 billion (US$12 billion), and formally listed that as one of the priorities in its Tenth Five-Year Plan (2001-2005).[42] The Beijing–Shanghai express link was planned to be completed before the 2008 Olympics in Beijing. As part of a nationwide experiment, the Shanghai Transrapid Maglev Line, the world's first high-speed (up to 430 kilometers an hour) commercial electromagnetic levitation commuter line was completed by the end of 2002.[43] The 30-kilometer (or 19-mile) German-designed maglev line, however, came with a prohibitive price tag of US$1.2 billion. As a result, the Chinese Ministry of Railways decided soon after that it would choose the traditional wheel-based system over the maglev technology for the Beijing–Shanghai railway, and invited tenders from German, Japanese, and French firms to build this line.[44] The Beijing–Shanghai railway project, the second largest one after the controversial Three Gorge Project, had attracted the attention of the Mitsubishi Corp., a Japanese consortium known for its Bullet Train or "Shinkansen" technology. In fact, the Japanese contender was the favored candidate of the Chinese Ministry of Railways from the start, so much so that the Ministry planned to send a mission to study the Shinkansen train system in Japan early in 2003.[45] To add incentives for the Chinese government to award the contract to the Japanese railway industry, the Japanese government was planning to prepare a package of financial aid, or official development assistance (ODA), to China.[46] In the meantime, the Japanese Transport Minister and the chairman of the powerful Japan Business Federation, among others, traveled to China to lobby on behalf of the Japanese bullet train technologies.[47]

By July 2003, China was reported to be "more than 90 percent certain" to choose the Japanese bullet train system for its Beijing–Shanghai express railway over its French and German competitors.[48] In August 2003, the three Japanese, French, and German competing entities received requests from the Chinese government to submit their responses to the Ministry of Railways by the end of that month.[49] While the official planning stage was vigorously under way, news about the government's inclination toward the Japanese bulletin train technologies spread quickly over the Internet through conventional media sources, online chat rooms, and bulletin boards. This immediately became a hot issue among Chinese netizens in their online conversations. One of the Web sites that hosted in-depth discussions was www.1931-9-18.org, the official online presence of a Beijing-based activist organization called the Patriots' Alliance Network. Participation was unusually popular and quickly spread to other major Chinese Web sites. One user submitted a proposal to the Web site calling for an online petition in opposition to adopting Japanese railway technologies, which was readily approved by the Web site administrator. A special section on the site was created for signatures and made public on July 19, 2003, which would end on midnight July 29. The petition opposed using the Japanese bulletin train system, called for public hearings involving the National People's Congress, urged the government to think about the long-term impact of the Beijing–Shanghai link, and implored the authorities to postpone the construction of the link.[50] Within ten days, the petition was signed by 82,752 Chinese netizens, and was widely publicized by the conventional media.[51] The signed petition was forwarded to the Ministry of Railways by two organizers of this event early in August with much fanfare by the online news sites as well as the conventional media.[52]

Nationalism ran high during these debates, with a lot of postings calling officials from the Ministry of Railways "traitors" and some calling for the removal of the Railway Minister; other issues that netizens expressed concerns with were future technological dependencies that the link would create in the future if Japan's bullet train system was implemented.[53] A few days later, Chikage Ogi, Japan's Transport Minister, who visited China to promote the Japanese bullet train system, was given a cold reception and did not even gain access to Chinese Premier Wen Jiabao and senior officials from the Ministry of Railways as she had planned.[54] At the same time, senior officials from the Ministry of Railways vehemently denied that they were leaning toward the Japanese bullet train system for the Beijing–Shanghai link while speaking to the national media.[55]

A public tender to select a contractor scheduled for the end of 2003 was aborted. In March 2004, a Chinese envoy told Japanese press that "Chinese people's feelings" might be behind the delay.[56] The diplomat's remark, of course, was in direct response to a recent visit to the Yasukuni Shrine by Japanese Prime Minister Junichiro Koizumi. The war shrine, which honors the 2.5 million Japanese who died in wars since 1853, also enshrines fourteen convicted World War II Class-A criminals. For its neighboring countries, especially China and South Korea, the shrine is a symbol of Japan's militarism and a reminiscence of the sufferings and humiliation those countries went through during Japan's occupation in World War II; any official visit to the shrine is considered by those countries to be an indication of Japan's reluctance to say good-bye to its military past and therefore hampers bilateral relations. Koizumi, under pressure from the rising force of right-wing groups in Japan, however, has visited the shrine every year since he took office in 2001, despite protest and anger from other countries. Every visit, expectedly, has been met with denunciations and protest from Chinese netizens on a variety of Internet platforms. While the Beijing–Shanghai route was still in its planning state as of late 2005, there were signs that Japan is losing its momentum in its bidding for the project. In July 2005, China's Ministry of Railways signed an agreement with Germany's Federal Ministry of Transport, Building and Housing to strengthen cooperation on designing and constructing high-speed passenger railway lines,[57] and the French bidder Alstom got the green light for large-scale business expansion in China.[58]

Throughout the process, debate has been kept alive on the Internet over Japan's role in and its possible impact on China's massive railway infrastructure. In addition to the technological, economic, and political considerations in the Chinese government's decision-making process on the railway link, online opinions and Internet debates have also played a significant role. The dramatic downturn of Japan's Shinkansen technologies from a leading candidate to a hot potato for the Chinese railway officials indicates that public sentiments as reflected in Chinese cyberspace are hard to bypass. Nationalism as a double-edged sword can be used by the government to its advantage sometimes, but it can also tie the government's hands in making strategic decisions.

So it is no wonder that Internet activists would mobilize quickly again when news was circulating about Japan gaining momentum in its UN Security Council permanent seat bid. This time, the signature drive against Japan's Security Council bid was the brainchild of an overseas activist group called the Alliance for Preserving the Truth of the Sino-Japanese War. The mission of the Northern California–based grassroots organization, according to its Web site, is to

> cause the Japanese government to shoulder the responsibility and finally accept the consequences of the Japanese unmerciful assaults of its neighbors during the war, offer apology to the Chinese people, pay appropriate compensation to victims and their families, and tell the truth of history to the Japanese citizens so that its people will never again bear the burden of any unconscionable act of aggression.[59]

As part of the effort to commemorate the sixtieth anniversary of the end of World War II, and to call on the Japanese government to "correctly face" its military past and "frankly acknowledge" the crimes it committed against its Asian neighbors during that period, the Alliance initiated the online petition with several other civil groups from different parts of the world on February 28, 2005, in Los Angeles with the goal of collecting at least 1 million signatures to be presented to the United Nations General Assembly in September 2005.[60]

The campaign started to quietly take shape in late February and quickly gained pace in early March among Net activists mainly in China. Nonetheless, there was little publicity from the conventional media, and circulation of the news about this movement was principally limited to a few online forums and news groups. A turning point came when the Chinese national media started to pay attention to this online campaign after Kofi Annan formally presented his proposals for reform at the Security Council on March 21, 2005. In a conference after his speech at the General Assembly, Annan openly expressed his approval for Japan as a candidate in the expanded Security Council.[61]

Although the first news story about the signature drive was reported by the *People's Daily* UN correspondent Zou Dehao to the Chinese audience on March 2, 2005, which appeared on its official Web site (people.com.cn) the next day and was also available on major Chinese portal sites,[62] public response was lukewarm and scope of participation in the online petition remained limited in early March. By March 20, 2005, the campaign collected 401,556 signatures.[63] However, the day after Annan's UN speech and public support for Japan's candidacy for a permanent seat in the Security Council, coverage of the online petition immediately became widespread in China among the online news sites as well as conventional media.[64] The coverage sparked massive participation in this signature campaign across China; in Internet chat rooms, and on BBS and popular forums people were urged to join an online petition against Japan's Security Council permanent seat effort. Most popular Chinese Web sites posted special sections for Chinese netizens to sign their petition.[65] A Web site that is exclusively devoted to the memory of the Japanese invasion of China, China918.net, listed more than 300 links available to solicit signatories at www.china918.net/qm/fenzhan.htm. At the same time, Internet activists also started to collect signatures from non–netizens by setting petition stands on busy streets of major Chinese cities. By the end of March, some 22 million signatures had been gathered in China.[66] Three of the most popular portal sites, Sina.com, 163.com, and Sohu.com, collected over 11.5 million signatories from March 23 (the date when these three Web sites joined the petition) to March 29.[67] On June 30, 2005, a petition signed by 41 million people from 41 countries against a permanent seat for Japan in the Security Council was formally presented to UN Secretary General Kofi Annan after a public demonstration in front of the UN headquarters in New York.[68]

The letter to the UN underwritten by the Global Alliance for Preserving the History of WW II in Asia states:

The GLOBAL ALLIANCE FOR PRESERVING THE HISTORY OF WORLD WAR II IN ASIA, a Northern California-based non-governmental organization, and several U.S. and Korean human rights activist groups started a petition drive on Internet on February 28, 2005. Our collective grassroots effort aims to raise the objection against Japan's bid for a permanent seat in the United Nations Security Council (UNSC) if the reorganization of the United Nations and the expansion of the UNSC are to be approved by the U.N. General Assembly in the coming session and later.

While all of us fully support the U.N. reforms and the restructure of the UNSC, we would support granting Japan a permanent seat in the UNSC only if Japan could meet certain conditions as follows:

"The Japanese government must explicitly affirm its contrition to its past misdeeds, its determination to right historical wrongs and bring all pending issues to a final closure, once and for all:

1. The apology must be based on a law duly enacted by the Japanese Diet, authorizing its Prime Minister and Emperor to make a public apology to all the aggrieved nations;
2. The same law must include an authorization for the government to compensate the victims of Japanese aggression and atrocities and a mechanism for determining the just compensation for the victims;
3. The law must also mandate a faithful collection, documentation, preservation, and distribution of the truths about Japanese aggression in the Pacific War, 1931-1945 (such as Nanjing Massacre, Comfort Women, Chemical Warfare and Biological Warfare);
4. The legislation must mandate the textbooks in Japan to reflect this history in perpetuity without distortion, omission, or deceptive manipulations;
5. The law must prohibit and punish any individual who denies these crimes; and those who are in public services or hold elected offices (including the Diet) shall be prohibited to worship war criminals, assist or finance the construction and building of facilities that glorify and commemorate militarism;
6. The law must stipulate that violation of any of the provisions above shall be prosecuted and punished by jail terms and fines. Those who work for the government or hold political offices or parliamentary position shall be expelled from public services or elected offices and barred from returning for life."[69]

Although the vast majority of the petitioners came from China, this signature campaign has been truly global in its scope. As already mentioned, the petition was formally launched in Los Angeles in the United States by a Northern California–based grassroots organization with the participation of groups worldwide. Next to China, the country with the most participants is South Korea, which, along with China, suffered immensely from Japan's colonial rule. In South Korea, public participation had been energized by two almost simultaneous developments: a series of new Japanese secondary school history textbooks written by radical rightist nationalists, which downplayed Japan's military aggression toward its neighboring nations during World War II, were submitted for approval by Japan's Education Ministry in March 2005[70]; the other development was the claim by the Japanese Ambassador to South Korea at a meeting of foreign reporters in late February that the disputed islets of Tokdo (called Takeshima by the Japanese) are "historically and legally Japan's territory."[71] The major Internet base for Korean activists is the Web site of a Los Angeles-based organization, Historical Justice Now (historicaljustice. org/HJN/), which published petition letters in both English and Korean and offered specific advice on how to participate. By March 24, 2005, over 60,000 Koreans had signed the online petition[72]; and by the time the petition was submitted to the UN headquarters on June 30, 2005, 164,255 signatories were gathered from South Korea, making South Korea second to China on the top ten list of countries in terms of the total number of individual signatures collected (the other eight are the United States, Canada, Japan, the United Kingdom, Australia, Germany, France, and New Zealand).[73] In the case of China, the demographic distribution of the signatories correlates perfectly with the Internet penetration in the different regions of the country, with heavy participation from six regions in terms of the total number of signatures gathered — Shanghai, Beijing, Guangdong, Shandong, Jiangsu, and Zhejiang.[74] Globally, this well-orchestrated movement would not have possible without the reach of the Internet.

In China, this online petition quickly spread to the offline world in triggering anti-Japanese protests in major Chinese cities such as Chengdu, Shengzhen, Beijing, Shanghai, and Hangzhou.[75] In all cases of these public protests, the Internet had played a pivotal role in organizing protests (e.g., time, place, and route of protest) and in disseminating news in relation to the protests to Chinese netizens as well as overseas Web sites, despite government orders to stop such public gatherings.[76] For example, in a Beijing protest involving more than 20,000 people on April 9, 2005, participants proceeded and followed the specific route in response to a call on the Internet.[77] The following text, which is titled "Detailed Manual Concerning Shanghai Region's Protest Activity against Japanese Right-Wingers," was posted ahead of the event, and got reposted on many popular Chinese Web sites and forums and widely circulated among bulletin boards and chat rooms. Additionally, the message was also sent to millions via short message services (SMS) to cell phone users both in and outside of the region. The following is an English translation of the text[78]:

Time: 9:00 am, April 16, 2005 (Saturday)

Place: Group 1 Gathers at the People's Hero Monument at the Bund; Group 2 Gathers at the People's Square

Route: People's Hero Monument at the Bund → Nanjing Road → People's Square → Japanese Consulate

(We suggest that those with disabilities take Bus 925B to Hongqiao Development District [where the Japanese Consulate is])

Precautions

If you bring your own food and drink, don't choose Japanese brands;

Don't bring expensive or valuable items with you, try to wear sport shoes for your convenience.

Cameras, video cameras, cell phones, tape recorders and other electronic products that are made in Japan should be avoided in order to prevent any unexpected accidents;

Bring your pen so that you can sign your name.

Don't hurl hard objects such as rocks and metal ware. Instead, we suggest that you bring tomatoes, eggs, Koizumi's head portrait, a cigarette lighter, or Japanese national flags, etc.

Recommended slogans and banners: "Boycott Japanese Products; Protest Against the Japanese Practice of Tampering with History Textbooks!" "Boycott Japanese Products; Support Domestic Products!" "Oppose Japan's Bid for a Permanent Seat in the UN Security Council!" "Return Diaoyu [Senkaku as called by Japan] Island to China!" etc.

Purpose

This event is intended to express our strongest outrage against the Japanese government's evil acts of protractedly refusing to acknowledge the crimes Japan committed during World War II, tampering with history textbooks, occupying the Diaoyu Island, and attempting to become a permanent member of the UN Security Council.

Important Reminders

This event is not targeting any Japanese friends in China but only Japanese ring-wing forces and their supporters, so don't show radical behaviors toward Japanese people who are friendly to China.

Police are people's public servants, and they are as patriotic as everybody else throughout the demonstration. But they have their own job to do — to make sure that the event be carried out safely. So please cooperate with Uncle Cops, especially in front of the Japanese consulate — do not throw anything as Uncle Cop is looking at you, and throw an egg or tomato if he is not looking at you; however, if you throw an egg or tomato and Uncle Cop sees it, just smile at him.

When passing by Japanese-funded stores or companies, don't strike with the intention to damage, because if you do, the Japanese are going to ask our government for compensation. So act wisely.

Show caution when burning Japanese flag or Koizumi's head portrait so that you don't set you clothes ablaze and burn yourself.

Exercising self-restraint is the key to the whole event; those in charge from every unit (school, company, social organization) should take proper control. Shanghai is an international metropolis and is the life line of our national economy. So take part in this event by showing your sense of reason.

Those are the points we have in mind. Feel welcome to add to the list, and remind your participating friends of them.

Person who drafted the text: Tang Ye@SHTel (Tel: 021-2883 1672 Email: bolide_2003@163.com QQ: 11002046

These detailed instructions became available two to three days ahead of this event, and were sent to people via chain e-mails and SMS so that many people around the Shanghai area were well informed before the protest. On April 16, 2005, as planned, tens of thousands of demonstrators took part in the protest, making it the biggest public protest in Shanghai since the 1999 massive demonstrations against the bombing of the Chinese Embassy in Belgrade by the U.S.-led NATO forces.[79] The message drew a lot of support and acclaim from Chinese netizens from over the country, and many organized similar events in their localities. As a result, in addition to Shanghai, public protests were also simultaneously organized via the Internet in at least sixteen other Chinese cities on April 16 and 17 through online messages circulated via Internet forums, BBS, SMS, instant messaging, and chain e-mail despite various official efforts to suppress these messages.[80] After (and sometimes in the process of) these protests, participants took pictures and posted them along with their eyewitness accounts of the protests over the Internet (most of which were unavailable from the conventional media) and shared other information (such as tips on organizing and taking part in such events).[81] Even during the protests, some participants sent real-time messages, pictures, and recruiting notes to call on others to join the ongoing events.[82]

On top of Japan's UN Security Council bid, another direct cause of the protests was the approval by Japan's Education Ministry on April 5, 2005, of newer versions of the previously mentioned secondary school history textbooks written by radical rightist nationalists, which downplay Japan's military aggression toward its neighboring nations during World War II. The textbooks blame China for the outbreak of the Sino-Japanese War (1894-1895) and argue that the historical evidence for the 1937 Nanjing Massacre (in which hundreds of thousands civilians were believed to be murdered by the Japanese) is "inconclusive" and "under debate"; they also justify the Japanese occupation of Korea, claiming that Japan's colonial rule helped modernize Korea.[83] Then to make things worse, the Japanese government initiated procedures to grant Japanese developers rights to test-drill for oil and gas deposits in the disputed waters of East China Sea on April 13, 2005,[84] provoking anger from the Chinese government as well as civilians.

Worried that public protests might spin out of control and backfire against the government (because when people gather at public protests, there is no guarantee that they won't use these occasions to address grievances over domestic or politically sensitive issues), the Chinese government acted rather quickly to try to put the situation under control. As early as April 6, the Central Propaganda Ministry under the Chinese Communist Party issued an eight-point circular ordering all Chinese media to stop coverage of anti-Japanese public protests and warned that journalists should not participate in these events or conduct interviews in relation to these protests. Moreover, the circular also reminded the media to be on high alert over any attempts to take advantage of public anti-Japanese sentiments to create pressure on the government on other domestic issues and asked the media to promote social stability in its coverage of news events.[85] Tang Ye, the author of the text calling for the protest in Shanghai on April 16, was arrested for creating and posting the message on the Internet.[86] Tang made it easy for the police to find him because he posted his name and other identifying information at the end of the message. Tang was sentenced to five years in prison on May 2, triggering numerous debates and protests from netizens online. In response to Tang's imprisonment, online postings and blog entries typically ridiculed the impotence of the government and expressed their indignation at the Shanghai authority.[87] One popular legal forum, totoolaw.com, which attracts Chinese netizens with legal expertise to offer self-support and legal advice on different issues, published a special page with fifty-seven messages, many of which challenge the legality of this sentence based on current laws. One discussant has this comment on China's legal system: "Everything under Control? Or Rather under Manipulation!"[88]

After rising tides of public protests and a quick expansion of the scope and scale of citizen participation throughout major Chinese cities in mid-April, the alarmed central regime stepped up its efforts at cybercontrol. Online messages calling for public protests were deleted, and Web sites that took part in the organizational effort and spread protest information were shut down.[89] Detailed notices of planned rallies and instructions for action, however, were still readily available on some popular Web sites at the time of heightened official crackdown.[90] Eruptions of widespread protests over the April 16 to 17 weekend in major Chinese cities, which led to street violence and property damage, added to the government's concern that it was losing control and led to an intensification of official intervention. With a major public holiday around the corner on May 1 (which is celebrated with a week-long vacation every year in China) and increasing signs that more protests were being planned for these days, the government orchestrated newspapers, television and radio stations, and major online news publications into a well-concerted effort to cool down anti-Japanese sentiments and to defuse grassroots protest activities. Television stations repeated calls to the public to express their feelings "in a lawful and orderly way" and to stay away from illegal protests, the *People's Daily* called for calm and stability among Chinese citizens, and articles bashing the boycott of Japanese goods and unruly behaviors during public protests were displayed prominently on major portal sites.[91]

Because most protesters were in their twenties and thirties, and college students were among the most active participants, the government organized concurrent efforts to coerce students into staying on campus. In late April, the Ministry of Public Security announced in a toughly worded public statement that organizing and encouraging protests through Internet postings and text message services were illegal, as was taking part in unauthorized public rallies; former diplomats were sent by the Central Propaganda Ministry to a six-day "speech tour" to major college campuses to tell college students that China and Japan should "co-exist peacefully, develop friendship for generations to come, carry out mutually beneficial cooperation and seek common development."[92] University authorities, meanwhile, joined the official efforts to dissuade students from taking to the streets through close monitoring and conventional ideological brainwashing via leaflets and circulars.[93]

The authorities also resorted to the very technologies that helped mobilize protesters to spread their own messages and warnings. In late April and early May, the police departments in a few cities such as Beijing, Shanghai, and Nanjing sent text messages en masse via cell phones to residents urging them to "be patriotic in a rational way," not to spread or believe rumors, and not to join or stage illegal demonstrations; the same messages also appeared on the Internet.[94] The government's aggressive efforts on multiple fronts paid off because no public incident of protest or demonstration was reported throughout major cities on May 4, 2005 despite repeated anonymous calls for protests on the Internet.[95] May 4 is a historically important but politically sensitive date in modern Chinese nationalism because it is the anniversary of the 1919 student movement in which over 50,000 students marched in Tiananmen Square against Western colonialism, especially the Japanese exploitation of China as specified in the Versailles Treaty. The student-led movement spread all over China and forced the Chinese government to abstain from signing the Treaty.

An ironic recent development in bilateral relations between China and Japan has been characterized by a senior Chinese official as "politically cold and economically warm."[96] Economically, China surpassed the United States to become Japan's largest trade partner in 2004, while Japan had been China's top trader for years up to 2003, and it remained China's third trade partner in 2004 (behind the European Union and the United States).[97] Apparently, further deterioration in bilateral diplomatic relations is not in the interest of either country. Spontaneous outburst of public sentiments in China created external pressure on the Japanese government. In a rare expression of Japan's remorse, Japanese Prime Minister Junichiro Koizumi, while addressing leaders at the Asia–Africa Summit in Jakarta, Indonesia, on April 22, 2005, expressed "deep remorse and heartfelt apology" for Japan's wartime acts and acknowledged that "[i]n the past Japan, through its colonial rule and aggression, caused tremendous damage and suffering for the people of many countries, particularly those of Asian nations."[98] As a symbol of defiance to cater to domestic feelings, however, 168 Japanese lawmakers, including a cabinet member, paid their respects to the Yasukuni Shrine in the meantime.[99]

Mounting public anger also pressured the Chinese government to take tough postures in its diplomatic relations with Japan. For the Chinese government, a stable relation with Japan is essential for continued economic growth; on the other hand, any move with Japan that may hurt national pride can backfire, and outpouring of public sentiment on and off the Internet weighs heavily in considering official action toward Japan. On April 18, 2005, the Chinese government bluntly rejected the request from Japan for an apology over the violent protests during an official visit by the Japanese foreign minister to China, and blamed its Japanese counterpart for "hurting the feelings" of the Chinese people.[100] In May 2005, during a goodwill visit to Japan, Chinese Vice Premier Wu Yi abruptly canceled a scheduled meeting with Japanese Prime Minister Junichiro Koizumi within a few hours' notice and left back for China. This diplomatic snub to the Japanese government was China's way of expressing its displeasure at Koizumi's recent remarks over his insistence on visiting Yasukuni Shrine in Tokyo.[101]

In May 2005, reversing its long-time practice of not commenting publicly about the G-4 plan for UN Security Council reform, China openly announced its opposition to the Japan-led G-4 resolution and called it "detrimental" to the process of UN reform.[102] A revised draft one month later also met with firm resistance from China as well as the United States.[103] The G-4 resolution failed to make it to the agenda of the September 2005 UN General Assembly because of lack of enthusiasm and support from key member states such as China and the United States.

Network Activism and Popular Participation in the Anti-Japan Protests: Concluding Remarks

The online petition against Japan's UN Security Council permanent seat bid has demonstrated the global nature of Internet activism in the network age. Unlike the Sun Zhigang case, which energized activists first in one city and then spread to the whole country in its organizational flow of protest, the petition over the Japanese UN effort originated from activists outside of the country and then spread to a domestic base of Net activists. The unprecedented speed and transborder reach of the Internet, however, made it possible for an internetwork of global activism to self-organize and act quickly. The Internet clearly fulfilled the three functions of mobilization, validation, and scope enlargement that are typically found with conventional media as observed by

Gamson and Wolfsfeld (1993): it mobilized diasporic Chinese communities across the globe and a large base of domestic Chinese individuals and groups in a way that no conventional media channel could have dreamed of doing; it provided a global platform for winning moral and emotional support; and it made the scope of the campaign global from the moment it started.

The Internet has created brand-new opportunities for Chinese civil society groups by interconnecting like-minded netizens into concerted action. One example is the Patriots' Alliance, which was started by Lu Yunfei, a Web designer, and a group of well-educated professionals who share the same anti-Japan sentiment. Its main base of activism is its Web site www.1931-9-18.org, which claims close to 80,000 registered users[104] and offers special Internet meeting places for netizens in twenty-one Chinese provinces.[105] The Web site publishes, among other information, latest news, major (past and future) events, announcements, forums, photos, essays, historical facts, and VIP pages. The Alliance has played a pivotal role in spreading the news about and organizing the online petition against both Japan's involvement in China's railway projects in 2003 and the Japanese UN Security Council bid in 2005. In recent years, a multitude of civil society organizations that cater to the interests of niche activist groups have established their online presence, and have made cyberspace their major base of action.

The common thread that connects this global petition movement has been the heavy dose of nationalism observable through its goal, its mobilizing strategy, and its organizing dynamics. Nationalism, of course, is nothing unique to China and has been a potent force of social change in all societies throughout history, especially during times of external conflicts and warfare. So in the wake of the bombing of the Chinese Embassy in Belgrade by U.S.-led NATO forces in 1999 and during the U.S.–China row over a plane collision involving a U.S. spy plane and a Chinese jet fighter in 2001, nationalism was running high in both the United States and China. The global petition against Japan's UN Security Council bid itself was in partial response to the rise of nationalism within Japan, which has lately witnessed the ascendancy of right-wing forces that try to whitewash the country's military past. What the case illustrates, however, is the changing nature of nationalism in the cyber-age: nationalism, when empowered by new technological developments, can transcend the borders of the nation-state. This is, in essence, one particularistic formation of Arjun Appadurai's (1996) "transnationalism" as a result of cross-national flows of ideas, people, images, and goods facilitated by emerging communication and transportation technologies.

This transnationalism, however, is deeply entwined with nationalistic sentiments in the globalized space of diasporas. This is likened to a practice of "long-distance nationalism" as envisioned by Benedict Anderson (1998: 58–76) who claims that advances in communication technologies enable transnational political diasporas to influence political events in their countries of origin and at the same time remain unaccountable in the safe havens of the host countries. This deterritorialization of nationalism finds new homesteading in cyberspace, which fundamentally changes the dynamics of transnational social movements in the new millennium.

We also see the dual nature of nationalism in this analysis. While the Chinese government has for long successfully used nationalism as a political tool in state policy making to its advantage, the regime may find nationalism a formidable hindrance under particular circumstances. The rising demand for a hard-line approach against Japan dominated by online discourses serves as an insurmountable barrier for the government's efforts to improve bilateral relations with Japan, because a government that is perceived to weaken its knee before a major rival like Japan will lose its legitimacy among some significant sectors of the domestic public, especially the techie-savvy Net Generation. In the petition against adopting Japanese bullet train technologies within China's own railway network, an otherwise smooth-going joint project was derailed by a burst of angry sentiments over the Internet, even though the Chinese government was keenly interested in the technologies.

Petition in the Sun Zhigang case has been largely limited to the cyberdomain. By contrast, the crusade against Japan's permanent seat at the UN Security Council quickly spread from the online landscape to the physical world and from overseas to the nation. This clearly represents an emerging trend of the interplay of online activism and offline protests in which campaigns starting originally in cyberspace can evolve into offline movements. Offline protests, which were mainly organized over the Internet and through personal communication devices, were meanwhile connected to the virtual diasporic space when news about these events was circulated over cell phones and cyberforums in real time and posted later on popular Web sites. This sophisticated integration of online and offline domains will in all likelihood be a defining feature of the dynamics of social movements in China in the twenty-first century.

Three phases can be observed in the offline protests among major Chinese cities. Phase one was the eruption stage and lasted from early April to April 10. Most of the protests took place over the April 3 to 4 and April 9 to 10 weekends, and the official line regarding these protests was noncommittal (thus leading to charges that the government was behind these destructive protests); the Internet as a major platform of organization and mobilization met with little government intervention. Conventional media covered these events extensively despite the April 6 circular to play down these events. Phase two, which lasted from April 11 to 17, was the intensification stage with protest events peaking during the April 16 to 17 weekend ahead of the visit by the Japanese foreign minister for bilateral talks. During this stage, there were clear signs of an escalation, and alarmed by the quick developments, officials at the national and local levels started to send clear signals to residents that the government wanted to be back in control. Mass mobilization on the Internet, at the same time, was reaching a new level with popular forums and BBS flooded with calls for more protests. The government, on the other hand, beefed up its efforts to clamp down these rallies and to clean cyberspace by ordering Web site administrators to delete messages and by closing selective Web sites. Conventional media started to bombard audience with official messages calling on people to cool down. Nonetheless, massive demonstrations across major cities took place over the April 16 to 17 weekend. Phase three, lasting from April 18 to early May, was the fade-out stage in which the government gained an upper hand over individual activists through a massive, well-coordinated propaganda campaign aimed at putting the brakes on fresh protests. The state-controlled mass media, in combination with major online channels of communication, joined the official call for "rational patriotism" and social stability. New communication technologies that had been used effectively by Net activists in organizing protests were incorporated into the official campaign in communicating pleas and warnings to the mass audience. As a result, the week-long May 4 holiday was free from public protests on streets of major cities in China. Some activists, meanwhile, shifted their protest platform from the streets to cyberspace by attacking Japanese Web sites and online interests[106]; this kind of Net hacktivism is becoming commonplace during international conflicts (Jordan and Taylor, 2004).

Chapter Summary

The analysis of the two cases in this chapter reveals that the Internet has become an empowering tool for Chinese civil society in the domain of social movements in at least three ways. First of all, the Internet (often along with other emerging new technologies such as cell phones and mobile personal communication devices) permits the creation of a brand new, transformative platform of public communication and discourse among Chinese netizens. As has also been shown in previous chapters, we see the recurring theme in the two cases discussed here that the Internet has remarkably expanded the scope of public communication by its speed and reach. News about particular events can be spread quickly to an ever wider audience base, and surging public interest and demand often in turn lead to the supply of more news by more (and often diversified) sources. While the primary model of communication with conventional mass media has been "few producers, many receivers," the dominant mode of communication in cyberspace is "many producers, massive receivers." This point was particularly prominent in the numerous instances of anti-Japanese demonstrations in a number of Chinese cities in April 2005 when participants provided eyewitness accounts of these events and oftentimes pictures on popular Internet forums, especially when news from conventional media was suppressed. In this sense, the Internet has become a viable alternative source of news, competing against the official media outlets.

The Internet-based platform of communication has crossed the conventional boundaries of nation-states by involving global Chinese diasporic communities, as clearly demonstrated by the global petition against Japan's UN Security Council permanent membership bid.

Second, a development that is closely related to the first point in Net activism has been the ability of the Internet to link like-minded netizens into collective action. In this regard, cyberspace has become a great gathering place for activists not only to share news but also to exchange views and ponder actions. While conventional media may fulfill a limited function for these purposes, the Internet has surpassed all mass media in that it can bring in massive participation in issues and topics that may lie outside the official agenda. Therefore, cyberspace has effectively become a space of public debate and engagement for Chinese netizens in spite of its numerous imperfections (such as official sanctions and harassments and limited access).

Third, the Internet has become a rather effective tool of mass mobilization and organization for social movements within Chinese civil society in the new millennium. Here, it is useful to borrow an observation from Howard Rheingold (2003: xviii; emphasis original) who says that Internet-related technologies *"enable people to act together in new ways and in new situations where collective action was not possible before"* by creating "smart mobs" or "associations of amateurs." Although this is applicable to all societies to varying degrees, it is a particularly significant point for China where there are generally more limitations on social movements, especially those that are not within the boundaries of activities granted by the authoritarian regime. In both the Sun Zhigang protest and the anti-Japanese petition, Chinese netizens self-organized largely in response to official inaction (in the former case) or what they perceived as unsatisfactory official action (in the latter case). Similar protests would have been much harder, and riskier, to organize in China in the offline world. Plus, it would have been impossible to mobilize protesting acts with such speed and with such popular participation off the Internet. Thus, cyber-roots activism has become revolutionary force in the evolving dynamics of social movements in China.

Finally, Internet populism may on occasions pose a threat to the Chinese government in its demands, its foci, and its mechanism. Petitions in both cases pressured the Chinese regime to address populist demands originating from the Internet. But these demands often come into conflict with government interests and may lead to either official responsiveness to address online grievances or heavy-handed official suppression once the demands go beyond boundaries tolerated by the government. As the veteran Chinese affairs reporter Paul Mooney comments, for the Chinese government, "riding the internet can be like riding the tiger: Once you get on, it can be very hard to get off."[107] That tug of war between the Chinese authorities and Internet populism will most likely remain a constant theme in Internet activism for years to come in the new century.

Conclusion

As the Internet population in China continues its current trend of fast growth and as available services expand, the social space that arises on the Internet for Chinese netizens to seek information and socialization will keep growing exponentially. The social consequences of Internet use will have a profound impact on the development of Chinese society in the new millennium. We need to look at how the Internet has affected the life of ordinary Chinese citizens to understand the cyber revolution that is taking place in China.

The policy of economic reform and openness initiated by Deng Xiaoping since 1978 has pluralized China's socioeconomic structure and has greatly weakened the state's dominance over society in China. Individual freedom in economic activities has spawned an expanding space for Chinese civil society because personal and group interests have become in many cases the most important motivational force in social life. Thus economic liberalization has cultivated a fertile ground for the growth and prosperity of Chinese civil society. The recent development of the Internet has become the latest catalyst for the strengthening of civil society in China.

China's enthusiastic embrace of the Internet by the authoritarian regime is based on two premises. First, it can serve as the newest engine of economic acceleration and productivity; through its state-orchestrated informatization efforts, Chinese authorities believe that the country can maintain its leading position in its pace of economic growth among all countries in the world into the new millennium. To accomplish that, information and communication technologies (ICTs) have been afforded a central place in China's national development strategy. Secondly, in the past decade or so, China has systematically put in place a regulative mechanism to filter out of the Chinese cyberspace politically incendiary and socially offensive content. The government believes that, with proper technologies at its hand, it can succeed in creating a cyber environment with all the information that's fit to see. As a result, the country has led the world in investing in and implementing filtering and surveillance technologies to build its Great Firewall of China in the cyber era.

Yet as the Internet has fundamentally transformed, and will continue to transform, every aspect of Chinese society, the actual course of events may not follow exactly what the Chinese regime has mapped out both in the short term and in the long run. What individuals or social groups may or may not do on the Internet will not likely follow the trajectory designed by the authorities, as we have seen throughout this book. In this regard, the law of unintended consequences may shed light on the nature of the impact of the Internet on Chinese society.

When Adam Smith used the metaphor of the Invisible Hand, he was merely talking about the (what he perceived to be positive) unintended consequences of the capitalist market to contribute to the common good of society. Adam Ferguson, one of the most original contributors to the law of unintended consequences, described it this way:

> Like the winds, that come we know not whence, and blow withersoever they list, the forms of society are derived from an obscure and distant origin; they arise, long before the date of philosophy, from the instincts, not from the speculations of men. The croud of mankind, are directed in their establishments and measures, by the circumstances in which they are placed; and seldom are turned from their way, to follow the plan of any single projector.
>
> Every stem and every movement of the multitude, even in what are turmed enlightened ages, are made with equal blindness to the future; and nations stumble upon establishments, which are indeed the result of human action, but not the execution of any human design. If Cromwell said, That a man never mounts higher, than when he knows not whither he is going; it may with more reason be affirmed of communities, that they admit of the greatest revolutions where no change is intended, and that the most refined politicians do not always know whither they are leading the state by their projects.

(Ferguson, 1995: 119)

Likewise, according to Ferguson, civil society is largely a result of unintended human action: "Men, in fact, while they pursue in society different objects, or separate views, procure a wide distribution of power, and by a species of chance, arrive at a posture than what human wisdom could ever calmly devise" (Ferguson 1995: 225). As a matter of fact, Ehrenberg (1999) points out that the law of unintended consequences is one of Ferguson's most important contributions to the theory of civil society.

The law of unintended consequences is particularly relevant to the understanding of the dynamics of the Internet and its social impact, as Zaheer Baber suggests:

> Thus, the idea that both social relations and technologies simultaneously affect each other with unpredictable mix of intended and unintended consequences, while certainly not absent, was not a dominant focus of the countless reiteration of studies in the constructivist mode. This perspective, while certainly useful for making sense of any technology, is particularly germane to the Internet as it generates a tremendous amount of social change even as it is simultaneously transformed by the

socially and culturally specific demands placed on it by diverse global constituencies of users.

(Baber, 2002a: 196)

Therefore, the real significance of the Internet in a society must be evaluated in the context of the social consequences that may or may not have been designed or expected by either the government or civil society. In that sense, social actualities, observable patterns, and creative use of the Internet by members and groups of civil society are the important aspects to study in our effort to develop an appreciation of the impact of the Internet on Chinese civil society — as I have tried to accomplish in this book.

Let me offer a justification for the methodological approaches I have taken in the book. Over the years, there has been a well-established line of scholarly inquiries into the social aspects of new media technologies with contributions from researchers with diversified training and academic traditions. As a result, our knowledge base has continued to expand as new theoretical perspectives are developed and old ones revitalized. However, there has also been the disconcerting tendency among many scholars to make sweeping conclusions based on single-factor analysis or reductionistic views of these new communication technologies. A particularly relevant approach to counter this trend is Peter Perdue's "equilibrium analysis" in which he argues that "[t]he interrelationship of all the elements, rather than any single one, determines the whole" (1994: 188). Perdue, of course, limits his discussion to comparative analysis of technological developments in agrarian societies, yet his model is well taken for Internet researchers in that contextual accounts that integrate technological, social, political, and cultural factors can lead us to a better understanding of key issues. This is why I believe a full-dimensional view into the interplay of civil society and the Internet in China can yield a more accurate picture for us to understand this important topic.

Findings in the research have identified clear evidence that the Internet has emerged as an emancipatory and empowering tool for Chinese civil society and has opened new opportunities for the revitalization of civil society forces. Even though the state still maintains a formidable presence in Chinese cyberspace, there are indications that the Internet marks a dramatic departure from previous types of communication technologies. The revolutionizing effect of the Internet in Chinese civil society can be summarized in the following aspects.

First and foremost, despite all its imperfections, the Internet has started to democratize communication of information in Chinese society. A brand-new information environment is taking shape on the Internet in China as more and more citizens are exposed to a growing body of information sources online, and individuals and social groups have enjoyed varying levels of success in developing creative ways to bypass official control and blockades in accessing information from alternative sources and in sending information to desired parties. Average Chinese netizens have become actively involved in the information dissemination and production process in Chinese cyberspace, a domain that used to be monopolized by the state-controlled conventional media channels. As shown by the numerous cases mentioned in the various chapters, civil society empowered by information has on many occasions created a powerful pressure for change on the part of the state.

Second, the Internet has created a public sphere for Chinese netizens to engage in public debates on social and political issues. Although still constrained by many limitations, that online public sphere has become an important barometer of public opinion and public sentiments. For an authoritarian regime that does not tolerate dissenting voices, the Internet has provided the only forum to assess the pulse of mass opinion in many cases. The Chinese authority has showed some attentiveness toward network opinion, and from time to time has displayed varying levels of responsiveness to the outpouring of public sentiments in its decision making and policy toward certain issues. In the meantime, a relatively sizeable proportion of Chinese netizens regularly engage in public communication in chat rooms, on BBS, and Internet forums. Overall displaying a much higher level of political efficacy on the Internet than their counterparts in other countries, they have developed a quite favorable attitude toward the ability of the Internet to allow them to express themselves, communicate with public officials, and extract a certain level of accountability from the government.

Third, there has emerged a growing body of autonomous individuals who are able to develop independent opinions and consciousness free from the sphere of state influence, and they regularly contribute to online communications in debates and deliberations through their own writings. That autonomy is made possible by economic independence and is facilitated by a favorable information environment on the Internet. For each major debate or event, there are usually commentaries or analytical writings from a rising group of opinion leaders that get circulated to hundreds or thousands or more of Chinese netizens via repostings and e-mail chains, and they often set the tone for discussion or become the starting point for action.

Fourth, the Internet has changed the traditional role of conventional media in Chinese life. While marketization of mass media in China has pushed the media more and more toward the side of the market, the Internet has stepped up that shift. Major portal sites in China have all teamed up with national and local media in sharing information sources, and news stories are no longer limited by geographic location in reaching potential audience members. Human interest stories and social events are emphasized over political news on the Internet, as the audience takes more control in what to look for and as traffic flow to the different pages is easily tracked. This in turn creates the incentive for journalists to produce more stories that cater to the tastes of the audience. As the various cases in Chapters 6 and 7 demonstrated, local stories have developed a national scope on the Internet and have triggered a new culture of vigorously pursuing events of major social interest in the traditional newsroom.

Fifth, the Internet has also turned into a hotbed of collective action for Chinese civil society. Online protests and signatory campaigns are becoming frequent ways for Chinese netizens to express their discontent with the status quo and call for attention from the authority. Because protests in physical places are highly monitored and are still risky in China, the Internet has offered an alternative channel for similar actions in cyberspace. The government has generally displayed a more tolerant approach toward online protests or signatory campaigns, partly because there is less perceived threat to the state and partly because technically it is virtually impossible to eliminate online gatherings. Alternatively, the government's tolerance may be explained by the fact that Internet users in China are still a small group who tend to be middle class and well educated; those are the people who are most likely to align themselves with the government's effort in its economic reform policy and who may not want to rock the boat by challenging the regime because they have the most to lose by doing so. Similarly for the government, there is not much to gain in alienating the core segment of Chinese civil society that it needs the most in its economic modernization campaigns. On the other hand, the law of unintended consequences of the Internet dictates that once people have access to a brand-new platform of online communication, what they can do on the Internet is only limited by their imagination and creativity. Consequently, the Internet has become a significant player in dissident movements, such as the Tiananmen Mothers campaign and the Falun Gong group.

Meanwhile, there are also significant inhibitory factors that still keep the Internet from becoming a fully democratic force in China. First of all, the Chinese state still maintains one of the most sophisticated control mechanisms in cyberspace and has enforced a stringent policy toward Internet surveillance. Its control at the state, organizational (institutional), and individual levels still is a Damocles' sword hanging over Net surfers' heads to remind them of the presence of the state power in the cyber world. Although the government has shown a more lenient approach toward behavior on the Internet and has allowed expressive activities that it does not perceive to be a direct threat, it has also from time to time selectively persecuted individual violators, depending on the political tide of the day.

Second, the diffusion rate of the Internet is still low in the country. Although China boasts the second largest Internet population in the world, the percentage of Chinese citizens enjoying Internet connectivity is still low. Two types of digital divide still prove to be a big hindrance to the development of the Internet in China: the gap between rural and urban areas, and the gap between economically developed regions and underdeveloped regions.

Notes

Introduction

1. The term "Network Opinion" is a translation of the Chinese phrase, *wangluo yulun*, which refers to the rise of public opinion on the Internet. Although it was in use before 2003, this term became a catch phrase among both online and offline media in China in 2003 because of the occurrence of several important events, the course of which were changed by opinions and actions from massive numbers of Chinese netizens. For some general discussions on the role of network opinion in China during 2003, see, for example: "Writings from Wang Yi: The Value of Network Opinion in 2003," a widely circulated essay on popular Chinese Web sites, which can be retrieved at "Network: Window to the Will of the Chinese People," published in January 2004 at the *Global Chinese Network Professionals Website* at http://www.networkchinese.com/region/china/wcno.html (Accessed on July 20, 2004); Wang Wei, "2003: Rising Waves of Network Opinion," originally published on February 2, 2004, in *Xinmin Weekly*, a popular, Shanghai-based newsweekly, and available at http://news.sina.com.cn/c/2004-02-02/08192742343.shtml (Accessed on July 18, 2004); "Roundtable Discussion: 2003 in Retrospect — the Rise of Network Opinion in China," a special program aired by *Radio Free Asia* on January 29, 2004, available at http://www.rfa.org/service/article.html?service=man&encoding=6&id=129099 (Accessed on July 20, 2004); "The Freedom to Express in Network Space," an online discussion by four prominent Chinese social scientists with Chinese netizens (or to use a popular Chinese term, *wangyou* — network pals) during the 2003 Chinese Online Media Forum, a conference organized by Chinese Internet Media and held in Beijing in October 2003, available at the official Xinhua News Agency Web site at http://news.xinhuanet.com/newmedia/2003-10/09/content_1115386.htm (Accessed on July 20, 2004).
2. See "CCTV 'Social Record': The Controversial BMW Incident," a documentary by China Central Television, the national Chinese TV station, and available on Xinhuanet.com (the official Web site of Xinhua News Agency) at http://news.xinhuanet.com/newscenter/2004-01/10/content_1269008_1.htm (Accessed on July 18, 2004).
3. Chua Chin Hon, "Chinese Internet Users Wield Clout: Bombarded by Thousands of Furious Online Postings, Police Reopen Case of a Woman Who Got Off Lightly after Causing a Peasant's Death," *The Straits Times* (Singapore), January 6, 2004.
4. For comprehensive coverage of this case, see the special page section on the Web site of Xinhua News Agency at http://www.hlj.xinhuanet.com/news/detail_news.asp?dataid=hljWeb_news_1000041550; the QianLong News Net special coverage page at http://china.qianlong.com/4352/2004/01/08/Zt1160@1812930.htm; special coverage section by Dayoo.com, a Chinese portal site, at http://zhuanti.dayoo.com/gb/node/node_4439.shtml. All other major Chinese portals or news sites have published similar pages in relation to this story.
5. For the full text of the verdict, see "Chinese Agency Gives Details of Alleged Crime Boss' Trial, Execution," *Financial Times Global News Wire*, December 23, 2003.
6. For a full account of this case and Internet comments, see special coverage pages online on the following sites: "The Supreme People's Court Hears the Case of Liu Yong the Ring Leader," by the China.com portal site at http://news.china.com/zh_cn/focus/liuyong/; "Focus on the Supreme People's Court Trial of the Liu Yong Case," by *Nanfang Wang* (*Southern Net*) at http://www.southcn.com/news/china/china04/ly/default.htm; "The Supreme People's Court Sentences Liu Yong to Death," by Sohu.com at http://news.sohu.com/1/0803/19/subject212561976.shtml; "Public Trial of the Case of Liu Yong from Shenyang," by Tom.com at http://news.tom.com/hot/liuyong/.
7. The exact number of the Chinese prostitutes is not clear, and varied from 200 to 500 according to the different Chinese media that reported this incident.

8. Chow Chung-yan and Irene Wang, "Reports of Japanese Orgy in Zhuhai Spark Outrage." *South China Morning Post*, September 29, 2003.

9. Oliver August, "China Angry at Japanese Tourist Orgy Claims." *South China Morning Post*, October 1, 2003.

10. The summary of this incident has used multiple online sources. See the following special coverage sites for more information: "Japanese Tourists Buy Sex Service in Zhuhai," by *Yahoo.com* at http://cn.news.yahoo.com/maichun/; "Hundreds of Japanese Involved in Sex Spree in Zhuhai on China's Day of National Shame," by Sohu.com at http://news.sohu.com/1/0903/79/subject213717992.shtml; "Zhuhai: Japanese Orgy Group Visits on China's Day of National Shame," by the official Web site of *People's Daily* at http://www1.people.com.cn/GB/guandian/8213/29975/; "Organized Sex Crime in Zhunai: Three Japanese Wanted by Police," by the official Web site of Xinhua News Agency at http://news.xinhuanet.com/legal/2003-12/17/content_1235919.htm; "Japanese Sex Spree on China's Day of National Shame," by Rednet.com at http://news.rednet.com.cn/template/Default-TopicTemplate.asp?TopicID=1746. All retrieved in October 2004.

11. A typical comment is, for example, "Strongly Protesting against the Humiliation of Murdered Children in North Ossetia by CCTV," which summarizes some common responses from Chinese netizens. Compiled by Zhao Dagong on September 6, 2004, and available at http://www.boxun.com/hero/zhaodagong/354_1.shtml (Retrieved August 2005). See also another posting at the time "Who Gives CCTV the Right to Such an Immoral Question?" Available at http://my.cnd.org/models/wfsection/print.phd?articleid=7666 (Retrieved September 2004).

12. "Entertainment Guess Game Going Wry: Don't Seek Entertainment by Exploiting Others' Pain," published on Xinhuanet.com on September 9, 2004. Available at http://news.xinhuanet.com/newmedia/2004-09/09/content_1961029.htm (Retrieved August 2005).

13. See, for example, two blogs at http://sxs.blogdriver.com/sxs/index.html and http://www.yourblog.org/Blogger/20043/CKXP_4679.html (Retrieved August, 2005).

14. "Barbarian Game Guessing and Humane Care." Special Topic section on 163.com. Available at http://news.163.com/special/t/tanzi14.html (Retrieved August 2005).

15. "Producers of *Today's Focus* Let Go," *Xi'an Daily Online*, September 16, 2004. Available at http://www.xawb.com/gb/rbpaper/2004-09/16/content_341880.htm (Retrieved August 2005).

16. "China: Regulator Orders TV Stations Cease Mobile Phone Text Competitions," *BBC Monitoring International Reports*, September 27, 2004.

17. Chua Chin Hon, "Online, China's Protesters Are Too Loud to Ignore." *The Straits Times* (Singapore), October 5, 2003.

Chapter 1: The Idea of Civil Society from Early Modern to Contemporary Social Thought in the West

1. Plato, *The Republic*. Edited by G. R. F. Ferrari and Translated by Tom Griffith, Cambridge University Press, Cambridge, U.K. 2000. All subsequent citations from Plato come from the same source.

2. All subsequent quotes come from Aristotle, *The Politics and the Constitution of Athens*; Edited by Stephen Everson, Cambridge University Press, Cambridge, UK, 1996.

Chapter 2: The Idea of Civil Society in the Chinese Context

1. For example, the College of Public Administration at Qinghua (Tsinghua) University in Beijing has set up an NGO Research Institute and publishes a Web site at http://www.ngorc.net.cn.

2. Su Xiaohui, "SARS in China — How Society Promotes Government Behavior." Available at http://www5.chinesenewsnet.com/gb/MainNews/Forums/BackStage/2003_4_27_1_28_16_46.html (Accessed April 30, 2003).

Chapter 3: Government Policy and State Control of the Internet in China

1. "China, US Look to the Future." *China Daily*, July 29, 1998.

2. "Chinese President Addresses Regional Leaders at APEC Gathering." *Xinhua Wire News*, November 19, 1998.

3. "Chinese President Addresses APEC Human Resources Forum." *Xinhua Wire News*, May 15, 2001.
4. "Chinese President Outlines Priorities for Studying Party Ideology." Translation of a report by *Qiushi* (Seeking Truth) by BBC Worldwide Monitoring, January 30, 2004.
5. Office of the Premier, State Council of the PRC, "Outline of the 10th Five-Year National Economic and Social Development Plan of the People's Republic of China (Draft)," released on March 5, 2001, in Chinese. English quotation from BBC's wire release of the translated text in English on March 15, 2001.
6. Wang Xudong, "Strengthening Cooperation, Promoting Development and Moving towards the Information Society Together," statement at the world summit on the Information Society, December 10, 2003. Available at http://www.itu.int/wsis/geneva/coverage/statements/china/cn.pdf (accessed January 31, 2004).
7. See, for example: "China Overheats: Slowdown Would Be Felt across Asia and around the World." *Financial Times* (London), May 4, 2004, p. 14; "Soft Landing for China Seems More Likely Now; Data Points to Reduced Chances of Economy Overheating, Say Analysts." *Straits Times* (Singapore), June 16, 2004, p. 16.
8. This was the focal point by Wang Qiming, Director of Information Networking Division, Ministry of Science and Technology of China, in his speech titled "Can ICT Promote Sustainable Development?" at The Second High-Level Forum on City Informatization in the Asia Pacific Region, Shanghai, China, May 2001. Available at http://unpan1.un.org/intradoc/groups/public/documents/apcity/unpan001465.pdf (Accessed January 31, 2004).
9. Xu Guanhua, Minister of Science and Technology, PRC, "A New Role of Science and Technology in Chinese Society," speech at the World Economic Forum, April 2001. Available at http://www.chinese-embassy.no/eng/15671.html (Accessed January 31, 2004).
10. "China Should Adjust to New FDI Parameters," Global News Wire, *Financial Times*, November 18, 2003.
11. "The Next Generation of Chinese IPOs Looks to Tap Capital Markets," *AFX News*, Asia, October 7, 2003.
12. "Portals Lured to Nasdaq Riches; NetEase's 11,571 pc Share Gain Whets the Appetite of Mainland Internet Companies for Listing in the US," *South China Morning Post*, October 7, 2003.
13. "Chinese Dotcoms on the Course to NASDAQ," SinaCast China IT Watch, *Comtex News Network, Inc.*, November 18, 2003.
14. "Yahoo Buys China Internet Firm 3721.com for 120 Mln Dollars Cash," *Agence France Presse*, November 21, 2003.
15. "M&A to Prevail Among Web Portals," Asia Africa Intelligence Wire, *Financial Times*, December 19, 2003.
16. Mure Dickie and Richard Waters, "Yahoo to Pay Dollars 1bn in Alibaba Venture." *Financial Times* (London), August 12, 2005.
17. "Chinese Dotcoms Planning for IPO," SinaCast China IT Watch, *Comtext News Network, Inc.*, October 13, 2003.
18. Wang Pufeng (1995), "The Challenge of Information Warfare," available at http://www.fas.org/irp/world/china/docs/iw mg wang.htm (Accessed on February 28, 2004).
19. "NATO's War Speeds PLA's Pace of Change," *South China Morning Post*, May 12, 2999, p. 17.
20. Michael Evans, "War Planners Warn of Digital Armageddon," *The Times* (London), November 20, 1999.
21. Andrew J. Glass, "Angry Hackers Blitz Web sites of FBI, Senate; 'Electronic Pearl Harbor' warning?" *The Atlanta Journal and Constitution*, May 29, 1999, p. 3A.
22. "U.S. Military Concerned over Possible Chinese Mao-style People's Cyber Warfare," available at http://www.chinesenewsnet.com (Accessed on February 11, 2004).
23. "China Investing in Information Warfare Technology, Doctrine." *Financial Times News Wire*, July 20, 2005.
24. "DVD Makers Face Key Issues." *Financial Times Global News Wire*, March 21, 2002.
25. "Japanese & American Magnates Impose DVD Writer Patent Fee." *Financial Times Global News Wire*, November 26, 2002.
26. David Hsieh, "Now, a 'Super DVD' Made in China." *The Strait Times* (Singapore), July 17, 2003.
27. "China Unleashes EVD Players." *Financial Times Global News Wire*, January 7, 2004.

28. "Hollywood Companies to Support Chinese EVD Standard." *Comtex News Network, Inc.*, February 24, 2004.
29. "EVD Becomes a Savior for Disc Player Industry." *Comtex News Network, Inc.*, July 24, 2004.
30. "China's Home-Grown EVD Technology Selected as National Standard — MII." *Xinhua Financial Network News*, February 24, 2005.
31. "EVD Comes to Its Own." *Comtex News Network, Inc.*, May 19, 2005.
32. "China Debuts New Standard for High-Definition Player Sector." *Financial Times Global News Wire*, April 25, 2005.
33. "China Challenges Microsoft with Red Flag Linux OS." *ChinaOnline*, August 13, 1999.
34. "China's Linux Market to See Reshuffle." Comtex News Network, Inc., April 1, 2005; "Linux Suitors Get out of the Wood." *Comtex News Network, Inc.*, August 17, 2005.
35. "Beijing 'to Drop Microsoft Over Security Fears.'" *South China Morning Post*, January 7, p. 1. See also "The *Yangcheng Evening News* Article on China's Microsoft Windows 2000 Ban." *Financial* Times Global News Wire, January 10, 2000.
36. "Quasi-ban Hits Windows 2000 in China." *Asia Computer Weekly*, January 24, 2000. See also "Microsoft Perceived as Security Risk Germany and China Have Dumped Microsoft Software over Concerns of a Built-In Espionage Back Door." *Financial Times Global News Wire*, April 3, 2001.
37. "Chinese Computer Firm to Use Linux Software in PCs." *Deutsche Presse-Agentur*, August 4, 2000.
38. "IBM Expands Linux Ambition in China." *Financial Times Global News Wire*, September 16, 2003.
39. "Dell Launches Servers Equipped with Red Flag Linux." *Comtex News Network, SinoCast*, December 9, 2003.
40. "Regulations for the Protection of Computer Information Systems Safety in the People's Republic of China." Available in Chinese at http://www.cnnic.net.cn/html/Dir/1994/02/18/0644.htm (Accessed March 25, 2004).
41. "Temporary Decree on the Management of Computer Information Network International Connectivity in the People's Republic of China." Available in Chinese at: http://www.cnnic.net.cn/html/Dir/1997/05/20/0646.htm (Accessed on March 25, 2004).
42. "Implementation Measures for Enforcing the Temporary Decree on the Management of Computer Information Network International Connectivity in the People's Republic of China." Available in Chinese at: http://www.cnnic.net.cn/html/Dir/1997/12/08/0649.htm (Accessed on March 25, 2004).
43. "State Secrets Protection Regulations for Computer Information Systems on the Internet." Available in Chinese at: http://www.cnnic.net.cn/html/Dir/2003/11/27/1482.htm (Accessed on March 25, 2004).
44. "Decree on the Management of Internet News/Information Services." http://www.cnnic.org.cn/html/Dir/2005/09/27/3184.htm (Accessed on October 1, 2005).
45. "Chinese Internet Police." *Xinhua General News Service*, August 4, 2000.
46. "Internet Police Ranks Swell to 300,000." *BBC Summary of World Broadcasts*, December 11, 2000.
47. For a complete list, see "China's Computer Information Network Policies, Laws and Regulations," available online in Chinese at http://www.cnnic.net.cn/index/0F/index.htm (Accessed March 26, 2004).
48. "Computer Information Network and Internet Security, Protection and Management Regulations." Available online at http://www.cnnic.net.cn/html/Dir/1997/12/11/0650.htm (Accessed on March 26, 2004).
49. "Tough New Rules Don't Faze Chinese Internet Start-ups." *New York Times*, October 4, 2000, p. C2.
50. "Temporary Ordinance on the Management of Internet News Publishing." Available in Chinese at: http://www.cnnic.net.cn/html/Dir/2000/11/07/0654.htm (Accessed on March 26, 2004).
51. Philip P. Pan, "Chinese Crack Down on Student Web Sites." *Washington Post*, March 24, 2005, p. A13.
52. "Chinese Agency Reports on University Websites after Intervention, Shutdown." *BBC Worldwide Monitoring*, May 30, 2005.
53. "China Closes Nearly 10,000 Websites." *BBC Worldwide Monitoring*, September 8, 2005.
54. Hiawatha Bray, "Netting a Market of 1 Billion." *Boston Globe*, April 30, 1997, p. F2.

55. "Chinese Websites, ISPs Sign Self-discipline Pact." *Xinhua News Service,* July 5, 2002.
56. "Media Freedom Body Condemns China Internet Self-censorship Pledge." *Agence France Presse,* July 16, 2002.
57. Verne Kopytoff, "Search Engines in China Face Balancing Act." *San Francisco Chronicle,* September 16, 2002, p. E1.
58. "China Pleads Ignorance over Google Ban." *Agence France Presse,* September 2, 2002
59. "Google Mystery Deepens as Site Unblocked Again in China." *Agence France Presse,* September 13, 2002.
60. Michael Laris, "Police on the Prowl in China; Free Flow of Ideas Worries Leaders." *Washington Post,* October 24, 1998, p. A12.
61. Seth Faison, "E-Mail to U.S. Lands Chinese Internet Entrepreneur in Jail." *New York Times,* January 21, 1999, p. A10.
62. "China Shuts Down Political Website, Arrests Founder." *Agence France Presse,* June 7, 2000.
63. "Internet Dissident in China Sentenced to Five Years Imprisonment." *Deutsche Presse-Agentur,* May 18, 2003.
64. "China Student Arrested for Posting Anti-government Essays on Internet." *Agence France Presse,* December 8, 2002.
65. Jim Yardley, "China Frees 3 'Cyber Dissidents'." *New York Times,* December 1, 2003, p. A3.
66. Paul Festa, "Software Rams Great Firewall of China." Available online at: http://news.com.com/2100-1028-997101.html?tag=fd_top (Accessed March 25, 2004). See also, Jim Hu, "Rights Group Looks at China and Techs." Available at http://news.com.com/2100-1023-975517.html?tag=nl (Accessed March 24, 2004).
67. Jiao Guobiao, "Declaration of the Campaign against the Central Propaganda Ministry." The posting is available on over two dozen popular Web sites. See, the original Chinese text as well as an English translation, for example, available at http://msittig.freeshell.org/docs/jian_guobiao_essay_utf8.html (Retrieved on August 20, 2004).
68. Jiao Guobiao, "My Follow-up Campaign against the Central Propaganda Ministry." Available at http://forum.netix.com/messages/1960.html (Retrieved on August 20, 2004).
69. Chris Buckley, "Daring to Publish: a Chinese Writer's Fight." *International Herald Tribune,* June 16, 2005.
70. See, for example, the support Web site at http://www.fillthesquare.org/chinese/factsheet.asp for more information.
71. For a chronology of the Tiananmen Mothers movement, see "About 'Tiananmen Mothers Campaign,'" published on the *Human Rights in China* Web site at http://gb.hrichina.org/gate/gb/big5.hrichina.org/big5/article.adp?article_id=1943&subcategory_id=221.
72. See http://tongmeng.org/gb/newsdetail.php?id=1046.
73. See the publications on the Human Rights in China Web site available at http://gb.hrichina.org/gate/gb/big5.hrichina.org/big5/article_listings3.adp?category_id=61&subcategory_id=196 and http://gb.hrichina.org/gate/gb/big5.hrichina.org/big5/article_listings3.adp?category_id=61&subcategory_id=205 (Retrieved on August 20, 2004). These same publications are also available at multiple Web sources.
74. Some examples can be seen at the *Human Rights in China* Web site at http://gb.hrichina.org/gate/gb/big5.hrichina.org/big5/article_listings.adp?category_id=61 (Retrieved on August 20, 2004). See also "Tiananmen Mothers' Declaration on the 12th Anniversary of the June 4th Event," at http://www.zhongguohun.com/viewpoint/64/004.html (Retrieved on August 20, 2004).
75. Wang Yi, "'Tiananmen Mothers': A Term That Is Blocked." Available at http://www.boxun.com/hero/wangyi/22_1.shtml (Retrieved on August 20, 2004). Original is in Chinese, and the English title is my translation.
76. "Nobel Prize Sought for Tiananmen Mothers." *China Support Network,* January 12, 2002. Available at http://www.chinasupport.net/topnews5.htm (Retried on August 20, 2004).
77. For a list and an introduction of these awards, see "A Brief Biography of Ding Zilin." Available at http://www.yangjianli.com/people/intro_dingzilin1_en.htm (Retrieved on August 20, 2004).
78. "Detained Relatives of June 4th Victims Testified for UN: Rights Group." *Agence France Presse,* March 30, 2004.
79. "Tiananmen Mothers Released Following International Campaign." *South China Morning Post,* April 3, 2004.

80. Christopher Bodeen, "China Releases Relatives of Tiananmen Crackdown Victims." *Associated Press*, April 2, 2004.

81. Most major Chinese news sites have special coverage (hot topic) sections on these incidents by publishing investigative stories from a variety of news sources. See, for example, *EasternNet* (http://news.eastday.com//eastday/news/xwzxzt/node5085/node18043/index. html), *Southern Net* (http://www.southcn.com/news/community/shzt/mp/), *Renmin Wang* (http://www.people.com.cn/GB/shehui/8217/33048/index.html).

82. See note 81.

83. See the special coverage section on Sina.com at: http://news.sina.com.cn/z/liuyongsy/1. shtml (Accessed on March 20, 2005).

84. A special coverage of the Huang Jing case can be found at Sina.com, at: http://news.sohu. com/1/0404/62/subject219996237.shtml (Accessed on March 20, 2005), as well as other major portal sites.

85. See the special coverage pages at two popular Chinese news portals: Sohu.com at http:// news.sohu.com/s2005/tengxingshan.shtml and NetEase.com at http://news.163.com/ special/y/000113A8/yuanan050615.html (Both accessed in August 2005).

86. See the comprehensive report at *Asian Times Online* (Chinese Version) at http://202.82.86.97:82/gate/gb/www.atchinese.com/index.php?option=com_content&ta sk=view&id=2178&Itemid=28 (Accessed in August 2005).

87. *South China Morning Post* (Singapore) Chinese Edition, September 19, 2005. Available at http://www.zaobao.com/special/realtime/2005/09/050919_16.html (Retrieved in September 2005).

88. For example, "See How Some Officials Respond to Public Opinion Supervision," available at http://news.xinhuanet.com/comments/2005-09/19/content_3509831.htm; "It is Futile to Interfere with Public Opinion Supervision," available at http://news.xinhuanet. com/comments/2005-09/19/content_3510155.htm; "To Suppress Negative Coverage is to Challenge Public Opinion Supervision," available at http://news.xinhuanet.com/comments/2005-09/19/content_3514516.htm. All accessed in September 2005.

Chapter 4: Historical Development of the Internet in China

1. "Domestic Cell Phone Users Hit 170 Million, the World's Most." *China Daily*, June 22, 2002.

2. "Monthly Statistics of the Telecommunications Industry, August 2005." Released by the Ministry of Information Industry, available at http://www.mii.gov.cn/mii/hyzw/tjxx.html.

3. "A Swiss Bank Found That Chinese Cell Phone Users May Be Inflated as High as 1/3." *Xinhuanet.com*, November 3, 2003.

4. "China Ranks First in Telephone Users." *Xinhua News Wire*, May 23, 2002.

5. See Note 2.

6. "China Decides It's Internet Crazy." *Wired News*, August 21, 2000. Available at http:// www.wired.com/news/politics/0,1283,38324,00.html. See also "Jiang Calls for 'Vigorous' Promotion of IT." *Financial Times*, August 22, 2000, p. 8.

7. "Internet Business Faces Wonderful Opportunities in China: Minister." *Xinhua News Wire*, November 25, 2002.

8. "Jiang Calls for 'Vigorous' Promotion of IT." See note 6.

9. "Milestone Events in China's Internet Development." Available from the China Internet Network Information Center Web site at: http://www.cnnic.org.cn/internet.shtml (Accessed 5/10/2003).

10. CAS Networking Center, "The Four (Chinese) Backbone Networks." Available at http:// www.kepu.com.cn/gb/technology/telecom/network/net712.html (Accessed May 18, 2003).

11. Barry M. Leiner et al (2003), "A Brief History of the Internet." Available: http://www. isoc.org/internet/history/brief.shtml (Accessed May 15, 2003); also David Patrick Chott (1997), "A Comparison of the Internet Revolution and the Printing Revolution." Available at http://www.chott.com/thesis.html (Accessed September 20, 2004).

12. John Thompson (2000), "Privatization of the New Communication Channel." Available: http://www.sit.wisc.edu/%7Ejcthomsonjr/j561/ (Accessed May 15, 2003).

13. "Security in Digitized Government Administration," Available from the Beijing Jingtai Network Security Inc. Web site at http://www.bhlnet.com.cn/news.files/GS2001102201. html (Accessed May 25, 2003).

14. "Less Than 4% Elementary and High Schools Are Connected to the Internet: Our Level of Education Informatization Needs Improvement." Huaxia Student Admission Online, April 27, 2004. Available at http://www.huaedu.cn/apps/readFile.asp?f=178 (Retried on August 28, 2004).
15. "China Joins Internet and Exposes Its Flank." *South China Morning Post*, January 10, 1995, p. 2.
16. Science Museum of China, "The Four Backbones." Available http://www.kepu.com.cn/gb/technology/telecom/network/net712.html (Accessed May 26, 2003).
17. "A Chronology of China Internet Development: 1986-2004." *Blogchina.com*, August 16, 2004. Available at http://www.blogchina.com/new/display/40827.html (Accessed on August 28, 2004).
18. See the previous note. Unless otherwise indicated, narrative information in this section is from the same source.
19. Teresa Poole, "China Seeks to Make the Internet Toe Party Line." *The Independent* (London), January 5, 1996, p. 8.
20. Tan Tarn How, "US Doctors Offer Help to Chinese Girl after Internet SOS Call." *The Straits Times* (Singapore), April 25, 1995, p. 14.
21. Sheila Tefft, "China Surfs the Internet, but Gingerly." *Christian Science Monitor*, April 13, 1995, p. 1.
22. Tony Walker and Shi Junbao, "China's Wave of Internet Surfers Sets Censors a Poser." *Financial Times* (London), June 24, 1995, p. 3.
23. Louise Lucas, "Media Futures: Net for China; No Smut, No Politics, No Decadent Culture." *Financial Times* (London), July 10, 1995, p. 13.
24. "See note 19.
25. Available at the CNNIC Web site at http://www.cnnic.org.cn/policy/5.shtml (Accessed May 20, 2003).
26. Available at the CNNIC Web site at http://www.cnnic.net.cn/policy/1.shtml (Accessed May 21, 2003).
27. "China's NPC Adopts Plan on New Ministries, Mergers." *Xinhua News Wire*, March 10, 1998.
28. "China's Internet Players Hope New Regulator Will Boost Prospects." *Agence France Presse*, March 25, 1998.
29. "E-Commerce Is Walking towards Us." *Zhongshan University Network and Information Center*, December 15, 1999. Available at http://www.zsu.edu.cn/WebNews/get/techs/280.html (Retrieved on August 29, 2004).
30. He Jiacheng, "China's E-Commerce Development." *Perspectives*, 2(2), 2000. Available: http://www.oycf.org/Perspectives/8_103100/ecommerce.htm (Accessed on May 30, 2003). He was Deputy Director of the State Internal Trade Administration and Director of E-Commerce Development in China.
31. "Speech by Minister Shi Guangsheng on the Opening Ceremony of the APEC High-Level Symposium on E-commerce and Paperless Trading." Available at the MOFTEC Web site at: http://www1.moftec.gov.cn/moftec_en/apec/report-2.html (Accessed on May 30, 2003).
32. See note 29.
33. See "Fast as a Rabbit, Patient as a Turtle." Available on the *Forbes* Web site at: http://www.forbes.com/best/2000/0717/074.html (Accessed on May 30, 2003).
34. "E-commerce in China: The CCIDnet Survey." *China Online Global News Wire*, May 5, 2000.
35. "China Passes Law Legalizing Electronic Deals." *Xinhua News Agency*, August 30, 2004.
36. "EachNet CEO Predicts E-Commerce Boom." *Financial Times Business Daily Update*, December 23, 2002.
37. "China Enters the 'Era of Network Merchants': Six Million Venture Business Activities Online." *Tom.com*, June 14, 2004. Available at http://tech.tom.com/1121/1794/2004614-104932.html (Retrieved on August 29, 2004).
38. "First Network Merchant Convention to Be Held in June; Online Merchants Surface as a Community." *Tom.com*, May 10, 2004. Available at http://tech.tom.com/1121/1794/2004510-97655.html (Retrieved on August 29, 2004).
39. "China Passes Law Legalizing Electronic Signatures." *BBC Monitoring International Reports*, August 28, 2004.

40. "China — CCIDnet Survey Details Chinese Enterprises' Use of IT." *China Online Global News Wire*, December 4, 2001.

41. Michael Logan, Sidney Luk, and Hui Yuk-min, "Old Ways Slow Path to e-Commerce; China's Online Retailers Face Obstacles Including Inefficient Infrastructure and Consumer Reluctance." *South China Morning Post*, August 3, 2004, p. 1.

42. "China's Cultural Revolution on the Web." *BBC Wire News*, July 14, 1999.

43. Stephen Seawright, "China.com Triples in Nasdaq Debut." *South China Morning Post* (Hong Kong), July 14, 1999, p. 1.

44. "China: Sina Soars with Nasdaq Listing." *China Daily*, April 16, 2000, p. 1.

45. Craig S. Smith, "Nasdaq Debut of Chinese Stock Dampens Internet Fever." *New York Times*, July 3, 2000, p. C2.

46. "China: Sohu Debuts on Nasdaq." *Asiainfo Daily China News*, July 20, 2000.

47. Russell Flannery, "NetEase Wins With Online Gaming." *Forbes Online*, April 19, 2003. Available: http://www.forbes.com/2003/04/29/cz_rf_0429netease.html (Accessed June 1, 2003).

48. See the timeline for China's WTO bid by AFP, "China's Long March to WTO Membership Reaches Destination." *Agence France Presse News Wire*, December 11, 2001.

49. John Burgess, "U.S., China Agree on Trade; Pact on Entry into WTO Climaxes 13 Years of Talks." *The Washington Post*, November 16, 1999, p. A1.

50. Yvonne Chan, "Web Wave to Break on Mainland Shores under WTO Membership." *South China Morning Post*, November 18, 1999, p. 3.

51. "Online Auction Giant Completes Acquisition." *China Daily*, June 13, 2003.

52. "EachNet Unveils Biz Expansion to Ride Upcoming E-Commerce." *Financial Times Information*, Business Daily Update, June 8, 2004.

53. "Google, Yahoo Extend Presence in China." *Financial Times Information*, Business Daily Update, June 22, 2004.

54. "Multinationals Eyeing Chinese Internet Industry." *Comtex News Network, Inc.*, June 28, 2004.

55. "Amazon Buys China Foothold in USD 75 MLN." *Financial Times Information*, SinoCast China IT Watch, August 30, 2004.

56. Francesco Guerrera and Fang Wang, "Chinese Online Groups Look to Raise Dollars 1bn in US Initial Public Offerings." *The Financial Times* (London), April 26, 2004, p. 26.

57. "Ctrip Going Public on Nasdaq." *Financial Times Information*, SinoCast China Business Daily News, December 12, 2003.

58. Hui Yuk-min and Sidney Luk, "Linktone Soars on Nasdaq Debut." *South China Morning Post*, March 5, 2004, p. 4.

59. "Tom Online Receives Cold Welcome on Debut." *Financial Times Information*, SinoCast China Business Daily News, March 12, 2004.

60. "Game Firm Raises US $154.2 M through IPO." *Financial Times Information*, Business Daily Update, May 14, 2004.

61. "Cyber Game Vendor Shanda in Full Swing." *Financial Times Information*, SinoCast China IT Watch, August 30, 2004.

62. "CNNIC 'Top Ten Web Site Ranking' Campaign Will Be Terminated at Year's End." *Sina. com*, November 13, 2000. Available at http://tech.sina.com.cn/i/c/41987.shtml (Retrieved on August 30, 2004).

63. "CNNIC: An Introduction." Available at http://www.cnnic.org.cn/about.shtml.

64. The world Internet population is an estimation from World Internet Stats, "World Internet Usage and Population Statistics," available at http://www.internetworldstats.com/stats.htm (Retrieved October 5, 2005).

65. "China Has World's 2nd Largest Number of Netizens: Report." *Xinhua News Agency*, January 17, 2003.

66. See, for example, "The Central Committee Has Decided to Revitalize the Northeast as Its National Policy." A special topic section at Sina.com, available at http://news.sina.com.cn/z/dongbei/index.shtml.

67. See the official Web site of the National Bureau of Statistics of China at http://www.stats.gov.cn/.

Chapter 5: Communication, Empowerment, and the Emergence of Network Public Opinion in Chinese Cyberspace

1. "First Release of Findings from the UCLA World Internet Project Shows Significant 'Digital Gender Gap' in Many Countries." *UCLA News*, January 14, 2004. Available at http://www.digitalcenter.org/downloads/World_Internet_Project.doc (Retrieved on September 2, 2005).

2. The Chinese bureaucracy has in place a sophisticated system to direct propaganda work at its various levels of government agencies and organizations that fall within the arms of the Communist Party. Party committees at the national and the local levels all have propaganda bureaus that are in charge of policy making in relation to propaganda tasks and campaigns. Propaganda bureaus are the administrative superiors over all media organizations in their districts of jurisdiction. Even state-run enterprises and universities have their own propaganda bureaus that work in coordination with the Propaganda Bureau of the Central Party Committee.

3. "Chinese President Addresses Propaganda Work Forum." *Financial Times* Global News Wire, December 8, 2003.

4. "China's Wen Jiabao Chairs State Council Meeting on Economy." *BBC Monitoring Asia Pacific*, October 20, 2003.

5. Melinda Liu with reporting by Leila Abbound and Kevin Platt, "Look Who's Talking." *Newsweek*, Atlantic Edition, May 7, 2001, 37-39.

6. "Gallup Explores China's Huge Consumer Market." *Xinhua New Agency*, February 15, 1995.

7. "Nationwide Gallup Poll." *China Economic Review*, November 23, 1997.

8. "Gallup Consumer Survey: Survey Shows Consumer Lifestyle." *China Economic Review*, March 13, 2001.

9. "Consumers Crowd Modern Stores." *China Daily*, December 16, 2002.

10. "Survey Shows Ten Most Favored Brands of Chinese." *Xinhua News Agency*, June 30, 2000.

11. "Broadcasting: Choice Attracts Cable Viewers." *China Economic Review*, March 9, 2001.

12. "Over 80 Percent Chinese Glued to World Cup." *Xinhua News Agency*, June 8, 2002.

13. "Lowest Car Prices, Highest Car Possession in Beijing." *Financial Times Global News Wire*, May 24, 2004.

14. "Poll: 94.9 Percent of Beijing Residents Back Olympic Bid." *Xinhua News Agency*, February 2, 2001.

15. "China: CCIDnet Unveils Online Survey Service for IT Firms." *Financial Times Global News Wire*, November 23, 2000.

16. Jaimie FlorCruz, "China Finds Opinions Count." *CNN.com*, February 18, 2002.

17. See note 16.

18. "Foreign Polling Services to Undergo Annual Scrutiny." *Financial Times Global News Wire*, August 3, 1999.

19. "Chinese Politburo Member Zeng Qinghong Reportedly Bans Opinion Polls." *Financial Times Global News Wire*, February 8, 2003.

20. See note 19.

21. The official line that is stressed year after year by the Chinese bureaucracy to the media professionals is the policy of *zhengmian xuanchuan weizhu*, or "positive propaganda as the main thread" in the coverage of issues, opinions, and events.

22. Li Xiguang, "The Internet's Impact on China's Press." Keynote speech at Asia-Pacific Journalists Meeting, 2001. Available at http://www.rthk.org.hk/mediadigest/20020115_76_10450.html (Accessed on June 30, 2004).

23. Anthony Kuhn, "China: Internet Boom Changes Face of News." *IPI Global Journalists Online*, 2001, 3rd Quarter. Available at http://www.globaljournalist.org/archive/Magazine/china.html (Retrieved on July 10, 2004).

24. "10th National People's Congress Delegate Zhou Hongyu Welcomes and Will Forward Netizens' Suggestions." Available at http://bbs.people.com.cn/bbs/ReadFile?whichfile=1057&typeid=97 (Retrieved June 2004).

25. "Netizens Constitute Most Active 'Constituency' in China." *Xinhua News Agency*, March 8, 2004.

26. Elaine Kurtenbach, "China's Politicians Ease into Digital Age." *Associated Press Wire News*, June 28, 2004. See also, Elaine Kurtenbach, "Chinese Politicians Tap into Public Opinion." *Associated Press Wire News*, May 13, 2004.

27. Full coverage can be found on Hangzhou Net at http://www.hangzhou.com.cn/20040101/ca652267.htm (Retrieved August 2005).

28. "Special Section: Network Supervision — Red Net Has Never Been Absent." Available at http://hn.rednet.com.cn/Articles/2004/01/513424.HTM (Retrieved June 2004).

29. Zhao Ying, "Participating and Talking about Politics with an e-Taste," *Renmin Wang*, May 11, 2005. Available at http://npc.people.com.cn/GB/15017/3377966.html (Retrieved August 2005).

30. Jane Cai, "Beijing City Hall Panned in Poll." *South China Morning Post*, December 6, 2003, p. 6.

31. See note 30.

32. "Cancellation of Decree an Encouraging Sign." *China Daily*, April 20, 2004.

33. "Ideas from News Network Netizens Become the No. 1 Document Submitted during the Citizens' Month," May 7, 2005, *Qingdaonews.com*. Available http://www.qingdaonews.com/gb/content/2005-07/05/content_5007424.htm (Retrieved July 2005).

34. "Premier Wen Jiabao: I Am Deeply Moved by Netizens." *Sohu.com*, March 16, 2005. Available at http://news.sohu.com/20050316/n224779609.shtml (Retrieved June 2005).

35. "Through Reading an Online Information Bulletin, Wen Jiabao Ordered that Urban Workers be Compensated for Their Salary." *Beijing Evening News*, November 11, 2004. See also Min Dahong,, "China's Internet Media of 2004." *Renmin Wang* (People's Net), December 12, 2004. Available at http://www.people.com.cn/GB/14677/3070327.html (Retrieved August 2005).

36. "China Goes Undercover to Sway Opinion on the Internet." Reuters Wire Service, May 23, 2005.

Chapter 6: A School Explosion, a Fatal Virus, and the Internet Factor

1. e11th Hour, "SARS Country Breakdown." Sources from BBC News, Centers for Disease Control, CNN, ReliefWeb, Reuters, World Health Organization. Available at http://www.e11th-hour.org/resources/timelines/sars.countries.html (Accessed May 20, 2004).

2. UNAIDS, "Epidemiological Fact Sheets on HIV/AIDS and Sexually Transmitted Infections: China." 2002 Update. Available at http://www.unaids.org/html/pub/Publications/Fact-Sheets01/China_EN_pdf.pdf (Accessed on May 20, 2004).

3. John Gittings, "The Aids Scandal China Could Not Hush Up: Health Officials' Blood-for-Cash Scheme Breeds HIV Tragedy." *The Guardian* (London), June 11, 2001, p. 15.

4. "UNAIDS Official to Chat Online with Chinese Netizens." China News Agency Online News Release, Available at http://www.chinanews.com.cn/news/2004year/2004-05-21/26/439348.shtml (Accessed on May 20, 2004).

5. "Chinese Activist Detained by Police, Immediate Action Needed — Wan Yanhai." *AIDS Treatment News*, September 6, 2002. Available at http://www.findarticles.com/p/articles/mi_m0HSW/is_2002_Sept_6/ai_92864512 (Accessed on September 12, 2004). See also "China Releases AIDS Activist for Leaking State Secrets." *Reuters Health Information*, September 23, 2002. Available at http://www.hivandhepatitis.com/recent/developing/092302b.html (Accessed on September 12, 2002).

6. "China AIDS Patient Uses Internet to Help Others." *Reuters NewMedia*, November 5, 2001. Available at http://www.aegis.com/news/re/2001/RE011104.html (Accessed on September 12, 2004).

7. See http://sh.netsh.com/bbs/8109/ for further information.

8. See, for example, "China and SARS: China's Chernobyl?" *The Economist*, 367 (8321), April 26, 2003, 9–10; "Diagnosing SARS in China," *New York Times*, May 19, 2003, p. A20; Anne Hyland, "SARS 'The Chinese Chernobyl,'" *Australian Financial Review*, April 28, 2003, p. 9.

9. Sin-Ming, Shaw, "China's Glasnost Moment?" *China Review* (London), No. 25, Summer 2003, 8–9.

10. China Elections and Governance Special Report, "Hu Angang Is Deadly Wrong on SARS." Available at http://www.chinaelections.org/Eng/readnews.asp?newsid=%7BB62DF8FB-62C0-4C76-B569-807F8D06E3FE%7D (Accessed on May 20, 2004). Hu's original comments were made in Shanghai-based *Wenhui Daily*, one of China's leading newspapers, on May 11, 2003.

11. For example, "Bird Flu Spreads to China as Alerts Issued." *Time Online*, January 27, 2004. Available at http://www.timesonline.co.uk/article/0,,9529-979375,00.html (Accessed on May 21, 2004); "China Showcases Anti-Bird Flu Efforts." *Associated Press Wire*, February 12, 2004.

12. See, for example, Jim Yardley, "China Reports Suspected Case of SARS in Beijing." *New York Times*, April 23, 2004, p. A6; Lawrence Altman, "New Cases Identified in China's SARS Outbreak." *New York Times*, April 26, p. A3.

13. "China Praised for Handling SARS Outbreak." *Associated Press Wire*, April 28, 2004.

14. "U.S. Congratulates Hu Jintao on Elevation to CPC Chief." *Agence France Presse Wire*, November 15, 2002. See also Josephine Ma and Wang Xiangwei, "Jiang Stands Down as Head of Party; Hu Jintao Is Poised to Take Over in China's First Orderly Power Transfer." *South China Morning Post* (Hong Kong), November 15, 2002.

15. For example, Martin Sieff, "Who's Hu." *United Press International News Wire*, November 15, 2002; Peter Harmsen, "AFP: Analyst Says China's Jiang to Continue Wielding Power behind Scenes." *Financial Times Global News Wire*, November 14, 2002; Jasper Becker, "China's New Orchestra Plays the Same Music." *The Independent* (London), November 16, 2002, p. 16.

16. "Congress Elects Hu Jintao New Chinese President, Zeng Qinghong Vice-President." *Xinhua News Agency* Wire News, March 15, 2003.

17. "New Chinese Premier, Central Military Commission Leaders Approved at NPC Meeting." *Xinhua News Agency* Wire News, March 16, 2003.

18. Joe McDonald, "Man of the People? China's Hu Stakes Out an Image as Champion of the Poor." *Associated Press*, January 23, 2003.

19. "China's Hu Jintao Stresses Importance of 'Plain Living, Hard Struggle.'" *BBC Monitoring International Reports*, December 7, 2002.

20. Erik Eckholm, "New Chinese Party Chief Strikes a Contrast; Champion of the Poor & Claiming Mao's Mantle." *New York Times*, January 13, 2003, p. A2.

21. "Chinese Party Leader Hu Jintao Pays New Year Visit to Public Workers, Police." *China News Agency Wire*, February 1, 2003.

22. "Pneumonia Outbreak under Control in Guangzhou." *Xinhua News Agency* Wire, February 11, 2003.

23. "Wen Jiabao, Zhu Rongji Urge Tighter Control on Atypical Pneumonia." *Financial Times Global News Wire*, March 27, 2003.

24. "China's State Council Discusses Atypical Pneumonia." *Xinhua News Agency*, April 2, 2003.

25. "AFP: China Seeks to Come Clean Over Sars as Global Criticism Mounts." *Financial Times Global News Wire*, April 3, 2003.

26. "Pneumonia Outbreak under Control in Guangzhou." *Xinhua News Agency*, February 11, 2003; "Pneumonia 'Under Control' in China's Guangdong Province after Five Dead." *Financial Times Global News Wire*, February 12, 2003.

27. See Mathew Forney, "Stalking a Killer: How Did a Deadly Virus Find Its Way from Southern China to the Rest of the World?" *Time Online*, April 14, 2003, for a narrative. Available at" http://www.time.com/time/asia/covers/501030421/tictoc.html (Accessed May 25, 2004).

28. Chen Hai and Jiang Hua, "Guangzhou kangji buming bingdu" (Guangzhou Fights against an Unknown Virus). *Nanfang Weekend Daily Online*, February 13, 2003. Available at http://www.nanfangdaily.com.cn/zm/20030213/xw/tb/200302130499.asp (Accessed on May 24, 2004).

29. See note 27.

30. See note 28.

31. "Guangzhou: 305 Infected with Atypical Pneumonia." *Renmin Wang* (*People's Net*, the online edition of *People's Daily*), February 11, 2003. Available at http://www.people.com.cn/GB/shehui/47/20030211/921420.html (Accessed on May 22, 2004).

32. John Pomfret, "China's Slow Reaction to Fast-Moving Illness." *Washington Post*, April 3, 2003, p. A18.

33. See note 32.
34. See note 28.
35. "Sars Crisis Brings Opportunity." *China Daily*, May 13, 2003.
36. "Analysis: China in Continued SARS Denial." *United Press International* Wire, April 8, 2003.
37. "An Informed Public Remains Key." *China Daily*, April 2, 2003.
38. "Guangdong Brings Atypical Pneumonia under Control." *Xinhua News Agency*, February 11, 2003.
39. See note 27.
40. See a series of stories on the February 20 issue of *Southern Weekend*, a popular news-weekly in Southern China: "Guangzhou: Five Days of Crisis." Available at http://www.nanfangdaily.com.cn/zm/20030220/cs/csfm/200302200863.asp (Accessed on May 21, 2004); "February 17: What Are They Worried About?" Available at http://www.nanfang-daily.com.cn/zm/20030220/cs/zt/200302200876.asp (Accessed on May 21, 2004).
41. "People Calm Down Once Told the Truth." *Southern Weekend*, February 20, 2003. Available at http://www.nanfangdaily.com.cn/zm/20030220/wh/bxcf/200302200906.asp (Accessed on May 21, 204).
42. See note 24.
43. Rong Jiaojiao and Xiong Lei, "Interview: International Editor of the Year Hu Shuli." *World Press Review Online*, July 30, 2003. Available at http://www.worldpress.org/Asia/1510.cfm (Retrieved on September 12, 2004).
44. John Pomfret, "Outbreak Gave China's Hu an Opening." *Washington Post*, May 13, 2003, p. A1; also David Wall, "SARS Set off Power Struggle in Beijing." *Japan Times*, May 19, 2003.
45. Liu Chang, "301 Military Hospital Rings the First Alarm for SARS in Beijing." *China Youth Daily*, June 5, 2003. Available at http://www.people.com.cn/GB/she-hui/47/20030606/1009738.html (Accessed on May 24, 2004).
46. Joseph Kahn with Elisabeth Rosenthal, "New Health Worry for China as SARS Hits the Hinterland ." *New York Times*, April 22, 2003, p. A1.
47. "Hong Kong Identifies Source of Hong Kong Atypical Pneumonia Cases." *Xinhua News Agency*, March 19, 2003.
48. John Pomfret and Peter S. Goodman, "Mysterious Illness Kills 2 in Beijing in Sign of Spread." *Washington Post*, March 22, 2003. p. A03.
49. See John Pomfret in note 44.
50. "Following Long Period of Suspicion, China Listed as SARS-Affected Area." *Xinhua News Agency*, March 28, 2003.
51. "Wen Jiabao Chairs State Council Exe Meeting, Discusses SARS, State Council Work." *Xinhua News Agency*, April 2, 2003.
52. "CCTV Program Provides SARS Prevention Information, MOH, CDC Web Address." *Financial Times Global News Wire*, April 2, 2003.
53. "WHO Team Travels to Southern China to Study the Origin of SARS." *Deutsche Presse-Agentur*, April 3, 2003.
54. "Chinese Government Figures Show SARS Outbreak in Southern Province May be Slowing Down." Associated Press Wire News, April 3, 2003; "Minister: Epidemic under Control." *China Daily*, April 3, 2003.
55. "Wu Yi Emphasizes Need to Build Emergency Mechanism for Epidemic Outbreaks." *Financial Times Global News Wire*, April 4, 2003.
56. "Chinese Premier Says SARS Epidemic under Control, Travel Safe." *BBC Monitoring International Reports*, April 7, 2003.
57. "SARS Outbreak Still 'Grave' in China, Premier Says." *Deutsche Presse-Agentur*, April 14, 2003.
58. Joe McDonald, "Chinese Leaders Express Worry about SARS, Canadian Team Breaks Illness' Genetic Code." *Associated Press*, April 14, 2003.
59. "China in Continued SARS Denial." *United Press International*, April 8, 2003; "WWP Report: Beijing Refutes Claims of 'Covering Up' SARS Situation." *Financial Times Global News Wire*, April 2, 2003; "Wen Wei Po: PRC Health Official Claims Guangdong Not 'Evading' SARS Questions." *Financial Times Global News Wire*, April 6, 2003.
60. Peter Harmsen, "Sings of Jitters in Beijing Over SARS." *Agence France Presse*, April 8, 2003.

61. Susan Jakes, "Beijing's SARS Attack." *Time Online*, April 8, 2003. Available at http://www.time.com/time/asia/news/daily/0,9754,441615,00.html (Accessed on May 19, 2004). Susan Jakes, "People Who Mattered: Jiang Yanyong." *Time Online*, December 29, 2003. Available at http://www.time.com/time/asia/printout/0,13675,501031229-565988,00.html (Accessed on May 19, 2004).

62. See a story run by the English version of Renmin Wang, the official Web site of *People's Daily*, titled "Feature: a Chinese Doctor's Extraordinary April in 2003," Available at http://english.peopledaily.com.cn/200306/13/eng20030613_118182.shtml (Accessed on May 28, 2004).

63. Leigh Dayton, "Lies, Damn Lies and Chinese Statistics on SARS Cases." *The Australian*, April 11, 2003, p. 11.

64. "Beijing Mayor Says SARS Under Control, Denies 60 Cases Detected in Army Hospital." *Financial Times Global News Wire*, April 14, 2003.

65. "Magazine Investigation Reveals 'Truth' Inside Beijing's SARS Wards." *Deutsche Presse Agentur*, April 14, 2003.

66. "China: Politburo Standing Committee Meets to Discuss SARS Control." *Financial Times Global News Wire*, April 17, 2003.

67. "Chinese Politburo Member Liu Qi Heads Beijing SARS Working Group." *BBC Worldwide Monitoring*, April 18, 2003.

68. Joe McDonald, "China Reports Spike in SARS Cases, Cancels One of Nation's Most Popular Holidays to Slow SARS Spread." *Associated Press*, April 20, 2003.

69. William Foreman, "China Fires Health Minister and Beijing Mayor, Cancels Massive Holiday after New Jump in SARS Deaths." *Associated Press*, April 20, 2003.

70. "China and SARS: China's Chernobyl?" *The Economist*, 367 (8321), April 26, 2003, 10.

71. "SARS Fallout Bodes Well for Winds of Change." *South China Morning Post*, April 21, 2003, p. 10.

72. James Skynge, "Admission on SARS Fractures Beijing's Wall of Secrecy: Rare Apology from Top Official Could Herald New Openness." *Financial Times* (London), April 22, 20003, p. 1.

73. See note 72.

74. Fong Tak-ho, "Leaders Get Tough with Local Officials; WHO Widens Its Mainland Travel Advisory as It Emerges 120 People Have Been Sacked." *South China Morning Post*, May 9, 2003, p. 1.

75. "China's Henan Punishes 891 Cadres for Incompetence in Fighting SARS." *Financial Times* Global News Wire, May 24, 2003.

76. "China Creates SARS Task Force, Special Fund." *Xinhua News Agency*, April 23, 2003.

77. "Wu Yi Says China to Build $421.7 Million Disease Control Network." *Xinhua News Agency*, April 25, 2003.

78. Eric Echholm, "Thousands Riot in Rural Chinese Town over SARS." *New York Times*, April 28, 2003.

79. Josephine Ma, "Farmers Barricade Roads Near the Capital; as SARS Panic Spreads; Villagers Have Set Up Checkpoints and Banned Any Visitors." *South China Morning Post*, May 1, 2003, p. 4.

80. Bill Savadove, "SARS-Wary Villagers Riot, Attack Officials." *South China Morning Post*, May 6, 2006, p. 3.

81. "SARS — Panic Grips Beijing as People Stock Up on Goods, Leave City." *AFX-Asia*, April 24, 2003.

82. "Chinese President in Tianjin Calls for 'People's War' against SARS." *Xinhua News Agency*, May 1, 2003.

83. Antoaneta Bezlova, "Health-China: Anti-Sars Drive No Less Than a People's War." *InterPress Service*, May 2, 2003.

84. "WHO Experts in China Praise 'Unique' SARS Surveillance System." *Financial Times Global News Wire*, May 13, 2003.

85. "AFP: Shanghai Quarantined Nearly 29,000 during SARS Fight." *Financial Times Global News Wire*, May 30, 2003.

86. "Chinese Capital Isolates 2,069 Suspected SARS Contacts." *Financial Times Global News Wire*, June 1, 2003.

87. Jason Leows, "Good News: China TV Reports the Bad News; Live Telecast Nationwide and Around the World of Beijing's Soaring Virus Toll Is an Important Step Towards Media 'Openness'." *The Straits Times* (Singapore), May 17, 2003.
88. "Substantial Headway Made in China's SARS Campaign: Gov't." *Asian Pulse*, May 26, 2003.
89. "WHO Lifts SARS Advisories against Chinese Capital." *Financial Times* Global News Wire, June 24, 2003.
90. Zhou Ruijin, "Putting 'Positive Propaganda as the Main Theme' in the Right Perspective." *Chinese Political Science Online*, July 10, 2003. Available at http://www.cp.org.cn/2233/ReadNews.asp?NewsID=1123&BigClassName=&BigClassID=24&SmallClassID=40&SmallClassName=&SpecialID=28 (Accessed on September 13, 2004).
91. Sun Zhengyi and Liu Tingting, "An Overview of Chinese Media: April of 2003." *Renmin Wang*, December 30, 2003. Available at http://www.people.com.cn/GB/14677/21963/2206 5/2271846.html (Retrieved on September 13, 2004).
92. "China: Official Says Former Health Minister Not Sacked for SARS Cover-up." *Financial Times Global News Wire*, May 30, 2003.
93. Chen Ke, "Being Accused of Finding Excuses for the Negligence of Zhang Wenkang: Gao Qiang Was Openly Criticized by the Chinese Media." *United Morning Post* (Singapore), June 11, 2003. Available at http://www.zaobao.com/special/pneumonia/pages2/pneumonia110603d.html (Accessed on September 13, 2004).
94. For example, Anthony Kuhn, "Chinese Learn True Scope of SARS from the Internet." May 5, 2003, *USC Annenberg Online Journalism Review*. Available at http://www.ojr.org/ojr/world_reports/1053657288.php. See also (Xiao, 2003a; 2003b). But see "Not Such a Threat After All." *Economist*, 367(83232), May 10, 2003, 26–27, a rebuttal of the above view. See also Sautedâe (2003).
95. "SMS Has Become the 'Fifth Medium?'" *Sina.com*, February 24, 2003. Available at http://tech.sina.com.cn/it/t/2003-02-24/1454167580.shtml (Accessed on May 30, 2004).
96. Huang Junying, "SMS Triggers the Economy of the Thumb: Secret of its Instantaneous Success." *Sina.com*, July 14, 2003. Available at http://tech.sina.com.cn/it/t/2003-07-14/1522209178.shtml (Accessed on May 30, 2004).
97. See note 28. See also Jiang Xun, "Perspective: A Periscope of SMS in China." *BBC Online* (in Chinese), June 16, 2003. Available at http://news.bbc.co.uk/hi/chinese/china_news/newsid_2993000/29935721.stm (Accessed on May 30, 2004).
98. Yu Xi and Zhang Jie, "Guangzhou: Five Days of Crisis." *Southern Weekend*, February 20, 2003. Available at http://www.nafangdaily.com.cn/zm/20030220/cs/csfm/200302200863.asp (Accessed on May 30, 2004).
99. See note 28.
100. See note 28.
101. See notes 28 and 98.
102. Henry Hoenig, "SARS Virus Attacks State Control of the News." *New Zealand Herald*, April 26, 2003.
103. Kuhn in note 94.
104. Robert J. Saiget, "China Gags SARS Talk on Internet Chatrooms." *Agence France Presse*, April 6, 2003; Christian M. Wade, "Analysis: China in Continued Denial." *United Press International*, April 8, 2003.
105. Tang Jianguang and Liu Liu, "China Builds a Net of Safety on the Internet." *News Weekly* (China), April 5, 2004. Available at http://my.cnd.org/modules/wfsection/print.php?articleid=6610 (Accessed on May 30, 2004).
106. See Kuhn in note 94.
107. See note 102.
108. See Kuhn in note 94.
109. Xiao Han, "Atypical Pneumonia: The Price of Silence." Posted on April 6, 2003. Available at http://caotong.vip.sina.com/csf/HS/cmdj.htm (Accessed on June 1, 2004).
110. Yu Minghui, "Obtaining Trust from the People: Reflections on This Atypical Pneumonia Epidemic." Originally posted on *People's Net* (*Renmin Wang*) on April 7, 2003. Available at http://www2.qglt.com.cn/wsrmlt/wyzs/2003/04/07/040702.html (Accessed on May 30, 2003).
111. Josephine Ma and Staff Reporters, "Party Leaders in Emergency Talks on SARS." *South China Morning Post*, April 18, 2003, p. 1. Josephine Ma and Staff Reporters, "Shanxi Medical School Sealed Off." *South China Morning Post*, May 2, 2003.

112. Josephine Ma and Staff Reporters, "Virus Spreads Panic among Beijing Students: The Education Ministry Remains Silent as Two Leading Universities Halt Classes after Lecturers Are Infected with SARS." *South China Morning Post*, April 17, 2003.
113. Meng Lingwei, "Broad Reflections on Atypical Pneumonia." Posted on June 11, 2003. Available at http://www.yypl.net/data/data5.jsp?db=sanjiao&id=view030609 (Accessed on May 30, 2003). Similar postings can be found at the same forum.
114. Benjamin Kang Lim, "Panicking Crowds Flee Chinese Capital." *New Zealand Herald*, April 24, 2003; See also Josephine Ma and Staff Reporters in note 112.
115. For example, "Magazine Investigation Reveals 'Truth' Inside Beijing's SARS Wards." *Deutsche Presse Agentur*, April 14, 2003; Hannah Beech, "Unmasking a Crisis: Time Investigates: As SARS Rages in China, Officials Seem More Intent on Saving Face than Saving Lives." *Time*, 161(16), April 21, 2003, 62–63.
116. "When SARS Collides with Chinese Media." *Nanfeng Chuang* (*South Wind Window*, a popular Chinese weekly published in Guangzhou), May 16, 2003. Available at http://www.mediaresearch.com.cn/user/yjzt.php?TxtID=555&&ClassID=32&&now_offset= (Accessed on May 30, 2004).
117. See Kuhn, note 94.
118. "Weekend: Opinion Survey on Atypical Pneumonia in Five Big Cities." Published on June 1, 2003, at Sina.com. Available at http://news.sina.com.cn/c/2003-06-01/19521123697.shtml (Accessed on May 31, 2004).
119. Zhang Yuhong, "Unprecedented Milestones: An Overview of Chinese Internet Events of 2003." December 14–16, 2003. Available at http://www.usc.edu.hk/wk_wzdetails.asp?id-2960 (Accessed on May 30, 2004).
120. "PRC Web sites Issue Joint Call for Battling SARS, Launch New Web site." *Financial Times Global News Wire*, April 27, 2003.
121. "Hangzhou Officials, Residents Give Support to SARS Quarantined." *Xinhua News Agency*, April 28, 2003. Also "Members Fought on the Frontlines of War Against SARS in Hangzhou." *Renmin Wang* (*People's Net*), May, 12, 2003. Available at http://news.sina.com.cn/o/2003-05-12/0155115216s.shtml.
122. For example, "Eight Web sites in Shanghai Join Hands for an Interactive 'May Fourth' across Time and Space." *China Netmedia*, May 13, 2003. Available at http://netmedia.academe.com.cn/115/2003-5-13/50012@803.htm "CCTV: Volunteers in Wuxi Fight SARS." Wuxi Spiritual Civilization Work Report, 29(107), May 7, 2003. Available at http://www.wxwmw.com/jb/107.htm.
123. See the speech by the Civil Affairs Minister, Li Xueju, at the award-giving ceremony. Available at http://www.crs.org.cn/crs/jianghua.htm. Also refer to the related report by *People's Daily* on July 11, 2003, titled "Ride the Same Boat and Build a Wall of Mass Determination: The Ministry of Civil Affairs Praise Civil Organizations in the Anti-SARS War." Available at http://www.crs.org.cn/crs/biaozhang.htm.
124. Eric Eckholm, "China Reports 70 Sailors Die in Submarine Accident in Yellow Sea." *New York Times*, May 2, 2003, p. A4.
125. "Casualties from Natural Disasters Are No Longer State Secrets." *Sina.com*, September 13, 2005. Available at http://news.sina.com.cn/c/2005-09-13/11306933367s.shtml.
126. This summary of the explosion is compiled from these news stories: "Inside the Jiangxi Elementary School Explosion: Students Were Asked to Manufacture Firecrackers While the Teachers Got Kick-backs." *Jiangxi Dushi Bao* (*Jiangxi Metropolitan Daily*), March 8, 2001. Available at http://www.hnby.com.cn/20010309/document/56430.htm (Accessed on June 1, 2004). "Witnessing the '3-6' Explosion at Wanzai." *Dahe Bao* (Big River Daily), March 10, 2001. Available at http://www.hnby.com.cn/20010309/document/56982.htm (Accessed on June 1, 2004). "Wanzai Fireworks Explosion Killed 41." *Nanfang Dushi Bao* (*Southern Metropolitan Daily*), March 6, 2001. Available at http://www.dajiyuan.com/gb/1/3/22/n61108.htm (Accessed on June 1, 2004). "Principal Organized Students in Self-dependent Money-Making: Another Disaster in the Township of Fireworks.'" *Xin Kuai Bao* (*New Express Daily*), March 7, 2001.
127. Calum MacLeod, "Dozens of Pupils Making Fireworks Killed in Explosion." *The Independent* (London), March 8, 2001, p. 11.
128. "Background Material." *Chengshi Zaobao* (*City Morning Post*), March 9, 2001. Available at http://www.hnby.com.cn/20010309/document/56430.htm (Accessed on June 1, 2004).
129. See note 125.

130. John Leicester, "Families Bury Dead, Officials Urge Tougher Laws after China School Blast." *Associated Press*, March 9, 2001. "Delegates Concerned about Elementary School Blast." *China News Service*, March 8, 2001. Available at http"//www.people.com.cn/GB/shehui/44/2001/0308/412181.html (Accessed on May 25, 2004).

131. Christopher Bodeen, "Parents Say Children Forced to Make Fireworks before China School Blast." *Associated Press*, March 8, 2001.

132. Kirk Troy, "Village Upset about Government Stories." *United Press International*, March 9, 2001.

133. "Chinese Premier Says Mentally Unstable Man Triggered School Blast." Text from a *Ta Kung Po* (Hong Kong) "Special Dispatch." *BBC Worldwide Monitoring*, March 9, 2001.

134. "China: Police Say Mentally Ill Man Blew up Jiangxi School." *BBC Worldwide Monitoring*, March 9, 2001.

135. "Facts for Explosion in School: Reporter's Coverage Notes." *Xinhua News Agency*, March 10, 2001.

136. "Sub-streams in the Tears: A Look at the Status Quo of Chinese Media from the Fangli School Explosion." *Sixiang de jingjie luntan (Spiritual World Forum)*, March 16, 2001. Available at http://www.dajiyuan.com/gb/1/3/16/n58890.htm (Accessed on May 30, 2004).

137. Various first-hand accounts by reporters on their personal experiences can be found at "An Overview of the Struggle to Get at the Truth of the Jiangxi School Blast." *Dajiyun.com*, March 22, 2001. Available at http://www.dajiyuan.com/gb/1/3/22/n61108.htm (Accessed on May 29, 2004).

138. "Roundup: Villagers Dispute 'Mad Bomber' Cause of 60 School Deaths." *Deutsche Presse Agentur*, March 8, 2001. Note that this report claimed that 60 people died in the accident. The total number of deaths was later confirmed to be 42, with 41 killed on the site at the explosion and one dead at the hospital later.

139. For example, Lynne O'Donnell, "Fury over School Fire Cover-up." *The Australian*, March 12, 2001. Peter Hessler, "School Explosion Finds Cracks in China's Media Control, Premier Scrambles to Counter Internet." *Boston Globe*, March 11, 2001, p. A4.

140. Craig S. Smith, "Chinese Leader and Parents in Dispute over School Explosion." *New York Times*, March 9, 2001, p. A8.

141. "China Says School Children in Blast Were Not Making Fireworks." *AFX News Wire*, March 13, 2001.

142. Wu Zhisen, "Premier Zhu Finds out the Truth through Overseas Media." *Apple Daily* (Hong Kong), March 22, 2001. *Big Reference*, vol. 1146, March 21, 2001. Available at http://www.bignews.org/20010321.txt (Accessed on May 31, 2004).

143. Peter Hessler, "China Leader Hints of Error." *Boston Globe*, March 16, 2001, p. A12.

144. For the script of Zhu's televised speech during the press conference, see "China: Premier Deeply Saddened by School Blast, Calls for Self-criticism." *BBC Worldwide Monitoring*, March 15, 2001. See also "Blast School Used to Make Fireworks, China Admits." *Deutsche Presse Agentur*, March 15, 2001.

145. "Top Officials Axed in Wake of Fatal School Explosion." *The Straits Times* (Singapore), April 3, 2001, p. A4.

146. John Schauble, "China Divided Over Facts behind Firework Tragedy." *The Age* (Melbourne), March 15, 2001, p. 11.

147. See the story at: http://www.peopledaily.com.cn/GB/shehui/47/20010308/412100.html (Accessed on May 29, 2004).

148. "Jiangxi School Blast Survivors: Students Were Not Making Firecrackers at That Time." *People.com.cn*, March 10, 2001. Available at http://gb.hrichina.org/gate/gb/big5.hrichina.org/subsite/big5/article.adp?article_id=2420&subsubcategory_id=178 (Accessed on May 28, 2004).

149. Leslie Chang, "School Explosion Further Illustrates China's Effort to Stifle Information." *Wall Street Journal*, March 16, 2001.

150. See the comprehensive report at *Big Reference*, vol. 1141, March 16, 2001. Available at http://www.bignews.org/20010316.txt (Accessed on May 29, 2004).

151. See note 150.

152. "Jiangxi School Blast: Government Keeps Close Watch on Parents for Fear of Information Leaks." *Dajiyuan.com*, March 10, 2001. Available at http://www.epochtimes.com/gb/1/3/10/n56620.htm (Accessed on May 30, 2004).

153. "Big Explosion in Wanzai Fireworks Factory Shocked the Nation, Citizens from the 'Township of Explosion' Criticized the Incompetence of Jiangxi Officials." *Renminbao. com*, December 31, 2001. Available at http://www.renmenbao.com/rmb/articles/2001/12/31/18022p.html (Accessed on June 1, 2004).

154. "Mainland Net Pals Doubted That the Government Shirks Responsibility in the Jiangxi Blast." *Dajiyuan.com*, March 9, 2001. Available at http://www.dajiyuan.com/gb/1/3/11/n56883.htm (Accessed on May 28, 2004).

155. For a detailed list of popular comments and postings concerning the Jiangxi school blast, see the special collection of reports on *Dajiyuan.com*, Available at http://www.dajiyuan.com/gb/nf2221.htm (Accessed on May 26, 2004). See also *Big Reference*, volumes 1132 through 1139, published from March 7 to March 14, available at http://www.bignews.org/2001.html (Accessed on June 1, 2004).

156. See note 155.

157. "Jiangxi School Blast: Villagers Protest, Netizens Express Anger, and the Governor May Lose his Job." *Dajiyuan.com*, March 8, 2001.Avaiulable at: http://www.dajiyuan.com/gb/1/3/11/n56883.htm (Accessed on May 30, 2004).

158. "Sina.com Shuts Chatroom over Jiangxi School Blast Comments." *AFX*, March 10, 2001.

159. See the March 10 *Voice of America* (VOA) report, "China: Web Site Chatroom Shutdown." Available at http://www.voa.gov/chinese/archive/worldfocus/mar2001/sat/0310012china-internetchatcontr.htm (Accessed on June 2, 2004).

160. Ibid.

161. "Jiangxi Blast Triggered Waves of Net Anger." *Dajiyuan.com*, March 11, 2001. Available at http://www.dajiyuan.com/gb/1/3/11/n56883.htm (Accessed on May 29, 2004).

Chapter 7: Online Activism, Internet Protest and Social Movements in Chinese Cyberspace

1. The whole text of the directive can be accessed at *Renmin Wang*, http://www.people.com.cn/GB/guandian/183/7123/7132/20011220/631520.html (Accessed on June 2, 2004).

2. The above account of Sun's death is based on two investigative stories from the Chinese media. One is "A College Student in Guangzhou was Detained and Beaten to Death for Not Having Temporary Residency Permit." *Nanfang Wang (Southern Net)*, April 25, 2003, Available at http://news.21cn.com/social/shixiang/2003-04-25/1021755.html (Accessed on June 3, 2004). The other is "Behind the Truth of Sun Zhigang's Death." *Xinwen Zhoukan* (Newsweekly), June 12, 2003, Available at http://www.tfol.com/news/china/block/html/2003061200459.html (Accessed on June 2, 2004).

3. See the first article of the previous note.

4. "Follow-up of the Death of a College Student at a Detention Center Clinic: Family Turned Down 2,000 Yuan from the Police." *Qianlong News Net*, May 1, 2003. Available at http://news.21cn.com/social/shixiang/2003-05-01/1028645.html (Accessed on June 4, 2004).

5. "13 Suspects Caught in the Investigation of the Beating to Death of Sun Zhigang." *Nanfang Wang (Southern Net)*, May 13, 2003. Available at http://news.21cn.com/domestic/guoshi/2003-05-13/1039463.html (Accessed on June 3, 2004).

6. "Witnessing the Trial of the Case Involving Sun Zhigang's Death." *Xinhua News Agency*, June 9, 2003. Available at http://www.rongwp.com/sunzg/sun8.htm (Accessed on June 4, 2003). Also "18 Involved in Sun Zhigang's Death Were Sentenced." *Renmin Wang*, June 9, 2003. Available at http://www.people.com.cn/GB/shehui/44/20030609/1012813.html (Accessed on June 4, 2004).

7. "23 Face Party or Administrative Disciplinary Punishment in the Sun Zhigang Case." *Remnin Wang*, June 10, 2003. Available at http://www.people.com.cn/GB/shehui/212/10857/10858/20030610/1012976.html (Accessed on June 1, 2004).

8. Anne Hyland, "Desire for Legal Reform Builds." *Australian Financial Review*, June 10, 2003, p. 12.

9. "Tragedy Spurs End to 21-Year-Old Rule on Vagrants." *China Daily*, June 20, 2003. Available at http://www.chinadaily.com.cn/en/doc/2003-06/20/content_239912.htm (Accessed on May 28, 2004).

10. Available at http://www.people.com.cn/GB/shehui/8217/27299/index.html (Accessed on May 25, 2004).

11. See other examples of special coverage at two of the most popular portals in China, Sina. com, at http://news.sina.com.cn/z/takein/index.shtml (Accessed on June 5, 2004), and Tom.com, at http://news.tom.com/hot/shourong/ (Accessed on June 5, 2004).

12. See the online memorial site at: http://www.netor.com/m/box200304/m26789. asp?BoardID=26789 (Accessed on June 6, 2004).

13. Ouyang Bin, "The Internet Shakes China's Social Ecological System." Posted on June 7, 2004. Available at http://home.banzhu.com/f/fengyuwuzu/prog/showDetail.asp?id=1602 (Accessed on June 9, 2004).

14. "New Perspectives from the Internet Media: Dialogue with Charles Zhang of Sohu. com." *Yangzhou Hotline* Web site, December 31, 2003. Available at http://news2.yzren. com/1094/2003-12-31/20031231-4952-1094.htm (Accessed on June 3, 2004).

15. "Migrant Population Deserves Better." *Financial Times Global News Wire*, November 18, 2003.

16. See the special page section of Sina.com at: http://comment2.sina.com.cn/cgi-bin/com-ment/comment.cgi?channel=gn&newsid=1184589&style=0 (Accessed on May 15, 2004).

17. See note 13.

18. Huo Jianrong, "The Significance of People's Daily Publishing Pieces from *Renmin Wang*." *Renmin Wang*, April 30, 2004. Available at http://www.people.com.cn/GB/guan-dian/1036/2476320.html (Accessed on June 5, 2004).

19. "The Sun Zhigang Case: Who Is Playing Deaf?" *Renmin Wang*, May 4, 2003. Available at http://www.people.com.cn/GB/guandian/30/20030504/984197.html (Accessed on June 1, 2004).

20. Lin Chufang and Zhao Ling, "The Glory and Dream of Online Public Opinions." *Nanfang Zhoumo* (*Southern Weekend*), June 5, 2003. Available at http://www.nanfangdaily.com. cn/zm/20030605/xw/szxw/200306050755.asp (Accessed on May 26, 2004).

21. "A Victim of Corruption and Greed." *The Straits Times* (Singapore), June 29, 2003.

22. See for example, "Unforgettable 2003." *Cncotton.com*, December 22, 2003. Available at http://bbs.cncotton.com.cn/showarticle.jsp?id=119&code=5011 (Accessed on June 2, 2004). And another well-circulated posting that has appeared in most chat rooms is "Sun Zhigang Died for Me." *Boxun.com*, May 25, 2003. Available at http://www.peacehall.com/ news/gb/yuanqing/2003/05/200305250106.shtml (Accessed on June 2, 2004).

23. "Follow-up of College Student's Death at the Deportation Center: Family's Inquiry into Cause of Death Got Nowhere." *21cn.com* (*21ˢᵗ Century Net*), April 28, 2003. Available at http:// news.21cn.com/social/shixiang/2003-04-28/1024957.html (Accessed on June 4, 2004).

24. Mo Ke, "My Three Suggestions on the Sun Zhigang Case." *Boxun News Net*, May 9, 2003. Available at http://peacehall.com/news/gb/pubvp/2003/05/200305091534.shtml (Accessed on June 5, 2004). "Reflections on the Sun Zhigang Case: Problems with the System." *Tom. com*, May 27, 2003. Available at http://news.tom.com/Archive/1002/2003/5/27-60597.html (Accessed on June 3, 2004). Many other similar pages can be found at the special sections on Renmin Wang (http://www.people.com.cn/GB/shehui/8217/27299/index.html), Sina.com (http://news.sina.com.cn/z/takein/index.shtml), and other major portal and news sites. Also a series of opinion pieces on the legal violations of citizen rights can be found at HiChinese Forum (http://www.hichinese.net/forums/list.php?f=24&t=1066634762&a=2).

25. The open letter from Ai can be found at http://peacehall.com/news/gb/yuanq-ing/2003/05/200305021247.shtml (Accessed on June 3, 2004).

26. A copy of this widely-circulated letter can be found at http://bolin.netfirms.com/index8. htm (accessed on June 8, 2004).

27. See the protest letter at: http://www.asiademo.org/gb/2003/05/20030506a.htm (Accessed on June 3, 2004).

28. "Open Letter to the Supreme People's Procuratorate by 270 Chinese Citizens." Available at http://www.chinaaffairs.org/gb/detail.asp?id=32429 (Accessed on June 4, 2004).

29. "Three Doctorates Claim the Custody and Repatriation Measures Violate the Constitution in Their Petition." *China Youth Daily*, May 16, 2003. Available at http://shlaw.com. cn/ReadNews.asp?NewsID=77 (Accessed on June 8, 2004).

30. "Legal Scholars Petition Again for a Special Investigation Procedure Regarding the Custody and Repatriation System." *China Youth Daily*, May 28, 2003. Available at http://news. rednet.com.cn/Articles/2003/05/421468.HTM (Accessed on June 8, 2004).

31. See for example, Zhang Shuguang, "A Breakthrough in Promoting Democratic Constitutional Polity." June 5, 2003. Available at http://www.china-review.com/content_files/zhangshuguang-zxzp-27.htm20030609/zhangshuguang-zxzp-27.htm (Accessed on June 12, 2004). Also "One Hundred Years of Chinese Constitutional Politics: From Monarchy to People's Constitutional Polity." *China Youth Daily*, December 4, 2003. Available at http://news.xinhuanet.com/legal/2003-12/04/content_1212785.htm (Accessed on June 12, 2004).

32. "Experts Say Citizen Petitions Promoted the End of the Custody and Repatriation Measures." *China Youth Daily*, June 20, 2003. Available at http://news.xinhuanet.com/legal/2003-12/04/content_1212785.htm (Accessed on June 12, 2004).

33. Unless otherwise noted, quotes and information come from "About the United Nations" section of the official UN Web site at http://www.un.org/aboutun/index.html (Retrieved October 2005).

34. Jon Sawyer, "Bush Appeals to UN on His Terms: He Offers No Apology and No Compromise on Operation in Iraq." *St. Louis Post-Dispatch*, September 24, 2003.

35. "Assembly to Focus on UN, Security Council Reform." *The Irish Times*, September 21, 2004.

36. See Wipepedia.com, the free encyclopedia online, the "United Nations" entry at http://en.wikipedia.org/wiki/United_Nations. Retrieved in October 2005.

37. Warren Hoge, "UN Tackles Issue of Imbalance of Power." *New York Times*, November 28, 2004.

38. Warren Hoge, "Annan to Offer Plans for Change in U.N. Structure." *New York Times*, March 21, 2005.

39. "Japan, 3 Other Nations Issue Joint Bid for Permanent UNSC Seats." *Jiji Ticker Service*, March 22, 2002.

40. See, for example, "Japan Diplomats Meet on Security Council Reform Ahead of Campaign." *Kyodo News Service*, March 29, 2005; "Nakayama, 5 Others Named Special Envoy for U.N. Reform." *Jiji Press Ticker Service*, March 25, 2005.

41. Kent Chen, "Beijing Super Train Planned to Shanghai." *South China Morning Post*, April 4, 1994.

42. "China to Build More Big Projects in Next 5 Years." *Xinhua News Service*, March 5, 2001.

43. Martin Fackler, "China Will Extend Route of Futuristic Rail Technology, German Leader Says." *Associated Press*, January 1, 2003.

44. "China Rejects Germany's 'Maglev' for Beijing-Shanghai High-Speed Train." *Agence France Presse*, September 25, 2003.

45. "Japan to Accept Chinese Railway Study Mission." Kyodo News Service, April 25, 2003.

46. "Focus: Japanese Aid May Be Ace in the Hole in China's Train Deal." *Kyodo News Service*, March 18, 2003.

47. Hiroshi Hiyama, "Japan's Transport Minister to Visit China to Promote Bullet Train." *Agence France Presse*, July 8, 2003.

48. "China Leaning towards Japan's Bullet Train on Beijing-Shanghai Line." *Agence France Presse*, July 14, 2003.

49. "Rivals Still in Mix for China Railway." *The Nikkei Weekly*, August 4, 2003.

50. In addition to the www.1931-9-18.org petition page at http://www.1931-9-18.org/bbs/guest_sign.asp, see also "Welcome to Sign the Petition Against Adopting Japanese Bulletin Train Technologies" on the LinuxForm.net (a forum for Chinese Linux users), available at http://www.linuxforum.net/forum/showflat.php?Cat=&Board=linuxnews&Number=429221&page=50&view=collapsed&sb=5&o=&fpart=1&vc=1; "Don't Ever Forget Our Hatred" on tjfootball.com (a Tijian-based soccer forum), available at http://www.tjfootball.com/bbs/topic.asp?topic_id=3667&forum_id=35&cat_id=9&CurPage=57; "Japan Waits for China's Courtship" on srzc.com (Shangrao Forum, a local online BBS in Zhejiang province), available at http://www.srzc.com/cgi-bin/printpage.cgi?forum=15&topic=461.

51. "Eighty Thousand Netizens Sign the Petition against Bullet Train." Available at major Chinese news portal sites, such as Sina.com (http://news.sina.com.cn/c/2003-07-31/18091452249.shtml), Sohu.com (http://news.sohu.com/62/47/news211694762.shtml), and Tom.com (http://news.tom.com/Archive/1002/2003/8/1-62062.html). (Retrieved in October 2005).

52. See related report at http://news.sohu.com/01/46/news212484601.shtml. (Retrieved in October 2005).

53. See the three previous notes.

54. Richard McGregor and Mariko Sanchanta, "Bullet Train Gets a Cool Reception in China Beijing-Shanghai Rail Link." *Financial Times* (London), August 7, 2003.
55. "The Shinkansen Puzzle." *Sohu.com*, August 14, 2003, available at http://news.sohu.com/69/36/news212123669.shtml. (Accessed in October 2005).
56. "Koizumi's Yasukuni Visits Affecting Railway Bid in China: Envoy." *Kyodo News Service*, March 16, 2004.
57. "China Signs Railway Cooperation Agreement with Germany." *Xinhua News Agency*, June 8, 2005.
58. Eric Ng, "French Energy Giant in Talks on China Ventures." *South China Morning Post*, June 20, 2005.
59. Mission statement from the official Web site of the Alliance for Preserving the Truth of the Sino-Japanese War, available at http://www.sjwar.org/htm/mission.html.
60. "Chinese American Initiated Online Petition against Japan's UN Security Council Permanent Seat Bid." *Sina.com*, March 22, 2005. Available at http://news.sina.com.cn/w/2005-03-22/06285425255s.shtml.
61. "Annan Eyes 'Representative' UNSC, Mentions Japan as Candidate." *Kyodo News Service*, March 21, 2005.
62. For example, "One Million Signatures across the Globe to Stop Japan from Becoming a Permanent Member on the UN Security Council." *Tom.com*, March 3, 2005, Available at http://news.tom.com/1002/20050303-1909549.html; and *Sina.com*, March 3, 2005, Available at http://news.sina.com.cn/w/2005-03-03/08255252423s.shtml. (Retrieved in October 2005).
63. "International Website Opposes UN Seat for Japan." *United Press International*, March 23, 2005.
64. For example, among the numerous portal sites, see multiple stories on the special topic section of Sohu.com at http://news.sohu.com/s2005/lianheguogaige.shtml; Sina.com at http://news.sina.com.cn/z/unnation/1.shtml; and Qianlong.com at http://china.qianlong.com/4352/2005/03/24/Zt42@2565021.htm.
65. For example, http://news.sina.com.cn/comment/index.shtml, http://news.sohu.com/comment/sign.html, http://www.sjwar.org/, http://news.sina.com.cn/comment/index.shtml, and http://news.qq.com/sign.htm. All retrieved in October 2005.
66. Joseph Kahn, "If 22 Million Chinese Prevail at U.N., Japan Won't." *New York Times*, April 1, 2005, p. A4.
67. "More Than Ten Million Online Oppose Japan's UN Campaign." *Xinhua News Agency*, March 29, 2005.
68. "41 Million Signatories against Japan's Permanent Seat at the Security Council Have Been Submitted to the United Nations." *163.com*, July 2, 2005. Available at http://news.163.com/05/0702/02/1NKE7HDH0001121S.html (Retrieved August 2005).
69. The full letter can be found at http://historicaljustice.org/HJN/pressreleases/2UN_052005.pdf. (Retrieved in October 2005).
70. "Stop Distorting History's Lessons." *China Daily*, March 19, 2005.
71. "Japanese Envoy to South Korea Says Disputed Islets 'Japan's Territory'." *Yonhap News Agency*, February 23, 2005.
72. "South Koreans Join Petition against Japan's UN Security Council Bid." *Yonhap News Agency*, March 24, 2005.
73. "Worldwide Data Distribution" (from data collected by the Global Alliance for Preserving the History of WW II in Asia) available at http://historicaljustice.org/HJN/notice/Signature-Worldwide-Dist(chart).htm; (Retrieved in September 2005).
74. See note 73.
75. For a more comprehensive list, see "Chronology of Japan-China Relations in Recent Weeks." *Kyodo News Service*, April 16, 2005.
76. Mark Magnier, "Letting Passions Burn May Backfire on China." *Los Angeles Times*, April 25, 2005; "China Orders Halt to Anti-Japanese Protests." *The Strait Times* (Singapore), April 5, 2005.
77. "Beijing Sees Biggest Protest since 1989." *South China Morning Post*, April 10, 2005.

78. This text can be found at multiple Web sites. For example, http://bbs.sjtu.edu.cn/file/Food/1113453157199051.doc; http://www.ruishi.info/forum/simple/index.php?t24441.html; http://chinaaffairs.org/gb/detail.asp?id=52952; http://www.veryzone.org/forum/index.php?showtopic=4990; http://www5.uuzone.com/club/12205/forum/205822.htm; http://www.donews.net/thjsword/archive/2005/04/15/336855.aspx. (All retrieved in October 2005).

79. See a posting of pictures and narratives of this event by a participant at http://www.blue2river.net/article.asp?type=qstd&id=1131 (Retrieved in October 2005).

80. For example, The Internet Merchants Community Web site at: http://www.51kk7.cn/BBS_XP/showArticle.aspx?ArticleID=61074; Big Reference News Web site at http://www.bignews.org/20050415.txt (retrieved in October 2005); Chinese Democratic Justice Party Web site at http://www.cdjp.org/gb/article.php/3187 (Accessed in October 2005). See also, "Jim Yardley, "Getting Around Beijing's Censors: How E-mail and Text Messaging Drove Anti-Japanese Protests." New York Times, April 26, 2005.

81. See, for example, stories about a protest in Shenzhen on April 3, 2005 at http://19190.com/reply.php?id=7149340&list=; (Retrieved in October 2005).

82. Jim Yardley, "A Hundred Cellphones Bloom, and Chinese Take to the Streets." New York Times, April 25, 2005.

83. "Textbook with Amendments on Colonization, Nanjing Massacre Approved." Kyodo News Service, April 5, 2005; "China Summons Japanese Ambassador over History Textbook Issue." Xinhua News Agency, April 5, 2005.

84. "Japan Starts Granting Drilling Rights in East China Sea." Xinhua News Agency, April 13, 2005; Mari Yamaguchi, "Japan Will Allow Test-drilling of East China Sea Gas Exploration." Associated Press, April 13, 2005.

85. "Propaganda Toned Down to Cool Anti-Japanese Sentiment; Censors Step In to Prevent the Media Whipping Up Trouble over Tokyo's Security Council Bid." South China Morning Post, April 6, 2005.

86. "Shanghai Resident Tang Ye Is Arrested for Spreading False Information and Inciting the April 16 Shanghai Protest." Sohu.com, April 27, 2005. Available at http://sh.sohu.com/20050427/n225361083.shtml (Accessed in October 2005).

87. A Google search turns up hundreds of Web sites with postings and messages on this topic. See, for example, Tianyuclub.com (http://www.tianyaclub.com/new/techforum/Content.asp?idWriter=0&Key=0&idItem=41&idArticle=601697), a personal blog site (http://zgd101.blogdriver.com/zgd101/652653.html), a popular BBS site (http://bbs.i7766.com/topicdisplay_safe.asp?TopicID=1923&Page=1&BoardID=-4), and at blogchina.com (http://www.bokee.com/new/display/71261.html). (All accessed in October 2005).

88. http://www.totoolaw.com/forum/printpage.asp?BoardID=102&ID=22067 (Accessed in October 2005).

89. "China Gears Up for Large-Scale Anti-Japanese Protests This Weekend." Xinhua Financial Network News, April 15, 2005.

90. Howard W. French and Joseph Kahn, "Thousands Rally in Shanghai, Attacking Japanese Consulate." New York Times, April 16, 2005.

91. Chua Chin Hon, "Media Drive to Douse Anti-Japan Passions in China; Message on State TV, Paper, Internet: Stay Calm, Rational and Don't Break Law." The Straits Times (Singapore), April 21, 2005.

92. Chua Chin Hon, "China Issues Warnings against Fresh Protests; Former Diplomats Also Sent on Tour to Explain Bilateral Ties to Students." The Straits Times (Singapore), April 22, 2005.

93. "China Says Net-Organized Anti-Japan Demonstrations Illegal." Kyodo News Service, April 21, 2005; "Security Tight in China to Head off Anti-Japan Protests." Kyodo News Service, May 1, 2005.

94. "Police in Nanjing Attempt to Scuttle Planned Anti-Japan Protest." Kyodo News Service, April 28, 2005; Robert Marquand, "Beijing Keeps Lid on Anti-Japan Sentiment." Christian Science Monitor, May 4, 2005.

95. Jim Yardley, "Chinese Police Head Off Anti-Japan Protests." New York Times, May 5, 2005.

96. Wang Xiangwei, "Escalating Outcry Poses Threat to Japanese Trade, Investments." South China Morning Post, April 4, 2005.

97. "China Now Japan's No. 1 Trade Partner." United Press International, January 26, 2005.

98. "Koizumi Expresses 'Heartfelt Apology.'" China Daily, April 23, 2005.

99. Antony Faiola, "Japan Honors War Dead and Opens Neighbors' Wounds." *Washington Posts*, April 23, 2005.

100. Audra Ang, "China Rebuffs Demand for Apology after Anti-Japanese Violence." *Associated Press*, April 18, 2005.

101. Chisaki, "China Cancels Meeting between Top Envoy and Japanese Prime Minister." *The Associated Press*, May 23, 2005.

102. "China Says G-4 Resolution on Security Council Reform 'Detrimental' to UN Reform Process." *Xinhua News Agency*, May 17, 2005.

103. "China Strongly Opposes G-4's Revised UN Reform Plan." *Kyodo News Service*, June 9, 2005; "US Task Force Fails to Agree on Security Council Expansion." *Kyodo News Service*, June 15, 2005.

104. Melinda Liu and Christian Caryl, "Asia: Furies Unleashed." *Newsweek* (Atlantic Edition), April 25, 2005, p. 22.

105. See its Web site at http://www.1931-9-18.org/.

106. Anthony Faiola, "Anti-Japanese Hostilities Move to the Internet: Chinese and South Korean Hackers Blamed for Digital Barrage Designed to Cripple Web Sites." *Washington Post*, May 10, 2005.

107. Paul Mooney, "Internet Fans Flames of Chinese Nationalism: Beijing Faces Dilemmas as Anti-Japanese Campaign in Cyberspace Hits the Streets." *YaleGlobal*, April 4, 2005. Available at http://yaleglobal.yale.edu/display.article?id=5516 (accessed in October 2005).

Bibliography (English)

Abramovitz, Moses (1986). Catching up, forging ahead, and falling behind. *Journal of Economic History* XLVI (2), 385–406.

Acock, Alan; Clarke, Horad D.; and Stewart, Marianne C. (1985). A new model for old measures: a covariance structure analysis of political efficacy. *The Journal of Politics* 47(4), 1062–1084.

Aczel, Tamas (1978). Intellectual aspect, in Kiraly, Bela K. and Jonas, Paul, Eds, *The Hungarian Revolution of 1956 in Retrospect*. East European Quarterly, Boulder, CO, pp. 25–32.

Afele, John Senyo C. (2003). *Digital Bridges: Developing Countries in the Knowledge Economy*. Idea Group, Hershey, PA.

Alexander, Arthur J. (1990). *Comparative Innovation in Japan and in the United States*. RAND Center for US-Japan Relations, Santa Monica, CA.

Alexander, Jeffrey C. (1997). The paradoxes of civil society. *International Sociology* 12(2), 115–33.

Alexander, Jeffrey C. (1998). Introduction — civil society I, II, III: Constructing an empirical concept from normative controversies and historical transformations, in Alexander, Jeffrey, Ed., *Real Civil Societies: Dilemmas of Institutionalization*. SAGE, Thousand Oaks, CA: pp. 1–19.

Allison, Juliann Emmons (Ed.) (2002). *Technology, Development, and Democracy: International Conflict and Cooperation in the Information Age*. State University of New York Press, Albany, NY.

Almond, Gabriel A. and Verba, Sidney (1989). *The Civic Culture: Political Attitudes and Democracy in Five Nations*. SAGE Thousand Oaks, CA. First published in 1963 by Princeton University Press.

Alvarez, Sonia E., Dagnino Evelina, and Escobar, Arturo (Eds.) (1998). *Cultures of Politics, Politics of Cultures: Re-visioning Latin American Social Movements*. Westview Press, Boulder, CO.

An Pyong-uk (1988). The growth of popular consciousness and the popular movement in the nineteenth century. *Korea Journal* 28(4), pp. 4–19.

Anderson, Benedict O'G (1991). *Imagined Communities: Reflections on the Origin and Spread of Nationalism, Rev. Extended Edition*. Verso, New York.

Anderson, Benedict O'G (1998). *The Spectre of Comparisons: Nationalism, Southeast Asia and the World*. Verso, London.

Appadurai, Arjun (1996). *Modernity at Large: Cultural Dimensions of Globalization*. University of Minnesota Press, Minneapolis, MN.

Aristotle (1996). *The Politics and the Constitution of Athens*. Everson, Stephen, Ed. Cambridge University Press, London.

Arquilla, John and Ronfeldt, David (Eds.) (1997). *In Athena's Camp: Preparing for Conflict in the Information Age*. RAND, Santa Monica, CA.

Asen, Robert (2000). Seeking the 'counter' in counterpublics. *Communication Theory* 10(4), 424–446.

Asen, Robert (2003). The multiple Mr. Dewey: multiple publics and permeable borders in John Dewey's theory of the public sphere. *Argumentation and Advocacy*, 39(3), 174–188.

Asen, Robert and Brouwer, Daniel C. (2003). Introduction: John Dewey and the public sphere. *Argumentation and Advocacy* 39(3), 157–160.

Ash, Timothy Garton (1989). *The Uses of Adversity: Essays on the Fate of Central Europe*. Random House, New York.

Avineri, Shlomo (1975). *The Social and Political Thought of Karl Marx*. Cambridge University Press, Cambridge, U.K..

Baber, Zaheer (2002a). The Internet and social change: key themes and issues. *Asian Journal of Social Science* 30(2), 195–198.

Baber, Zaheer (2002b). Engendering or endangering democracy? The Internet, civil society and the public sphere. *Asian Journal of Social Science* 39(2), 287–303.

Baddeley, Simon (1997). Governmentality, in Loader, Brian D., Ed., *The Governance of Cyberspace: Politics, Technology and Global Restructuring*. Routledge, New York, pp. 64–96.

Baer, Aalter S. (1997). Will the global information infrastructure need transnational (or any) governance? in Kahin, Brian, and Wilson, Ernest J., III, Eds., *National Information Infrastructure Initiatives: Vision and Policy Design*. The MIT Press, Cambridge, MA, pp. 532–552.

Bakardjieva, Maria (2003). Virtual togetherness: An everyday-life perspective. *Media, Culture & Society* 25(3), 291–313.

Baker, Keith Michael (1992). Defining the public sphere in eighteenth-century France: Variations on a theme by Habermas, in Calhoun, Craig, Ed., *Habermas and the Public Sphere*, The MIT Press, Cambridge, MA, pp. 181–211.

Balch, George S. (1974). Multiple indicators in survey research: The concept 'sense of political efficacy.' *Political Methodology* 1(2), 1–43.

Ball-Rokeach, Sandra J. and Reardon, Katherine (1988). Monologue, dialogue, and telelogue: Comparing an emergent form of communication with traditional forms, in Hawkins, Robert P.; Wiemann, John M.; and Pingree Suzanne, Eds., *Advancing Communication Science: Merging Mass and Interpersonal Processes*. SAGE, Thousand Oaks, CA, pp. 135–161.

Bandura. Albert (1977). Self-efficacy: Toward a unifying theory of behavioral change. *Psychological Review* 84 (2), 191-215.

Bandura, Albert (1997). *Self-efficacy: The Exercise of Control*. Freeman, New York.

Banfield, Edward (1958). *The Moral Basis of a Backward Society*. Free Press, New York.

Barber, Ben (1984). *Strong Democracy: Participatory Politics for a New Age*. University of California Press, Berkeley, CA.

Barber, Benjamin (1998). *A Place for Us: How to Make Society Civil and Democracy Strong*. Hill and Wang, New York.

Barro, Robert J. and Sala-i-Martin, Xavier (1995). *Economic Growth*. McGraw-Hill, New York.

Barth, Richard C. and Smith, Clint N. (1997). International regulation of encription: technology will drive policy, in Kahin; Brian and Nesson; Charles; Eds., *Borders in Cyberspace: Information Policy and the Global Information Infrastructure*. The MIT Press, Cambridge, MA, pp. 283–299.

Baum, Richard and Shvchenko, Alexei (1999). The 'state of the state', in Goldman, Merle, and MacFarquhar, Roderick, Eds., *The Paradox of China's Post-Mao Reforms*. Harvard University Press, Cambridge, MA, pp. 333–360.

Baym, Nancy K. (1997). Interpreting soap operas and creating community: inside an electronic fan culture, in Kiesler, Sara, Ed., *Culture of the Internet*. Erbaum, Mahwah, NJ, pp. 103–120.

Beem, Christopher. (1999). *The Necessity of Politics: Reclaiming American Public Life*. University of Chicago Press, Chicago, IL.

Bell, Daniel (1973). *The Coming of Post-Industrial Society: A Venture in Social Forecasting*. Basic Books, New York.

Bellah, Robert N.; Madsen, Richard;, Sullivan, William M.; Swidler, Ann; and Tipton Steven M. (1991). *The Good Society*. Knopf, New York.

Benhabib, Seyla (1984). Obligation, contract and exchange: on the significance of Hegel's abstract right, in Pelczynski, Z.A., Ed., *The State and Civil Society: Studies in Hegel's Political Philosophy*. Cambridge University Press. New York. pp. 150–177.

Benhabib, Seyla (1996). Toward a deliberative model of democratic legitimacy, in Benhabib, Seyla, Ed., *Democracy and Difference: Contesting the Boundaries of the Political*. Princeton University Press, Princeton, NJ, pp. 67–94.

Benkert, Gerald Francis (1942). *The Thomistic Conception of an International Society*. The Catholic University of America Philosophical Studies, Vol. 70. The Catholic University of America Press, Washington, DC.

Bergère, Marie-Claire (1989). *The Golden Age of the Chinese Bourgeoisie, 1917–1937*. Cambridge University Press, Cambridge, U.K.

Bergère, Marie-Claire (1997). Civil society and urban change in Republican China. *China Quarterly* 150, 309–328.

Berners-Lee, Tim (1999). *Weaving the Web: The Original Design and Ultimate Destiny of the World Wide Web by Its Inventor*. With Mark Fischetti. Harper San Francisco, San Francisco, CA.

Bernhard, Michael H. (1993). *The Origins of Democratization in Poland: Workers, Intellectuals, and Oppositional Politics, 1976–1980*. Columbia University Press, New York.

Bianchi, Robert (1989). *Unruly Corporatism: Associational Life in Twentieth Century Egypt*. Oxford University Press, Oxford.

Blumler, Jay G. (1992). *Television and the Public Interest: Vulnerable Values in Western European Broadcasting*. SAGE, Thousand Oaks, CA.

Boczkowski, Pablo J. (1999). Mutual shaping of users and technologies in a national virtual community. *Journal of Communication* 49(2), 86–108.

Boggs, Carl (2001). *The End of Politics: Corporate Power and the Decline of the Public Sphere*. Guildford Press, New York.

Bolter, Jay David and Grusin, Richard (1999). *Remediation: Understanding New Media*. The MIT Press, Cambridge, MA.

Bonnin, Michel and Chevrier, Yves (1991). The intellectual and the state: social dynamics of intellectual autonomy during the post-Mao era. *China Quarterly* 127, 569–593.

Bradley, A.C. (1991). Aristotle's conception of the state, in Keyt, David and Miller, Fred D., Jr., Eds., *A Companion to Aristotle's Politics*. Blackwell, Cambridge, MA, pp. 13–56.

Brady, Anne-Marie (2002). Regimenting the public mind: the modernization of propaganda in the PRC. *International Journal* 57(4), 563–578.

Brandts, Kees, Hermes, Joke, and van Zoonen, Liesbet (Eds.) (1998). *The Media in Question: Popular Cultures and Public Interests*. SAGE, Thousand Oaks, CA.

Breckman, Warren (1999). *Marx, the Young Hegelians, and the Origins of Radical Social Theory: Dethroning the Self*. Cambridge University Press, New York.

Brod, Harry (1992). *Hegel's Philosophy of Politics: Idealism, Identity, and Modernity*. Westview, Boulder, CO.

Brook, Timothy (1993). *Praying for Power: Buddhism and the Formation of Gentry Society in China*. M.E. Sharpe, Armonk, NY.

Brook, Timothy (1997). Auto-organizations in Chinese society, in Brook, Timothy and Frolic, B. Michael, Eds., *Civil Society in China*. M.E. Sharpe, Armonk, NY, pp. 19–45.

Brook, Timothy and Frolic, B. Michael (Eds.) (1997). *Civil Society in China*. M.E. Sharpe, Armonk, NY.

Bryant, Christopher G.A. (1995). Civic nation, civil society, civil religion, in Hall, John A., (Ed.), *Civil Society: Theory, History, Comparison*. Polity, Cambridge, MA. pp. 136–157.

Burk, Dan L. (1997). The market for digital piracy, in Kahin, Brian and Nesson, Charles, Eds., *Borders in Cyberspace: Information Policy and the Global Information Infrastructure*. The MIT Press, Cambridge, MA, pp. 205–234.

Cahoone, Lawrence E. (2002). *Civil Society: The Conservative Meaning of Liberal Politics*. Blackwell, Malden, MA.

Calhoun, Craig (1992). Introduction: Habermas and the public sphere, in Calhoun, Craig, Ed., *Habermas and the Public Sphere*. The MIT Press, Cambridge, MA, pp. 1–48.

Calhoun, Craig (1994). *Neither Gods nor Emperors: Students and the Struggle for Democracy in China*. University of California Press, Berkeley, CA.

Calhoun, Craig (1995). *Critical Social Theory: Culture, History, and the Challenge of Difference*. Blackwell, Cambridge, MA.

Callahan, William A. (2002). Diaspora, Cosmopolitanism and Nationalism: Overseas Chinese and Neo-Nationalism in China and Thailand. Working Paper Series (No. 35), The Southeast Asia Research Center (SEARC) of the City University of Hong Kong. Available online at: www.cityu.edu.hk/searc/WP35_02_Callahan.pdf (Accessed March 1, 2004).

Campbell, Angus; Gurin, Gerald; and Miller, Warren (1954). *The Voter Decides*. Row, Peterson, Evanston, IL.

Campbell, Donald T. (1988a). 'Degrees of freedom' and the case study, in Campbell, Donald T., *Methodology and Epistemology for Social Science: Selected Papers*. Overman, E. Samuel, Ed., University of Chicago Press, Chicago, pp. 377–388. Originally published in 1975.

Campbell, Donald T. (1988b). Qualitative knowing in action research, in Campbell, Donald T., *Methodology and Epistemology for Social Science: Selected Papers*, (Overman, E. Samuel, Ed.). University of Chicago Press. Chicago, pp. 360–376. Originally published in 1978.

Campbell, Donald T. and Stanley, Julian C. (1963). Experimental and quasi-experimental designs for research on teaching, in Gage, N.L., Ed., *Handbook of Research on Teaching*. Rand McNally, Chicago, pp. 171–246.

Caplan, Scott E. (2001). Challenging the mass-interpersonal communication dichotomy: are we witnessing the emergence of an entirely new communication system? *Electronic Journal of Communication* 11(1). Available at: http://www.cios.org/getfile/Caplan_v11n101 (Accessed on June 20, 2004).

Cardoso, Fernado Henrique (2001). *Charting a New Course: The Politics of Globalization and Social Transformation*. Edited and Introduced by Mauricio A. Font. Rowman & Littlefield, New York.

CASS (Chinese Academy of Social Sciences) Research Center for Social Development (2003). *Surveying Internet Usage and Impact in Twelve Chinese Cities*. Directed by Guo Liang. Chinese Academy of Social Sciences, Beijing, China.

CASS (Chinese Academy of Social Sciences) Research Center for Social Development (2005). *2005 Survey Report on Internet Use and Impact in Five Chinese Cities*. Chinese Academy of Social Sciences, Beijing, China.

Castells, Manuel (1996). *The Rise of the Network Society*. Blackwell, Cambridge, MA.

Castells, Manuel (2001). *The Internet Galaxy: Reflections on the Internet, Business, and Society*. Oxford University Press, New York.

CDSR (Communicable Disease Surveillance and Response) (2003). Severe Acute Respiratory Syndrome (SARS). Geneva: World Health Organization. Available at http://www.who.int/csr/media/sars_wha.pdf (Accessed May 18, 2004).

Chadwick, Andrew (2003). Bringing E-democracy back in: why it matters for future research on E-governance. *Social Science Computer Review* 21(4), 443–455.

Chan, Alex (2002). From propaganda to hegemony: Jiaodian Fangtan and China's media policy. *Journal of Contemporary China* 11(30), 35–51.

Chan, Anita (1994). Revolution or corporatism: workers and trade unions in post-Mao China, in Goodman, David S.G. and Hooper, Beverley, Eds., *China Quiet Revolution: New Interactions Between State and Society*. St. Martin's Press, New York, pp. 162–93

Chan, Man Joseph (1993). Commercialization without independence: trends and tensions of media development in China, in Cheng, Joseph Yu-shek and Brosseau, Maurice, Eds., *China Review 1993*. Chinese University Press, Hong Kong, pp. 25.1–25.21.

Chang, Hao (1996). The intellectual heritage of the Confucian ideal of *Ching-shih*, in Tu, Wei-ming, Ed., *Confucian Traditions in East Asian Modernity*. Harvard University Press, Cambridge, MA, pp. 72–91.

Chang, Maria Hsia (2001). *Return of the Dragon: China's Wounded Nationalism*. Westview, Boulder, CO.

Chang, Tsan-Kuo and Tai, Zixue (2002). Freedom of the press in the eyes of the dragon: a matter of Chinese relativism and pragmatism, in Anokwa, Kwadwo; Lin, Carolyn A.; and Salwen, Michael B., Eds., *International Communication: Concepts and Cases*. Wadsworth. pp. 24–46

Chase, Michael S. and Mulvenon, James C. (2002). *You've Got Dissent! Chinese Dissident Use of the Internet and Beijing's Counter-Strategies*. RAND, National Security Research Division Center for Asia Pacific Policy, Santa Monica, CA.

Cheek, T. (1992). From priests to professionals: intellectuals and the state under the CCP, in Wasserstrom, Jeffrey N. and Perry, Elizabeth J., Eds., *Popular Protest and Political Culture in Modern China: Learning from 1989*. Westview, Boulder, CO, pp. 124–145.

Chen, Feng (2003). Between the state and labour: the conflict of Chinese trade unions' double identity in market reform. *China Quarterly* 176, 1006–1028.

Chen, Huailin and Chan, Joseph M. (1998). Bird-caged press freedom in China, in Cheng, Joseph Y.S., Ed., *China in the Post-Deng Era*. Chinese University Press, Hong Kong, pp. 645–667.

Chesneaux, Jean (1969). *The Chinese Labor Movement, 1919–1927*. Stanford University Press, Stanford, CA.

China Internet Network Information Center (CNNIC) (1997–2005). *Statistical Survey Report on the Internet Development in China* (No. 1–No. 16). Available at: http://www.cnnic.org.cn/index/0E/00/11/index.htm

Chvaja, Adam; Mokudai, Ikuichiro; and Efendic, Nedim (2001). E-commerce in China Challenge of the 21st Century. Available at: http://www.nhh.no/geo/chinese/2001/papers/e-commerce.pdf.

Cirtautas, Arista Maria (1996). *The Polish Solidarity Movement: Revolution, Democracy and Natural Rights*. Routledge, New York.

Coe, David T. and Helpman, Elhanan (1995). International R&D spillovers, *European Economic Review* 39 (5), 859–887.

Cohen, Jean L. (1982). *Class and Civil Society: The Limits of Marxian Critical Theory*. The University of Massachusetts Press, Amherst, MA.

Cohen, Jean L. and Arato, Andrew (1992). *Civil Society and Political Theory*. The MIT Press, Cambridge, MA.

Cohen, Jodi R. (1998). The significance of critical communication skills in a democracy, in Salvador, Michael and Sias, Patricia M., Eds., *The Public Voice in a Democracy at Risk*. Praeger, Westport, CT, pp. 41–56.

Cohen, Joshua and Rogers, Joel (1992). Secondary associations and democratic governance. *Politics and Society* 20(4), 393–472.

Cohen, Robin and Goulbourne, Harry, Eds, (1991). *Democracy and Socialism in Africa*. Westview, Boulder, CO.

Colas, Dominique (1997). *Civil Society and Fanaticism: Conjoined Histories*. Stanford University Press, Stanford, CA. Translated from the French by Amy Jacobs.

Coleman, James S. (1990). *Foundations of Social Theory*. Belknap, Cambridge, MA.

Compton, James (2000). Communicative politics and public journalism. *Journalism Studies*, 1(3), 449–467.

Congressional Executive Commission on China (2003). Information Control and Self-censorship in the PRC and the Spread of SARS. Available at: http://www.cecc.gov/pages/news/prcControl_SARS.php (Accessed May 20, 2004).

Converse, Philip E. (1972). Change in the American electorate, in Campbell, Angus and Converse, Phillip E., Eds., *The Human Meaning of Social Change*. Russell Sage, New York, pp. 267–337.

Cook, Colleen; Heath, Fred; and Thompson, Russel L. (2000). A meta-analysis of response rates in Web- or Internet-based surveys. *Educational and Psychological Measurement* 60(6), 821–836.

Cottrell, R.L.A.; Granieri, Charles; Fan, Lan; Xu, Rongsheng; and Karita, Yukio (1994). Networking with China. Paper contributed to the Conference on Computing in High Energy Physics, San Francisco, CA, April 21–27, 1994.

Couper, Mick P. (2000). Review: Web surveys: a review of issues and approaches. *Public Opinion Quarterly* 64(4), 464–494.

Couto, Richard A. (with Catherine S. Guthrie) (1999). *Making Democracy Work Better: Mediating Structures, Social Capital and the Democratic Prospect*. The University of North Carolina Press, Chapel Hill, NC.

Cullen, Bernard (1979). *Hegel's Social and Political Thought: An Introduction*. St. Martin's Press, New York.

Cunningham, Philip J. (2003). Constraints on China's coverage of SARS: for a variety of reasons, neither the government nor the press handled the medical crisis well. *Nieman Reports* 57(2), 50–53.

Curley, Melissa and Thomas, Nicholas (2004). Human security and public health in Southeast Asia: the SARS outbreak. *Australian Journal of International Affairs* 58(1), 17–32.

Curry, Jane Leftwich and Fajfer, Luba (Eds.) (1996). *Poland's Permanent Revolution: People vs. Elites, 1956 to the Present*. The American University Press, Washington, DC.

Dahlberg, Lincoln (2001a). The Internet and democratic discourse: exploring the prospects of online deliberative forums extending the public sphere. *Information, Communication & Society* 4(4), 615–633.

Dahlberg, Lincoln (2001b). Democracy via cyberspace: mapping the rhetoric and practices of three prominent camps. *New Media & Society*, 3(2), 157–177.

Dahlgren, Peter (1991). Introduction, in Dahlgren, Peter and Sparks Colin, Eds., *Communication and Citizenship: Journalism and the Public Sphere in the New Media Age*. Routlege, New York, pp. 1–24

Dahlgren, Peter (1995). *Television and the Public Sphere: Citizenship, Democracy and the Media*. SAGE, Thousand Oaks, CA.

Dahlgren, Peter (2001). The transformation of democracy?, in Axford, Barrie and Huggins, Richard, Eds., *New Media and Politics*. SAGE, Thousand Oaks, CA, pp. 64–89.

Dahlgren, Peter (2004). Foreword, in van de Donk, Wim; Loader, Brian D.; Nixon, Paul G.; and Rucht, Dieter, Eds., *Cyberprotest: New Media, Citizens and Social Movements*. Routledge, New York, pp. xi–xvi.

Dahlgren, Peter and Sparks, Colin (Eds.) (1991). *Communication and Citizenship: Journalism and the Public Sphere in the New Media Age*. Routledge, New York.

Dahlman, Carl J. and Aubert, Jean-Eric (2001). *China and the Knowledge Economy: Seizing the 21ˢᵗ Century*. The World Bank, Washington, DC.

Dai, Qing (1999). Guiding public opinion. *Media Studies Journal* 13(1), 78–81.

Dai, Xiudian (2003). ICTs in China's development strategy, in Hughes, Christopher R. and Wacker, Gudrun, Eds., *China and the Internet: Politics of the Digital Leap Forward*. Routledge Curzon, New York, pp. 8–29.

De Bary, Wm. Theodore (1991). *The Trouble with Confucianism*. Harvard University Press Cambridge, MA.

De Bary, Wm. Theodore (1998). *Asian Values and Human Rights: A Confucian Communitarian Perspective*. Harvard University Press, Cambridge, MA.

Deakin, Nicholas (2001). *In Search of Civil Society*. Palgrave, New York.

Deibert, Ronald J. (2002). Dark guests and Great Firewalls: The Internet and Chinese security policy. *Journal of Social Issues* 58(1), 143–159.

DeLisle, Jacques (2003). SARS, greater China, and the pathologies of globalization and transition. *Orbis* 47(4), 587–604.

Denning, Dorothy E. (1997). The future of cryptography, in Loader, Brian D., Ed., *The Governance of Cyberspace: Politics, Technology and Global Restructuring*. Routledge, New York, pp. 175–189.

Des Forges, Roger V. (1997). States, societies, and civil societies in Chinese history, in Brook, Timothy, and Frolic, B. Michael, Eds., *Civil Society in China*. M.E. Sharpe, Armonk, NY, pp. 68–95.

Dewey, John (1946). *The Public and Its Problems: An Essay in Political Inquiry*. Gateway Books, Chicago. Originally published in 1927.

Dewey, John (1966). *Democracy and Education: An Introduction to the Philosophy of Education*. Free Press, New York. Originally published in 1916.

Dewey, John (1981a). Creative democracy — the task before us, in Boydston, Jo Ann, Ed., *John Dewey: The Later Works, 1925–1953*. Vol. 14: 1929–1941. Southern Illinois University Press, Carbondale, IL, pp. 224–234. Originally published in 1939.

Dewey, John (1981b). The basic values and loyalties of democracy, in Boydston, Jo Ann, Ed., *John Dewey: The Later Works, 1925–1953*. Vol. 14: 1929–1941. Southern Illinois University Press, Carbondale, IL, pp. 275–277. Originally published in 1941.

Diamond, Larry (1994). Rethinking civil society: toward democratic consolidation. *Journal of Democracy* 5(3), 3–17.

Dickson, Bruce J. (2003). *Red Capitalists in China: The Party, Private Entrepreneurs, and Prospects for Political Change*. Cambridge University Press, London.

Ding, X.L. (1994). Institutional amphibiousness and the transition from communism: the case of China. *British Journal of Political Science* 24(3), 293–318.

Ding, Yijiang (2001). *Chinese Democracy after Tiananmen*. The University of British Columbia Press, Vancouver, BC.

Doctor, Sharon and Dutton, William H. (1998). The first amendment online: Santa Monica's public electronic network, in Tsagarousianous, Roza; Tambini, Damian; and Bryan, Cathy, Eds., *Cyberdemocracy: Technology, Cities and Civic Networks*. Routledge, New York, pp. 125–166.

Doctor, Sharon and Dutton, William H. (1999). The social shaping of the democracy network (DNet), in Hague, Barry N., and Loader, Brian D., Eds., *Digital Democracy: Discourse and Decision Making in the Information Age*. Routledge, New York, pp. 222–242.

Doheny-Farina, Stephen (1996). *The Wired Neighborhood*. Yale University Press, New Haven, CT.

Doleželová-Velingerová, Milena and Král, Oldřich (2001) *The Appropriation of Cultural Capital: China's May Fourth Project*. Harvard University Press, Cambridge, MA.

Donald, Stephanie Hemelryk; Keane, Michael; and Hong, Yin (Eds.) (2002). *Media in China: Consumption, Content and Crisis*. Routledge Curzon, New York.

Downing, John D.H. (with Ford, Tamara Villarreal; Gil, Genève; and Stein, Laura) (2001). *Radical Media: Rebellious Communication and Social Movements*. SAGE, Thousand Oaks, CA.

DTI (1998). Our Competitive Future: Building the Knowledge Driven Economy. The U.K. Department of Trade and Industry White Paper. Available at the U.K. DTI website: http://www.dti.gov.uk/comp/competitive/main.htm.

Dyson, R. W. (2001). *The Pilgrim City: Social and Political Ideas in the Writings of St Augustine of Hippo*. Boydell, Rochester, NY.

Edwards, Michael (2004). *Civil Society*. Polity, Malden, MA.

Ehrenberg, John (1999). *Civil Society: The Critical History of an Idea*. New York University Press, New York.

Eisenstadt, Abraham S. (1988). Introduction, in Eisenstadt, Abraham S., Ed., *Reconsidering Tocqueville's Democracy in America*. Rutgers University Press, New Brunswick, NJ, pp. 3–21.

Ekiert, Grzegorz (1996). *The State against Society: Political Crises and Their Aftermath in East Central Europe*. Princeton University Press, Princeton, NJ.

Eley, Geoff (1992). Nations, publics, and political cultures: placing Habermas in the nineteenth century, in Calhoun, Craig, Ed., *Habermas and the Public Sphere*. The MIT Press, Cambridge, MA, pp. 289–339.

Elshtain, Jean Bethke (1995). *Augustine and the Limits of Politics*. University of Notre Dame Press, Notre Dame, IN.

Ester, Peter and Vinken, Henk (2003). Debating civil society: on the fear for civic decline and hope for the Internet alternative. *International Sociology* 28(4), 659–680.

Etzioni, Amitai (1972). Minerva: an electronic town hall. *Policy Science* 3(4), 457–474.

Etzioni, Amitai (1993). Teledemocracy, the electronic town meeting. *Current* 350, 26–29.

European Institute for the Media (EIM) (2002). *Germany and the Digital World*. Düsseldorf, Germany. Available at: http://www.eim.de/DigWorld/Downloads/WIP_Report_Germany_2002.pdf (Retrieved July 2005).

Everard, Jerry (2000). *Virtual States: The Internet and the Boundaries of the Nation-State*. Routledge, New York.

Feenberg, Andrew and Bakardjieva, Maria (2004). Virtual community: no 'killer implication.' *New Media & Society* 6(1), 37–43.

Ferguson, Adam (1995). *An Essay on the History of Civil Society*. Fania Oz-Salzberger, Ed. Cambridge University Press, London. Initially published in 1767.

Ferguson, Sherry Devereaux (2000). *Researching the Public Opinion Environment: Theories and Methods*. SAGE, Thousand Oaks, CA.

Fernback, Jan (1999). There is a there there: notes toward a definition of cyberspace, in Jones, Steve, Ed., *Doing Internet Research: Critical Issues and Methods for Examining the Net*. SAGE, Thousand Oaks, CA. pp. 203–220.

Fewsmith, Joseph (1985). *Party, State, and Local Elites in Republican China: Merchant Organizations and Politics in Shanghai, 1890–1930*. University of Hawaii Press, Honolulu, HI.

Fewsmith, Joseph (2002). China's domestic agenda: social pressures and public opinion. *China Leadership Monitor* 6, 48–64..

Finley, Moses I. (1985). *Democracy Ancient and Modern*. rev. ed.. Rutgers University Press. New Brunswick, NJ.

Finnis, John (1998). *Aquinas: Moral, Political, and Legal Theory*. Oxford University Press, Oxford.

Firestone, William A. and Herriott, Robert E. (1986). Multisite qualitative policy research: some design and implementation issues, in Fetterman, David, Ed., *Ethnographic Evaluation: Ethnography in Theory, Practice and Politics*. SAGE, Beverly Hills, CA, pp. 63–88.

Fitzgibbons, Athol (1995). *Adam Smith's System of Liberty, Wealth, and Virtue*. Oxford University Press, New York.

Fogel, Joshua A. and Zarrow, Peter G. (Eds.) (1997). *Imagining the People: Chinese Intellectuals and the Concept of Citizenship, 1890–1920*. M.E. Sharpe, Armonk, NY.

Fornäs, Johan; Klein, Kajsa; Ladendorf, Martina; Sundén, Jenny; and Sveningsson, Malin (2002). Into digital borderlands, in Fornäs, Johan; Klein, Kajsa; Ladendorf, Martina; Sundén, Jenny; and Sveningsson, Malin, Eds. *Digital Borderlands: Cultural Studies of Identity and Interactivity on the Internet*. Peter Lang, New York, pp. 1–47.

Foster, William and Goodman Seymour E. (2000). *The Diffusion of the Internet in China*. International Security and Cooperation (CISAC) Report, Stanford University.

Franco, Paul (1999). *Hegel's Philosophy of Freedom*. Yale University Press, New Haven, CT.

Fraser, Nancy (1992). Rethinking the public sphere: a contribution to the critique of actually existing democracy, in Calhoun, Craig, Ed., *Habermas and the Public Sphere*. The MIT Press, Cambridge, MA, pp. 109–142.

Frissen, Paul (1997). The virtual state: postmodernisation, informatisation and public administration, in Loader, Brian D., Ed., *The Governance of Cyberspace: Politics, Technology and Global Restructuring*. Routledge, New York, pp. 111–125.

Frolic, Michael B. (1997). State-led civil society, in Brook, Timothy, and Frolic, B. Michael, Eds., *Civil Society in China*. M.E. Sharpe, Armonk, NY, pp. 46–67

Froomkin, A. Michael (1997). The Internet as a source of regulatory arbitrage, in Kahin, Brian and Nesson, Charles, Eds., *Borders in Cyberspace: Information Policy and the Global Information Infrastructure*. The MIT Press, Cambridge, MA, pp. 129–163.

Fukuyama, Francis (1995). *Trust: Social Virtues and the Creation of Prosperity*. Free Press, New York.

Fullinwider, Robert K. (Ed.) (1999). *Civil Society, Democracy, and Civic Renewal*. Rowman & Littlefield, New York.

Gamson, William A. and Wolfsfeld, Gadi (1993). Movements and media as interacting systems. *Annals of the American Academy of Political and Social Science* 526, pp. 114–127.

Garnham, Nicholas (1986). The media and the public sphere, in Golding, Peter; Murdock, Graham; and Schlesinger, Philip, Eds., *Communicating Politics: Mass Communications and the Political Process*. Holmes and Meier, New York, pp. 37–53.

Garnham, Nicholas (1990). *Capitalism and Communication: Global Culture and the Economics of Information*. SAGE, Newbury Park, CA.

Garver, John W. (1993). *Foreign Policy of the People's Republic of China*. Prentice Hall, Englewood Cliffs, NJ.

Gasster, Michael (1969). *Chinese Intellectuals and the Revolution of 1911: The Birth of Modern Chinese Radicalism*. University of Washington Press, Seattle, WA.

Gellner, Ernest (1994). *Conditions of Liberty: Civil Society and Its Rivals*. Hamish Hamilton, London.

Gellman, Robert (1997). Conflict and overlap in piracy regulation: national, international, and private, in Kahin, Brian and Nesson, Charles, Eds., *Borders in Cyberspace: Information Policy and the Global Information Infrastructure*. MIT Press, Cambridge, MA, pp. 255–282.

Gerschenkron, Alexander (1962). *Economic Backwardness in Historical Perspective: A Book of Essays*. Belknap, Cambridge, MA.

Giddens, Anthony (1994). *Beyond Left and Right: The Future of Radical Capitalism*. Stanford University Press, Stanford, CA.

Giddens, Anthony (2000). *The Third Way and Its Critics*. Blackwell, Malden, MA.

Giese, Karsten (2003). Internet growth and the digital divide: implications for spatial development, in Hughes, Christopher R. and Wacker, Gudrun, Eds., *China and the Internet: Politics of the Digital Leap Forward*. Routledge Curzon, New York, pp. 30–57.

Gilbert, Alan (1991). Political philosophy: Marx and radical democracy, in Carver, Terrell, Ed., *The Cambridge Companion to Marx*. Cambridge University Press, London, pp. 168–195.

Gill, Bates; Chang, Jennifer; and Palmer, Sarah (2002). China's HIV crisis. *Foreign Affairs* 81(2), 96–110.

Ginsberg, Benjamin (1986). *The Captive Public: How Mass Opinion Promotes State Power*. Basic Books, New York.

Gitlin, Todd (1980). *The Whole World is Watching: Mass Media in the Making & Unmaking of the New Left*. The University of California Press, Berkeley, CA.

Goetz, Judith and LeCompte, Margret D. (1984). *Ethnography and Qualitative Design in Educational Research*. Academic Press, New York.

Godwin, Mike (2003). *Cyber Rights: Defending Free Speech in the Digital Age*, rev., updated ed.,The MIT Press, Cambridge, MA.

Gold, Thomas (1990). The resurgence of civil society in China. *Journal of Democracy* 1(1), 18–31.

Gold, Thomas (1998). Bases for civil society in reform China, in Brødsgaard, Kjeld Erik and Strand, David, Eds., *Reconstructing Twentieth-Century China: State Control, Civil Society, and National Identity*. Clarendon Press, Oxford, pp. 161–188.

Goldring, John (1991). Netting the cybershark: consumer protection, cyberspace, the nation-state, and democracy, in Kahin, Brian and Nesson, Charles, Eds., *Borders in Cyberspace: Information Policy and the Global Information Infrastructure*. The MIT Press, Cambridge, MA, pp. 322–354.

Gomez, James (2002). Think center: the Internet and politics in the new economy. *Asian Journal of Social Science* 30(2), 304–318.

Gomm, Roger; Hammersley, Martyn; and Foster, Peter (Eds.) (2000). *Case Study Method: Key Issues, Key Texts.* SAGE, Thousand Oaks, CA.

Goodman, David and Hooper, Beverley (Eds.) (1996). *China's Quiet Revolution: New Interactions between State and Society.* St. Martins Press, New York.

Goodwyn, Lawrence (1991). *Breaking the Barrier: The Rise of Solidarity in Poland.* Oxford University Press, Oxford.

Graham, Stephen (2004). Beyond the 'dazzling light': from dreams of transcendence to the 'remediation' of urban life: a research manifesto. *New Media & Society*, 6(1), 16–25.

Green, Eileen and Adam, Alison (Eds.) (2001). *Virtual Gender: Technology, Consumption and Identity.* Routledge, New York.

Grossman, Gene and Helpman, Elhanan (1991). *Innovation and Growth in the Global Economy* The MIT Press, Cambridge, MA.

Grossman, Lawrence K. (1995). *The Electronic Republic.* Penguin, New York.

Gurak, Laura J. (1997). *Persuasion and Privacy in Cyberspace: The Online Protests over Lotus MarketPlace and the Clipper Chip.* Yale University Press, New Haven, CT.

Habermas, Jürgen (1989). *The Structural Transformation of the Public Sphere.* Polity, Cambridge, MA.

Habermas, Jürgen (1992). Further reflections on the public sphere, in Calhoun, Craig, Ed., *Habermas and the Public Sphere*, Burger, Thomas, Transl., The MIT Press, Cambridge, MA, pp. 421–461.

Hachigian, Nina (2001). China's cyber-strategy. *Foreign Affairs* 80(2), 118–133.

Hall, John A. (1995). In search of civil society, in Hall, John A., Ed., *Civil Society: Theory, History, Comparison.* Polity, Cambridge, MA, pp. 1–31.

Hall, John A. (1998). Genealogies of civility, in Hefner, Robert W., Ed., *Democratic Civility: The History and Cross-Cultural Possibility of a Modern Political Ideal.* Transaction Publishers, New Brunswick, NJ, pp. 53–77.

Hall, John A. (1999). Reflections on the making of civility in society, in Trentmann, Frank, Ed., *Paradoxes of Civil Society: New Perspectives on Modern German and British History.* Berghahn, New York, pp. 47–57.

Hamel, Jacques (with Dufour, Stéphane, and Fortin, Dominic) (1993). *Case Study Methods.* SAGE, Thousand Oaks, CA.

Hammersley, Martyn and Gomm, Roger (2000). Introduction, in Gomm, Roger: Hammersley, Martyn; and Foster, Peter, Eds., *Case Study Method: Key Issues, Key Texts.* SAGE, Thousand Oaks, CA, pp. 1–16.

Hanson, Jarice and Narula, Uma (1990). Introduction: technology in developing countries. In Hanson, Jarice, and Narula, Uma, Eds., *New Communication Technologies in Developing Countries.* Erlbaum, Hillsdale, NJ.

Hann, Chris (1996). Introduction: political society and civil anthropology. In Hann, Chris, and Dunn, Elizabeth, Eds., *Civil Society: Challenging Western Models.* Routledge, New York.

Hao, Xiaoming; Yu, Huang; and Kewen, Zhang (1998). Free market vs. political control in China: convenience or contradiction? *Media Development* 45(1), 35–38.

Haraway, Donna J. (1991). *Simians, Cyberorgs, and Women: The Reinvention of Nature.* Routledge, New York.

Hardimon, Michael O. (1994). *Hegel's Social Philosophy: The Project of Reconciliation.* Cambridge University Press, London.

He, Baogang (1994). Dual roles of semi-civil society in Chinese democracy. *Australian Journal of Political Science* 29(1), 154–71.

He, Baogang (1996). *The Democratization of China.* Routledge, New York.

He, Baogang (1997). *The Democratic Implications of Civil Society in China.* St. Martin's, New York.

Heerwegh, Dirk and Loosveldt, Geert (2002). An evaluation of the effect of response formats on data quality in web surveys. *Social Science Computer Review* 29(4), 471–484.

Hegel, G. W. F. (1962). *Hegel's Philosophy of Right.* Oxford University Press, Oxford. Translated with notes by T.M. Knox.

Hegel, G. W. F. (1991). *Elements of the Philosophy of Right.* Cambridge University Press, London. Edited by Allen W. Wood and translated by H.B. Nisbet.

Heith, Diane J. (2004). *Polling to Govern: Public Opinion and Presidential Leadership.* Stanford Law and Politics, Stanford, CA.

Herring, Susan C. (2004). Slouching toward the ordinary: current trends in computer-mediated communication. *New Media & Society* 6(1), 26–36.

Herriott, Robert E. and Firestone, William A. (1983). Multisite qualitative policy research: optimizing description and generalizability. *Educational Researcher* 12(2), 14–19.

Hershatter, Gail (1986). *The Workers of Tianjin, 1900–1949.* Stanford University Press, Stanford, CA.

Hirschman, Albert O. (1977). *The Passions and the Interests: Political Arguments for Capitalism before Its Triumph.* Princeton University Press, Princeton, NJ.

Hirschman, Albert O. (1984). Against parsimony: three easy ways of complicating some categories of economic discourse. *American Economic Association Papers and Proceedings* 74(2), 89–96.

Hirst, Paul (1993). Associative democracy, in Held, David, Ed., *Prospects for Democracy.* Stanford University Press, Stanford, CA, pp. 112–135.

Hirst, Paul (1994). *Associative Democracy: New Forms of Economic and Social Governance.* The University of Massachusetts Press, Amherst, MA.

Hobbs, Renee (1998). Building citizenship skills through media literacy education, in Salvador, Michael, and Sias, Patricia M., Eds., *The Public Voice in a Democracy at Risk.* Praeger, Westport, CT, pp. 57–76.

Hohendahl, Peter Uwe (1992). The public sphere: models and boundaries, in Calhoun, Craig, Ed., *Habermas and the Public Sphere.* The MIT Press, Cambridge, MA, pp. 99–108.

Hohendahl, Peter Uwe (1997). *From Statism to Pluralism: Democracy, Civil Society and Global Politics.* UCL Press, Bristol, PA.

Horrigan, John B. and Rainie, Lee (2001). Online Communities: Networks that Nurture Long-Distance Relationships and Local Ties. Pew Internet & American Life Project, Washington, DC. Available at http://www.pewtrusts.com/pdf/vf_pew_internet_community.pdf (Retrieved on September 9, 2004).

Howell, Jude and Pearce, Jenny (2001). *Civil Society and Development: A Critical Exploration.* Lynne Rienner, Boulder, CO.

Howland, Jacob (1993). *The Republic: The Odyssey of Philosophy.* Twayne, New York.

Hoynes, William (1994). *Public Television for Sale: Media, the Market, and the Public Sphere.* Westview, Boulder, CO.

Huang, Philip C.C. (1993). 'Public sphere'/'civil society' in China? The third realm between state and society. *Modern China* 19(2), 216–240.

Huang, Yanzhong (2004). The SARS epidemic and its aftermath in China: A political perspective, in Knobler, Stacey; Mahmoud, Adel; Lemon, Stanley; Mack, Alison; Sivitz, Laura; and Oberholtzer, Katherine, Eds. *Learning from SARS: Preparing for the Next Disease Outbreak.* The National Academies Press, Washington, DC, pp. 116–136.

Hughes, Christopher Rene (2000). Nationalism in Chinese cyberspace. *Cambridge Review of International Affairs* 13(2), 195–209.

Information Society and Trend Research Institute (ITTK) and Social Research Centre Inc. (TARKI Rt). (ISTRI-TARKI) (2002). *Mapping the Digital Future: Hungarian Society and the Internet.* Hungary: Infonia Foundation. Available at: (http://www.worldinternetproject.net/reports/WIP_2002_HU_report.pdf (Retrieved August 2005).

Inkeles, Alex (1950). *Public Opinion in Soviet Russia: A Study in Mass Persuasion.* Harvard University Press, Cambridge, MA.

Innis, Harold A. (1951). *The Bias of Communication.* University of Toronto Press, Toronto.

Inwood, Michael (1992). *A Hegel Dictionary.* Blackwell Publishers, Oxford.

James, Michael Rabinder (2004). *Deliberative Democracy and the Public Plurality.* University of Kansas Press, Lawrence, KS.

Jeffrey, Lawrence (2000). *China's Wired: Your Guide to the Internet in China.* Asia Law & Practice, Hong Kong.

Jeong, Kuk-Hwan and King, John Leslie (1997). Korea's national information infrastructure: vision and issues, in Kahin, Brian and Wilson, Ernest J., III, Eds., *National Information Infrastructure Initiatives: Vision and Policy Design.* The MIT Press, Cambridge, MA, pp. 112–49.

Jiang, Cecilia (2003). SMS in China. Available at: http://journalism.berkeley.edu/projects/chinadn/en/archives/SMS%20in%20China.doc (Accessed on May 30, 2004).

Johnson, David R. and Post, David G. (1997). The rise of law on the global network, in Kahin, Brian, and Nesson, Charles, Eds., *Borders in Cyberspace: Information Policy and the Global Information Infrastructure.* The MIT Press, Cambridge, MA, pp. 3–47.

Jones, Steven G. (Ed.) (1995). *Cybersociety: Computer-Mediated Communication and Community.* SAGE, Thousand Oaks, CA.

Jones, Steven G. (Ed.) (1998). *Cybersociety 2.0: Revisiting Computer-Mediated Communication and Community*. SAGE, Thousand Oaks, CA.

Jones, Steve (1999). Studying the Net: intricacies and issues, in Jones, Steve, Ed., *Doing Internet Research: Critical Issues and Methods for Examining the Net*. SAGE, Thousand Oaks, CA, pp. 1–28.

Jordan, Tim (1999). *Cyberpower: The Culture and Politics of Cyberspace and the Internet*. Routledge, New York.

Jordan, Tim and Taylor, Paul A. (2004). *Hacktivism and Cyberwars: Rebels with a Cause?* Routledge, New York.

Kahin, Brian (1997). The U.S. national information infrastructure initiative: the market, the web, and the virtual project, in Kahin, Brian and Wilson, Ernest J., III (Eds.), *National Information Infrastructure Initiatives: Vision and Policy Design*. The MIT Press, Cambridge, MA, pp. 150–189.

Kahin, Brian and Nesson, Charles (Eds.) (1997). *Borders in Cyberspace: Information Policy and the Global Information Infrastructure*. The MIT Press, Cambridge, MA.

Kahin, Brian and Wilson, Ernest J., III (Eds.) (1997). *National Information Infrastructure Initiatives: Vision and Policy Design*. The MIT Press, Cambridge, MA.

Kain, Philip J. (1993). *Marx and Modern Political Theory: From Hobbes to Contemporary Feminism*. Rowman & Littlefield, Lanham, MD.

Kalathil, Shanthi (2002). Community and communalism in the information age. *The Brown Journal of World Affairs*, 9(1), 347–354.

Kalathil, Shanthi and Boas Taylor C. (2001). The Internet and State Control in Authoritarian Regimes: China, Cuba, and the Counterrevolution. Working Paper 21, Carnegie Endowment for International Peace. Available at http://www.google.com/url?sa=U&start=2&q=http://www.ceip.org/files/pdf/21KalathilBoas.pdf&e=7413.

Kaplowitz, Michael D.; Hadlock, Timothy D.; and Levine, Ralph (2004). A comparison of Web and mail survey response rate. *Public Opinion Quarterly* 68(1), 94–101.

Katz, James E. and Rice, Ronald E. (2002). *Social Consequences of Internet Use: Access, Involvement, and Interaction*. The MIT Press, Cambridge, MA.

Keane, John (1988a). *Democracy and Civil Society on the Predicaments of European Socialism, the Prospects for Democracy, and the Problem of Controlling Social and Political Power*. Verso, London.

Keane, John (1988b). Introduction, in Keane, John, Ed., *Civil Society and the State: New European Perspectives*. Verso, London, pp. 1–31.

Keane, John (1998). *Civil Society: Old Images, New Visions*. Stanford University Press, Stanford, CA.

Keane, John (2000). Structural transformations of the public sphere, in Hacker, Kenneth L. and van Dijk, Jan, Eds., *Digital Democracy: Issues of Theory and Practice*. SAGE, Thousand Oaks, CA, pp. 70–89.

Kellogg, Tom (2002). Whitewashing criminal negligence: health officials seek to avoid responsibility for the spread of HIV/AIDS in rural Henan. *China Rights Forum* 3, 16–19.

Kessler, Lauren (1984). *The Dissident Press: Alternative Journalism in American History*. Sage Publications, Beverly Hills, CA.

Khilnani, Sunil (2001). The development of civil society, in Kaviraj, Sudipta and Khilnani, Sunil, Eds., *Civil Society: History and Possibilities*. Cambridge University Press, London, pp. 11–32.

Kidd, Dorothy (2003). Indymedia.org: a new communications commons, in van de Donk, Wim; Loader, Brian D.; Nixon, Paul G.; and Rucht, Dieter, Eds., *Cyberprotest: New Media, Citizens and Social Movements*. Routledge, New York, pp. 47–69.

Klosko, George (1986). *The Development of Plato's Political Theory*. Methuen, New York.

Kluver, Randy and Powers, John H. (Eds.) (1999). *Civic Discourse, Civil Society and Chinese Communities*. Ablex, Stamford, CT.

Kuhn, Philip A. (1980). *Rebellion and Its Enemies in Late Imperial China: Militarization and Social Structure*. Harvard University Press, Cambridge, MA.

Kuron, Jacek (1977). Reflection on a programme of action. *The Polish Review* XXII(3), 51–69.

Kwan, Man Bun (2001). *The Salt Merchants of Tianjin: State-Making and Civil Society in Late Imperial China*. University of Hawaii Press, Honolulu, HI.

Lacharite, Jason (2002). Electronic decentralisation in China: a critical analysis of Internet filtering policies in the People's Republic of China. *Australian Journal of Political Science* 37(2), 333–346.

Lampton, David. (1992). A plum for a peach: bargaining, interest and bureaucratic politics in China, in Lieberthal, Kenneth and Lampton, David, Eds., *Bureaucracy, Politics and Decision Making in Post-Mao China*. University of California Press, Berkeley, CA, pp. 35–36.

Lary, Diana (1985). Violence, fear, and insecurity: the mood of Republican China. *Republican China* 10(2), 55–63.

Lasar, Matthew (1999). *Pacifica Radio: The Rise of an Alternative Network*. Temple University Press, Philadelphia, PA.

Lash, Scott and Urry, John (1994). *Economies of Signs and Space*. SAGE, Thousand Oaks, CA.

Lee, Chin-chuan (1994). Ambiguities and contradictions: issues in China's changing political communication, in Lee, Chin-chuan, Ed., *China's Media, Media's China*. Westview, Boulder, CO, pp. 3–29.

Lenk, Klaus (1997). The challenge of cyberspatial forms of human interaction to territorial governance and policing, in Loader, Brian D., Ed., *The Governance of Cyberspace: Politics, Technology and Global Restructuring*. Routledge, New York, pp. 126–135.

Lerner, Daniel (1958). *The Passing of Traditional Society: Modernizing the Middle East*. Free Press, New York. With the assistance of Lucille W. Pevsner and an introduction by David Riesman.

Levine, Peter (2002). Can the Internet rescue democracy? Towards an online commons, in Hayduck, Ronald and Mattson, Kevin, Eds., *Democracy's Moment: Reforming the American Political System for the 21st Century*. Rowman & Littlefield, New York, pp. 121–137.

Leys, Colin (1996). *The Rise and Fall of Development Theory*. Indiana University Press, Bloomington, IN.

Li, Xiaoping (2002). 'Focus' (*Jiaodian Fangtan*) and the changes in the Chinese television industry. *Journal of Contemporary China* 11(30), 17–34.

Lichtenberg, Judith (1999). Beyond the public journalism controversy, in Fullinwider, Robert K., Ed., *Civil Society, Democracy, and Civic Renewal*. Rowman & Littlefield, New York, pp. 341–354.

Lieberthal, Kenneth (2004). *Governing China: From Revolution through Reform*. 2nd Ed., Norton, New York.

Lieberthal, Kenneth G. and Lampton, David M. (1992). Introduction: the 'fragmented authoritarianism' model and its implications, in Lieberthal, Kenneth G. and Lampton, David M., Eds., *Bureaucracy, Politics and Decision Making in Post-Mao China*. University of California Press, Berkeley, CA, pp. 1–30.

Lieberthal, Kenneth G. and Oksenberg, Michel (1988). *Policy Making in China: Leaders, Structures and Processes*. Princeton University Press, Princeton, NJ.

Lievrouw, Leah A. (2001). New media and the 'pluralization of life-worlds.' *New Media & Society* 3(1), 7–28.

Lievrouw, Leah A. (2004). What's changed about new media? Introduction to the fifth anniversary issue of *New Media & Society*. *New Media & Society* 6(1), 9–15.

Light, Jennifer S. (1999). From city space to cyberspace, in Crang, Mike; Crang, Phil; and May, Jon, Eds., *Virtual Geographies: Bodies, Space and Relations*. Routledge, New York, pp. 109–130.

Lin, Nan (2002). *Social Capital: A Theory of Social Structure and Action*. Cambridge University Press, New York.

Lincoln, Yvonna S. and Guba, Egon G. (2000). The only generalization is: there is no generalization, in Gomm, Roger; Hammersley, Martyn; and Foster, Peter, Eds., *Case Study Method: Key Issues, Key Texts*. SAGE, Thousand Oaks, CA, pp. 27–44. Originally published in 1979.

Lipski, Jan Józef (1985). *KOR: A History of the Workers' Defence Committee in Poland, 1976–1981*. Amsterdamska, Olga and Moore, Gene M., Transl.; University of California Press, Berkeley, CA.

Little, Daniel (1989). *Understanding Peasant China*. Yale University Press, New Haven, CT.

Liu, Xiaobo (2003). The rise of civil society in China. *China Rights Forum* No. 3, 16–21.

Livingston, Sonia (2004). The challenge of changing audiences: or, what is the audience researcher to do in the age of the Internet? *European Journal of Communication* 19(1), 75–86.

Livingstone, Sonia and Lunt, Peter (1994). *Talk on Television: Audience Participation and Public Debate*. Routledge, New York.

Loader, Brian D. (1997). The governance of cyberspace: politics, technology and global restructuring, in Loader, Brian D., Ed., *The Governance of Cyberspace: Politics, Technology and Global Restructuring*. Routledge, New York, pp. 1–19.

Lu, Wei; Du, Jia; Zhang, Jin; Ma, Feicheng; and Le, Taowen (2002). Internet development in China. *Journal of Information Science* 28(3), 207–233.

Lynch, Daniel C. (1999). *After the Propaganda State: Media, Politics, and "Thought Work" in Reformed China.* Stanford University Press, Stanford, CA.

Lyon, David (1993). An electronic panopticon? A sociological critique of surveillance theory. *Sociological Review* 41(4), 653–678.

Ma, Shu-yun (1994). The Chinese discourse on civil society. *China Quarterly* 138, 180–193.

Machlup, Fritz (1962). *The Production and Distribution of Knowledge in the United States.* Princeton University Press, Princeton, NJ.

Machlup, Fritz (1980). *Knowledge, Its Creation, Distribution, and Economic Significance. Volume I: Knowledge and Knowledge Production.* Princeton University Press, NJ.

Machlup, Fritz (1982). *Knowledge, Its Creation, Distribution, and Economic Significance. Volume II: The Branches of Learning.* Princeton University Press, Princeton, NJ.

Machlup, Fritz (Ed. with Una Mansfield) (1983). *The Study of Information: Interdisciplinary Messages.* Wiley, New York.

Machlup, Fritz (1984). *Knowledge, Its Creation, Distribution, and Economic Significance. Volume III: The Economics of Information and Human Capital.* Princeton University Press, Princeton, NJ.

Madison, G. B. (1998). *The Political Economy of Civil Society and Human Rights.* Routledge, New York.

Makawatsakul, Nantaporn; Tio, Julianto; Kietparadorn, Worawut; and Chiradet, Manophars (2001). *Internet and E-Commerce in China. First Draft.* Available: http://faculty.fullerton.edu/schen/ISDS%20553/Week%2015/T5%20-%20China.doc (Accessed May 30, 2003).

Manxa, Jeff; Lomax Cook, Fay; and Page, Benjamin I. (Eds.) (2002). *Navigating Public Opinion: Polls, Policy, and the Future of American Democracy.* Oxford University Press, New York.

Margolis, Michael and Resnick, David (2000). *Politics as Usual: The Cyberspace "Revolution."* SAGE, Thousand Oaks, CA.

Markham, James W. (1967). *Voices of the Red Giants.* Iowa State University Press, Ames, IA.

Martinson, David L. (2002). Public opinion, constitutional democracy, and the new technology: essential components in the secondary school social studies curriculum. *Social Studies* 93(2), 68–72.

Marx, Karl (1970a). *Critique of Hegel's "Philosophy of Right."* Cambridge University Press, New York. Translated from the German by Annette Jolin and Joseph O'Malley, Edited with an Introduction and Notes by Joseph O'Malley.

Marx, Karl (1970b). *A Contribution to the Critique of Hegel's "Philosophy of Right": Introduction.* Cambridge University Press, New York. Translated from the German by Annette Jolin and Joseph O'Malley, Edited with an Introduction and Notes by Joseph O'Malley.

Marx, Karl (1974). *Political Writings, Vol. 1: The Revolution of 1848,* Fernbach, David, Ed., Random House/Vintage Books and Monthly Review Press, New York.

Marx, Karl and Friedrich Engels (1976). *The German Ideology.* rev. ed.. Progressive Publishers, Moscow, Russia.

Marx, Karl and Friedrich Engels (1992). *The Communist Manifesto..* Oxford University Press, New York. Edited with an introduction by David McLellan.

Mayer-Schönberger, Viktor and Foster, Teree E. (1997). A regulatory Web: free speech and the global information infrastructure, in Kahin, Brian and Nesson, Charles, Eds., *Borders in Cyberspace: Information Policy and the Global Information Infrastructure.* The MIT Press, Cambridge, MA, pp. 235–254.

Mayhew, Robert (1997). *Aristotle's Criticism of Plato's Republic.* Rowman & Littlefield, New York.

McCarthy, George E. (1990). *Marx and the Ancients: Classical Ethics, Social Justice, and Nineteenth-Century Political Economy.* Rowman & Littlefield, Savage, MD.

McCaughey, Martha and Ayers, Michael D. (Eds.) (2003). *Cyberactivism: Online Activism in Theory and Practice.* Routledge, New York.

McChesney, Robert W. (1995). The Internet and U.S. communication policy-making in historical and critical perspective. *Journal of Computer-Mediated Communication* 1(4). Available at: http://www.ascusc.org/jcmc/vol1/issue4/vol1no4.html (Accessed on June 22, 2004).

McChesney, Robert W. (2004). *The Problem of the Media: U.S. Communication Politics in the 21st Century.* Monthly Review, New York.

McGuigan, Jim (1996). *Culture and the Public Sphere.* Routledge, New York.

McNair, Brian (2000). *Journalism and Democracy: An Evaluation of the Political Public Sphere.* Routlege, New York.

Meikle, Graham (2002). *Future Active: Media Activism and the Internet.* Routledge, New York.

Meikle, Scott (1991). Aristotle and exchange value, in Keyt, David and Miller, Fred D., Jr., Eds., *A Companion to Aristotle's Politics.* Blackwell, Cambridge, MA, pp. 156–181.

Merrill, John C.; Gade, Peter J.; and Blevens, Frederick R. (2001). *Twilight of Press Freedom: The Rise of People's Journalism.* Erlbaum, Mahwah, NJ.

Merritt, Davis (1998). *Public Journalism and Public Life: Why Telling the News is Not Enough,* 2nd Ed. Erlbaum, Mahwah, NJ.

Michnik, Adam (1985). *Letters from Prison and Other Essays.* University of California Press, Berkeley, CA. Translated by Maya Latynski, Foreword by Czesław Miłosz, Introduction by Jonathan Schell.

Mikami, Shunji (2003). *WIP Japan: Trends in Internet Usage 2000-2003.* Tokyo, Japan. Available at: http://www.soc.toyo.ac.jp/~mikami/wip/wip_meeting/materials/country_report_japan.sit (Retrieved August 2005).

Miller, Arthur; Erbring, Lutz; and Goldenberg, Edie (1979). Type-set politics: impact of newspapers on public confidence. *American Political Science Review* 73(1), 67–84.

Miller, David (1993). Deliberative democracy and social choice, in Held, David, Ed., *Prospects for Democracy.* Stanford University Press, Stanford, CA, pp. 74–89.

Miller, Fred D., Jr. (1995). *Nature, Justice, and Rights in Aristotle's Politics.* Clarendon Press, Oxford.

Miller, Warren E., Miller, Arthur H., and Schneider, Edward J. (1980). *American National Election Studies Data Sourcebook, 1952–1978.* Harvard University Press, Cambridge, MA.

Miller, Warren E. and Traugott, Santa (1989). *American National Election Studies Data Sourcebook, 1952–1986.* Harvard University Press, Cambridge, MA.

Milner, Henry (2002). *Civic Literacy: How Informed Citizens Make Democracy Work.* Tufts University Press, Hanover, NH.

Mitchell, J. Clyde (1983/2000). Case and situation analysis, in Gomm, Roger; Hammersley, Martyn; and Foster, Peter, Eds., *Case Study Method: Key Issues, Key Texts.* SAGE, Thousand Oaks, CA, pp. 165–186.

Mok, Ka-ho (1998). *Intellectuals and the State in Post-Mao China.* St. Martin's, New York.

Monoson, S. Sara (2000). *Plato's Democratic Entanglements.* Princeton University Press, Princeton, NJ.

Moore, Rebecca R. (2001). China's fledgling civil society: a force for democratization? *World Policy Journal* XVIII (1), 56–66.

Morgan Stanley (2004). *The China Internet Report.* Available at: http://www.morganstanley.com/institutional/techresearch/pdfs/China_Internet_Report0404.pdf (Retrieved July 2004).

Morrell, Michael E. (2003). Survey and experimental evidence for a reliable and valid measure of internal political efficacy. *Public Opinion Quarterly* 67(4), 589–602.

Morris, Merrill and Ogan, Christine (1996). The Internet as mass medium. *Journal of Computer-mediated Communication* 1(4). Available at: http://www.ascusc.org/jcmc/vol1/issue4/morris.html (Accessed on June 10, 2004).

Mu, Lin (2004). Changes and consistency: China's media market after WTO entry. *Journal of Media Economics* 17(3), 177–192.

Mueller, Franz (1987). *Person and Society According to St. Thomas Aquinas.* Aquinas Papers, No. 17. College of St. Thomas, St. Paul, MN.

Mueller, Milton and Tan, Zixiang (1997). *China in the Information Age: Telecommunications and the Dilemmas of Reform.* The Washington Papers/169. Praeger, Westport, CT.

Muller, Jerry Z. (1993). *Adam Smith in His Time and Ours: Designing the Decent Society.* Free Press, New York.

Mulvenon, James C. and Yang, Richard H. (1999). *The People's Liberation Army in the Information Age.* RAND, Santa Monica, CA.

Munro, Donald J. (1977). *The Concept of Man in Contemporary China.* The University of Michigan Press, Ann Arbor, MI.

Munt, Sally R. (2002). *Technospaces: Inside the New Media.* Continuum, New York.

Naisbitt, John (1982). *Megatrends: Ten New Directions for Transforming Our Lives.* Warner, New York.

Ndegwa, Stephen N. (1996). *The Two Faces of Civil Society: NGOs and Politics in Africa.* Kumarian, West Hartford, CT.

Negroponte, Nicholas (1995). *Being Digital.* Knopf, New York.

Newhagen, John E. and Rafaeli, Sheizaf (1996). Why communication scholars should study the Internet: a dialogue. *Journal of Computer-Mediated Communication* 1(4). Available at: http://www.ascusc.org/jcmc/vol1/issue4/rafaeli.html (Accessed on June 10, 2004).

Nguyen, Dan Thu and Alexander, Jon (1996) The coming of cyberspacetime and the end of the polity, in Shields, Rob, Ed., *Cultures of Internet: Virtual Spaces, Real Histories, Living Bodies.* SAGE, Thousand Oaks, CA, pp. 99–124.

Nichols, Mary P. (1987). *Socrates and the Political Community: An Ancient Debate.* State University of New York Press, Albany, NY.

Niemi, Richard G.: Craig, Stephen C.: and Mattei, Franco (1991). Measuring internal political efficacy in the 1988 national election study. *American Political Science Review* 85(4), 1407–1413.

Nisbet, Robert A. (1969). *The Quest for Community.* Oxford University Press, Oxford. First published in 1953.

Norris, Pippa (2001). *Digital Divide: Civic Engagement, Information Poverty, and the Internet Worldwide.* Cambridge University Press, New York.

Norris, Pippa (2004). The bridging and bonding role of online communities, in Howard, Philip N., and Jones, Steve, Eds., *Society Online: The Internet in Context.* SAGE, Thousand Oaks, CA, pp. 31–41.

Nosco, Peter (2002). Confucian perspectives on civil society and government, in Rosenblum, Nancy L. and Post, Robert C., Eds, *Civil Society and Government.* Princeton University Press, Princeton, NJ, pp. 334–359.

O'Brien, Kevin J. (1994). Chinese People's Congress and legislative embeddedness: understanding early organizational development. *Comparative Political Studies* 27(1), 99–101.

O'Connell, Brian (1999). *Civil Society: The Underpinning of American Democracy.* Tufts University, Hanover, NH.

O'Connor, James (1973). *The Fiscal Crisis of the State.* St. Martin's Press, New York.

OECD (Organization for Economic Cooperation and Development) (1997). Materials from the special session on information infrastructures, in Kahin, Brian and Wilson, Ernest J., III (Eds.), *National Information Infrastructure Initiatives: Vision and Policy Design.* The MIT Press, Cambridge, MA, pp. 569–612.

Oi, Jean C. (1992). Fiscal reform and the economic foundations of local state corporatism in China. *World Politics* 45(1), 99–126.

Oldenburg, Ray (1997). *The Great Good Place: Cafés, Coffee Shops, Community Centers, Beauty Parlors, General Stores, Bars, Hangouts and How They Get You Through the Day.* Marlowe, New York.

Olson, Kathleen K. (2005). Cyberspace as place and the limits of metaphor. *Convergence* 11(1), 10–18.

O'Malley, Joseph (1970). Editor's introduction. In Karl Marx, *Critique of Hegel's 'Philosophy of Right',* O'Malley, Joseph, Ed.,. Cambridge University Press, London.

Ophir, Adi (1991). *Plato's Invisible Cities: Discourse and Power in the Republic.* Barnes & Noble, Savage, MD.

Oxhorn, Philip (1995). *Organizing Civil Society: The Popular Sectors and the Struggle for Democracy in Chile.* The Pennsylvania State University Press, University Park, PA.

Oz-Salzberger, Fania (Ed.) (1995). Introduction, in Ferguson, Adam, *An Essay on the History of Civil Society,* Cambridge University Press, London, pp. vii–xxv. Initially published in 1767.

Palmer, Tom G. (2002). Classical liberalism and civil society: definitions, history, and relations, in Rosenblum, Nancy L., and Post, Robert C., Eds., *Civil Society and Government.* Princeton University Press, Princeton, NJ, pp. 48–78.

Pan, Zhongdang (2000). Improvising reform activities: the changing reality of journalistic practice in China, in Lee, Chin-chuan, Ed., *Power, Money, and Media: Communication Patterns and Bureaucratic Control in Cultural China.* Northwestern University Press, Evanston, IL, pp. 68–111.

Papacharissi, Zizi (2002). The virtual sphere: The Internet as a public sphere. *New Media & Society* 4(1), 9–27.

Parsons, Talcott (1971). *The System of Modern Societies.* Prentice-Hall, Englewood, NJ.

Pavlik, John V. (1994). Citizen access, involvement, and freedom of expression in an electronic environment, in Williams, Fredrick and Pavlik, John V., Eds., *The People's Rights to Know: Media, Democracy, and the Information Highway.* Erlbaum, Hillsdale, NJ, pp. 139–162.

Pei, Minxin (1994). *From Reform to Revolution: The Demise of Communism in China and the Soviet Union.* Harvard University Press, Cambridge, MA.

Pelczynski, Z.A. (1984). Nation, civil society, state: Hegelian sources of the Marxian non-theory of nationality, in Pelczynski, Z.A., Ed., *The State and Civil Society: Studies in Hegel's Political Philosophy.* Cambridge University Press, New York, pp. 262–278.

Perdue, Peter C. (1994). Technological determinism in agrarian societies, in Smith, Merritt Roe and Marx, Leo, Eds., *Does Technology Drive History? The Dilemma of Technological Determinism.* MIT Press, Cambridge, MA, pp. 169–200.

Perritt, Henry H., Jr. (1997). Jurisdiction in cyberspace: the role of intermediaries, in Kahin, Brian and Nesson, Charles, Eds., *Borders in Cyberspace: Information Policy and the Global Information Infrastructure.* The MIT Press, Cambridge, MA, pp. 164–202.

Perry, Elizabeth and Fuller, Ellen V. (1991). China's long march to democracy. *World Policy Journal* 4(3), 663–683.

Perse, Elizabeth M. (2001). *Media Effects and Society.* Erlbaum, Mahwah, NJ.

Pew Research Center (2000–2003). Pew Internet Project Reports. Multiple years. Available at: http://www.pewinternet.org/reports/index.asp.

Pigg, Kenneth E. (2001). Applications of community informatics for building community and enhancing civic society. *Information, Communication & Society* 4(4), 507–527.

Plamenatz, John (1992). *Man & Society: Political and Social Theories from Machiavelli to Marx.* Vol. II. Longman, New York. A new edition revised by M.E. Plamenatz and Robert Wokler.

Plato (2000). *Republic,* Cambridge University Press, London. Edited by G.R.F. Ferrari and translated by Tom Griffith.

Polumbaum, Judy (1990). The tribulations of China's journalists after a decade of reform, in Lee, Chin-chuan, Ed., *Voices of China: The Interplay of Politics and Journalism.* Guilford, New York, pp. 33–68.

Polumbaum, Judy (2001). China's media: between politics and the market. *Current History* 100(647), 269–277.

Post, Ken (1991). The state, civil society, and democracy in Africa: Some theoretical issues, in Cohen, Robin and Goulbourne, Harry, Eds., *Democracy and Socialism in Africa.* Westview, Boulder, CO, pp. 34–52.

Poster, Mark (1997). Cyberdemocracy: the Internet and the public sphere, in Holmes, David, Ed., *Virtual Politics: Identity and Community in Cyberspace.* SAGE, Thousand Oaks, CA, pp. 212–229.

Postman, Neil (1985). *Amusing Ourselves to Death: Public Discourse in the Age of Show Business.* Viking, New York.

Preston, Paschal (2001). *Reshaping Communications: Technology, Information and Social Change.* SAGE, Thousand Oaks, CA.

Pruijt, Hans (2002). Social capital and the equalizing potential of the Internet. *Social Science Computer Review* 20(2), 109–115.

Putnam, Robert D. (with Robert Leonardi and Raffaella Y. Nanetti) (1993). *Making Democracy Work: Civic Traditions in Modern Italy.* Princeton University Press, Princeton, NJ.

Putnam, Robert D. (1995). Tuning in, tuning out: the strange disappearance of social capital in America. *PS: Political Science and Politics* 28(4), 664–683.

Putnam, Robert D. (2000). *Bowling Alone: The Collapse and Revival of American Community.* Simon & Schuster, New York.

Putnam, Robert D. and Feldstein, Lewis M. (with Don Cohen) (2003). *Better Together: Restoring the American Community.* Simon & Schuster New York.

Pye, Lucian W. (1985). *Asian Power and Politics.* Harvard University Press, Cambridge, MA.

Pye, Lucian W. (1991). The state and the individual: an overview interpretation. *China Quarterly* 127, 443–466.

Qi, Yanli (2000). The current situation and prospect of Chinese information resources on the Web. *Social Science Computer Review* 18(4), 484–489.

Qiu, Jack Linchuan (2000/1999). Virtual censorship in China: keeping the gate between the cyberspaces. *International Journal of Communication Law and Policy* 4. Available online at: http://www.ijclp.org/4_2000/pdf/ijclp_webdoc_1_4_2000.pdf (Accessed January 26, 2004).

Raab, Charles D. (1997). Privacy, democracy, information, in Loader, Brian D., Ed., *The Governance of Cyberspace: Politics, Technology and Global Restructuring.* Routledge, New York, pp. 155–174.

Ragin, Charles C. and Becker, Howard S., (Eds.) (1992). *What Is a Case? Exploring the Foundations of Social Inquiry.* Cambridge University Press, London.

Raina, Peter (1981). *Independent Social Movements in Poland.* London School of Economics, London.

Rainie, Lee and Bell, Peter (2004). The numbers that count. *New Media & Society* 6(1), 44–54.

Rankin, Mary Backus (1986). *Elite Activism and Political Transformation in China: Zhejiang Province, 1865–1911.* Stanford University Press, Stanford, CA.

Rankin, Mary Backus (1997). State and society in early republican politics, 1912–1918. *The China Quarterly* 150, 260–281.

Rauch, Leo (1981). *The Political Animal: Studies in Political Philosophy from Machiavelli to Marx.* The University of Massachusetts Press, Amherst, MA.

Reidenberg, Joel R. (1997). Governing networks and rule-making in cyberspace, in Kahin, Brian and Nesson, Charles, Eds., *Borders in Cyberspace: Information Policy and the Global Information Infrastructure.* The MIT Press, Cambridge, MA, pp. 84–105.

Reis, Elisa P. (1998). Uncivil hierarchies. In Alexander, J.C., Ed., *Real Civil Societies: Dilemmas of Institutionalization.* SAGE, Thousand Oaks, CA, pp. 21–39.

Reisman, David A. (1976). *Adam Smith's Sociological Economics.* Harper & Row, New York.

Rheingold, Howard (1993). *The Virtual Community: Homesteading on the Electronic Frontier.* Addison-Wesley, Reading, MA.

Rheingold, Howard (2003). *Smart Mobs: The Next Social Revolution.* Perseus, Cambridge, MA.

Riedel, Manfred (1984). *Between Tradition and Revolution: The Hegelian Transformation of Political Philosophy.* Walter Wright, Transl. Cambridge University Press, New York.

Roberts, Moss (2001). Introduction, in Laozi, *Dao De Jing: The Book of the Way.* University of California Press, Berkeley, CA, pp. 1–23. Translation and commentary by Moss Roberts.

Rodgers, Daniel T. (1988). Of prophets and prophecy, in Eisenstadt, Abraham S., Ed., *Reconsidering Tocqueville's Democracy in America.* New Rutgers University Press, Brunswick, NJ, pp. 192–206.

Rosen, Stanley (1989). Public opinion and reform in the People's Republic of China. *Studies in Comparative Communism* XXII(2/3), 153–170.

Rosen, Stanley (1987). Survey research in the People's Republic of China: some methodological problems. *Canadian and International Education* 16(1), 190–197.

Rosen, Stanley and Chu, David S. K. (1987). *Survey Research in the People's Republic of China.* United States Information Agency, Washington, DC.

Rosenbaum, Arthur Lewis (Ed.) (1992). *State and Society in China: The Consequences of Reform.* Westview, Boulder, CO.

Rosenblum, Nancy L. (1998). *Membership and Morals: The Personal Uses of Pluralism in America.* Princeton University Press, Princeton, NJ.

Rowe, William T. (1984). *Hankow: Commerce and Society in a Chinese City, 1796–1889.* Stanford University Press, Stanford, CA.

Rowe, William T. (1989). *Hankow: Conflict and Community in a Chinese City, 1796–1895.* Stanford University Press, Stanford, CA.

Rowe, William T. (1990a). The public sphere in Modern China. *Modern China* 16(3), 309–329.

Rowe, William T. (1990b). *"Civil Society" and "Public Sphere" in Modern China: A Perspective on Popular Movements in Beijing, 1919–1989.* Working Papers in Asian/Pacific Studies Series. Duke University, Durham, NC.

Rucht, Dieter (2004). The quadruple 'A': media strategies of protest movements since the 1960s, in van de Donk, Wim; Loader, Brian D.; Nixon, Paul G.; and Rucht, Dieter, Eds., *Cyberprotest: New Media, Citizens and Social Movements.* Routledge, New York, pp. 29–56.

Rutherford, Paul (2000). *Endless Propaganda: The Advertising of Public Goods.* University of Toronto Press, Toronto.

Ryan, Charlotte (1991). *Prime Time Activism: Media Strategies for Grassroots Organizing.* South End Press, Boston.

Saco, Diana (2002). *Cybering Democracy: Public Space and the Internet.* University of Minnesota Press, Minneapolis, MN.

Salvador, Michael (1998). Practicing democracy, in Salvador, Michael, and Sias, Patricia M., Eds. *The Public Voice in a Democracy at Risk.* Praeger, Westport, CT, pp. 4–10.

Sassi, Sinikka (1996). The network and the fragmentation of the public sphere. *Electronic Journal of Communication* 6(2). Available at: http://www.cios.org/getfile/Sassi_V6N296 (Accessed on June 30, 2004).

Sautedâe, Eric (2003). The snares of modernity: Internet, information and the SARS crisis in China. *China Perspectives* 47, 21–27.

Savigny, Heather (2002). Public opinion, political communication and the Internet. *Politics* 22(1), 1–8.

Schak, David C. and Hudson, Wayne (Eds.) (2003a). *Civil Society in Asia.* Ashgate, Burlington, VT.

Schak, David C. and Hudson, Wayne (2003b). Civil society in Asia, in Schak, David C. and Hudson, Wayne, Eds., *Civil Society in Asia.*: Ashgate, Burlington, VT, pp. 1–8.

Schell, Jonathan (1985). Introduction,. in Michnik, Adam, *Letters from Prison and Other Essays.* University of California Press, Berkeley, CA.

Schmitter, Philippe C. (1974). Still the century of corporatism? *Review of Politics* 36(1) (January), 85–131.

Schneider, Steven M. (1996). Creating a democratic public sphere through political discussion: a case study of abortion conversation on the Internet. *Social Science Computer Review* 14(4), 373–393.

Schofield, Janet Ward (2000). Increasing the generalizability of qualitative research, in Gomm, Roger, Hammersley, Martyn, and Foster, Peter, Eds., *Case Study Method: Key Issues, Key Texts.* SAGE, Thousand Oaks, CA, pp. 69–97. Originally published in 1990.

Schoppa, R. Keith (1989). *Xiang Lake: Nine Centuries of Chinese Life.* Yale University Press, New Haven, CT.

Schram, Stuart R. (Ed.) (1985). *The Scope of State Power in China.* The Chinese University of Hong Kong, Hong Kong.

Schudson, Michael (1999). What public journalism knows about journalism, but does not know about 'public,' in Glasser, Theodore, Ed., *The Idea of Public Journalism.* Guilford, New York, pp. 118–133.

Schuler, Douglas (1996). *New Community Networks: Wired for Change.* Addison-Wesley, Reading, MA.

Schuurman, Fran J. (Ed.) (1993). *Beyond the Impasse: New Directions in Development Theory.* Zed, London.

Schwarcz, Vera (1986). *The Chinese Enlightenment: Intellectuals and the Legacy of the May Fourth Movement of 1919.* University of California Press, Berkeley, CA.

Schwartz, Benjamin I. (1985). *The World of Thought in Ancient China.* Harvard University Press, Cambridge, MA.

SDA (School of Management) Bocconi University (2002). World *Internet Project: Italy.* Available at: http://www.worldinternetproject.net/reports/wip2002-rel-15-luglio.pdf (Retrieved July 2005).

Seligman, Adam. (1992). *The Idea of Civil Society.* Free Press, New York.

Seligman, Adam B. (1995). Animadversions upon civil society and civic virtue in the last decade of the twentieth century, in Hall, John A., Ed., *Civil Society: Theory, History, Comparison.* Polity, Cambridge, MA, pp. 200–223.

Setton, Mark (1997). *Chông Yagyong: Korea's Challenge to Orthodox Neo-Confucianism.* State University of New York Press, Albany, NY.

Shade, Leslie Regan (1996). Is there free speech on the Net? Censorship in the global information infrastructure, in Shields, Rob, Ed., *Cultures of Internet: Virtual Spaces, Real Histories, Living Bodies.* SAGE, Thousand Oaks, CA, pp. 11–32.

Shapiro, Andrew L. (1999). *The Control Revolution: How the Internet is Putting Individuals in Charge and Changing the World We Know.* Century Foundation, New York.

Sharp, Elaine B. (1999). *The Sometimes Connection: Public Opinion and Social Policy.* State University of New York Press, Albany, NY.

Shaw, Donald; Hamm, Bradley; and Knott, Diana (2000). Technological change, agenda challenge and social melding: mass media studies and the four ages of place, class, mass and space. *Journalism Studies,* 1(1), 57–79.

Sheridan, James E. (1975). *China in Disintegration: The Republican Era in Chinese History, 1912–1949.* Free Press, New York.

Shils, Edwards (1991). The virtue of civil society. *Government and Opposition* 26(1), 3–20.

Shue, Vivienne (1994). State power and social organisation in China, in Migdal, Joel S.; Kohli, Atul; and Shue, Vivienne, Eds., *State Power and Social Forces: Domination and Transformation in the Third World.* Cambridge University Press, London, pp. 65–88.

Siebert, Fred S.; Peterson, Theodore; and Schramm, Wilbur (1956). *Four Theories of the Press.* University of Illinois Press Urbana, IL.

Sills, Stephen J. and Song, Chunyan (2002). Innovations in survey research: an application of Web-based surveys. *Social Science Computer Review* 20(1), 22–30.

Simons, Helen (1996). The paradox of case study. *Cambridge Journal of Education* 26(2), 225–240.

Sirianni, Carmen and Friedland, Lewis (2001). *Civic Innovation in America: Community Empowerment, Public Policy, and the Movement for Civic Renewal*. University of California Press, Berkeley, CA.

Slack, Roger S. and Williams, Robin A. (2000). The dialectic of place and space: on community in the 'information age.' *New Media & Society* 2(3), 313–334.

Smith, Adam (1892). *The Theory of Moral Sentiments; to Which Is Added, A Dissertation on the Origin of Languages*. George Bell & Sons, New York. new edition, with a biographical and critical memoir of the author, by Dugald Steward.

Smith, Adam. (1976). *An Inquiry Into the Nature and Cause of the Wealth of Nations*. The University of Chicago Press, Chicago. Edited by Edwin Cannan, with a new preface by George J. Stigler. Two volumes in one.

Smith, Joanna F. Handlin (1987). Benevolent societies: the reshaping of charity during the Late Ming and Early Ch'ing. *Journal of Asian Studies* 46(2), 309–337.

So, Alvin Y. (1990). *Social Change and Development: Modernization, Dependency, and World-system Theories*. SAGE, Newbury Park, CA.

Solinger, Dorothy J. (1992). Urban entrepreneurs and the state: the merger of state and society. in Rosenbaum, Arthur Lewis, Ed., *State and Society in China: The Consequences of Reform*. Westview, Boulder, CO, pp. 121–141.

Spacek, Thomas R. (1997). Approaches for maximizing GII impacts on sustainable development, in Kahin, Brian, and Wilson, Ernest J., III, Eds., *National Information Infrastructure Initiatives: Vision and Policy Design*. The MIT Press, Cambridge, MA, pp. 508–531.

Sproull, Lee and Faraj, Samer (1997). Atheism, sex, and databases: the Net as a social technology, in Kiesler, Sara, Ed., *Culture of the Internet*. Erbaum, Mahwah, NJ, pp. 35–51.

Sproull, Lee and Kiesler, Sara (1986). Reducing social context cues: electronic mail in organizational communication. *Management Science* 32(11), 1492–1512.

Stake, Robert E. (1995). *The Art of Case Study Research*. SAGE, Thousand Oaks, CA.

Stake, Robert E. (2000a). The case study method in social inquiry, in Gomm, Roger; Hammersley, Martyn; and Foster, Peter, Eds., *Case Study Method: Key Issues, Key Texts*. SAGE, Thousand Oaks, CA, pp. 19–26. Originally published in 1978.

Stake, Robert E. (2000b). Case studies, in Denzin, Norman K. and Lincoln, Yvonna S., Eds., *Handbook of Qualitative Research*, 2nd ed. SAGE, Thousand Oaks, CA, pp. 435–454.

Stalley, R.F. (1991). Aristotle's criticism of "Plato's Republic," in Keyt, David and Miller, Fred D., Jr., Eds., *A Companion to Aristotle's Politics*. Blackwell, Cambridge, MA, pp. 182–199.

Staniszkis, Jadwiga (1984). *Poland's Self-Limiting Revolution*. Gross, Jan T., Ed., Princeton University Press, Princeton, NJ.

Stepan, Alfred (1978). *The State and Society: Peru in Comparative Perspective*. Princeton University Press, Princeton, NJ.

Stepan, Alfred (1988). *Rethinking Military Politics: Brazil and the Southern Cone*. Princeton University Press, Princeton, NJ.

Sterling, Bruce (1993). *The Hacker Crackdown: Law and Disorder on the Electronic Frontier*. Bantam, New York.

Strand, David (1989). *Rickshaw Beijing: City People and Politics in 1920s China*. University of California Press, Berkeley, CA.

Streck, John. M. (1998). Pulling the plug on electronic town meeting: participatory democracy and the reality of the Usenet, in Toulouse, Chris and Luke, Timothy W., Eds., *The Politics of Cyberspace: A New Political Science Reader*. Routledge, New York, pp. 18–47.

Streitmatter, Rodger (2001). *Voices of Revolution: Dissident Press in America*. Columbia University Press, New York.

Stubbs, Paul (2001). Imagining Croatia? Exploring computer-mediated diasporic public spheres, in Frykman, Maja Povrzanovic, Ed., *Beyond Integration: Challenges of Belonging in Diaspora and Exile*. Nordic Academic Press, Lund, Sweden, pp. 195–224.

Sun, Yu (2003). Lessons from SARS coverage. *Nieman Reports* 57(4), 91–93.

Swaine, Michael D. and Tellis, Ashely J. (2000). *Interpreting China's Grand Strategy: Past, Present, and Future*. RAND, Santa Monica, CA.

Tan, Zixiang (Alex) (1999). Regulating China's Internet: convergence toward a coherent regulatory regime. *Telecommunications Policy* 23(3/4), 261–276.

Tan, Zixiang (Alex), Foster, William, and Goodman, Seymour (1999). China's state-coordinated Internet infrastructure. *Communications of the ACM* 42(6), 44–52.

Tao Te Ching (1999). Title in *The Collected Translations of Thomas Cleary, The Taoist Classics, Volume One*. Cleary, Thomas, Transl., Shambhala Boston, pp. 9–47.

Taylor, Charles (1995). *Philosophical Arguments*. Harvard University Press, Cambridge, MA.

Teeple, Gary (1984). *Marx's Critique of Politics: 1842–1847*. University of Toronto Press, Buffalo, NY.

Temple, Jonathan (1999). The new growth evidence, *Journal of Economic Literature* XXXVII: 112–156.

Tester, Keith (1992). *Civil Society*. Routledge, New York.

Thiers, Paul (2003). Risk society comes to China: SARS, transparency, and public accountability. *Asian Perspectives* 27(2), 241–251.

Thompson, John B. (1995). *The Media and Modernity: A Social Theory of the Media*. Polity, Cambridge, MA.

Thompson, Roger (1995). *China's Local Councils in the Age of Constitutional Reform, 1898–1911*. Council on East Asian Studies, Harvard University, Cambridge, MA.

Tilly, Charles (1978). *From Mobilization to Revolution*. Addison-Wesley, Reading, MA.

Tismaneanu, Vladimir (Ed.) (1990). *In Search of Civil Society: Independent Peace Movements in the Soviet Bloc*. Routledge, New York.

Tocqueville, Alexis de (1985a). *Democracy in America*, Vol. I. New York: Alfred A. Knopf, Inc. The Henry Reeve text as revised by Francis Bowen, further corrected and edited with Introduction, Editorial Notes, and Bibliographies by Phillips Bradley.

Tocqueville, Alexis de (1985b). *Democracy in America*, Vol. II. Knopf, New York. The Henry Reeve text as revised by Francis Bowen, further corrected and edited with Introduction, Editorial Notes, and Bibliographies by Philips Bradley.

Toffler, Alvin (1983). *The Third Wave*. Bantam, New York.

Tong, James (2002). An organizational analysis of the Falun Gong: structure, communications, financing. *China Quarterly* 171, 636–660.

Trentmann, Frank (1999). Introduction: paradoxes of civil society, in Trentmann, F., Ed., *Paradoxes of Civil Society: New Perspectives on Modern German and British History*. Berghahn, New York, pp. 3–46.

Trouteaud, Alex R. (2004). How you ask counts: a test of Internet-related components of response rates to a Web-based survey. *Social Science Computer Review* 22(3), 385–392.

Tsin, Michael (1997). Imagining 'society' in early twentieth-century China, in Fogel, Joshua A. and Zarrow, Peter G., Eds. *Imagining the People: Chinese Intellectuals and the Concept of Citizenship, 1890–1920*. M.E. Sharpe, Armonk, NY pp. 212–231, 257.

Tu, Wei-ming (1988). *Centrality and Commonality: An Essay on Confucian Religiousness*. The State University of New York Press, Albany, NY.

Turkle, Sherry (1995). *Life on the Screen: Identity in the Age of the Internet*. Simon & Schuster, New York.

Tyson, James and Tyson, Ann (1995). *Chinese Awakenings: Life Stories from the Unofficial China*. Westview, Boulder, CO.

UCLA Center for Communication Policy (2000). UCLA Internet Report: Surveying the Digital Future. Available at: http://ccp.ucla.edu/UCLA-Internet-Report-2000.pdf.

UCLA Center for Communication Policy (2001). UCLA Internet Report: Surveying the Digital Future. Year Two. Available at: http://ccp.ucla.edu/pdf/UCLA-Internet-Report-2001.pdf.

UCLA Center for Communication Policy (2003). UCLA Internet Report: Surveying the Digital Future. Year Three. Available at: http://ccp.ucla.edu/pdf/UCLA-Internet-Report-Year-Three.pdf.

Unger, Jonathan and Chan, Anita (1995). China, corporatism, and the East Asian model. *The Australian Journal of Chinese Affairs*,33 (January), 29–53.

United Nations General Assembly (2004). *A More Secure World: Our Shared Responsibility — Report of the High-level Panel on Threats, Challenges and Change*. United Nations, New York. Available online at: http://www.un.org/secureworld/report2.pdf (Accessed October 2005).

U.S. Helsinki Watch Committee (1986). *Reinventing Civil Society: Poland's Quiet Revolution*. U.S. Helsinki Watch Committee, New York.

Van de Donk, Wim; Loader, Brian D.; Nixon, Paul G.; and Rucht, Dieter (2004). Introduction: social movements and ICTs, in van de Donk, Wim; Loader, Brian D.; Nixon, Paul G.; and Rucht, Dieter, Eds., *Cyberprotest: New Media, Citizens and Social Movements*. Routledge, New York, pp. 1–25.

Venturelli, Shalini (1997). Information liberalization in the European Union, in Kahin, Brian and Wilson, Ernest J., III, Eds., *National Information Infrastructure Initiatives: Vision and Policy Design*. MIT Press, Cambridge, MA, pp. 457–489.

Verba, Sidney; Schlozman, Kay Lehman; and Brady, Henry E. (1995). *Voice and Equality: Civic Voluntarism in American Politics*. Harvard University Press, Cambridge, MA.

Verma, V. P. (1974). *Political Philosophy of Hegel*. Trimurti, New Delhi.

Verstraeten, Hans (1996). The media and the transformation of the public sphere: a contribution for a critical political economy of the public sphere. *European Journal of Communication* 11(3), 347–370.

Volkmer, Ingrid (1997). Universalism and particularism: the problem of cultural sovereignty and global information flow, in Kahin, Brian and Nesson, Charles, Eds., *Borders in Cyberspace: Information Policy and the Global Information Infrastructure*. MIT Press, Cambridge, MA, pp. 48–83.

Von Heyking, John (2001). *Augustine and Politics as Longing in the World*. University of Missouri Press, Columbia, MO.

Wacker, Gudrun (2003). The Internet and censorship in China, in Hughes, Christopher R. and Wacker, Gudrun, Eds., *China and the Internet: Politics of the Digital Leap Forward*. Routledge Curzon, New York, pp. 58–82.

Wakeman, Jr., Frederic (1985). *The Great Enterprise: The Manchu Reconstruction of Imperial Order in Seventeenth-Century China*. University of California Press, Berkeley, CA.

Wakeman, Jr., Frederic (1991). Models of historical change: The Chinese state and society, 1839–1989, in Lieberthal, Kenneth; Kallgren, Joyce; MacFarquhar, Roderick; and Wakeman, Frederic, Jr., Eds. *Perspectives on Modern China: Four Anniversaries*. M.E. Sharpe, Armonk, NY, pp. 68–102.

Wakeman, Jr., Frederic (1993). The civil society and public sphere debate: Western reflections on Chinese political culture. *Modern China* 19(2), 108–138.

Walder, Andrew (1989). The political sociology of the Beijing upheaval of 1989. *Problems of Communism* (September–October), 30–40.

Walder, Andrew G. (1995). The quiet revolution from within: economic reform as a source of political decline, in Walder, Andrew, Ed., *The Waning of the Communist State: Economic Origins of Political Decline in China and Hungary*. University of California Press, Berkeley, CA, pp. 1–24.

Walker, Jesse (2004). *Rebels on the Air: An Alternative History of Radio in America*. New York University Press, New York.

Wallach, John R. (2001). *The Platonic Political Art: A Study of Critical Reason and Democracy*. Pennsylvania State University Press, University Park, PA.

Walther, Joseph B.; Gay, Geri; and Hancock, Jeffrey T. (2005). How do communication and technology researchers study the Internet? *Journal of Communication* 55(3), 632–657.

Wang, Fei-Ling (1998). *Institutions and Institutional Change in China: Premodernity and Modernization*. St. Martin's, New York.

Wang, Fei-Ling (Translated) (2003a). China's Pre-SARS legal framework for disease control. *Chinese Law and Government* 36(4), 58–75.

Wang, Fei-Ling (Translated) (2003b). Speedy and consequential new laws and policies on SARS and information flow. *Chinese Law and Government* 36(4), 76–98.

Wang, Yanlai; Rees, Nicholas; and Andreosso-O'Callaghan, Bernadette (2004). Economic change and political development in China: findings from a public opinion survey. *Journal of Contemporary China* 13(39), 203–222.

Wank, David L. (1995). Civil society in Communist China? Private business and political alliance, 1989. in Hall, John A., Ed., *Civil Society: Theory, History, Comparison*. Polity, Cambridge, MA, pp. 56–79.

Warren, Mark E. (2001). *Democracy and Association*. Princeton University Press, Princeton, NJ.

Weber, Ian (2002). Reconfiguring Chinese propaganda and control modalities: a case study of Shanghai's television system. *Journal of Contemporary China* 11(30), 53–75.

Weber, Max (1951). *The Religion of China: Confucianism and Taoism*. Free Press, New York. Translated and edited by Hans. H. Gerth.

Weber, Max (1976). *The Protestant Ethic and the Spirit of Capitalism*. Scribner, New York:. Translated by Talcott Parsons; introduction by Anthony Giddens.

Wei, C.X. George and Liu, Xiaoyuan (Eds.) (2002). *Exploring Nationalisms of China: Themes and Conflicts*. Greenwood, Westport, CT. Foreword by William C. Kirby.

Weiss, Peter N. and Backlund, Peter (1997). International information policy in conflict: open and unrestricted access versus government commercialization, in Kahin, Brian and Nesson, Charles, Eds., *Borders in Cyberspace: Information Policy and the Global Information Infrastructure*. The MIT Press, Cambridge, MA, pp. 300–321.

Weller, Robert P. (1999). *Alternate Civilities: Democracy and Culture in China and Taiwan*. Westview, Boulder, CO.

Wellman, Barry (1997). An electronic group is virtually a social network, in Kiesler, Sara, Ed., *Culture of the Internet*. Erbaum, Mahwah, NJ, pp. 179–205.

Wellman, Barry and Haythornthwaite, Caroline (Eds.) (2002). *The Internet and Everyday Life*. Blackwell, Cambridge, MA.

Werhane, Patricia H. (1991). *Adam Smith and His Legacy for Modern Capitalism*. Oxford University Press, New York.

Westphal, Merold (1992). *Hegel, Freedom, and Modernity*. State University of New York Press, Albany, NY.

Wheeler, Mark C. (1997). *Politics and the Mass Media*. Blackwell, Cambridge, MA.

White, Gordon (1993). *Riding the Tiger: The Politics of Economic Reform in Post-Mao China*. Stanford University Press, Stanford, CA.

White, Gordon (1994). Prospects for civil society: a case study of Xiaoshan city, in Goodman, David S.G. and Hooper, Beverley, Eds, *China Quiet Revolution: New Interactions Between State and Society*. St. Martin's, New York, pp. 194–218.

White, Gordon: Howell, Jude: and Xiaoyuan, Shang (1996). *In Search of Civil Society: Market Reform and Social Change in Contemporary China*. Clarendon Press, New York.

Wilhelm, Anthony G. (1999). Virtual sounding boards: how deliberative is online political discussion? in Hague, Barry N. and Loader, Brian D., Eds., *Digital Democracy: Discourse and Decision Making in the Information Age*. Routledge, New York, pp. 154–178.

Williams, Raymond (1974). *Television: Technology and Cultural Form*. Fontana, London.

Wilhelm, Anthony (2000). *Democracy in the Digital Age*. Routledge, New York.

Wilson, Richard (1992). *Compliance Ideologies: Rethinking Political Culture*. Cambridge University Press, New York.

Wiseman, John A. (Ed.) (1995). *Democracy and Political Change in Sub-Saharan Africa*. Routledge, New York.

Woesler, Martin (2002). The Internet transforms China into a Western-style information society, in Zhang, Junhua and Woesler, Martin, Eds., *China's Digital Dream — The Impact of the Internet on Chinese Society*. The University Press Bochum, Rodondo Beach, CA, pp. 129–146.

Wolfe, Alan (2003). Is civil society obsolete: revisiting predictions of the decline of civil society in 'Whose Keeper'? *The Brookings Review* 21, 9–12.

Wolfsfeld, Gadi (1984). The symbiosis of press and protest: an exchange analysis. *Journalism Quarterly* 61(3), 550–556.

Wolfsfeld, Gadi (1991). Media, protest, and political violence: a transnational analysis. *Journalism Monographs* No. 127.

Wolin, Sheldon S. (2001). *Tocqueville between Two Worlds: The Making of a Political and Theoretical Life*. Princeton University Press, Princeton, NJ.

Wong, John and Seok Ling, Nah (2001). *China's Emerging New Economy: The Internet and E-Commerce*. Singapore University Press and World Scientific Publishing Co., Singapore

Wong, Poh-Kam (1997). Implementing the NII vision: Singapore's experience and future challenges, in Kahin, Brian and Wilson, Ernest J., III, Eds., *National Information Infrastructure Initiatives: Vision and Policy Design*. MIT Press, Cambridge, MA, pp. 24–60.

Woodside, Alexander B. (1976). *Community and Revolution in Modern Vietnam*. Houghton Mifflin, Boston.

Wright, James D. (1976). *The Dissent of the Governed: Alienation and Democracy in America*. Academic Press, New York.

Xiao, Qiang (2003a). Testimony before the U.S.-China Economic and Security Review Commission. Available at http://www.uscc.gov/researchreports/2000–2003/reports/qiates.htm (Accessed on May 21, 2004).

Xiao, Qiang (2003b). Cyber speech: catalyzing free expression and civil society. *Harvard International Review* 25(2), 70–75.

Xu, Bin (2000), Multinational enterprises, technology diffusion, and host country productivity growth, *Journal of Development Economic*, 62(2), 477–493.

Xu, Xiaoqun (2001). *Chinese Professionals and the Republican State: The Rise of Professional Associations in Shanghai, 1912–1937*. Cambridge University Press, Cambridge, U.K.

Yang, Dali (1997). *Beyond Beijing: Liberalization and the Regions in China*. Routledge, New York.

Yin, Robert K. (1994). *Case Study Research: Design and Methods*. Sage Publications, Thousand Oaks, CA.

Yurcik, William and Tan, Zixiang (1996). The great (fire)wall of China: Internet security and information policy issues in the People's Republic of China. Available online at: http://www.tprc.org/abstracts/tan.txt (Accessed March 26, 2004).

Zappen, James P.; Gurak, Laura; and Doheny-Farina, Stephen (1997). Rhetoric, community, and cyberspace. *Rhetoric Review* 15(2), 400–419.

Zarrow, Peter (1997). Liang Qichao and the notion of civil society in Republican China, in Fogel, Joshua A. and Zarrow, Peter G., Eds. *Imagining the People: Chinese Intellectuals and the Concept of Citizenship, 1890–1920*. M.E. Sharpe, Armonk, NY, pp. 232–257.

Zeigler, Harmon (1988). *Pluralism, Corporatism, and Confucianism: Political Association and Conflict Regulation in the United States, Europe, and Taiwan*. Temple University Press, Philadelphia.

Zhan, Jiang and Gang, Zhao (2002). 'Now broadcasting': another trump card in Central TV's efforts to strengthen the media's supervisory role. *Chinese Education and Society* 35(4), 95–101.

Zhang, Yunqiu (1997). From state corporatism to social representation: local trade unions in the reform years, in Brook, Timothy and Frolic, B. Michael, Eds., *Civil Society in China*. M.E. Sharpe, Armonk, NY, pp. 124–148.

Zhao, Suisheng (2000). China's nationalism and its international orientations. *Political Science Quarterly* 115(1), 1–33.

Zhao, Yuezhi (1998). *Media, Market, and Democracy in China: Between the Party Line and the Bottom Line*. University of Illinois Press, Urbana, IL.

Zhao, Yuezhi (2000). From commercialization to conglomeration: the transformation of the Chinese press Within the orbit of the party state. *Journal of Communication* 50(2), 3–26.

Zheng, Yongnian (1999). *Discovering Chinese Nationalism in China: Modernization, Identity and International Relations*. Cambridge University Press, London.

Zhong, Yong (2003). In search of loyal audiences — what did I find? An ethnographic study of Chinese television audiences. *Continuum: Journal of Media & Cultural Studies* 17(3), 233–246.

Zhou (sic) [Zhao], Yuezhi (2000). Watchdogs on party leashes? Contexts and implications of investigative journalism in post-Deng China. *Journalism Studies* 1(2), 577–597.

Znaniecki, Florian (1934). *The Method of Sociology*. Farrar & Rinehart, New York.

Zoubir, Yahia H. (Ed.) (1999). *North Africa in Transition: State, Society, and Economic Transformation in the 1990s*. University Press of Florida, Gainesville, FL.

Bibliography (Chinese)

陈宝良:《中国的社与会》。浙江人民出版社1996年版。
Chen Baoliang (1996). *China's she and hui*. Zhejiang People's Press.

陈炎:《Internet改变中国》。北京大学出版社1999年版。
Chen Yan (1999). *Internet Changes China*. Beijing University Press.

陈甬祥:《创新与未来——面向知识经济时代的国家创新体系》。科学出版社1998年5月版。
Chen Yongxiang (1998). *Creativity and the Future: the National Creative System in the Face of the Knowledge Economy*. Science Press, Beijing.

《中国电子商务年鉴:2002》。北京:中国电子商务年鉴编辑部编辑、出版。
China E-Commerce Yearbook (2002). China E-Commerce Yearbook Editorial Board, Beijing.

中国现代化战略研究课题组 & 中国科学院中国现代化研究中心:《2004中国现代化报告》。北京大学出版社2004年版。
China Modernization Strategy Research Group and China Modernization Research Center of the Chinese Academy of Sciences (2004). *China Modernization Report 2004*. Beijing University Press.

中华人民共和国国家统计局: 中华人民共和国2002年国民经济和社会发展统计公报。2003年2月28日。见:http://www.stats.gov.cn/tjgb/ndtjgb/qgndtjgb/1200302280214.htm。
China National Bureau of Statistics (2003). Statistical Report of National Economic and Social Development of the People's Republic of China 2002. Available at http://www.stats.gov.cn/tjgb/ndtjgb/qgndtjgb/1200302280214.htm.

《中国人口统计年鉴: 1990》。北京:中国统计出版社1990年版。
China Population Statistical Yearbook: 1990 (1990). China Statistical Publishing House, Beijing.

《中国人口统计年鉴: 1997》。北京:中国统计出版社1997年版。
China Population Statistical Yearbook: 1997 (1997). China Statistical Publishing House, Beijing.

《中国人口统计年鉴: 2000》。北京:中国统计出版社2000年版。
China Population Statistical Yearbook: 2000 (2000). China Statistical Publishing House, Beijing.

《中国人口统计年鉴: 2002》。北京:中国统计出版社2002年版。
China Population Statistical Yearbook: 2002 (2002). China Statistical Publishing House, Beijing.

中国社会科学院:《当代中国社会阶层研究报告》。社会科学文献出版社2004年版。
Chinese Academy of Social Sciences (CASS) (2004). *Research Report of Contemporary Social Stratification in China*. Social Science Literature Press, Beijing:.

邓正来:《国家与社会:中国市民社会研究》。成都:四川人民出版1997年版。
Deng Zhenglai (1997). *State and Society: Studies in Chinese Civil Society*. Sichuan People's Press, China.

方朝晖:"对90年代市民社会研究的一个反思。"《天津社会科学》 1999年第5期。
Fang Zhaohui (1999). Reflections on research in civil societies in the 1990s. *Tianjin Social Sciences*, No. 5.

冯之浚:《知识经济与中国发展》。中央党校出版社1998年5月版。
Feng Zhijun (1998). *Knowledge Economy and China's Development*. Central Party School Press, Beijing.

李凡:《静悄悄的革命:中国当代市民社会》,明镜出版社1998年出版。
Li Fan: *A Silent Revolution: Contemporary Chinese Civil Society*. Mirror Books, Hong Kong.

梁治平："'民间'、'民间社会'和Civil Society — Civil Society概念再探讨。"《当代中国研究》，72（1），2001年。见: http://www.chinayj.net/StubArticle.asp?issue=010106&total=72。
Liang Zhiping (2001). Minjian, minjian shehui and civil society: another exploration of the concept of civil society. *Contemporary China Studies* 72(1). Available at: http://www.chinayj.net/StubArticle.asp?issue=010106&total=72 (Accessed on August 29, 2003).

林毓生:《热烈与冷静》，上海文艺出版社1997年版。
Lin Yusheng (1997). *Enthusiasm and Calmness*. Shanghai Literature and Art Publishing House.

刘小波："民间的升值与政治民主化。" 《民主中国》，38(3)，2003年3月号。见: http://www.chinamz.org/115issue/115gbdl1.html。
Liu Xiaobo (2003). The rising value of civil-ness and political democratization. *China Monthly* 38(3). Available at: http://www.chinamz.org/115issue/115gbdl1.html (Accessed January 10, 2003).

毛泽东:《毛泽东论新闻宣传》。新华出版社 2000版。
Mao Tze-tung (Mao Zedong) (2000). *Mao Tze-tung on Journalistic Propaganda*. Xinhua Press, Beijing.

王绍光:"关于'市民社会'的几点思考。" 《二十一世纪》，8（十二月号），102—114。
Wang Shaoguang (1991). Some reflections on 'civil society.' *21st Century* 8, 102–114.

吴季松:《知识经济——21世纪社会的新趋势》。北京科技出版社1998年3月版。
Wu Jisong (1998). *Knowledge Economy: A New Trend in the 21st Century*. Beijing Science and Technology Press.

虞和平:《商会与中国早期现代化》。上海人民出版社1993年版。
Yu Heping (1993). *Chamber of Commerce and China's Early Modernization*. Shanghai People's Press.

张祖桦:关于公民社会研究的综述。《当代中国研究》，79（4），2002年。见：http://www.chinayj.net/StubArticle.asp?issue=020409&total=79。
Zhang Zuhua (2002). An overview of civil society research. *Contemporary China Studies*, 79(4). Available at: http://www.chinayj.net/StubArticle.asp?issue=020409&total=79 (Accessed February 10, 2003).

张祖桦:中国公民社会的兴起。2003年2月16日。北京大军网。见：http://www.dajun.com/gongminshehui.htm。
Zhang Zuhua (2003). "The rise of civil society in China. Beijing Dajun Net. Available at http://www.dajun.com/gongminshehui.htm (Accessed February 13, 2003).

赵弘:《知识经济呼唤中国》。改革出版社1998年7月版。
Zhao Hong (1998). *Knowledge Economy Calls for China*. Reform Press, Beijing.

周晓虹: 传播的畸变 ——对"SARS"传言的一种社会心理学分析. 见：http://www.folkcn.com/shownews.asp?newsid=630。
Zhou Xiaohong (2004). A transmutation of communication: a social psychological analysis of rumors in relation to SARS. Available at: http://www.folkcn.com/shownews.asp?newsid=630 (Accessed May 24, 2004).

Index

T - #0150 - 071024 - C0 - 229/152/17 - PB - 9780415535885 - Gloss Lamination